2087 A.D.

THERE WAS THIS WAR...

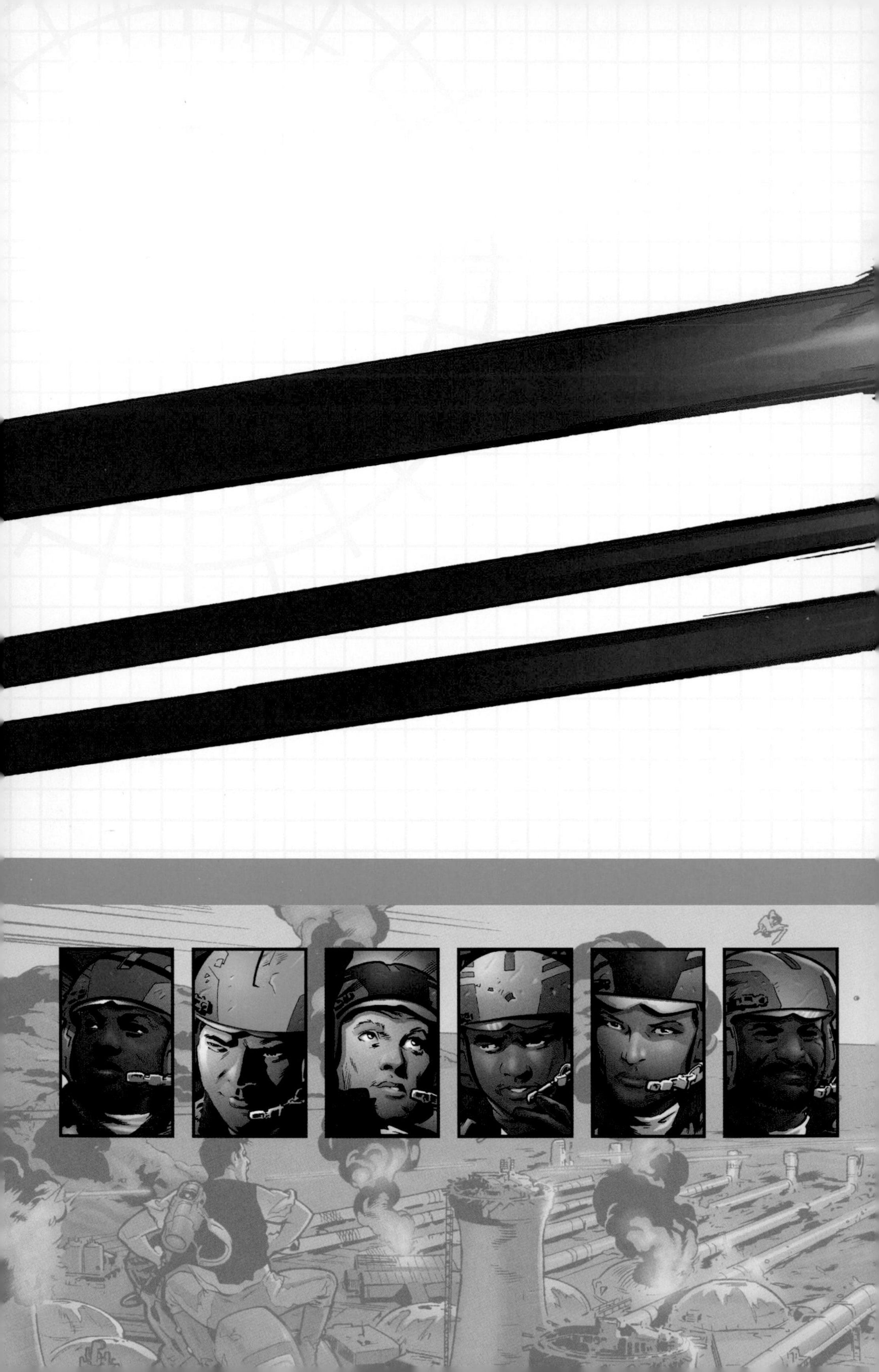

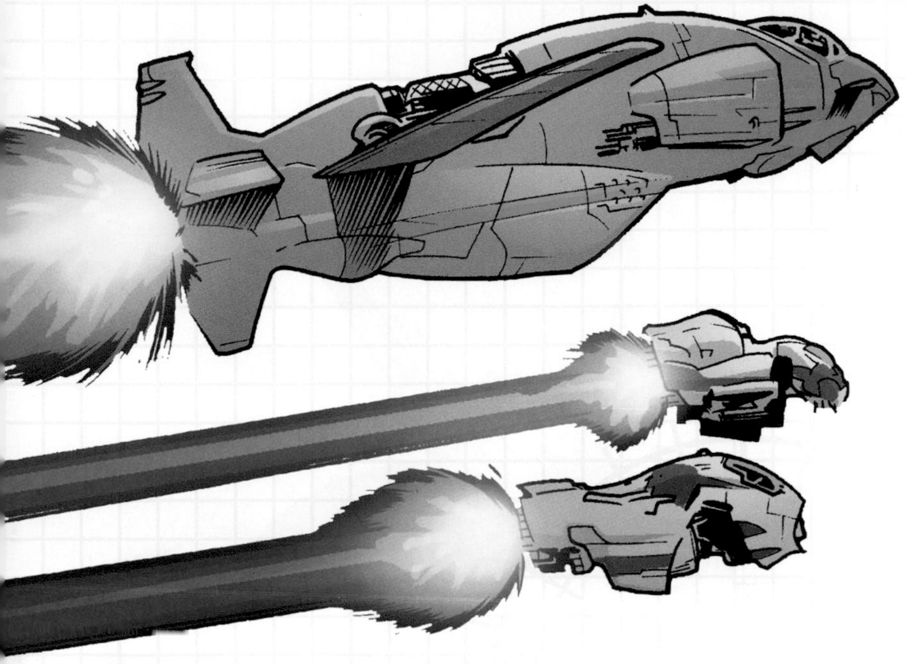

SHOCKROCKETS

WE HAVE IGNITION

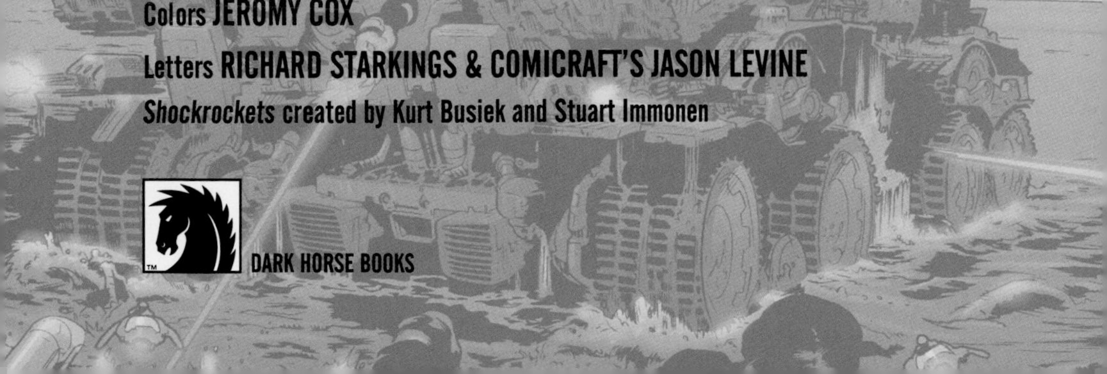

Script KURT BUSIEK

Pencils STUART IMMONEN

Inks WADE VON GRAWBADGER

Colors JEROMY COX

Letters RICHARD STARKINGS & COMICRAFT'S JASON LEVINE

Shockrockets created by Kurt Busiek and Stuart Immonen

DARK HORSE BOOKS

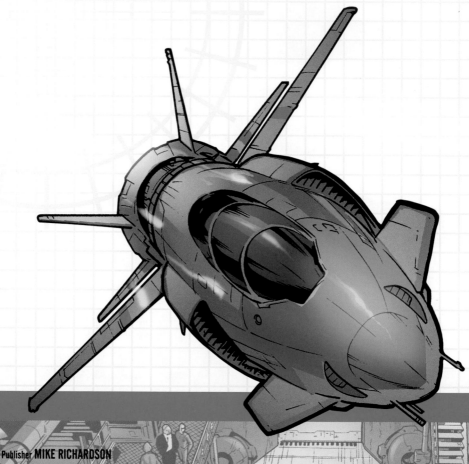

Publisher **MIKE RICHARDSON**

Collection Designer **DEBRA BAILEY**

Editorial Assistant **KATIE MOODY**

Editor **DAVE LAND**

SHOCKROCKETS

This book collects issues 1 through 6 of the comic-book series *Shockrockets*, originally published by Image Comics.

Dark Horse Comics, Inc.
10956 SE Main Street
Milwaukie, OR 97222
www.darkhorse.com

To find a comics shop in your area call the Comic Shop Locator Service toll-free at (888) 266-4226

First edition: August 2004
ISBN: 1-59307-129-9

10 9 8 7 6 5 4 3 2 1
PRINTED IN CHINA

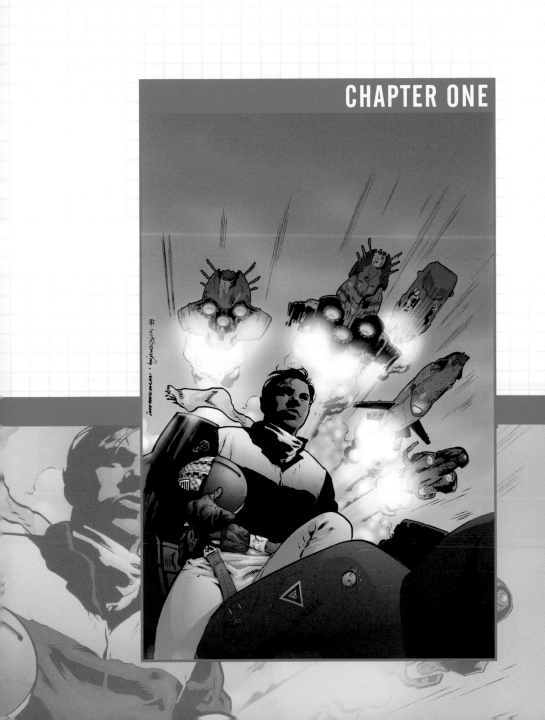

CHAPTER ONE

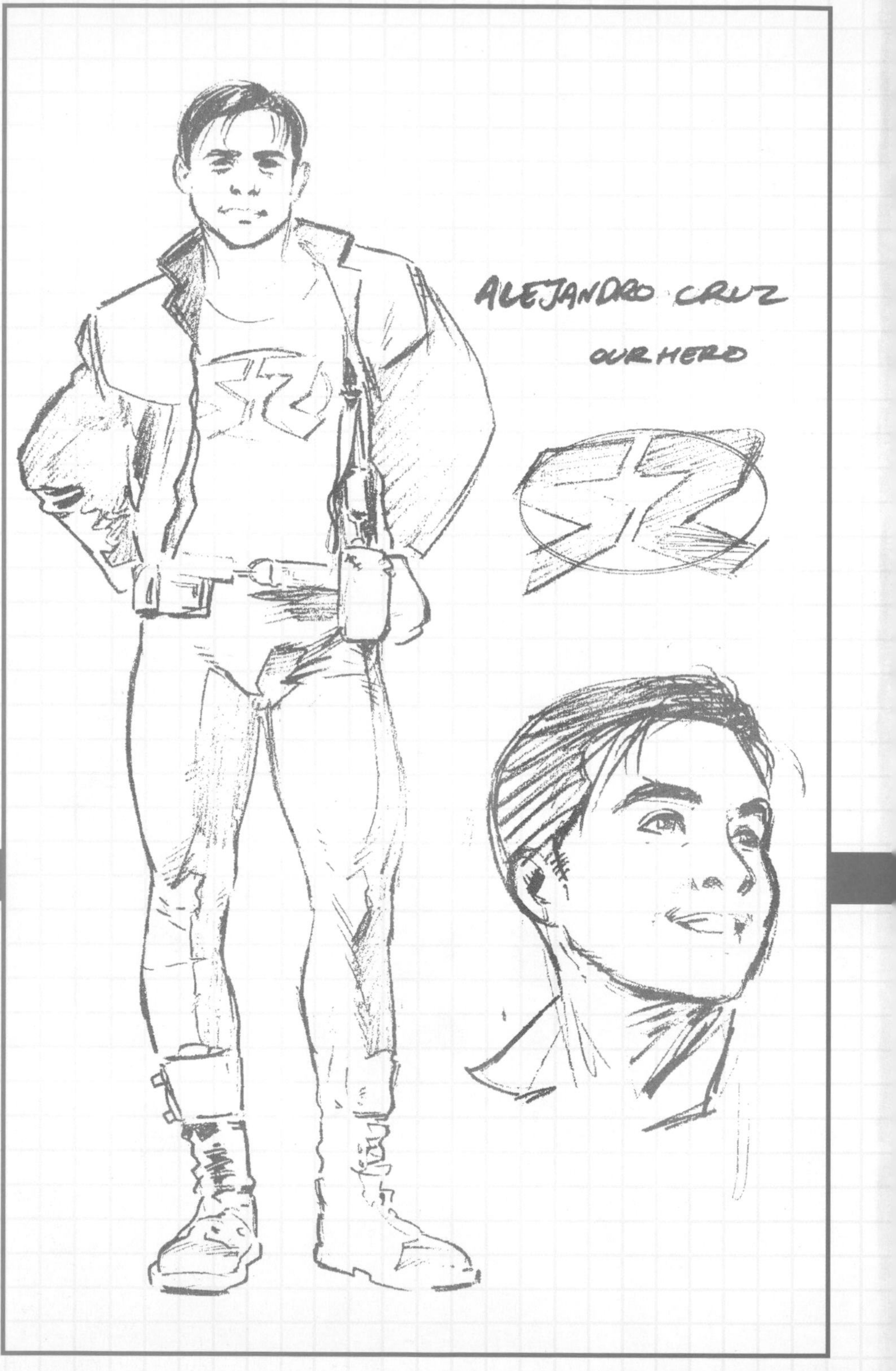
ALEJANDRO CRUZ
OUR HERO

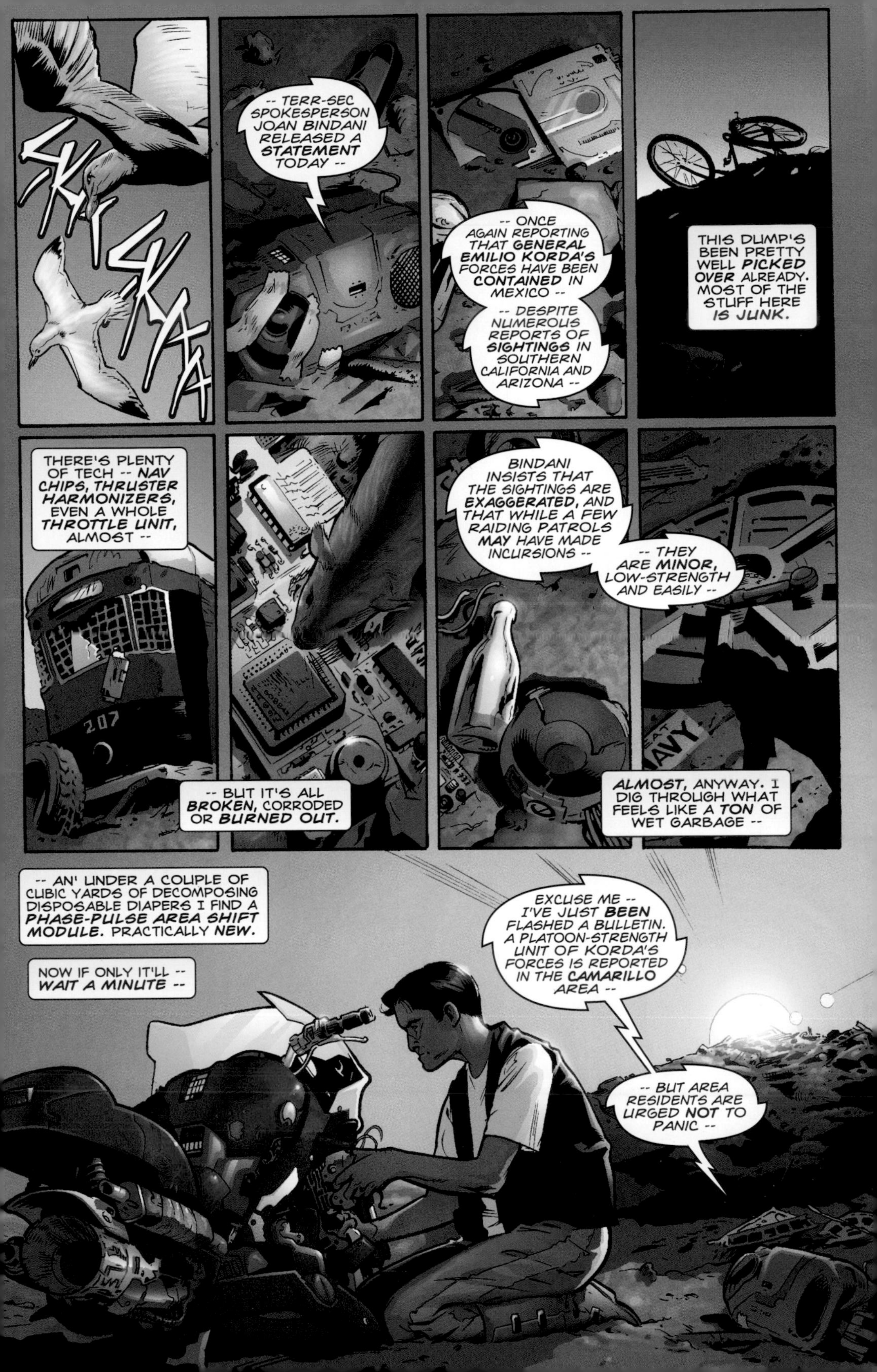
SKKKSKAAA
-- TERR-SEC SPOKESPERSON JOAN BINDANI RELEASED A STATEMENT TODAY --
-- ONCE AGAIN REPORTING THAT GENERAL EMILIO KORDA'S FORCES HAVE BEEN CONTAINED IN MEXICO --
-- DESPITE NUMEROUS REPORTS OF SIGHTINGS IN SOUTHERN CALIFORNIA AND ARIZONA --
THIS DUMP'S BEEN PRETTY WELL PICKED OVER ALREADY. MOST OF THE STUFF HERE IS JUNK.
THERE'S PLENTY OF TECH -- NAV CHIPS, THRUSTER HARMONIZERS, EVEN A WHOLE THROTTLE UNIT, ALMOST --
207
-- BUT IT'S ALL BROKEN, CORRODED OR BURNED OUT.
BINDANI INSISTS THAT THE SIGHTINGS ARE EXAGGERATED, AND THAT WHILE A FEW RAIDING PATROLS MAY HAVE MADE INCURSIONS --
-- THEY ARE MINOR, LOW-STRENGTH AND EASILY --
ALMOST, ANYWAY. I DIG THROUGH WHAT FEELS LIKE A TON OF WET GARBAGE --
-- AN' UNDER A COUPLE OF CUBIC YARDS OF DECOMPOSING DISPOSABLE DIAPERS I FIND A PHASE-PULSE AREA SHIFT MODULE. PRACTICALLY NEW.
NOW IF ONLY IT'LL -- WAIT A MINUTE --
EXCUSE ME -- I'VE JUST BEEN FLASHED A BULLETIN. A PLATOON-STRENGTH UNIT OF KORDA'S FORCES IS REPORTED IN THE CAMARILLO AREA --
-- BUT AREA RESIDENTS ARE URGED NOT TO PANIC --

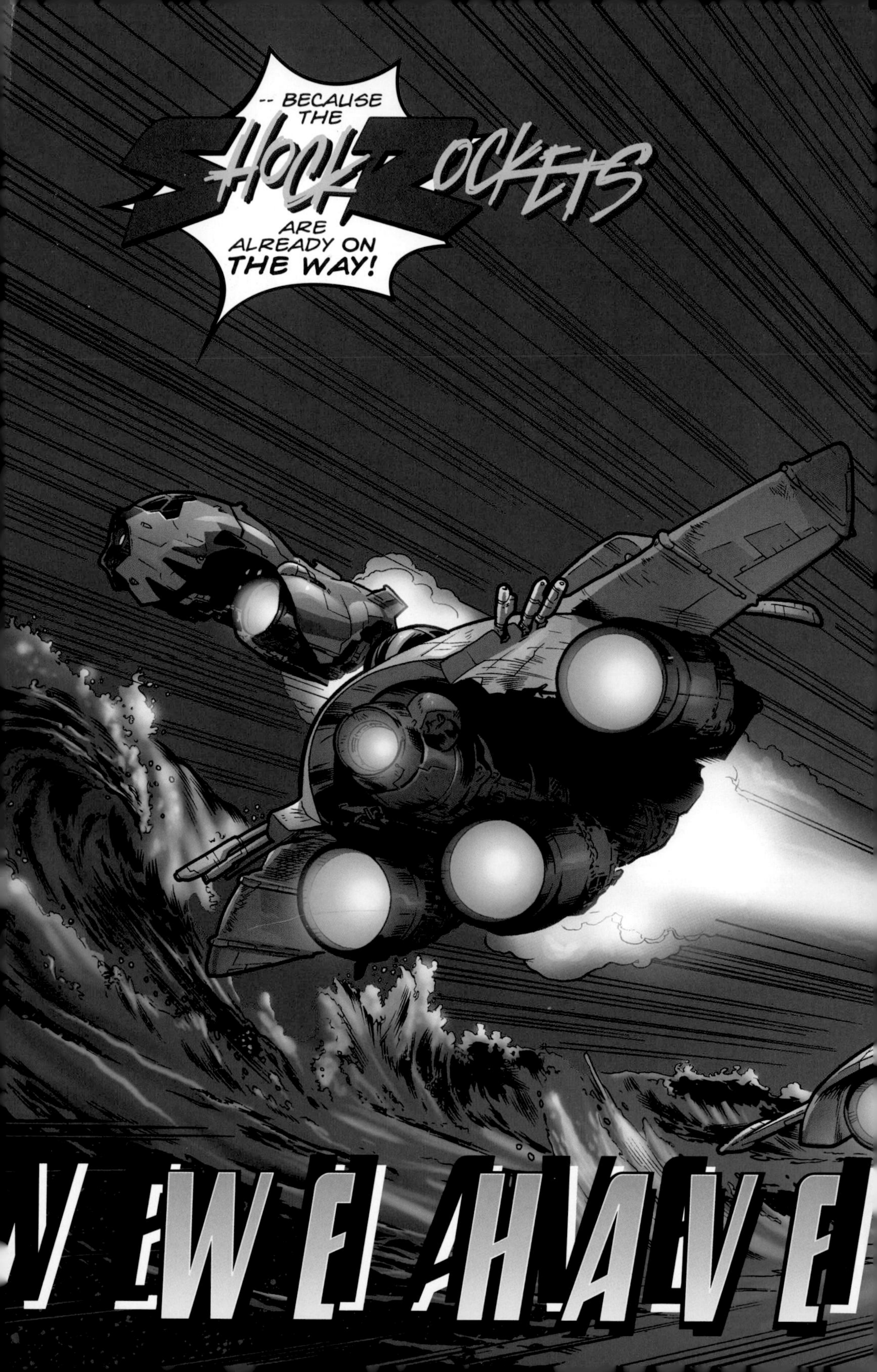
-- BECAUSE THE SHOCK ROCKETS ARE ALREADY ON THE WAY!
WE HAVE

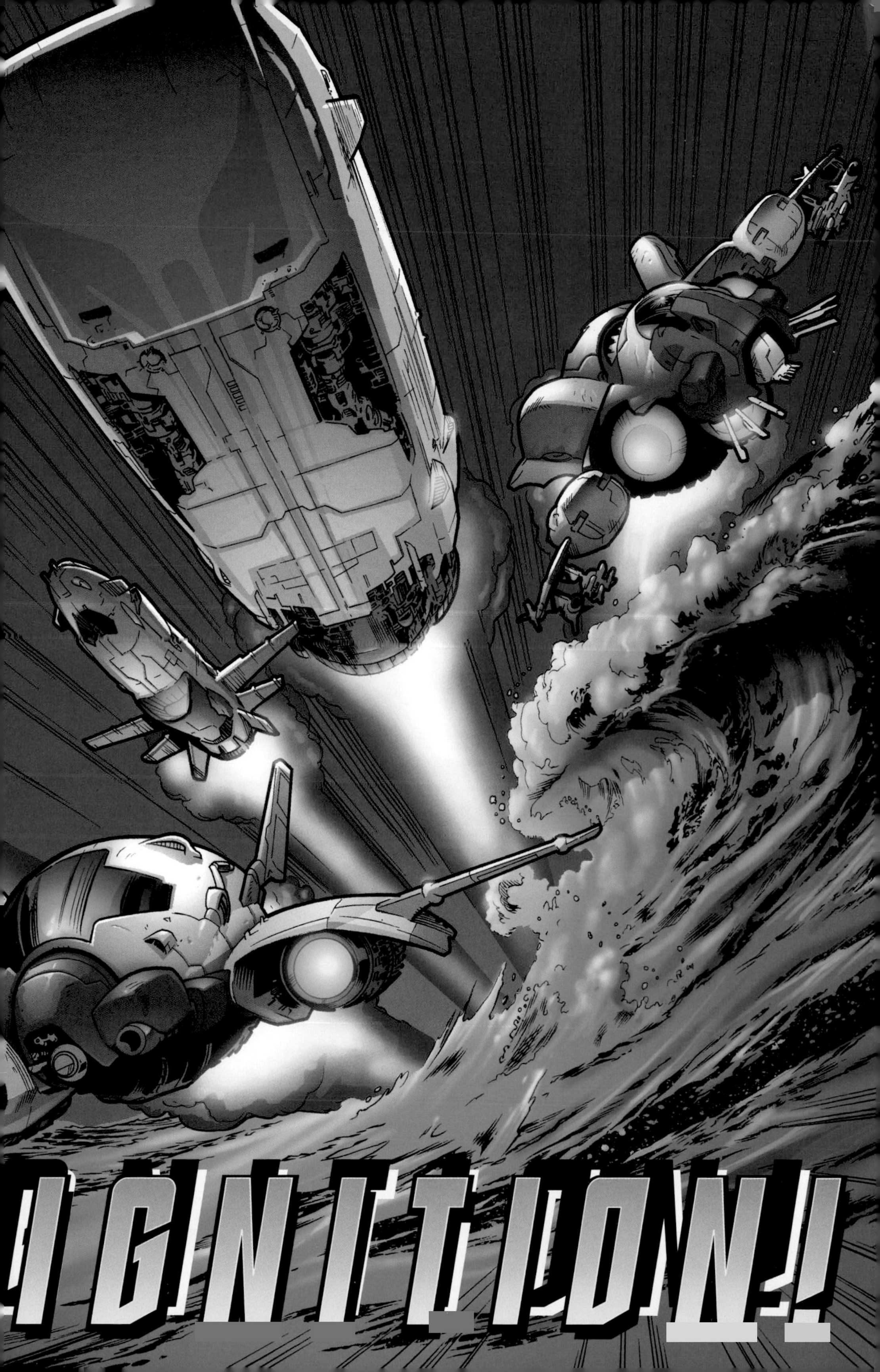
IGNITION!

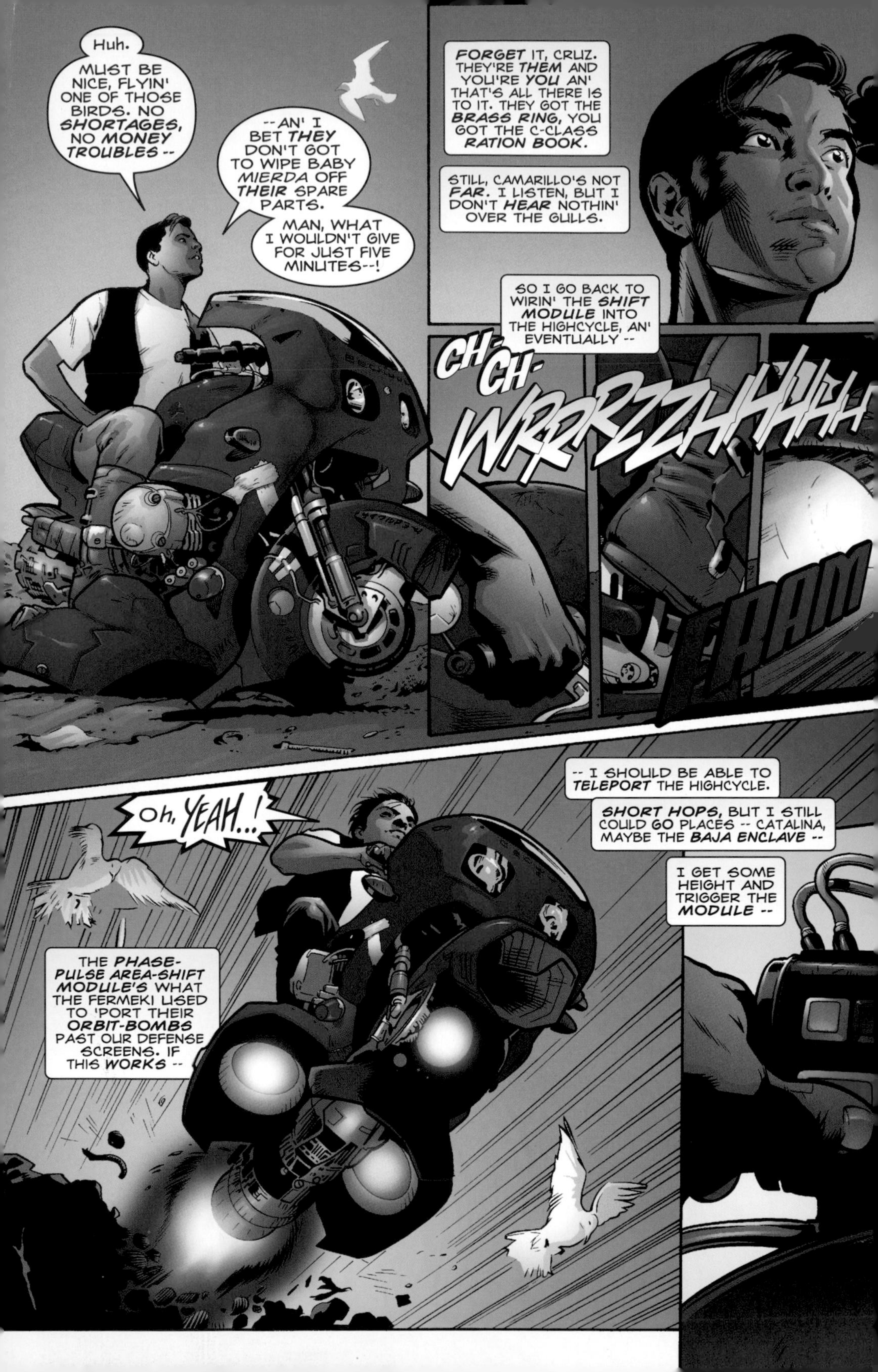
Huh.
MUST BE NICE, FLYIN' ONE OF THOSE BIRDS. NO SHORTAGES, NO MONEY TROUBLES --
--AN' I BET THEY DON'T GOT TO WIPE BABY MIERDA OFF THEIR SPARE PARTS.
MAN, WHAT I WOULDN'T GIVE FOR JUST FIVE MINUTES--!
FORGET IT, CRUZ. THEY'RE THEM AND YOU'RE YOU AN' THAT'S ALL THERE IS TO IT. THEY GOT THE BRASS RING, YOU GOT THE C-CLASS RATION BOOK.
STILL, CAMARILLO'S NOT FAR. I LISTEN, BUT I DON'T HEAR NOTHIN' OVER THE GULLS.
SO I GO BACK TO WIRIN' THE SHIFT MODULE INTO THE HIGHCYCLE, AN' EVENTUALLY --
CH-CH-WRRRZZHHHHH
-- I SHOULD BE ABLE TO TELEPORT THE HIGHCYCLE.
SHORT HOPS, BUT I STILL COULD GO PLACES -- CATALINA, MAYBE THE BAJA ENCLAVE --
Oh, YEAH...!
I GET SOME HEIGHT AND TRIGGER THE MODULE --
THE PHASE-PULSE AREA-SHIFT MODULE'S WHAT THE FERMEKI USED TO 'PORT THEIR ORBIT-BOMBS PAST OUR DEFENSE SCREENS. IF THIS WORKS --

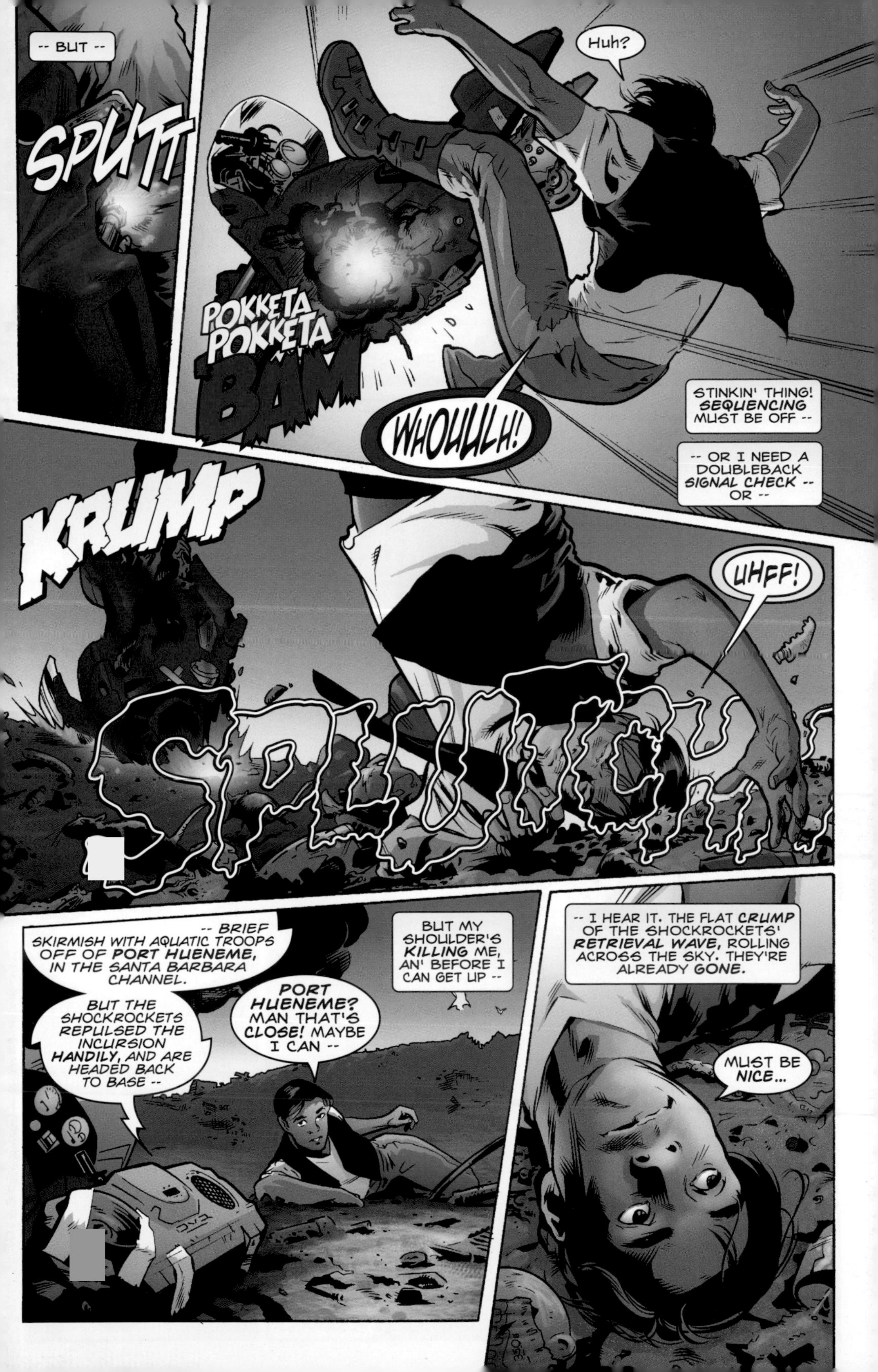
-- BUT --
SPUTT
Huh?
POKKETA POKKETA BAM
WHOUULH!
STINKIN' THING! SEQUENCING MUST BE OFF --
-- OR I NEED A DOUBLEBACK SIGNAL CHECK -- OR --
KRUMP
UHFF!
SPLUTCH
-- BRIEF SKIRMISH WITH AQUATIC TROOPS OFF OF PORT HUENEME, IN THE SANTA BARBARA CHANNEL.
BUT THE SHOCKROCKETS REPULSED THE INCURSION HANDILY, AND ARE HEADED BACK TO BASE --
BUT MY SHOULDER'S KILLING ME, AN' BEFORE I CAN GET UP --
PORT HUENEME? MAN THAT'S CLOSE! MAYBE I CAN --
-- I HEAR IT. THE FLAT CRUMP OF THE SHOCKROCKETS' RETRIEVAL WAVE, ROLLING ACROSS THE SKY. THEY'RE ALREADY GONE.
MUST BE NICE...

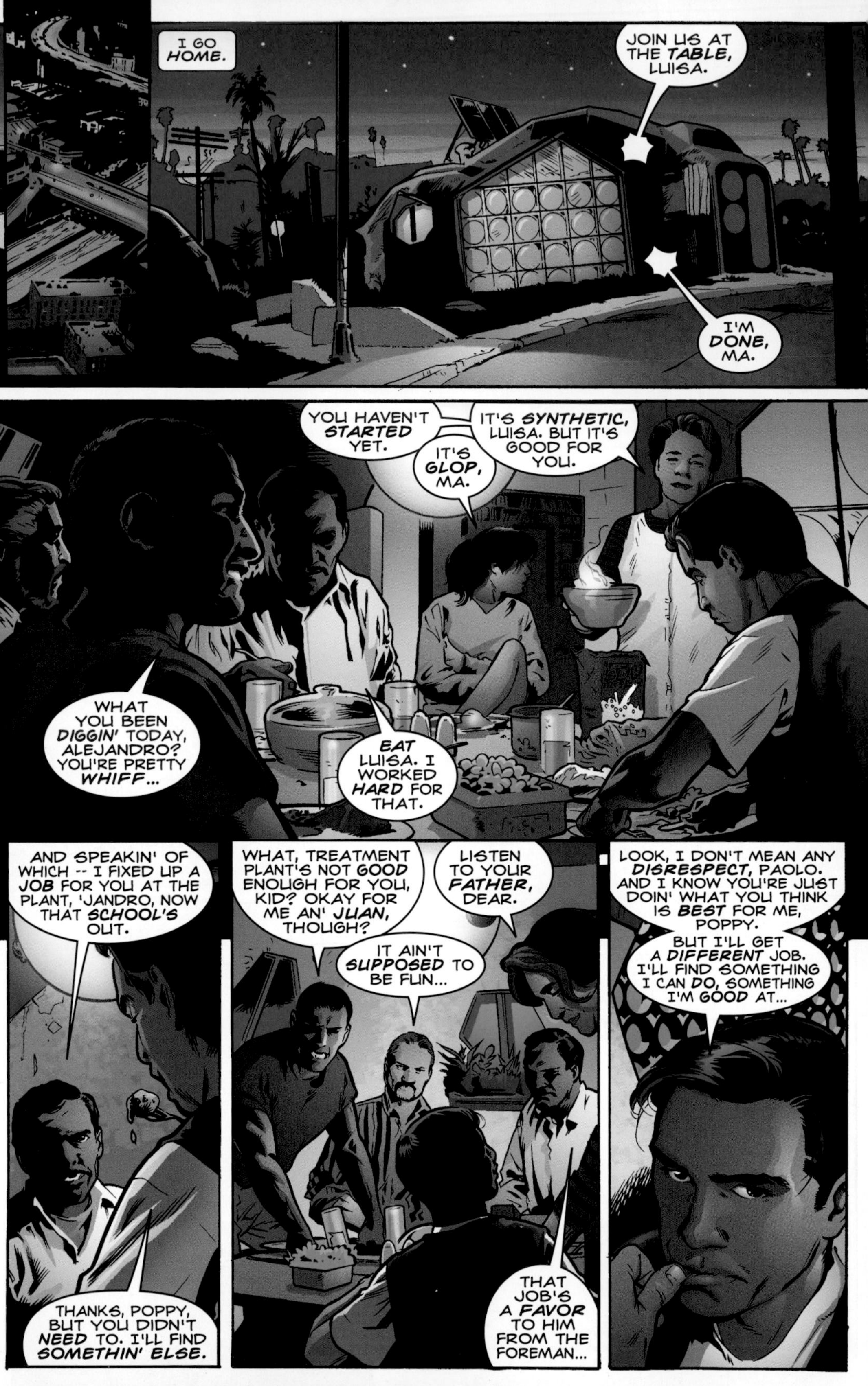

I GO HOME.
JOIN US AT THE TABLE, LUISA.
I'M DONE, MA.
YOU HAVEN'T STARTED YET.
IT'S GLOP, MA.
IT'S SYNTHETIC, LUISA. BUT IT'S GOOD FOR YOU.
WHAT YOU BEEN DIGGIN' TODAY, ALEJANDRO? YOU'RE PRETTY WHIFF...
EAT LUISA. I WORKED HARD FOR THAT.
AND SPEAKIN' OF WHICH -- I FIXED UP A JOB FOR YOU AT THE PLANT, 'JANDRO, NOW THAT SCHOOL'S OUT.
THANKS, POPPY, BUT YOU DIDN'T NEED TO. I'LL FIND SOMETHIN' ELSE.
WHAT, TREATMENT PLANT'S NOT GOOD ENOUGH FOR YOU, KID? OKAY FOR ME AN' JUAN, THOUGH?
IT AIN'T SUPPOSED TO BE FUN...
LISTEN TO YOUR FATHER, DEAR.
THAT JOB'S A FAVOR TO HIM FROM THE FOREMAN...
LOOK, I DON'T MEAN ANY DISRESPECT, PAOLO. AND I KNOW YOU'RE JUST DOIN' WHAT YOU THINK IS BEST FOR ME, POPPY.
BUT I'LL GET A DIFFERENT JOB. I'LL FIND SOMETHING I CAN DO, SOMETHING I'M GOOD AT...

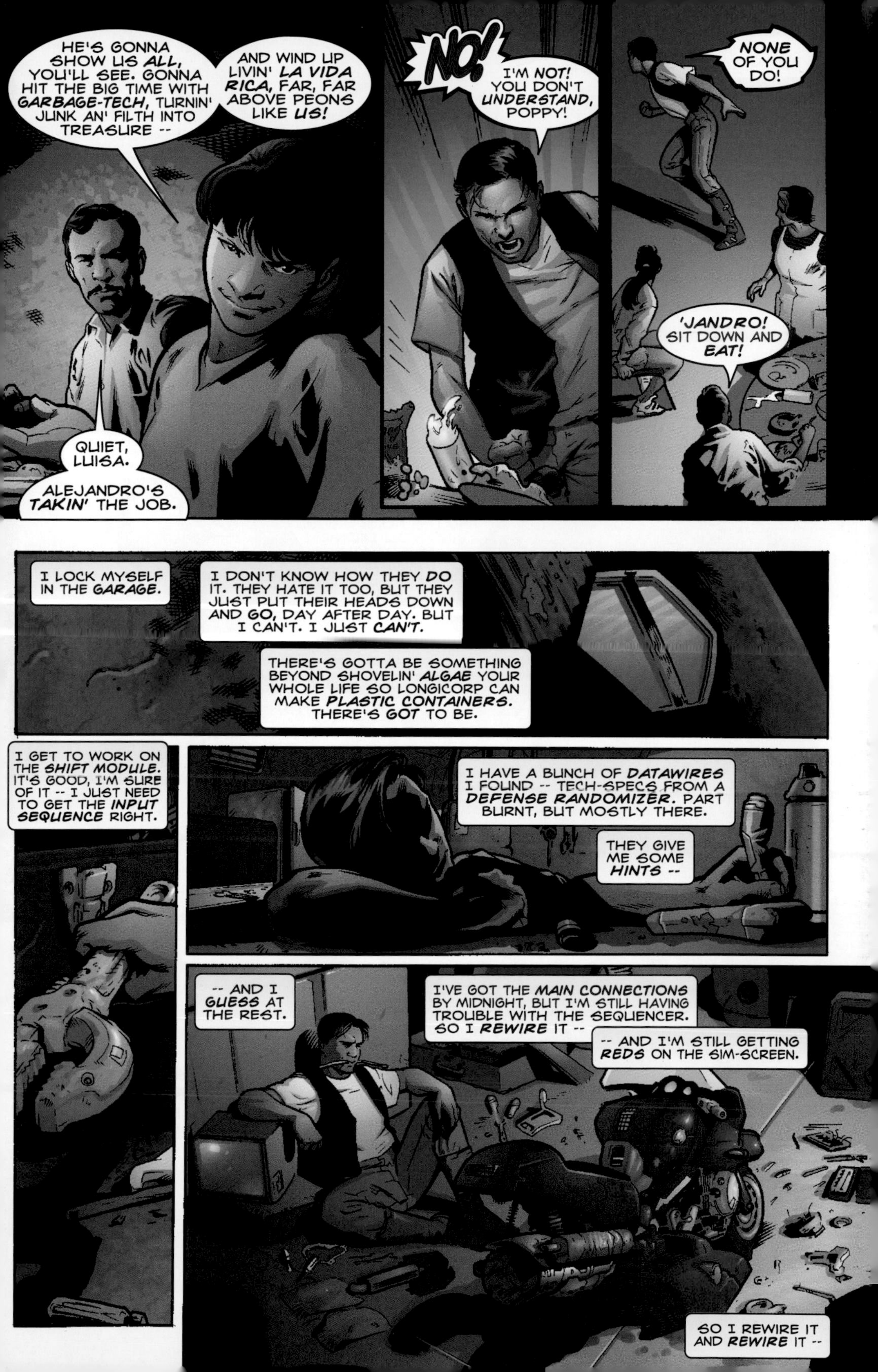
HE'S GONNA SHOW US ALL, YOU'LL SEE. GONNA HIT THE BIG TIME WITH GARBAGE-TECH, TURNIN' JUNK AN' FILTH INTO TREASURE --
AND WIND UP LIVIN' LA VIDA RICA, FAR, FAR ABOVE PEONS LIKE US!
QUIET, LUISA.
ALEJANDRO'S TAKIN' THE JOB.
NO!
I'M NOT! YOU DON'T UNDERSTAND, POPPY!
NONE OF YOU DO!
'JANDRO! SIT DOWN AND EAT!
I LOCK MYSELF IN THE GARAGE.
I DON'T KNOW HOW THEY DO IT. THEY HATE IT TOO, BUT THEY JUST PUT THEIR HEADS DOWN AND GO, DAY AFTER DAY. BUT I CAN'T. I JUST CAN'T.
THERE'S GOTTA BE SOMETHING BEYOND SHOVELIN' ALGAE YOUR WHOLE LIFE SO LONGICORP CAN MAKE PLASTIC CONTAINERS. THERE'S GOT TO BE.
I GET TO WORK ON THE SHIFT MODULE. IT'S GOOD, I'M SURE OF IT -- I JUST NEED TO GET THE INPUT SEQUENCE RIGHT.
I HAVE A BUNCH OF DATAWIRES I FOUND -- TECH-SPECS FROM A DEFENSE RANDOMIZER. PART BURNT, BUT MOSTLY THERE.
THEY GIVE ME SOME HINTS --
-- AND I GUESS AT THE REST.
I'VE GOT THE MAIN CONNECTIONS BY MIDNIGHT, BUT I'M STILL HAVING TROUBLE WITH THE SEQUENCER. SO I REWIRE IT --
-- AND I'M STILL GETTING REDS ON THE SIM-SCREEN.
SO I REWIRE IT AND REWIRE IT --

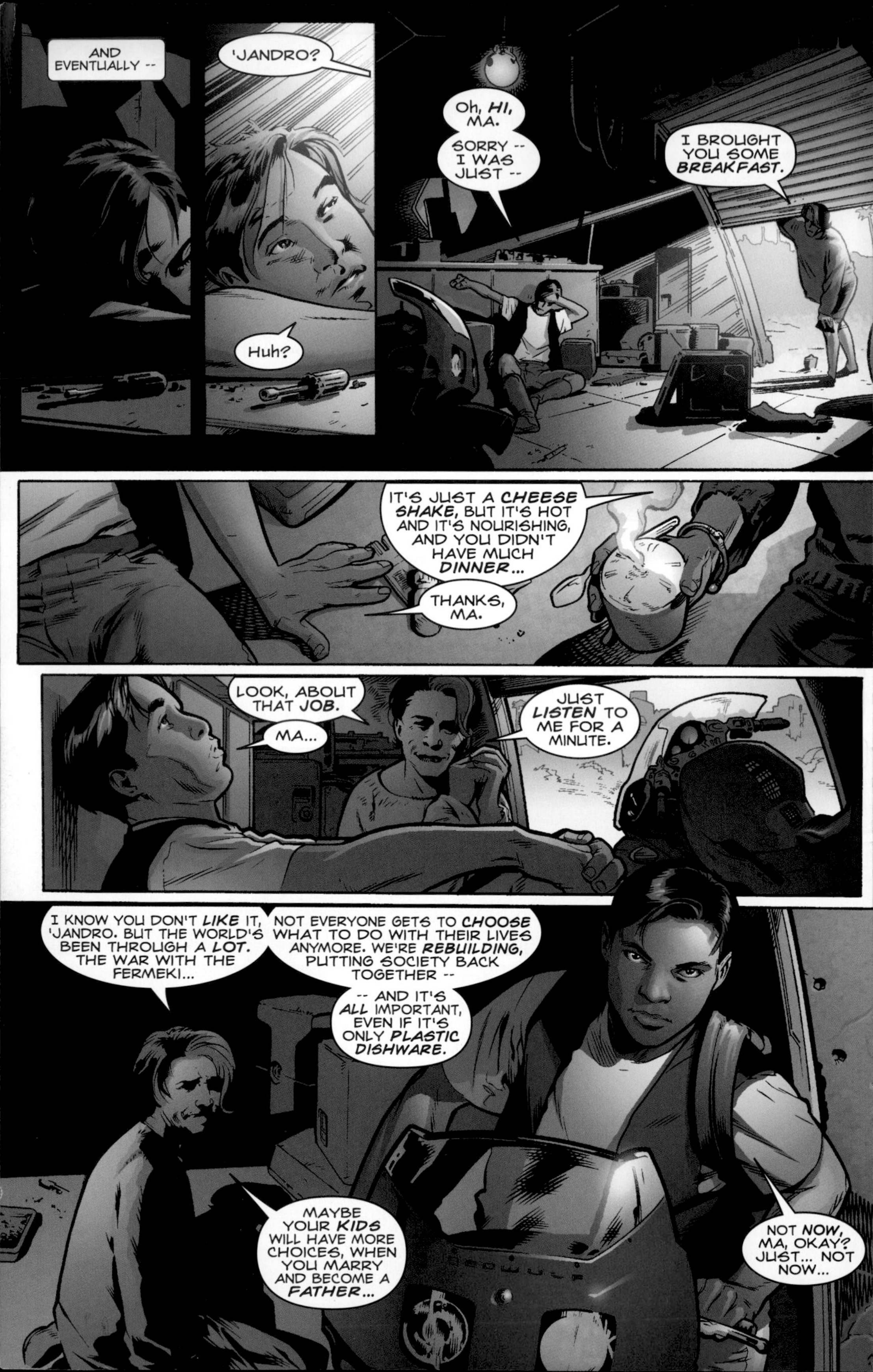
AND EVENTUALLY --
'JANDRO?
Huh?
Oh, HI, MA.
SORRY -- I WAS JUST --
I BROUGHT YOU SOME BREAKFAST.
IT'S JUST A CHEESE SHAKE, BUT IT'S HOT AND IT'S NOURISHING, AND YOU DIDN'T HAVE MUCH DINNER...
THANKS, MA.
LOOK, ABOUT THAT JOB.
MA...
JUST LISTEN TO ME FOR A MINUTE.
I KNOW YOU DON'T LIKE IT, 'JANDRO. BUT THE WORLD'S BEEN THROUGH A LOT. THE WAR WITH THE FERMEKI...
NOT EVERYONE GETS TO CHOOSE WHAT TO DO WITH THEIR LIVES ANYMORE. WE'RE REBUILDING, PUTTING SOCIETY BACK TOGETHER --
-- AND IT'S ALL IMPORTANT, EVEN IF IT'S ONLY PLASTIC DISHWARE.
MAYBE YOUR KIDS WILL HAVE MORE CHOICES, WHEN YOU MARRY AND BECOME A FATHER...
NOT NOW, MA, OKAY? JUST... NOT NOW...

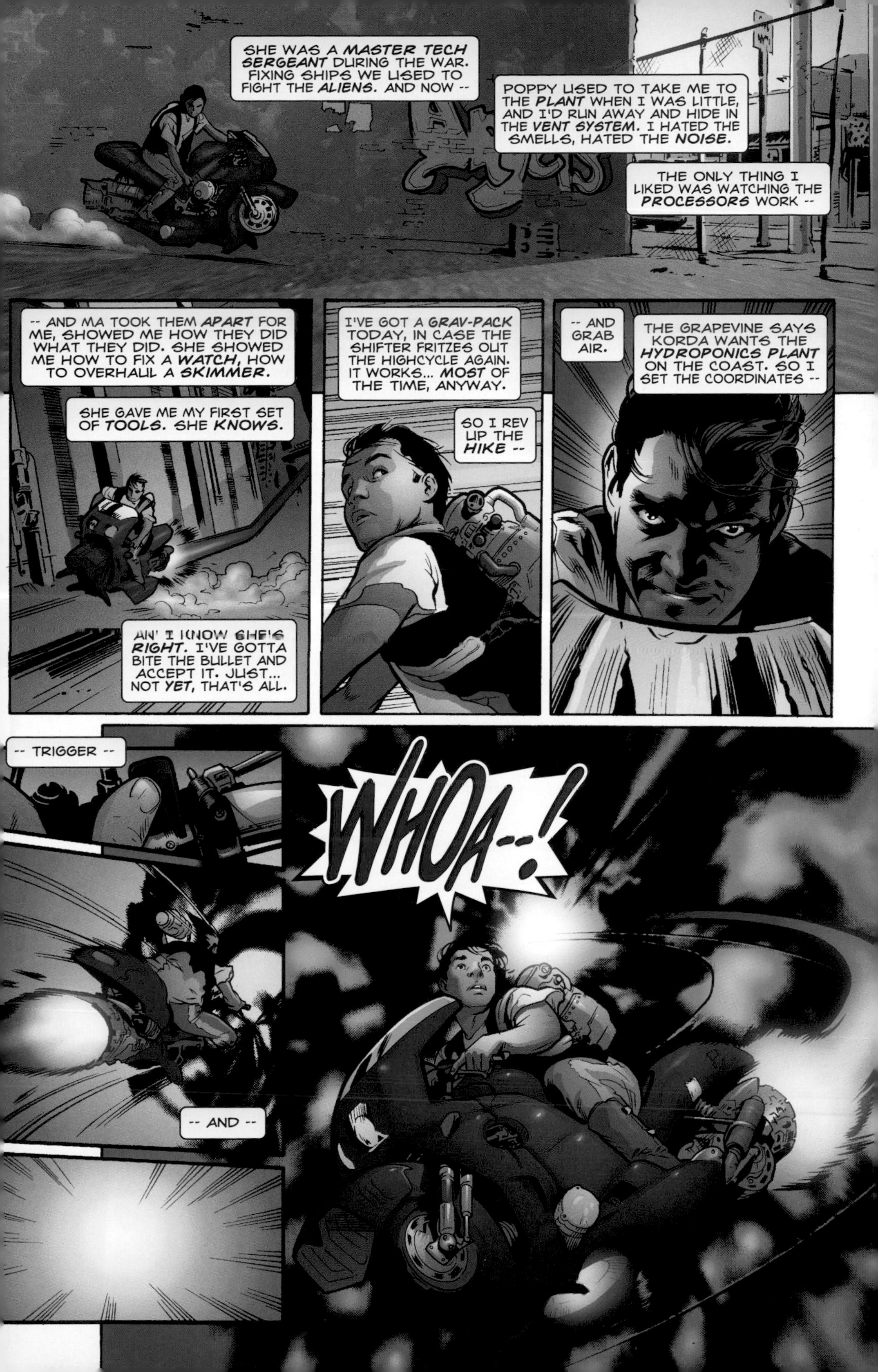
SHE WAS A MASTER TECH SERGEANT DURING THE WAR. FIXING SHIPS WE USED TO FIGHT THE ALIENS. AND NOW --
POPPY USED TO TAKE ME TO THE PLANT WHEN I WAS LITTLE, AND I'D RUN AWAY AND HIDE IN THE VENT SYSTEM. I HATED THE SMELLS, HATED THE NOISE.
THE ONLY THING I LIKED WAS WATCHING THE PROCESSORS WORK --
-- AND MA TOOK THEM APART FOR ME, SHOWED ME HOW THEY DID WHAT THEY DID. SHE SHOWED ME HOW TO FIX A WATCH, HOW TO OVERHAUL A SKIMMER.
SHE GAVE ME MY FIRST SET OF TOOLS. SHE KNOWS.
AN' I KNOW SHE'S RIGHT. I'VE GOTTA BITE THE BULLET AND ACCEPT IT. JUST... NOT YET, THAT'S ALL.
I'VE GOT A GRAV-PACK TODAY, IN CASE THE SHIFTER FRITZES OUT THE HIGHCYCLE AGAIN. IT WORKS... MOST OF THE TIME, ANYWAY.
SO I REV UP THE HIKE --
-- AND GRAB AIR.
THE GRAPEVINE SAYS KORDA WANTS THE HYDROPONICS PLANT ON THE COAST. SO I SET THE COORDINATES --
-- TRIGGER --
WHOA--!
-- AND --

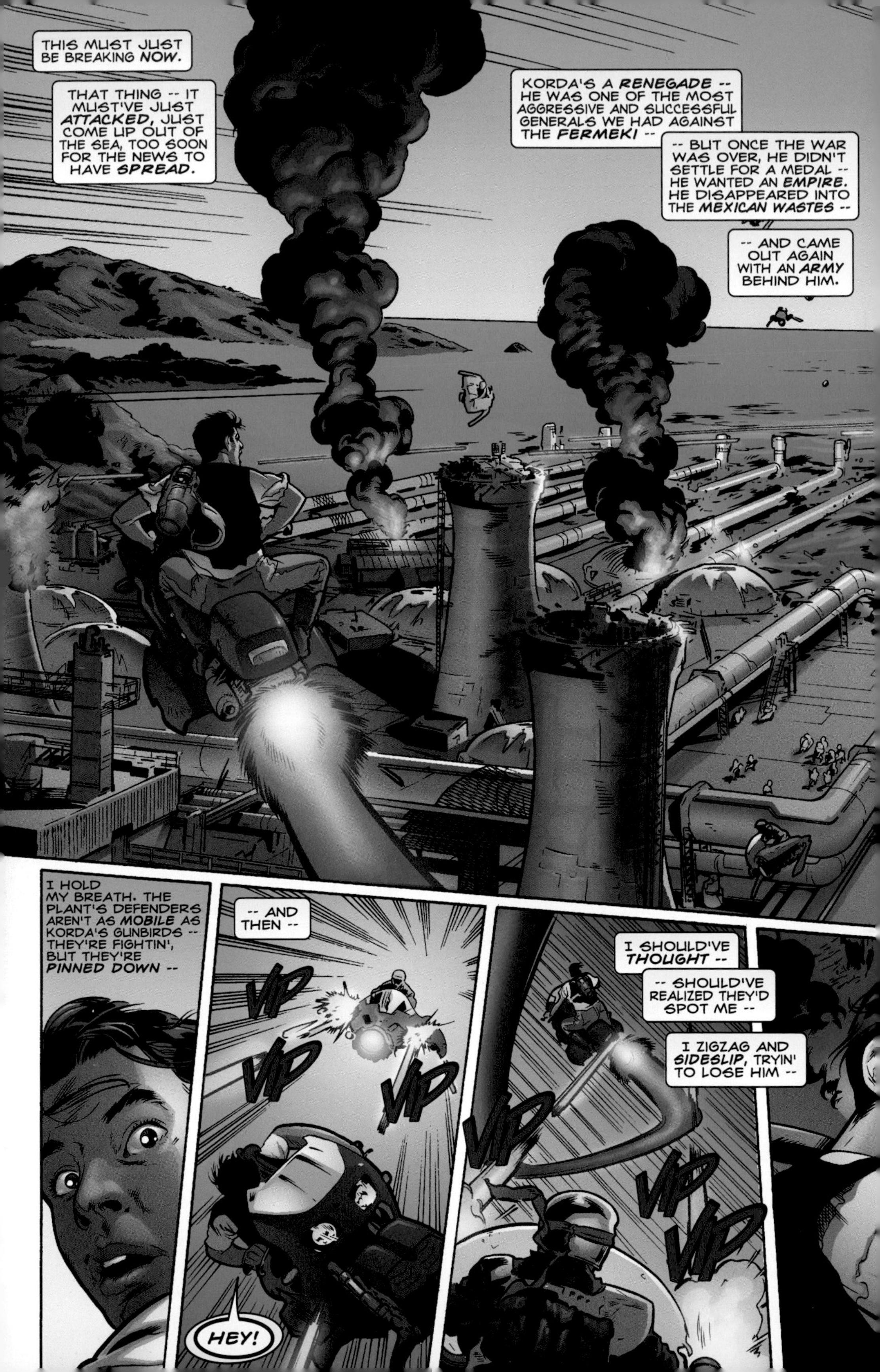
THIS MUST JUST BE BREAKING NOW.
THAT THING -- IT MUST'VE JUST ATTACKED, JUST COME UP OUT OF THE SEA, TOO SOON FOR THE NEWS TO HAVE SPREAD.
KORDA'S A RENEGADE -- HE WAS ONE OF THE MOST AGGRESSIVE AND SUCCESSFUL GENERALS WE HAD AGAINST THE FERMEKI --
-- BUT ONCE THE WAR WAS OVER, HE DIDN'T SETTLE FOR A MEDAL -- HE WANTED AN EMPIRE. HE DISAPPEARED INTO THE MEXICAN WASTES --
-- AND CAME OUT AGAIN WITH AN ARMY BEHIND HIM.
I HOLD MY BREATH. THE PLANT'S DEFENDERS AREN'T AS MOBILE AS KORDA'S GUNBIRDS -- THEY'RE FIGHTIN', BUT THEY'RE PINNED DOWN --
HEY!
-- AND THEN --
VIP
VIP
VIP
I SHOULD'VE THOUGHT --
-- SHOULD'VE REALIZED THEY'D SPOT ME --
I ZIGZAG AND SIDESLIP, TRYIN' TO LOSE HIM --
VIP
VIP
VIP
VIP

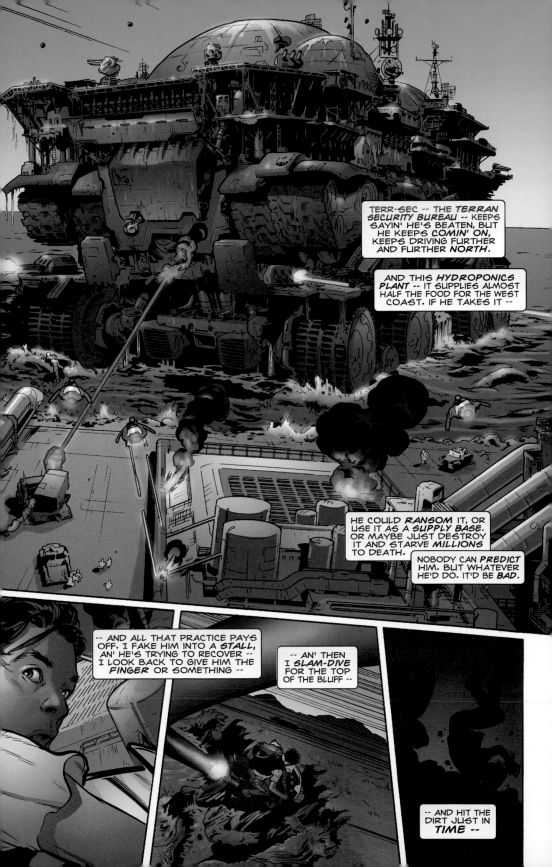

TERR-SEC -- THE *TERRAN SECURITY BUREAU* -- KEEPS SAYIN' HE'S BEATEN, BUT HE KEEPS *COMIN' ON,* KEEPS DRIVING FURTHER AND FURTHER *NORTH.*

AND THIS *HYDROPONICS PLANT* -- IT SUPPLIES ALMOST HALF THE FOOD FOR THE WEST COAST. IF HE TAKES IT --

HE COULD *RANSOM* IT, OR USE IT AS A *SUPPLY BASE.* OR MAYBE JUST DESTROY IT AND STARVE *MILLIONS* TO DEATH.

NOBODY CAN *PREDICT* HIM. BUT WHATEVER HE'D DO. IT'D BE *BAD.*

-- AND ALL THAT PRACTICE PAYS OFF. I FAKE HIM INTO A *STALL,* AN' HE'S TRYING TO RECOVER -- I LOOK BACK TO GIVE HIM THE *FINGER* OR SOMETHING --

-- AN' THEN I *SLAM-DIVE* FOR THE TOP OF THE BLUFF --

-- AND HIT THE DIRT JUST IN *TIME* --

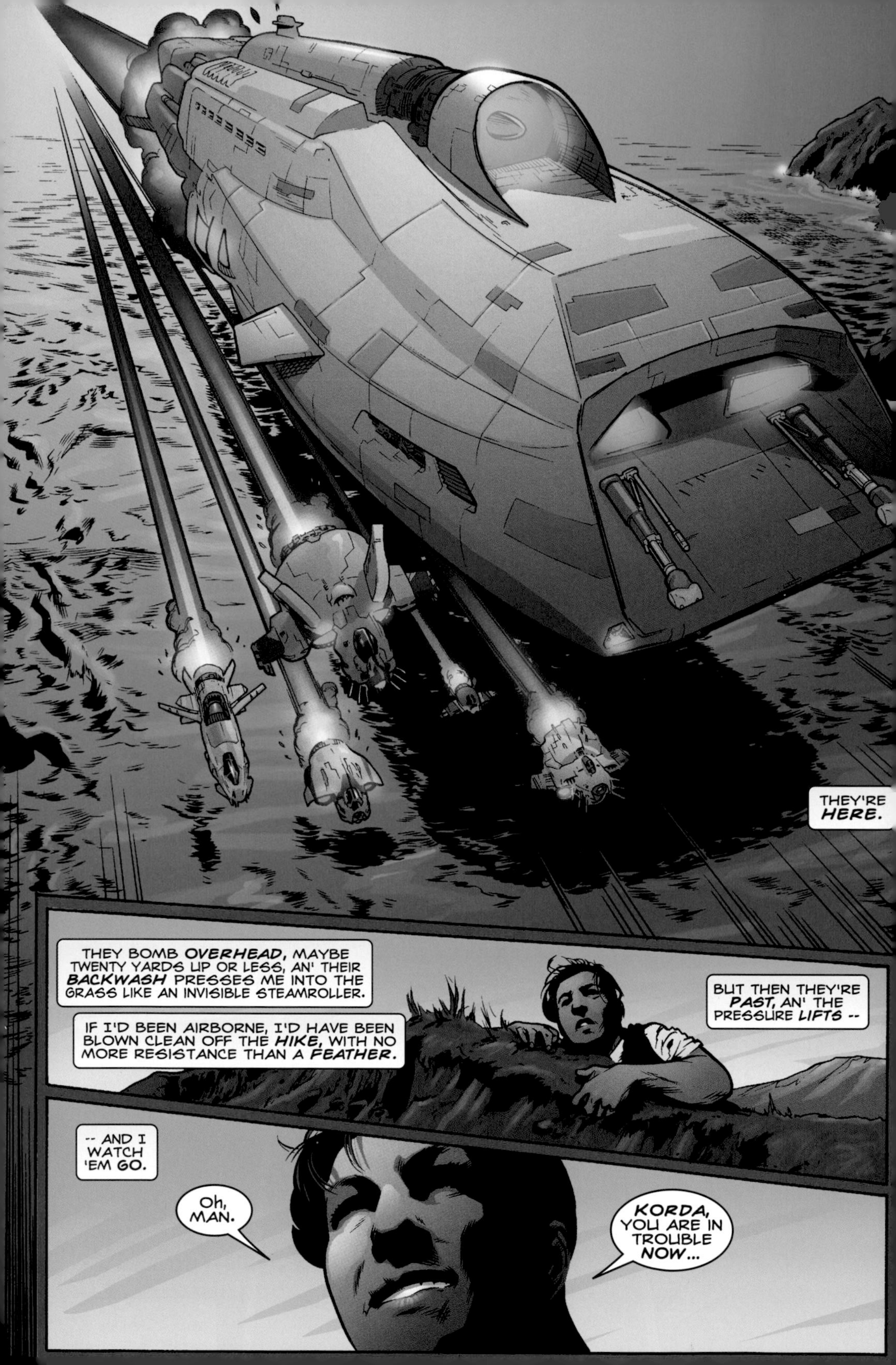
THEY'RE HERE.
THEY BOMB OVERHEAD, MAYBE TWENTY YARDS UP OR LESS, AN' THEIR BACKWASH PRESSES ME INTO THE GRASS LIKE AN INVISIBLE STEAMROLLER.
IF I'D BEEN AIRBORNE, I'D HAVE BEEN BLOWN CLEAN OFF THE HIKE, WITH NO MORE RESISTANCE THAN A FEATHER.
BUT THEN THEY'RE PAST, AN' THE PRESSURE LIFTS --
-- AND I WATCH 'EM GO.
Oh, MAN.
KORDA, YOU ARE IN TROUBLE NOW...

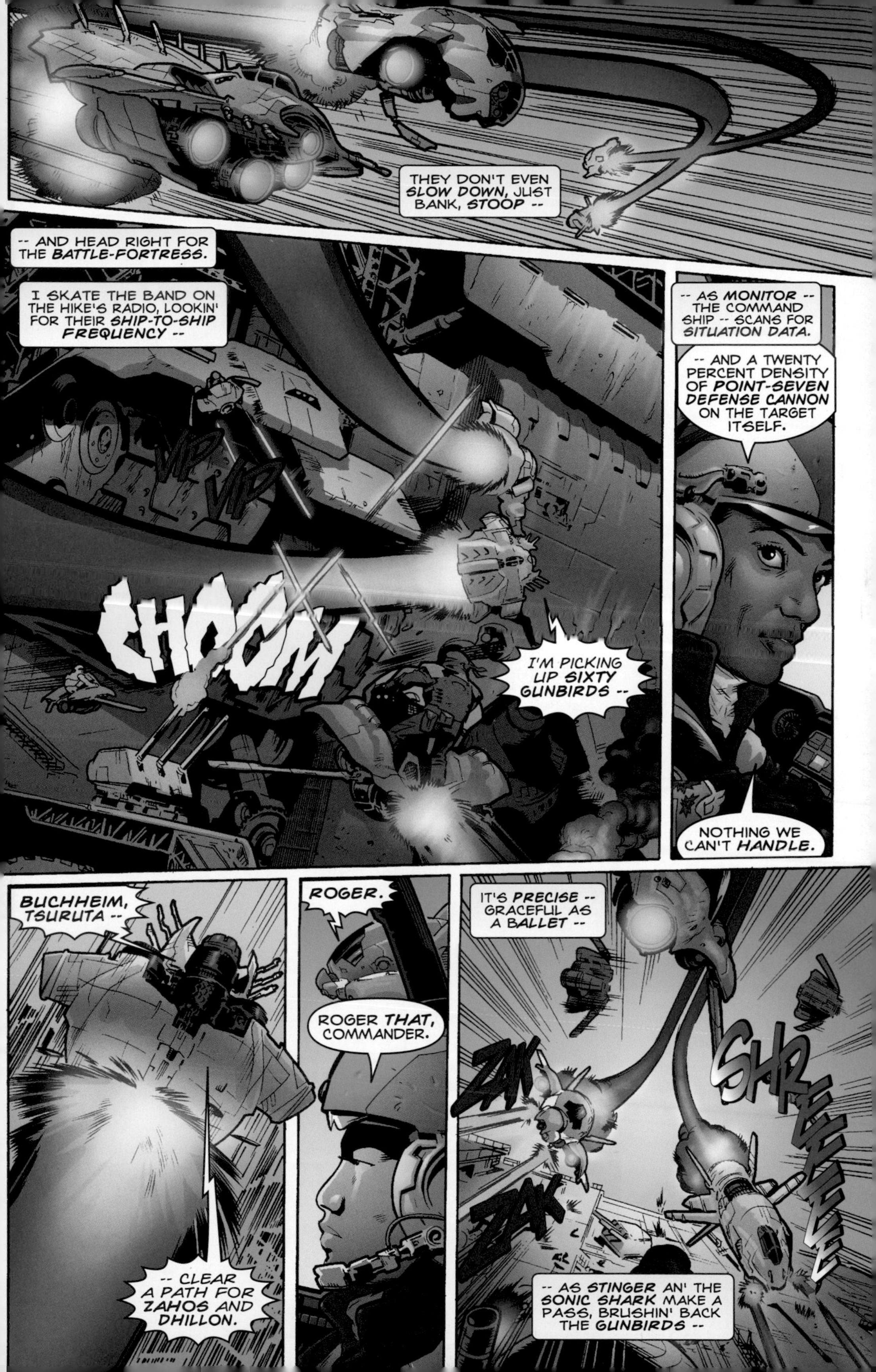
THEY DON'T EVEN SLOW DOWN, JUST BANK, STOOP --
-- AND HEAD RIGHT FOR THE BATTLE-FORTRESS.
I SKATE THE BAND ON THE HIKE'S RADIO, LOOKIN' FOR THEIR SHIP-TO-SHIP FREQUENCY --
VIP VIP
CHOOM
I'M PICKING UP SIXTY GUNBIRDS --
-- AS MONITOR -- THE COMMAND SHIP -- SCANS FOR SITUATION DATA.
-- AND A TWENTY PERCENT DENSITY OF POINT-SEVEN DEFENSE CANNON ON THE TARGET ITSELF.
NOTHING WE CAN'T HANDLE.
BUCHHEIM, TSURUTA --
-- CLEAR A PATH FOR ZAHOS AND DHILLON.
ROGER.
ROGER THAT, COMMANDER.
IT'S PRECISE -- GRACEFUL AS A BALLET --
ZAK
ZAK
SHREEEEEE
-- AS STINGER AN' THE SONIC SHARK MAKE A PASS, BRUSHIN' BACK THE GUNBIRDS --

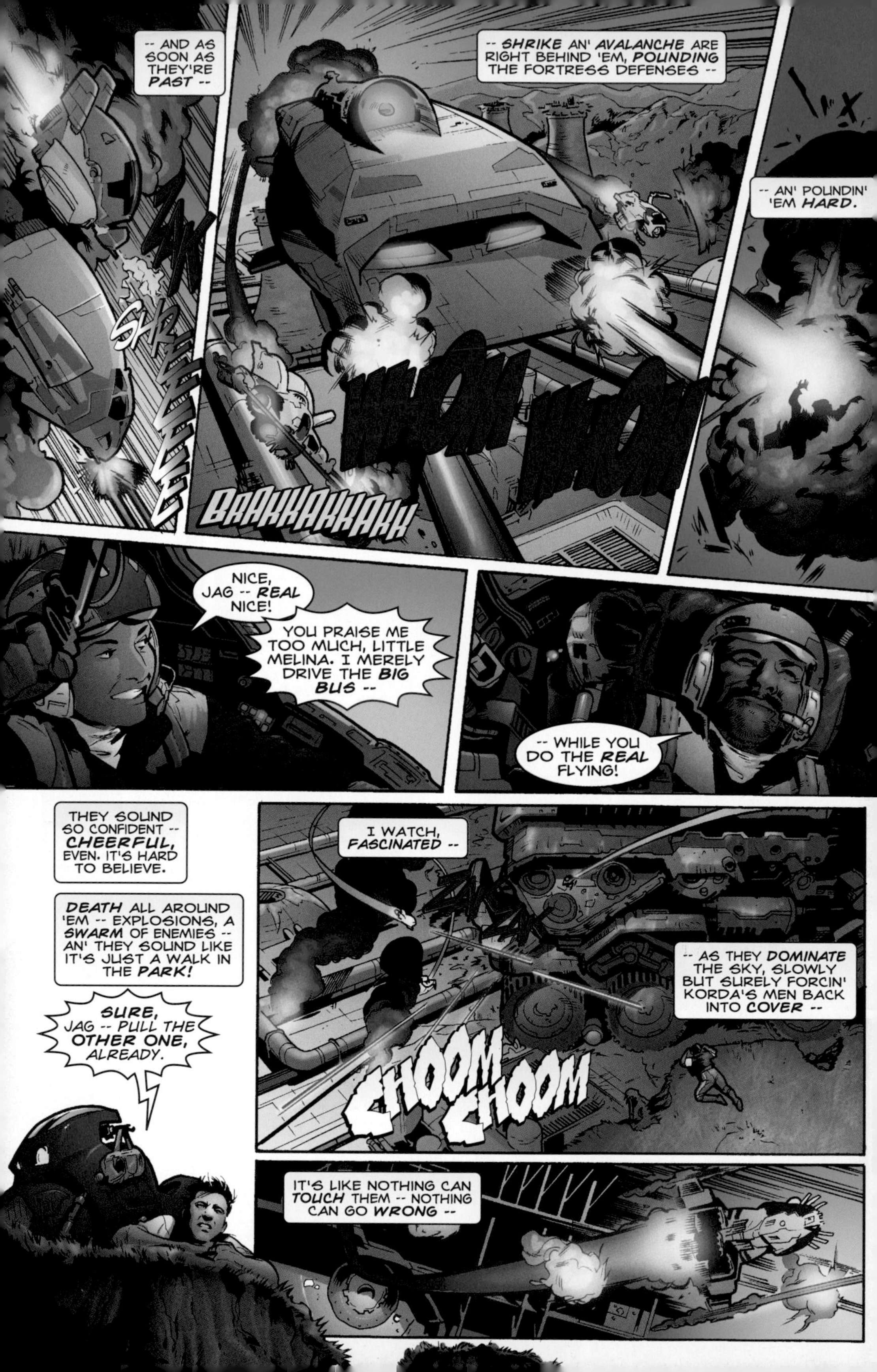
-- AND AS SOON AS THEY'RE PAST --
ZAK
SHRWWWWW
-- SHRIKE AN' AVALANCHE ARE RIGHT BEHIND 'EM, POUNDING THE FORTRESS DEFENSES --
WHOM WHOM
BRAKKAKKAKK
-- AN' POUNDIN' 'EM HARD.
NICE, JAG -- REAL NICE!
YOU PRAISE ME TOO MUCH, LITTLE MELINA. I MERELY DRIVE THE BIG BUS --
-- WHILE YOU DO THE REAL FLYING!
THEY SOUND SO CONFIDENT -- CHEERFUL, EVEN. IT'S HARD TO BELIEVE.
DEATH ALL AROUND 'EM -- EXPLOSIONS, A SWARM OF ENEMIES -- AN' THEY SOUND LIKE IT'S JUST A WALK IN THE PARK!
SURE, JAG -- PULL THE OTHER ONE, ALREADY.
I WATCH, FASCINATED --
ZAK ZAK
-- AS THEY DOMINATE THE SKY, SLOWLY BUT SURELY FORCIN' KORDA'S MEN BACK INTO COVER --
CHOOM CHOOM
IT'S LIKE NOTHING CAN TOUCH THEM -- NOTHING CAN GO WRONG --

BUT THEN, AS THE BATTLE-FORTRESS *RETREATS* --

-- 'AN THEY MAKE ANOTHER PASS TO *NUDGE* IT *ALONG* --

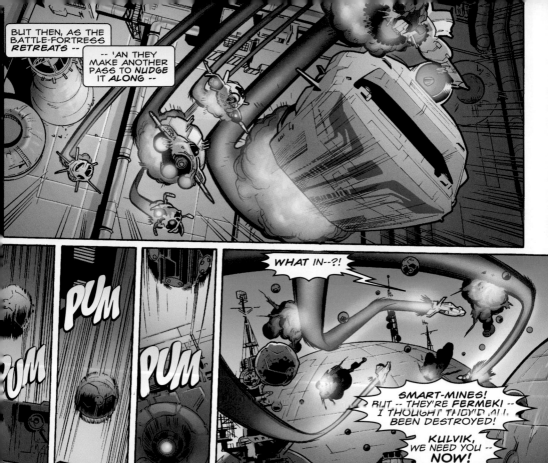

PUM

PUM

PUM

WHAT IN--?!

SMART-MINES! BUT -- THEY'RE *FERMEKI* -- I THOUGHT THEY'D ALL BEEN *DESTROYED!*

KULVIK, WE NEED YOU -- *NOW!*

YES, COMMANDER. I'LL USE *WINDSCREEN'S* FORCE-SHIELDS TO *DETONATE* AS MANY AS I CAN --

-- BUT THERE ARE *SCORES* OF THEM -- AND THEY'RE MOVING TO INTERCEPT THE *OTHERS!* THEY'LL BLOCK US IN--!

RIGHT -- WHILE KORDA'S *GUNBIRDS* HAVE A *CLEAR SKY.* BUT THERE'S GOT TO BE A *LINE-OF-SIGHT CONTROL UNIT* --

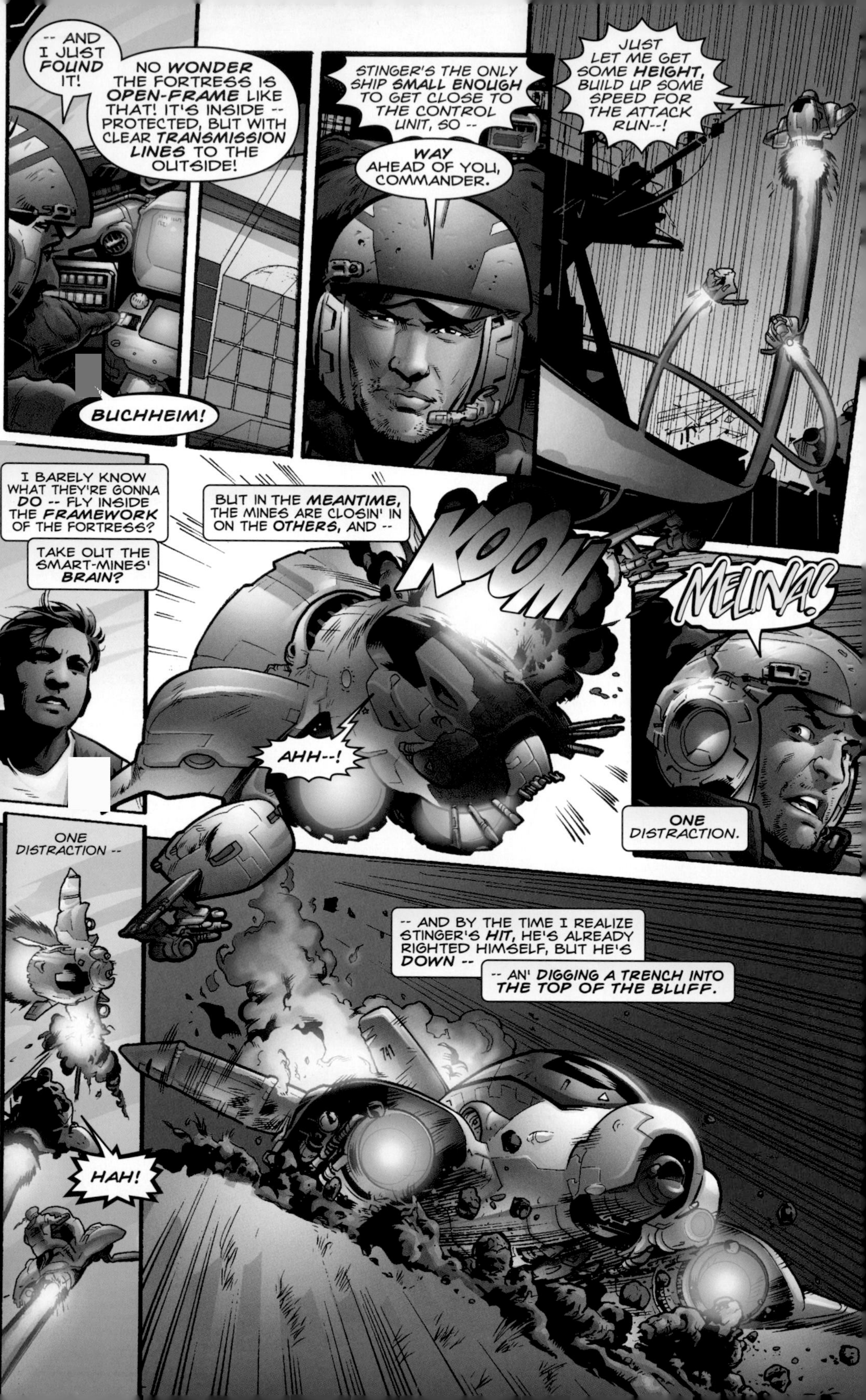
-- AND I JUST FOUND IT!
NO WONDER THE FORTRESS IS OPEN-FRAME LIKE THAT! IT'S INSIDE -- PROTECTED, BUT WITH CLEAR TRANSMISSION LINES TO THE OUTSIDE!
BUCHHEIM!
STINGER'S THE ONLY SHIP SMALL ENOUGH TO GET CLOSE TO THE CONTROL UNIT, SO --
WAY AHEAD OF YOU, COMMANDER.
JUST LET ME GET SOME HEIGHT, BUILD UP SOME SPEED FOR THE ATTACK RUN--!
I BARELY KNOW WHAT THEY'RE GONNA DO -- FLY INSIDE THE FRAMEWORK OF THE FORTRESS?
TAKE OUT THE SMART-MINES' BRAIN?
BUT IN THE MEANTIME, THE MINES ARE CLOSIN' IN ON THE OTHERS, AND --
KOOM
AHH--!
MELINA!
ONE DISTRACTION.
ONE DISTRACTION --
HAH!
-- AND BY THE TIME I REALIZE STINGER'S HIT, HE'S ALREADY RIGHTED HIMSELF, BUT HE'S DOWN --
-- AN' DIGGING A TRENCH INTO THE TOP OF THE BLUFF.

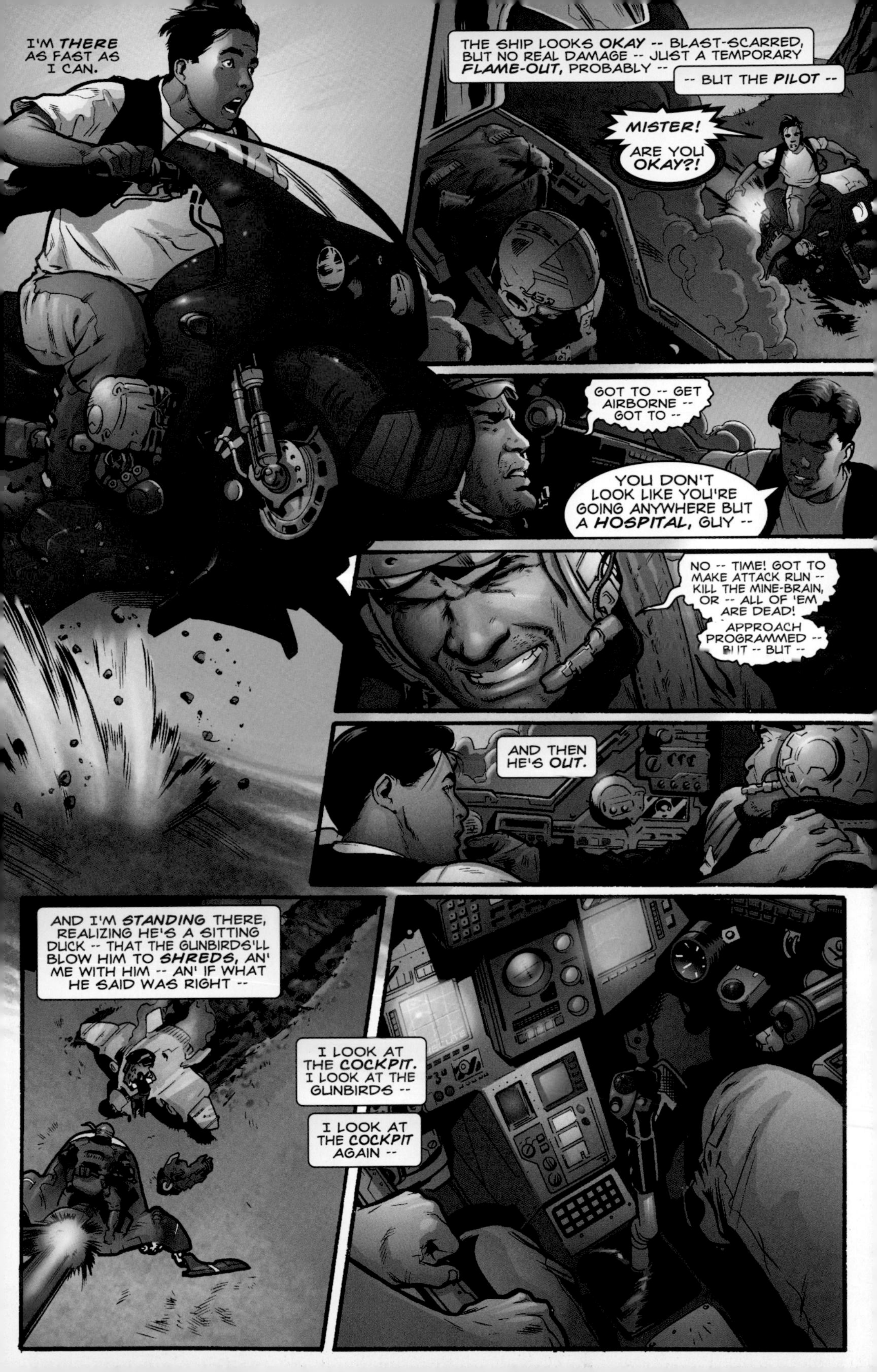
I'M THERE AS FAST AS I CAN.
THE SHIP LOOKS OKAY -- BLAST-SCARRED, BUT NO REAL DAMAGE -- JUST A TEMPORARY FLAME-OUT, PROBABLY --
-- BUT THE PILOT --
MISTER!
ARE YOU OKAY?!
GOT TO -- GET AIRBORNE -- GOT TO --
YOU DON'T LOOK LIKE YOU'RE GOING ANYWHERE BUT A HOSPITAL, GUY --
NO -- TIME! GOT TO MAKE ATTACK RUN -- KILL THE MINE-BRAIN, OR -- ALL OF 'EM ARE DEAD!
APPROACH PROGRAMMED -- BUT -- BUT --
AND THEN HE'S OUT.
AND I'M STANDING THERE, REALIZING HE'S A SITTING DUCK -- THAT THE GUNBIRDS'LL BLOW HIM TO SHREDS, AN' ME WITH HIM -- AN' IF WHAT HE SAID WAS RIGHT --
I LOOK AT THE COCKPIT. I LOOK AT THE GUNBIRDS --
I LOOK AT THE COCKPIT AGAIN --

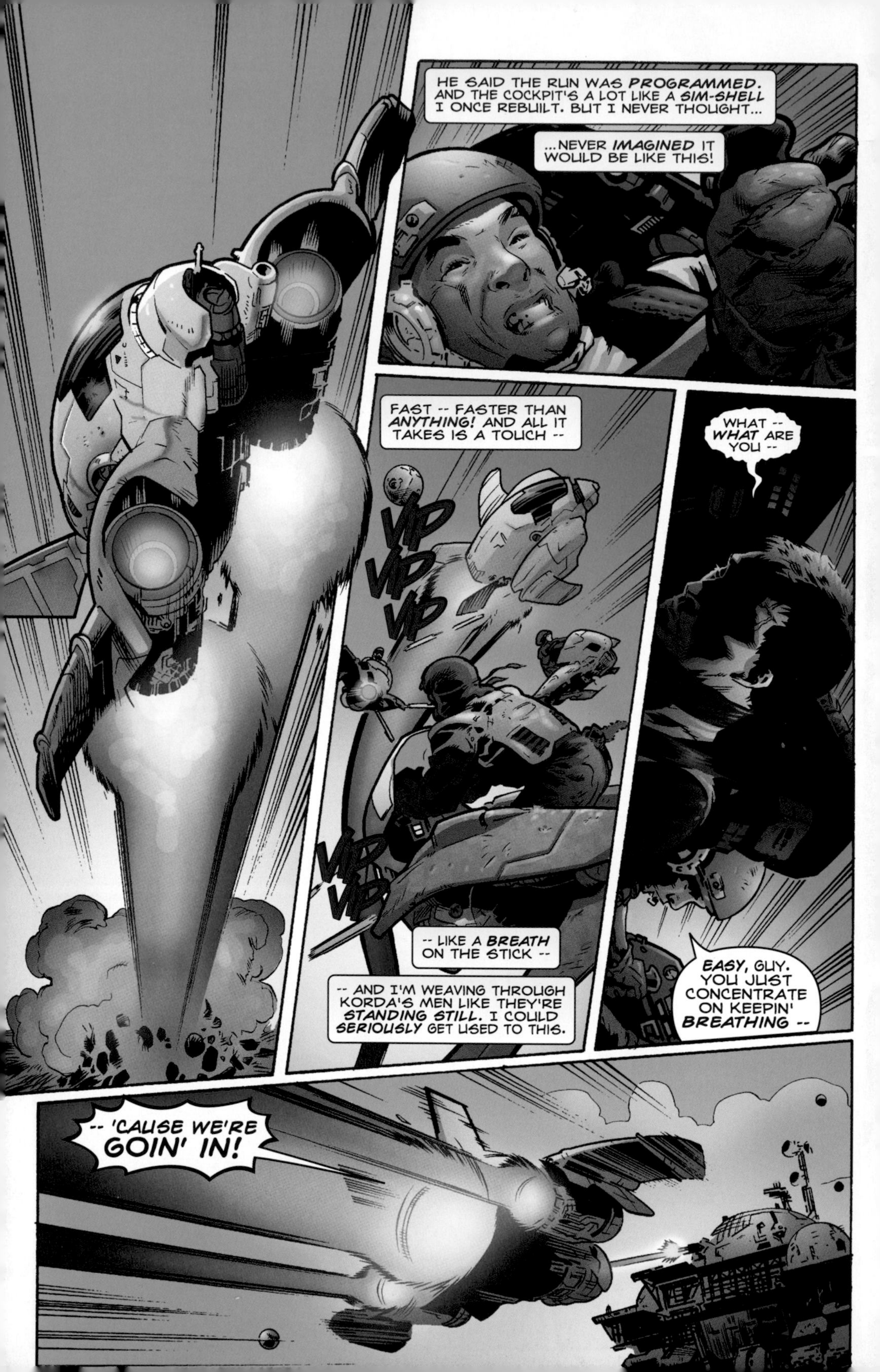
HE SAID THE RUN WAS *PROGRAMMED*. AND THE COCKPIT'S A LOT LIKE A *SIM-SHELL* I ONCE REBUILT. BUT I NEVER THOUGHT...
...NEVER *IMAGINED* IT WOULD BE LIKE THIS!
FAST -- FASTER THAN *ANYTHING!* AND ALL IT TAKES IS A TOUCH --
VIP VIP VIP
VIP VIP
-- LIKE A *BREATH* ON THE STICK --
-- AND I'M WEAVING THROUGH KORDA'S MEN LIKE THEY'RE *STANDING STILL*. I COULD *SERIOUSLY* GET USED TO THIS.
WHAT -- *WHAT* ARE YOU --
EASY, GUY. YOU JUST CONCENTRATE ON KEEPIN' *BREATHING* --
-- 'CAUSE WE'RE GOIN' IN!

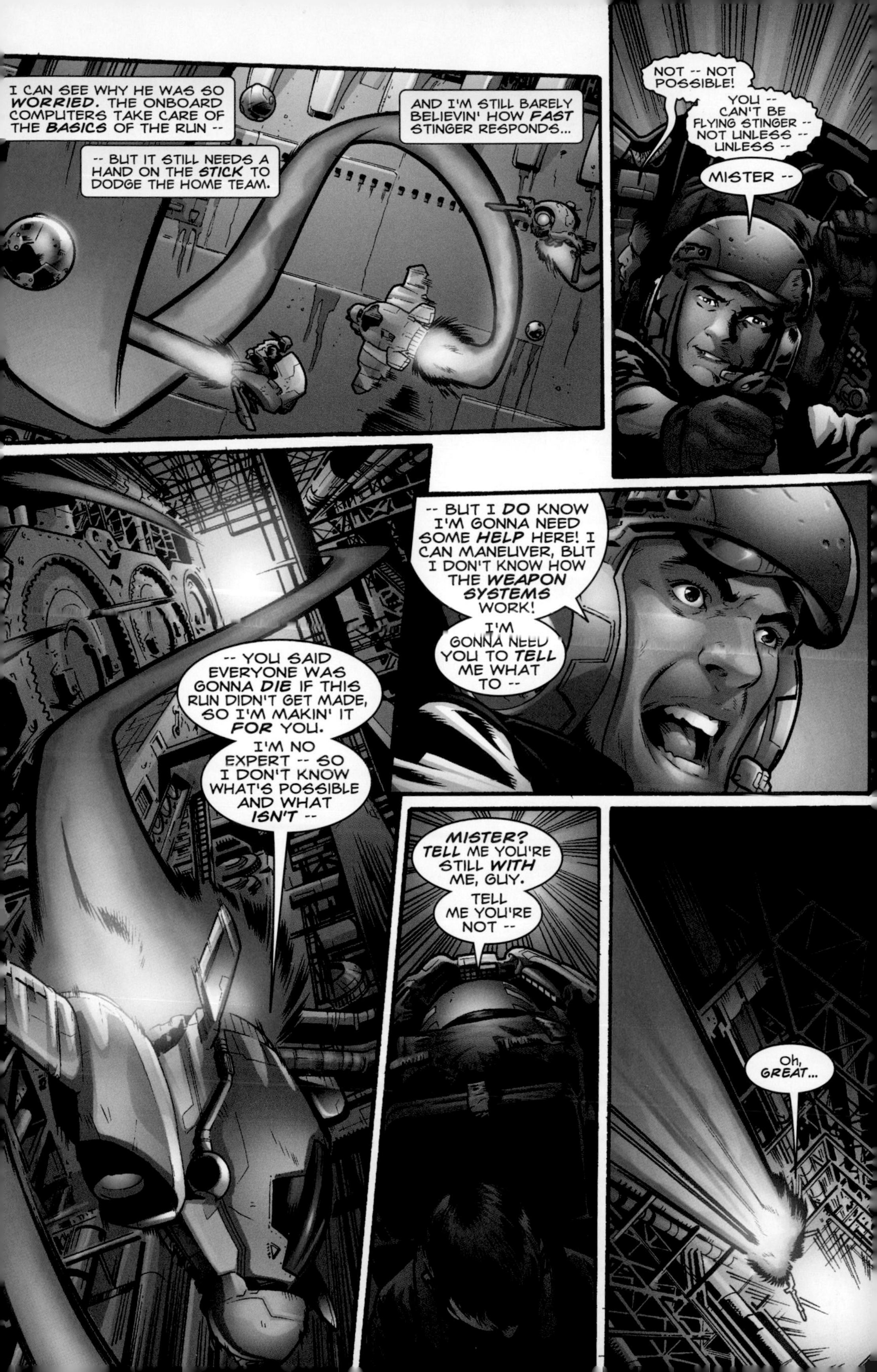
I CAN SEE WHY HE WAS SO WORRIED. THE ONBOARD COMPUTERS TAKE CARE OF THE BASICS OF THE RUN --
-- BUT IT STILL NEEDS A HAND ON THE STICK TO DODGE THE HOME TEAM.
AND I'M STILL BARELY BELIEVIN' HOW FAST STINGER RESPONDS...
NOT -- NOT POSSIBLE!
YOU -- CAN'T BE FLYING STINGER -- NOT UNLESS -- UNLESS --
MISTER --
-- YOU SAID EVERYONE WAS GONNA DIE IF THIS RUN DIDN'T GET MADE, SO I'M MAKIN' IT FOR YOU.
I'M NO EXPERT -- SO I DON'T KNOW WHAT'S POSSIBLE AND WHAT ISN'T --
-- BUT I DO KNOW I'M GONNA NEED SOME HELP HERE! I CAN MANEUVER, BUT I DON'T KNOW HOW THE WEAPON SYSTEMS WORK!
I'M GONNA NEED YOU TO TELL ME WHAT TO --
MISTER? TELL ME YOU'RE STILL WITH ME, GUY.
TELL ME YOU'RE NOT --
Oh, GREAT...

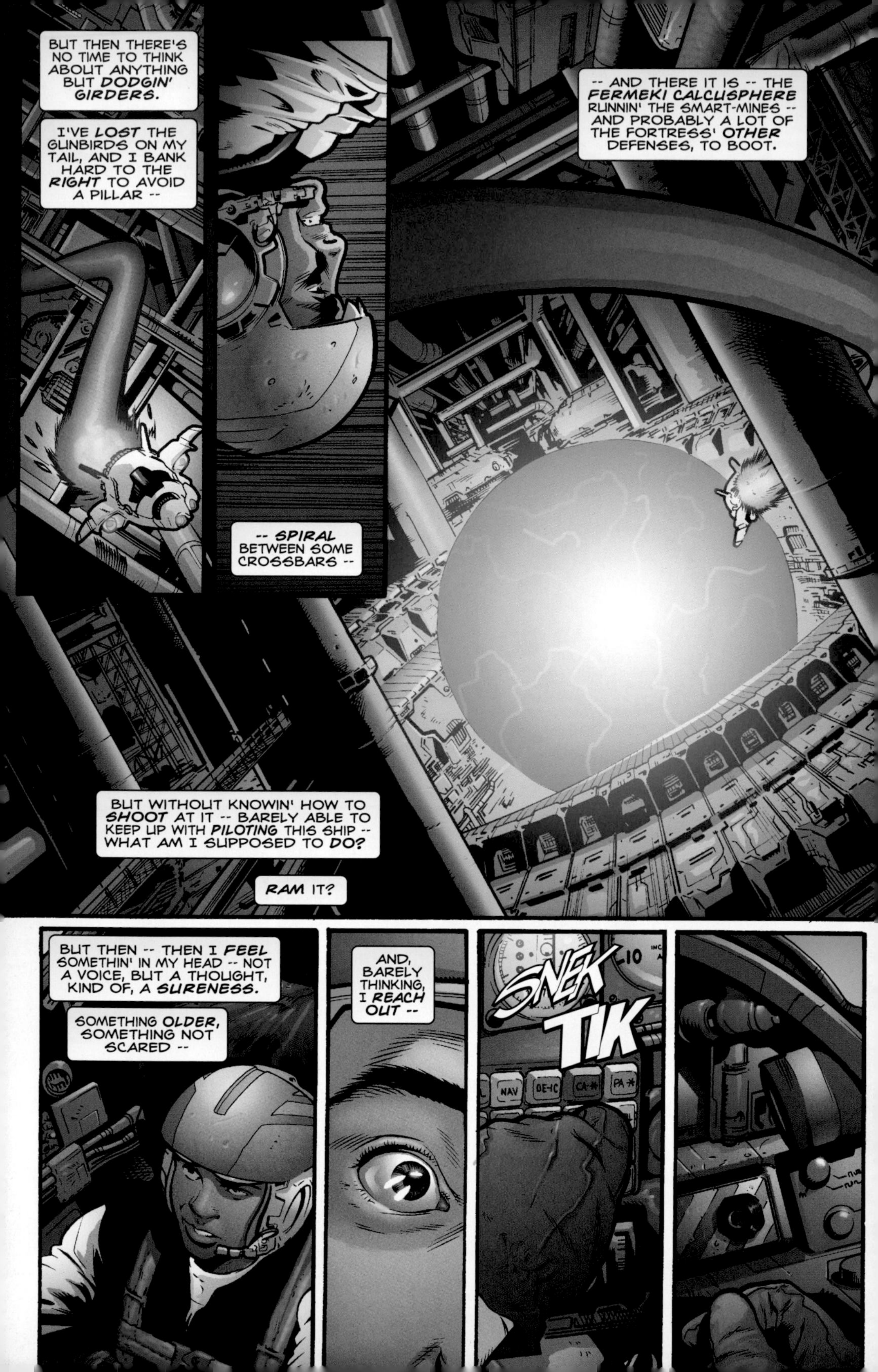
BUT THEN THERE'S NO TIME TO THINK ABOUT ANYTHING BUT DODGIN' GIRDERS.
I'VE LOST THE GUNBIRDS ON MY TAIL, AND I BANK HARD TO THE RIGHT TO AVOID A PILLAR --
-- SPIRAL BETWEEN SOME CROSSBARS --
-- AND THERE IT IS -- THE FERMEKI CALCUSPHERE RUNNIN' THE SMART-MINES -- AND PROBABLY A LOT OF THE FORTRESS' OTHER DEFENSES, TO BOOT.
BUT WITHOUT KNOWIN' HOW TO SHOOT AT IT -- BARELY ABLE TO KEEP UP WITH PILOTING THIS SHIP -- WHAT AM I SUPPOSED TO DO?
RAM IT?
BUT THEN -- THEN I FEEL SOMETHIN' IN MY HEAD -- NOT A VOICE, BUT A THOUGHT, KIND OF, A SURENESS.
SOMETHING OLDER, SOMETHING NOT SCARED --
AND, BARELY THINKING, I REACH OUT --
SNEK
TIK
NAV
DE-IC
CA-*
PA *

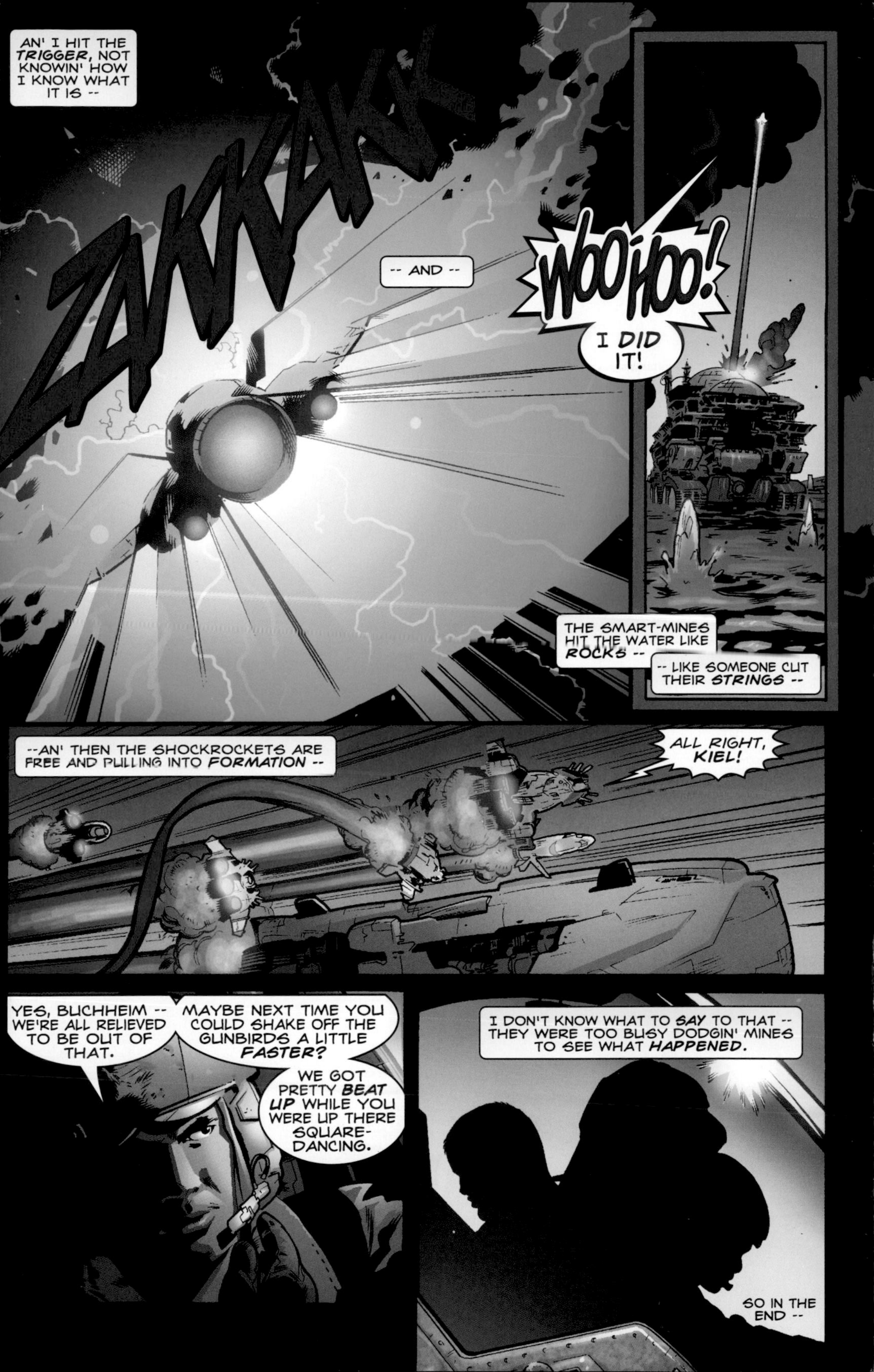
AN' I HIT THE TRIGGER, NOT KNOWIN' HOW I KNOW WHAT IT IS --
ZAKKAKK
-- AND --
WOO HOO!
I DID IT!
THE SMART-MINES HIT THE WATER LIKE ROCKS --
-- LIKE SOMEONE CUT THEIR STRINGS --
--AN' THEN THE SHOCKROCKETS ARE FREE AND PULLING INTO FORMATION --
ALL RIGHT, KIEL!
YES, BUCHHEIM -- WE'RE ALL RELIEVED TO BE OUT OF THAT.
MAYBE NEXT TIME YOU COULD SHAKE OFF THE GUNBIRDS A LITTLE FASTER?
WE GOT PRETTY BEAT UP WHILE YOU WERE UP THERE SQUARE-DANCING.
I DON'T KNOW WHAT TO SAY TO THAT -- THEY WERE TOO BUSY DODGIN' MINES TO SEE WHAT HAPPENED.
SO IN THE END --

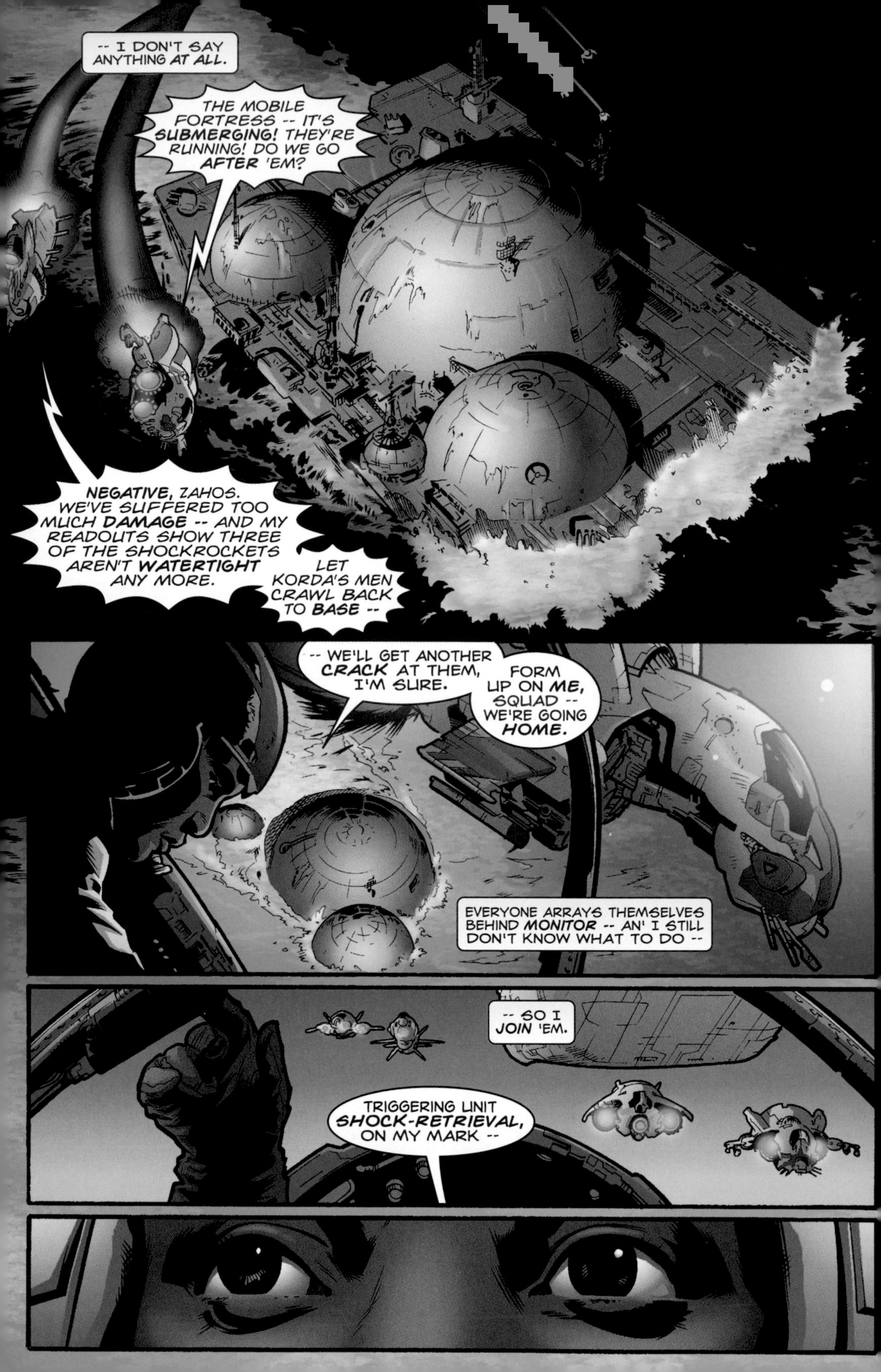
-- I DON'T SAY ANYTHING AT ALL.
THE MOBILE FORTRESS -- IT'S SUBMERGING! THEY'RE RUNNING! DO WE GO AFTER 'EM?
NEGATIVE, ZAHOS. WE'VE SUFFERED TOO MUCH DAMAGE -- AND MY READOUTS SHOW THREE OF THE SHOCKROCKETS AREN'T WATERTIGHT ANY MORE.
LET KORDA'S MEN CRAWL BACK TO BASE --
-- WE'LL GET ANOTHER CRACK AT THEM, I'M SURE.
FORM UP ON ME, SQUAD -- WE'RE GOING HOME.
EVERYONE ARRAYS THEMSELVES BEHIND MONITOR -- AN' I STILL DON'T KNOW WHAT TO DO --
-- SO I JOIN 'EM.
TRIGGERING UNIT SHOCK-RETRIEVAL, ON MY MARK --

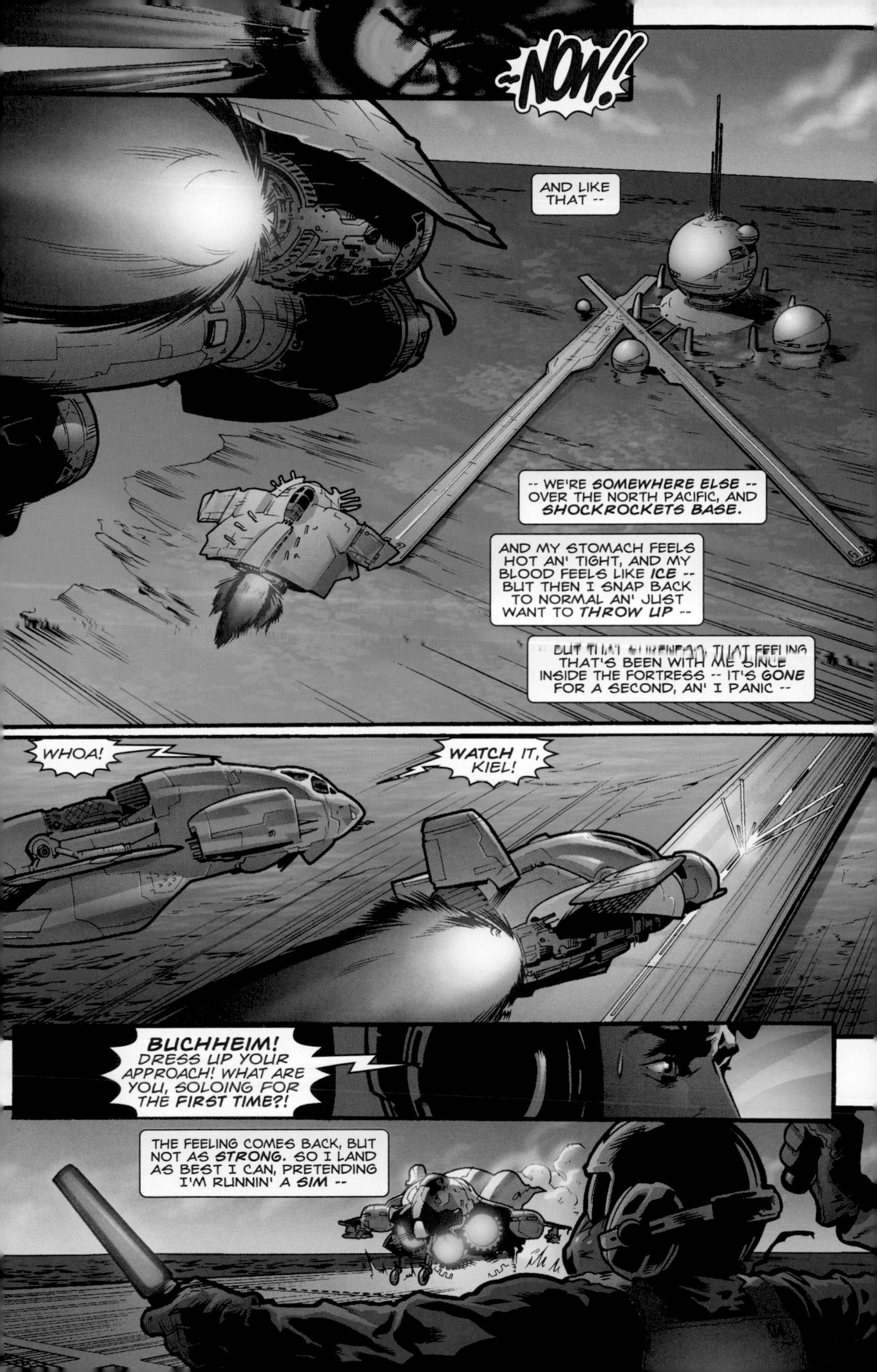
-- NOW!!
AND LIKE THAT --
-- WE'RE SOMEWHERE ELSE -- OVER THE NORTH PACIFIC, AND SHOCKROCKETS BASE.
AND MY STOMACH FEELS HOT AN' TIGHT, AND MY BLOOD FEELS LIKE ICE -- BUT THEN I SNAP BACK TO NORMAL AN' JUST WANT TO THROW UP --
THAT FEELING THAT'S BEEN WITH ME SINCE INSIDE THE FORTRESS -- IT'S GONE FOR A SECOND, AN' I PANIC --
WHOA!
WATCH IT, KIEL!
BUCHHEIM! DRESS UP YOUR APPROACH! WHAT ARE YOU, SOLOING FOR THE FIRST TIME?!
THE FEELING COMES BACK, BUT NOT AS STRONG. SO I LAND AS BEST I CAN, PRETENDING I'M RUNNIN' A SIM --

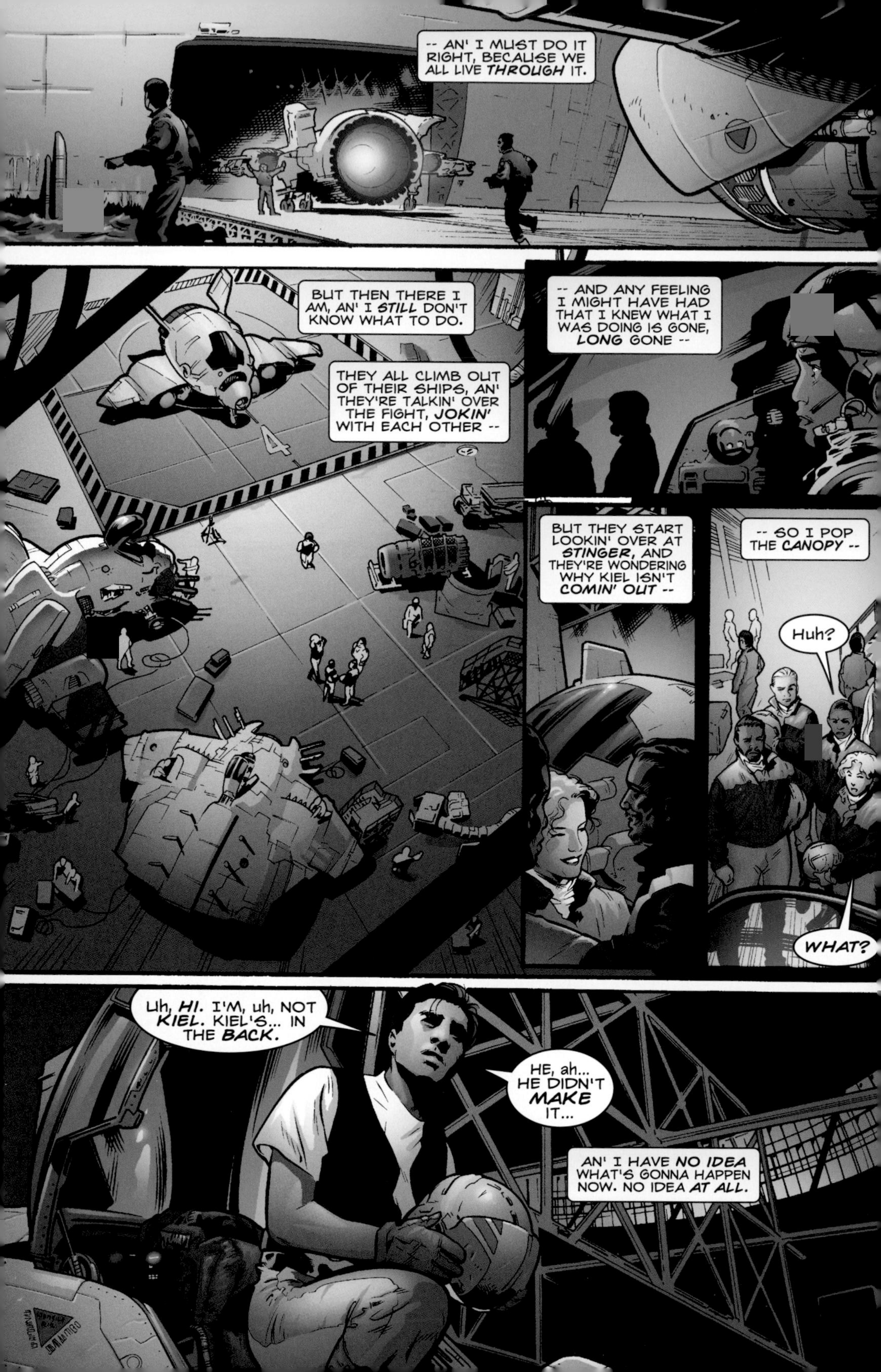
-- AN' I MUST DO IT RIGHT, BECAUSE WE ALL LIVE THROUGH IT.
BUT THEN THERE I AM, AN' I STILL DON'T KNOW WHAT TO DO.
THEY ALL CLIMB OUT OF THEIR SHIPS, AN' THEY'RE TALKIN' OVER THE FIGHT, JOKIN' WITH EACH OTHER --
4
-- AND ANY FEELING I MIGHT HAVE HAD THAT I KNEW WHAT I WAS DOING IS GONE, LONG GONE --
BUT THEY START LOOKIN' OVER AT STINGER, AND THEY'RE WONDERING WHY KIEL ISN'T COMIN' OUT --
-- SO I POP THE CANOPY --
Huh?
WHAT?
Uh, HI. I'M, uh, NOT KIEL. KIEL'S... IN THE BACK.
HE, ah... HE DIDN'T MAKE IT...
AN' I HAVE NO IDEA WHAT'S GONNA HAPPEN NOW. NO IDEA AT ALL.

CHAPTER TWO

x2 convert...1

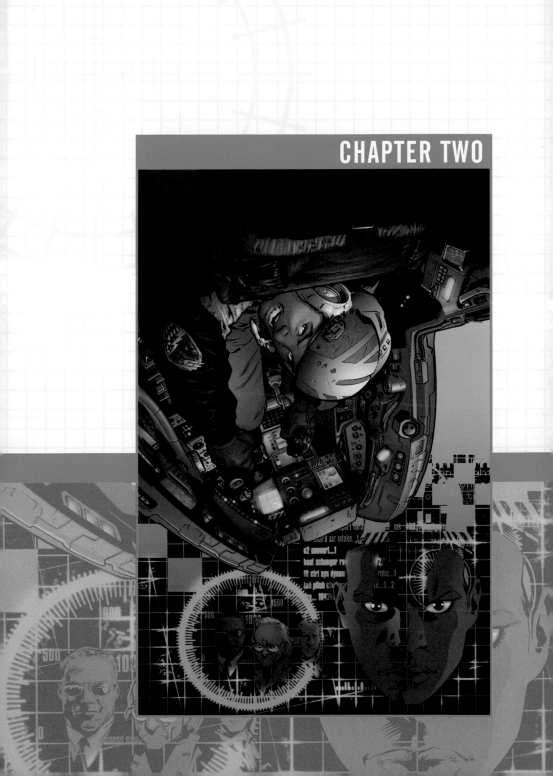

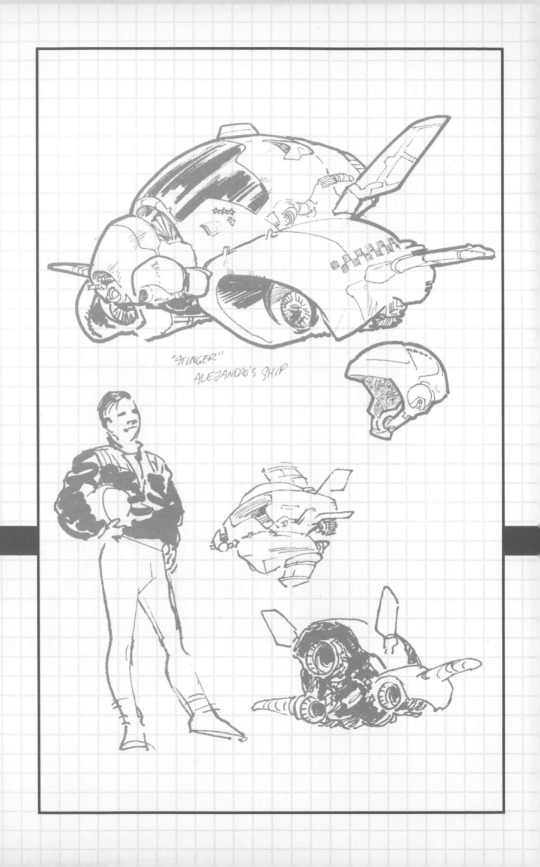

"STINGER"
ALEJANDRO'S SHIP

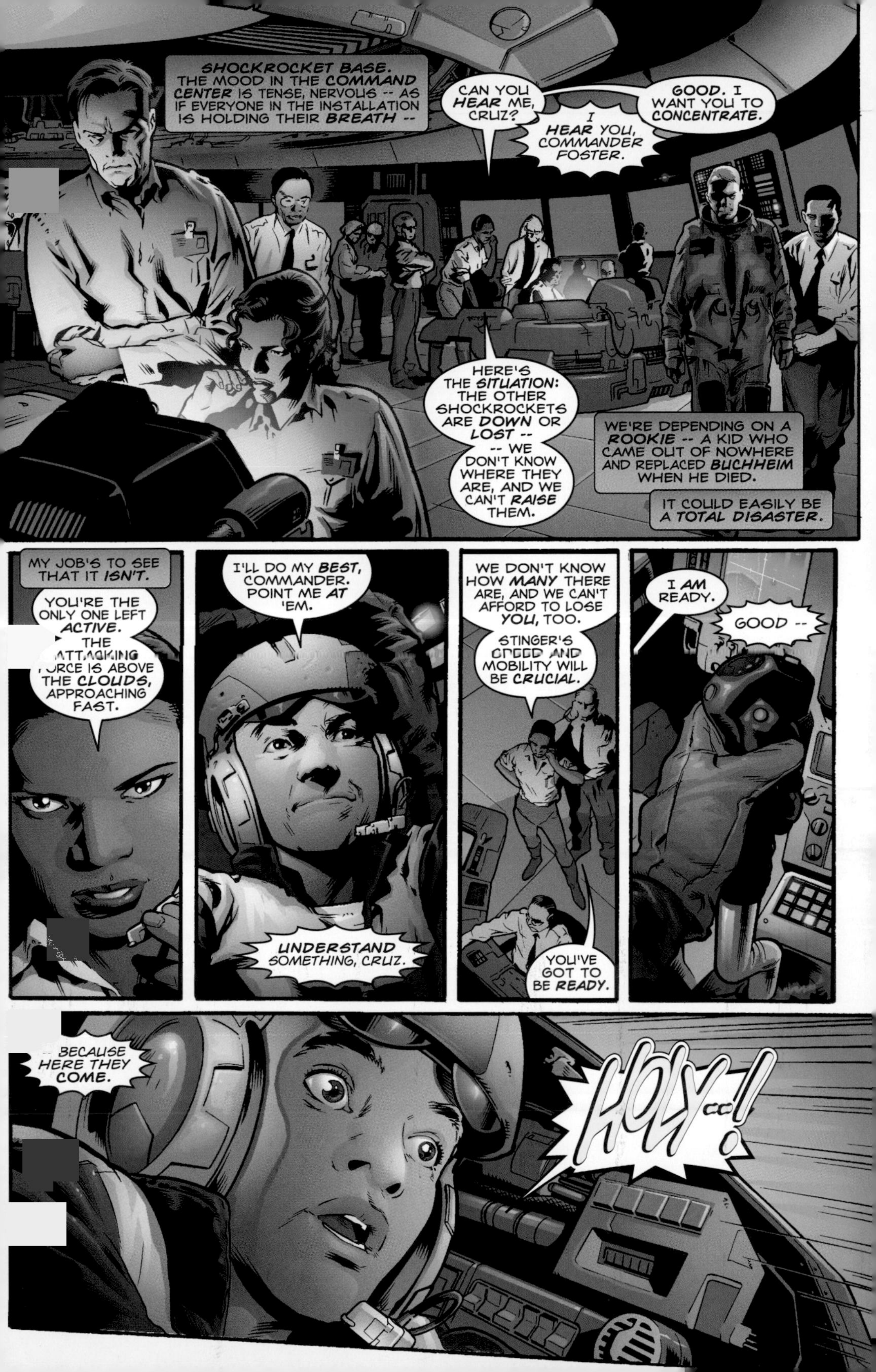
SHOCKROCKET BASE. THE MOOD IN THE COMMAND CENTER IS TENSE, NERVOUS -- AS IF EVERYONE IN THE INSTALLATION IS HOLDING THEIR BREATH --
CAN YOU HEAR ME, CRUZ?
I HEAR YOU, COMMANDER FOSTER.
GOOD. I WANT YOU TO CONCENTRATE.
HERE'S THE SITUATION: THE OTHER SHOCKROCKETS ARE DOWN OR LOST --
-- WE DON'T KNOW WHERE THEY ARE, AND WE CAN'T RAISE THEM.
WE'RE DEPENDING ON A ROOKIE -- A KID WHO CAME OUT OF NOWHERE AND REPLACED BUCHHEIM WHEN HE DIED.
IT COULD EASILY BE A TOTAL DISASTER.
MY JOB'S TO SEE THAT IT ISN'T.
YOU'RE THE ONLY ONE LEFT ACTIVE. THE ATTACKING FORCE IS ABOVE THE CLOUDS, APPROACHING FAST.
I'LL DO MY BEST, COMMANDER. POINT ME AT 'EM.
UNDERSTAND SOMETHING, CRUZ.
WE DON'T KNOW HOW MANY THERE ARE, AND WE CAN'T AFFORD TO LOSE YOU, TOO.
STINGER'S SPEED AND MOBILITY WILL BE CRUCIAL.
YOU'VE GOT TO BE READY.
I AM READY.
GOOD --
-- BECAUSE HERE THEY COME.
HOLY--!

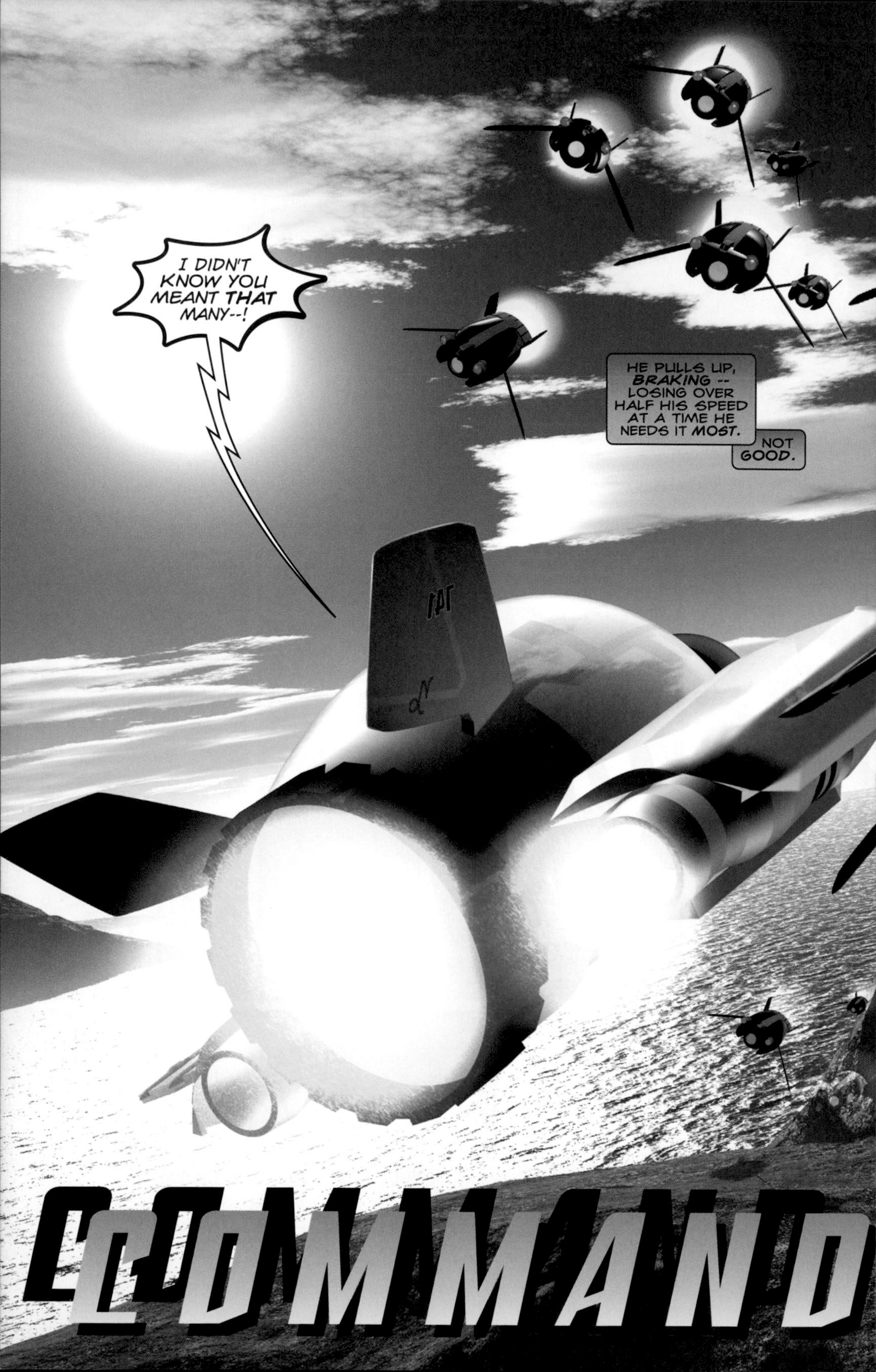
I DIDN'T KNOW YOU MEANT THAT MANY--!
HE PULLS UP, BRAKING -- LOSING OVER HALF HIS SPEED AT A TIME HE NEEDS IT MOST.
NOT GOOD.
COMMAND

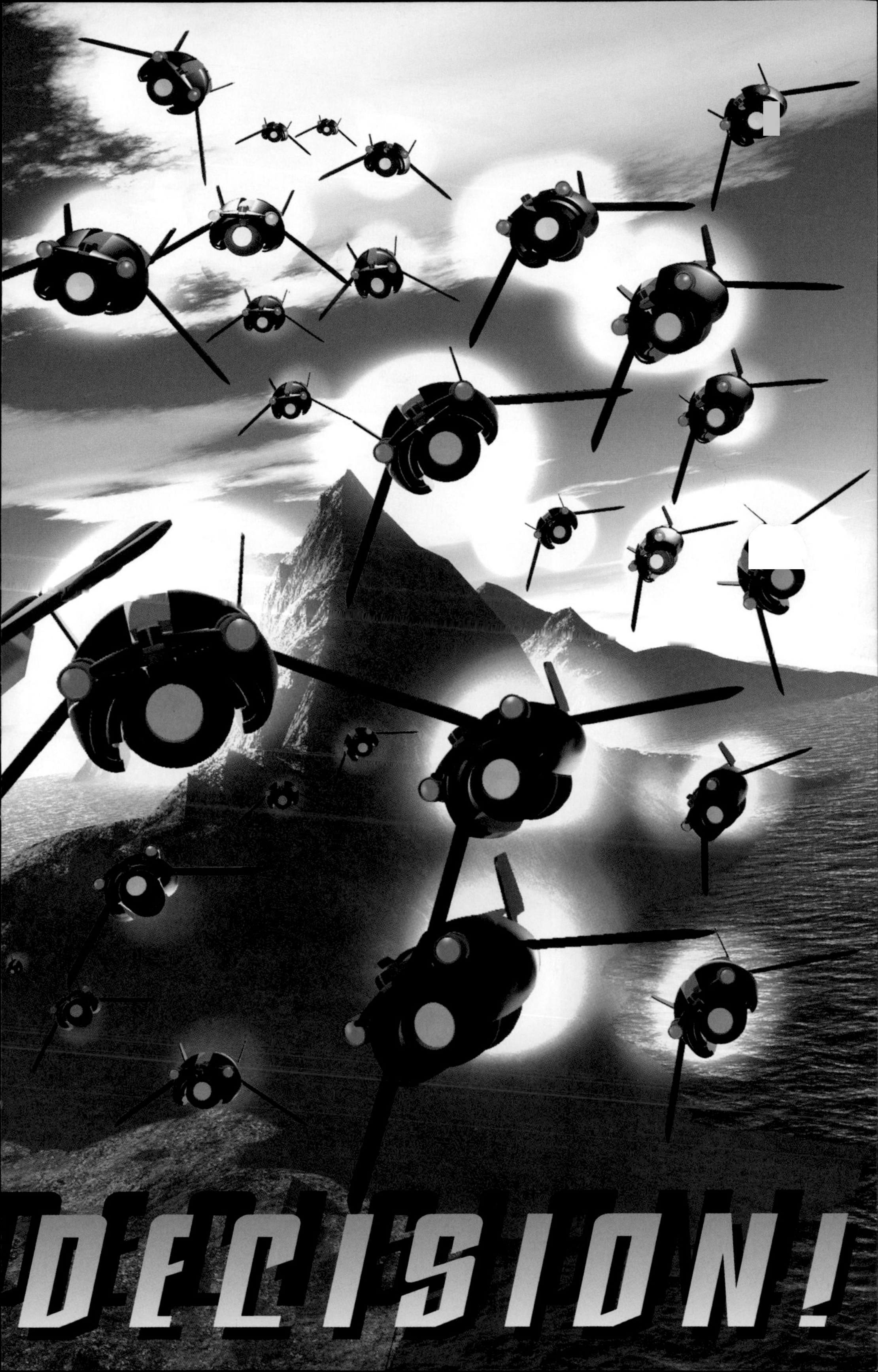
DECISION!

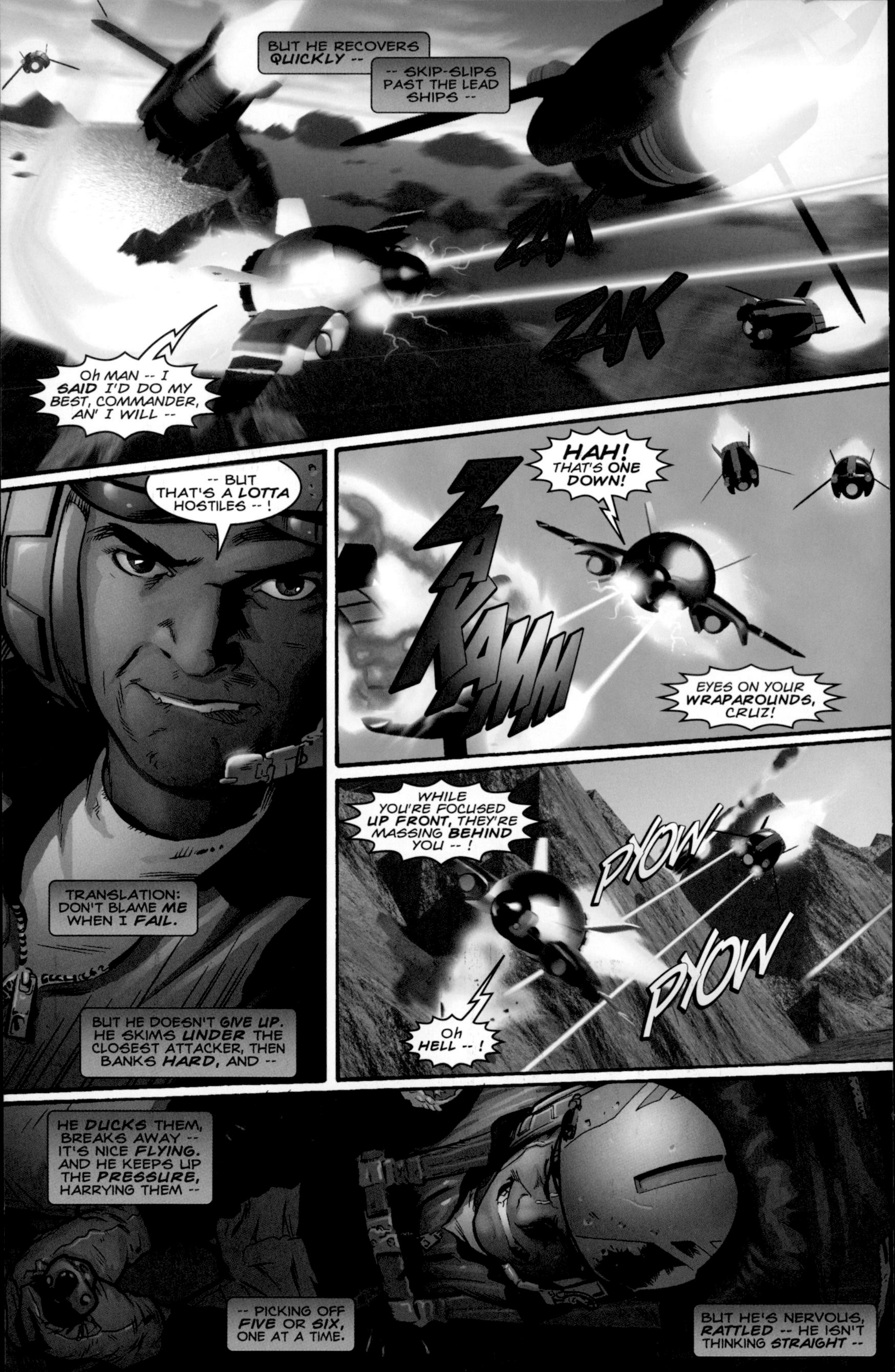

BUT HE RECOVERS QUICKLY --
-- SKIP-SLIPS PAST THE LEAD SHIPS --
ZAK
ZAK
Oh MAN -- I SAID I'D DO MY BEST, COMMANDER, AN' I WILL --
-- BUT THAT'S A LOTTA HOSTILES -- !
HAH! THAT'S ONE DOWN!
ZAKAMM
EYES ON YOUR WRAPAROUNDS, CRUZ!
TRANSLATION: DON'T BLAME ME WHEN I FAIL.
WHILE YOU'RE FOCUSED UP FRONT, THEY'RE MASSING BEHIND YOU -- !
PYOW
PYOW
Oh HELL -- !
BUT HE DOESN'T GIVE UP. HE SKIMS UNDER THE CLOSEST ATTACKER, THEN BANKS HARD, AND --
HE DUCKS THEM, BREAKS AWAY -- IT'S NICE FLYING. AND HE KEEPS UP THE PRESSURE, HARRYING THEM --
-- PICKING OFF FIVE OR SIX, ONE AT A TIME.
BUT HE'S NERVOUS, RATTLED -- HE ISN'T THINKING STRAIGHT --

LOOSEN UP, CRUZ. REMEMBER STINGER'S *OTHER* CAPABILITIES.

D'OHH! SORRY! I'M AN IDIOT!

TAK

SWITCHING TO *WEB*-CONFIG NOW...

AND AGAIN, HE'S FAST AND DECISIVE. HE DIVES INTO THEIR *MIDST*, EVADING THEIR FIRE --

-- AND HE TRIGGERS THE *WEB*.

ZAK ZAKK ZAKK ZAK ZAK

YEAH--!

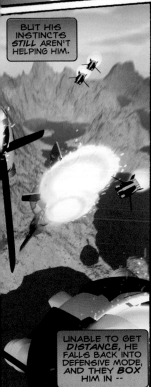

BUT HIS INSTINCTS *STILL* AREN'T HELPING HIM.

UNABLE TO GET *DISTANCE*, HE FALLS BACK INTO DEFENSIVE MODE, AND THEY *BOX* HIM IN --

-- AND THE END IS *INEVITABLE* --

PYOW PYOW

BKAMM

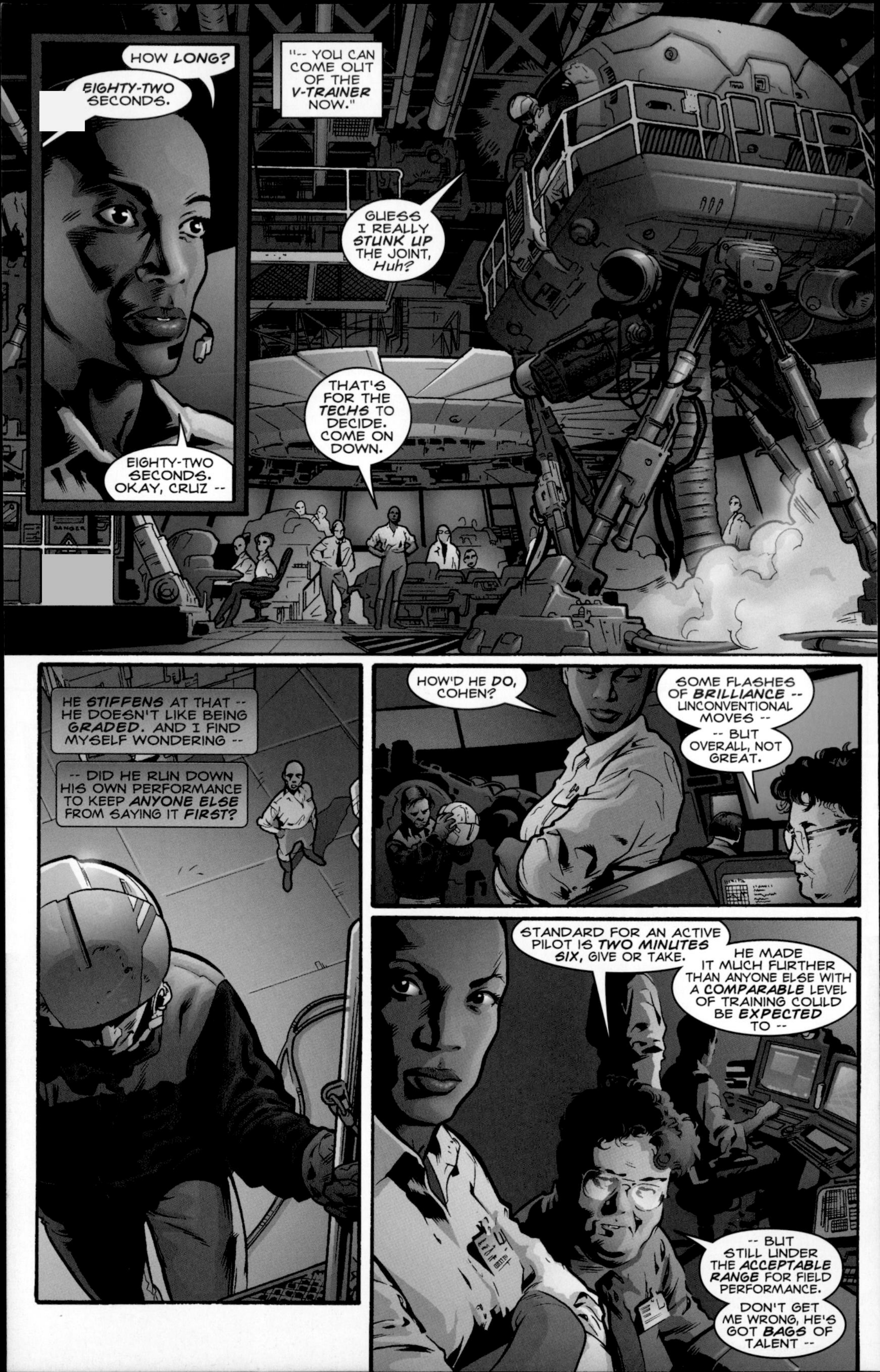
HOW LONG?
EIGHTY-TWO SECONDS.
"-- YOU CAN COME OUT OF THE V-TRAINER NOW."
GUESS I REALLY STUNK UP THE JOINT, Huh?
THAT'S FOR THE TECHS TO DECIDE. COME ON DOWN.
EIGHTY-TWO SECONDS. OKAY, CRUZ --
HE STIFFENS AT THAT -- HE DOESN'T LIKE BEING GRADED. AND I FIND MYSELF WONDERING --
-- DID HE RUN DOWN HIS OWN PERFORMANCE TO KEEP ANYONE ELSE FROM SAYING IT FIRST?
HOW'D HE DO, COHEN?
SOME FLASHES OF BRILLIANCE -- UNCONVENTIONAL MOVES --
-- BUT OVERALL, NOT GREAT.
STANDARD FOR AN ACTIVE PILOT IS TWO MINUTES SIX, GIVE OR TAKE.
HE MADE IT MUCH FURTHER THAN ANYONE ELSE WITH A COMPARABLE LEVEL OF TRAINING COULD BE EXPECTED TO --
-- BUT STILL UNDER THE ACCEPTABLE RANGE FOR FIELD PERFORMANCE.
DON'T GET ME WRONG, HE'S GOT BAGS OF TALENT --

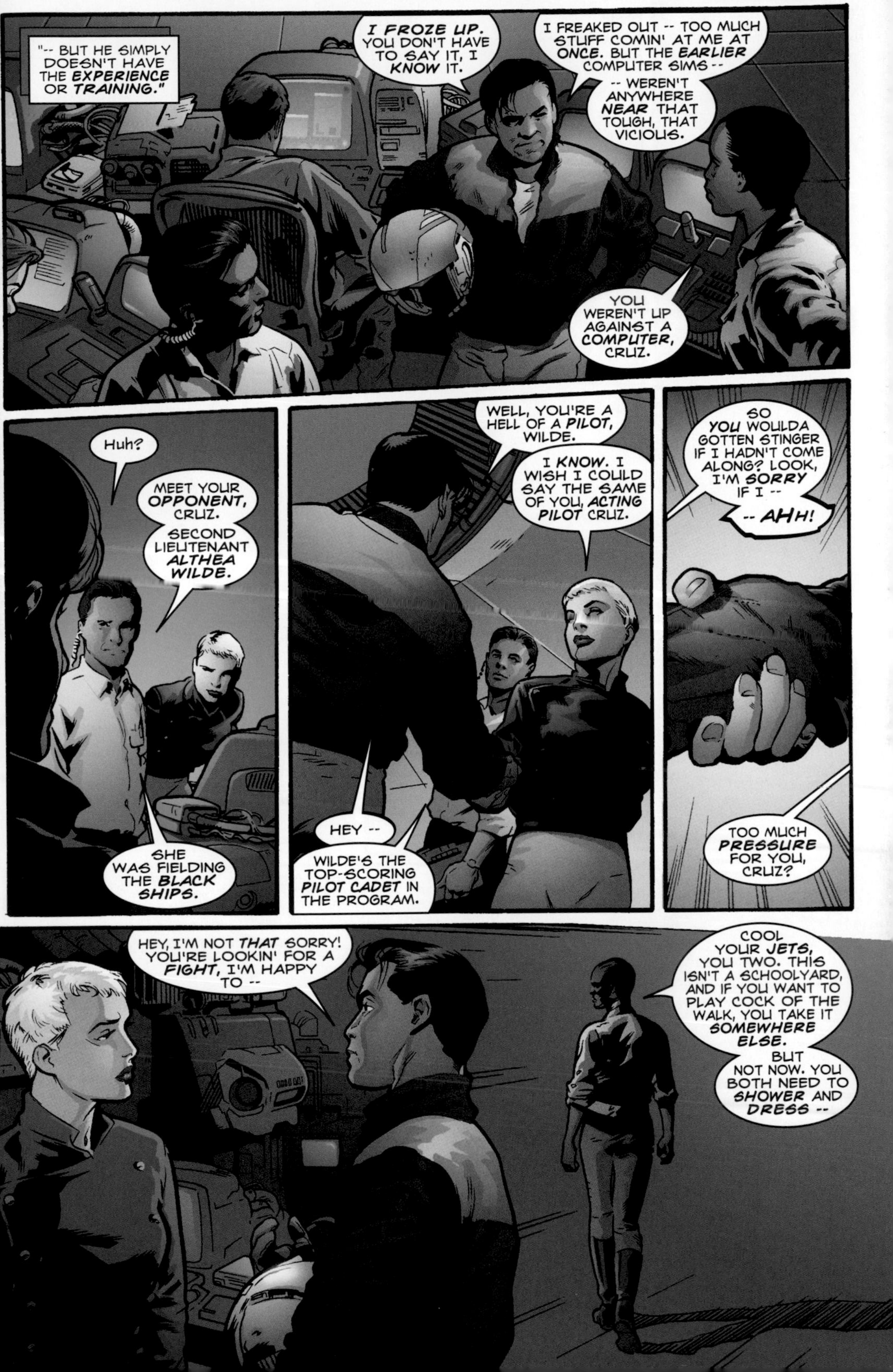
"-- BUT HE SIMPLY DOESN'T HAVE THE EXPERIENCE OR TRAINING."
I FROZE UP. YOU DON'T HAVE TO SAY IT, I KNOW IT.
I FREAKED OUT -- TOO MUCH STUFF COMIN' AT ME AT ONCE. BUT THE EARLIER COMPUTER SIMS --
-- WEREN'T ANYWHERE NEAR THAT TOUGH, THAT VICIOUS.
YOU WEREN'T UP AGAINST A COMPUTER, CRUZ.
Huh?
MEET YOUR OPPONENT, CRUZ.
SECOND LIEUTENANT ALTHEA WILDE.
SHE WAS FIELDING THE BLACK SHIPS.
WELL, YOU'RE A HELL OF A PILOT, WILDE.
I KNOW. I WISH I COULD SAY THE SAME OF YOU, ACTING PILOT CRUZ.
HEY --
WILDE'S THE TOP-SCORING PILOT CADET IN THE PROGRAM.
SO YOU WOULDA GOTTEN STINGER IF I HADN'T COME ALONG? LOOK, I'M SORRY IF I --
-- AHH!
TOO MUCH PRESSURE FOR YOU, CRUZ?
HEY, I'M NOT THAT SORRY! YOU'RE LOOKIN' FOR A FIGHT, I'M HAPPY TO --
COOL YOUR JETS, YOU TWO. THIS ISN'T A SCHOOLYARD, AND IF YOU WANT TO PLAY COCK OF THE WALK, YOU TAKE IT SOMEWHERE ELSE.
BUT NOT NOW. YOU BOTH NEED TO SHOWER AND DRESS --

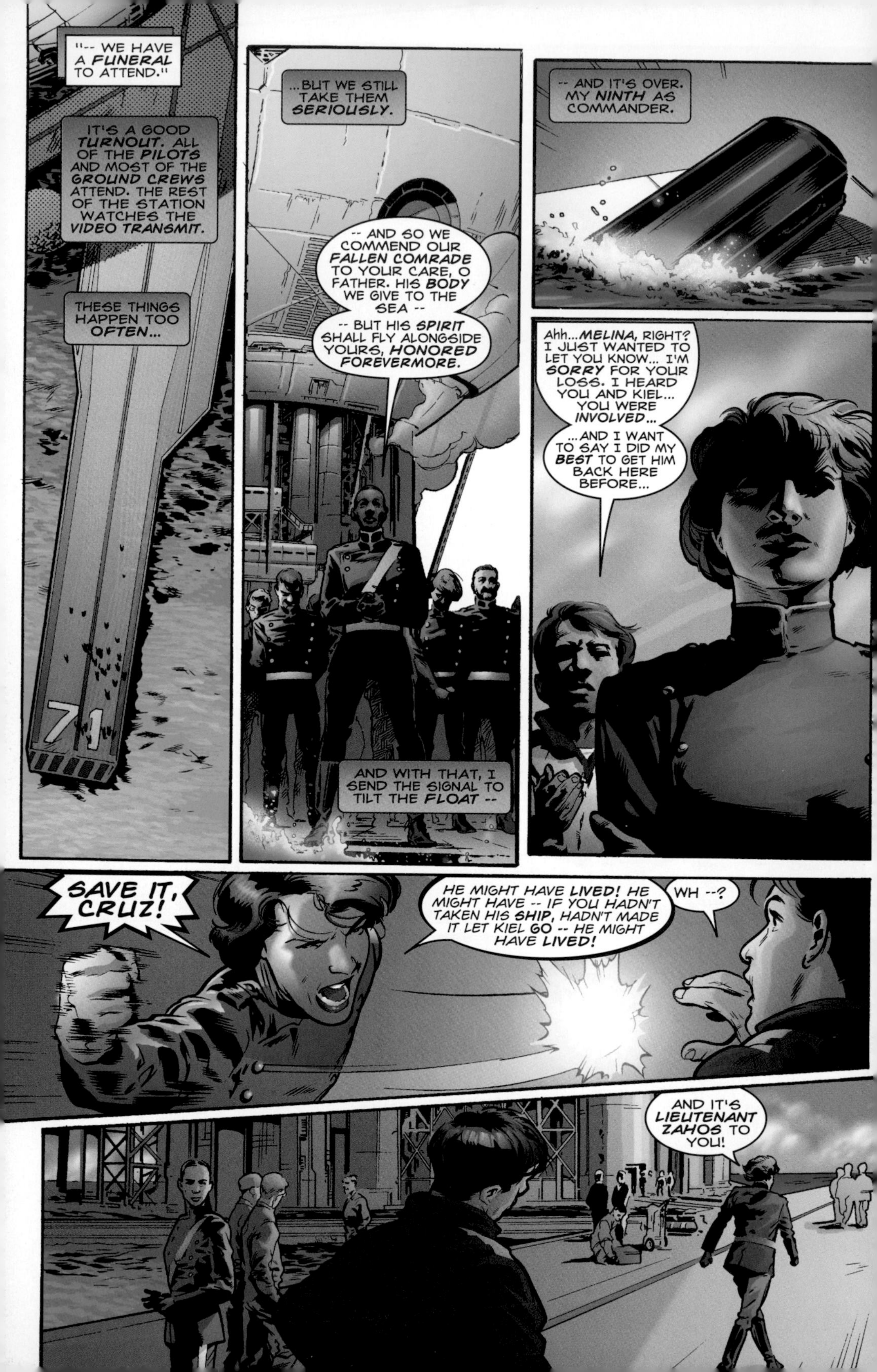
"-- WE HAVE A FUNERAL TO ATTEND."
IT'S A GOOD TURNOUT. ALL OF THE PILOTS AND MOST OF THE GROUND CREWS ATTEND. THE REST OF THE STATION WATCHES THE VIDEO TRANSMIT.
THESE THINGS HAPPEN TOO OFTEN...
...BUT WE STILL TAKE THEM SERIOUSLY.
-- AND SO WE COMMEND OUR FALLEN COMRADE TO YOUR CARE, O FATHER. HIS BODY WE GIVE TO THE SEA --
-- BUT HIS SPIRIT SHALL FLY ALONGSIDE YOURS, HONORED FOREVERMORE.
AND WITH THAT, I SEND THE SIGNAL TO TILT THE FLOAT --
-- AND IT'S OVER. MY NINTH AS COMMANDER.
Ahh...MELINA, RIGHT? I JUST WANTED TO LET YOU KNOW... I'M SORRY FOR YOUR LOSS. I HEARD YOU AND KIEL... YOU WERE INVOLVED...
...AND I WANT TO SAY I DID MY BEST TO GET HIM BACK HERE BEFORE...
SAVE IT, CRUZ!
HE MIGHT HAVE LIVED! HE MIGHT HAVE -- IF YOU HADN'T TAKEN HIS SHIP, HADN'T MADE IT LET KIEL GO -- HE MIGHT HAVE LIVED!
WH --?
AND IT'S LIEUTENANT ZAHOS TO YOU!

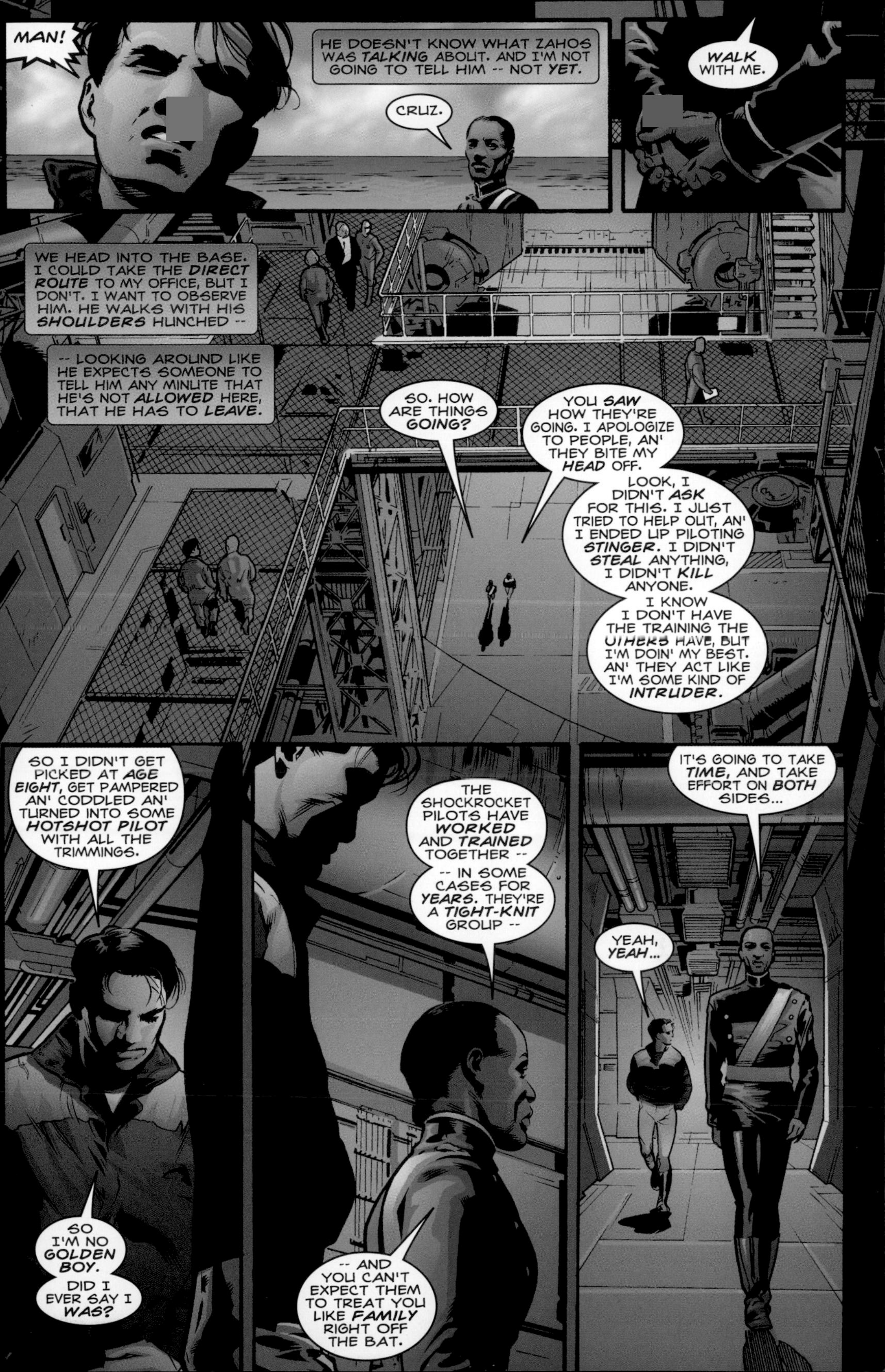
MAN!
HE DOESN'T KNOW WHAT ZAHOS WAS TALKING ABOUT. AND I'M NOT GOING TO TELL HIM -- NOT YET.
CRUZ.
WALK WITH ME.
WE HEAD INTO THE BASE. I COULD TAKE THE DIRECT ROUTE TO MY OFFICE, BUT I DON'T. I WANT TO OBSERVE HIM. HE WALKS WITH HIS SHOULDERS HUNCHED --
-- LOOKING AROUND LIKE HE EXPECTS SOMEONE TO TELL HIM ANY MINUTE THAT HE'S NOT ALLOWED HERE, THAT HE HAS TO LEAVE.
SO. HOW ARE THINGS GOING?
YOU SAW HOW THEY'RE GOING. I APOLOGIZE TO PEOPLE, AN' THEY BITE MY HEAD OFF.
LOOK, I DIDN'T ASK FOR THIS. I JUST TRIED TO HELP OUT, AN' I ENDED UP PILOTING STINGER. I DIDN'T STEAL ANYTHING, I DIDN'T KILL ANYONE.
I KNOW I DON'T HAVE THE TRAINING THE OTHERS HAVE, BUT I'M DOIN' MY BEST. AN' THEY ACT LIKE I'M SOME KIND OF INTRUDER.
SO I DIDN'T GET PICKED AT AGE EIGHT, GET PAMPERED AN' CODDLED AN' TURNED INTO SOME HOTSHOT PILOT WITH ALL THE TRIMMINGS.
SO I'M NO GOLDEN BOY.
DID I EVER SAY I WAS?
THE SHOCKROCKET PILOTS HAVE WORKED AND TRAINED TOGETHER --
-- IN SOME CASES FOR YEARS. THEY'RE A TIGHT-KNIT GROUP --
-- AND YOU CAN'T EXPECT THEM TO TREAT YOU LIKE FAMILY RIGHT OFF THE BAT.
IT'S GOING TO TAKE TIME, AND TAKE EFFORT ON BOTH SIDES...
YEAH, YEAH...

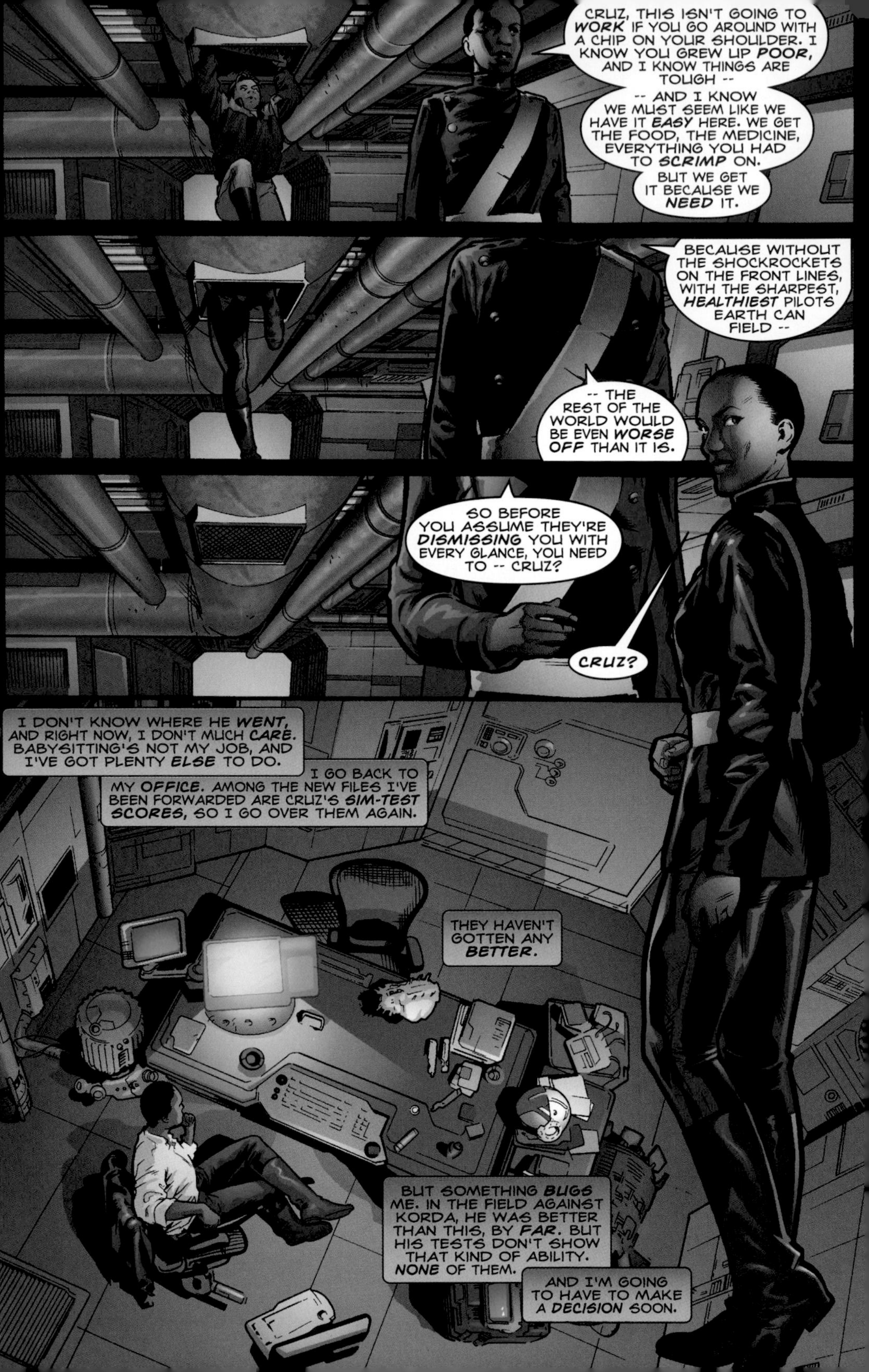

CRUZ, THIS ISN'T GOING TO WORK IF YOU GO AROUND WITH A CHIP ON YOUR SHOULDER. I KNOW YOU GREW UP POOR, AND I KNOW THINGS ARE TOUGH --
-- AND I KNOW WE MUST SEEM LIKE WE HAVE IT EASY HERE. WE GET THE FOOD, THE MEDICINE, EVERYTHING YOU HAD TO SCRIMP ON.
BUT WE GET IT BECAUSE WE NEED IT.
BECAUSE WITHOUT THE SHOCKROCKETS ON THE FRONT LINES, WITH THE SHARPEST, HEALTHIEST PILOTS EARTH CAN FIELD --
-- THE REST OF THE WORLD WOULD BE EVEN WORSE OFF THAN IT IS.
SO BEFORE YOU ASSUME THEY'RE DISMISSING YOU WITH EVERY GLANCE, YOU NEED TO -- CRUZ?
CRUZ?
I DON'T KNOW WHERE HE WENT, AND RIGHT NOW, I DON'T MUCH CARE. BABYSITTING'S NOT MY JOB, AND I'VE GOT PLENTY ELSE TO DO.
I GO BACK TO MY OFFICE. AMONG THE NEW FILES I'VE BEEN FORWARDED ARE CRUZ'S SIM-TEST SCORES, SO I GO OVER THEM AGAIN.
THEY HAVEN'T GOTTEN ANY BETTER.
BUT SOMETHING BUGS ME. IN THE FIELD AGAINST KORDA, HE WAS BETTER THAN THIS, BY FAR. BUT HIS TESTS DON'T SHOW THAT KIND OF ABILITY. NONE OF THEM.
AND I'M GOING TO HAVE TO MAKE A DECISION SOON.

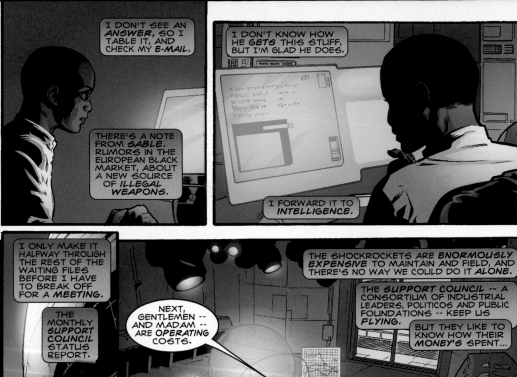

I DON'T SEE AN ANSWER, SO I TABLE IT, AND CHECK MY E-MAIL.

THERE'S A NOTE FROM *SABLE*. RUMORS IN THE EUROPEAN BLACK MARKET, ABOUT A NEW SOURCE OF *ILLEGAL WEAPONS*.

I DON'T KNOW HOW HE *GETS* THIS STUFF, BUT I'M GLAD HE DOES.

I FORWARD IT TO *INTELLIGENCE*.

I ONLY MAKE IT HALFWAY THROUGH THE REST OF THE WAITING FILES BEFORE I HAVE TO BREAK OFF FOR A *MEETING*.

THE *MONTHLY SUPPORT COUNCIL STATUS* REPORT.

NEXT, GENTLEMEN -- AND MADAM -- ARE *OPERATING* COSTS.

THE *SHOCKROCKETS* ARE *ENORMOUSLY EXPENSIVE* TO MAINTAIN AND FIELD, AND THERE'S NO WAY WE COULD DO IT *ALONE*.

THE *SUPPORT COUNCIL* -- A CONSORTIUM OF INDUSTRIAL LEADERS, POLITICOS AND PUBLIC FOUNDATIONS -- KEEP US *FLYING*.

BUT THEY LIKE TO KNOW HOW THEIR *MONEY'S* SPENT...

-- SO PLEASE NOTE OUR CONCERN ABOUT *COST OVERRUNS* IN THE RESEARCH DIVISION. WHAT'S *NEXT*?

AS YOU CAN SEE FROM THE *CHARTS* -- INCLUDING *PROJECTED* COST --

-- WE'RE TWENTY PERCENT OVER BUDGET *ALREADY*, AND EXPECT TO GET WORSE, THANKS TO THE COST OF HOLDING *KORDA* BACK.

WE'RE DOING OUR BEST TO *ECONOMIZE* IN OTHER AREAS, BUT --

Ah, Dr. *BISHOP*, IF I *MIGHT*? I DON'T SEE ANY REASON TO *SKIMP* ON OPERATIONS.

THE *SHOCKROCKETS* ARE *CRUCIAL* TO WORLD STABILITY, AND I'D HATE TO LOSE A CITY BECAUSE WE TRIED TO DO THINGS ON THE *CHEAP*.

THE SUPPORT COUNCIL WILL FIND WHATEVER YOU *NEED* ON THAT SCORE.

THANK YOU, Mr. DeANDRIA. NEXT, THEN, IS *INTELLIGENCE*...

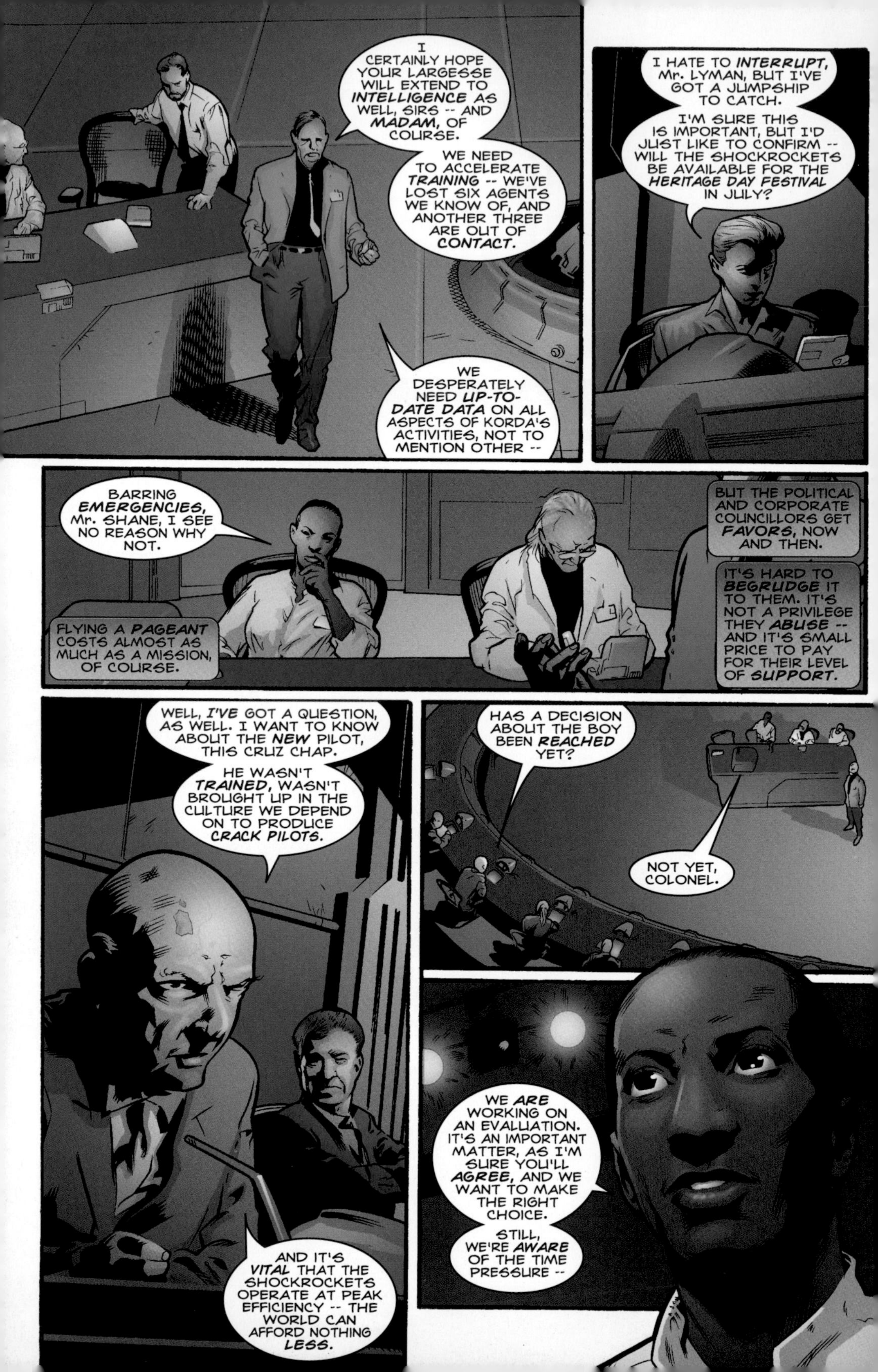
I CERTAINLY HOPE YOUR LARGESSE WILL EXTEND TO INTELLIGENCE AS WELL, SIRS -- AND MADAM, OF COURSE.
WE NEED TO ACCELERATE TRAINING -- WE'VE LOST SIX AGENTS WE KNOW OF, AND ANOTHER THREE ARE OUT OF CONTACT.
WE DESPERATELY NEED UP-TO-DATE DATA ON ALL ASPECTS OF KORDA'S ACTIVITIES, NOT TO MENTION OTHER --
I HATE TO INTERRUPT, Mr. LYMAN, BUT I'VE GOT A JUMPSHIP TO CATCH.
I'M SURE THIS IS IMPORTANT, BUT I'D JUST LIKE TO CONFIRM -- WILL THE SHOCKROCKETS BE AVAILABLE FOR THE HERITAGE DAY FESTIVAL IN JULY?
BARRING EMERGENCIES, Mr. SHANE, I SEE NO REASON WHY NOT.
FLYING A PAGEANT COSTS ALMOST AS MUCH AS A MISSION, OF COURSE.
BUT THE POLITICAL AND CORPORATE COUNCILLORS GET FAVORS, NOW AND THEN.
IT'S HARD TO BEGRUDGE IT TO THEM. IT'S NOT A PRIVILEGE THEY ABUSE -- AND IT'S SMALL PRICE TO PAY FOR THEIR LEVEL OF SUPPORT.
WELL, I'VE GOT A QUESTION, AS WELL. I WANT TO KNOW ABOUT THE NEW PILOT, THIS CRUZ CHAP.
HE WASN'T TRAINED, WASN'T BROUGHT UP IN THE CULTURE WE DEPEND ON TO PRODUCE CRACK PILOTS.
AND IT'S VITAL THAT THE SHOCKROCKETS OPERATE AT PEAK EFFICIENCY -- THE WORLD CAN AFFORD NOTHING LESS.
HAS A DECISION ABOUT THE BOY BEEN REACHED YET?
NOT YET, COLONEL.
WE ARE WORKING ON AN EVALUATION. IT'S AN IMPORTANT MATTER, AS I'M SURE YOU'LL AGREE, AND WE WANT TO MAKE THE RIGHT CHOICE.
STILL, WE'RE AWARE OF THE TIME PRESSURE --

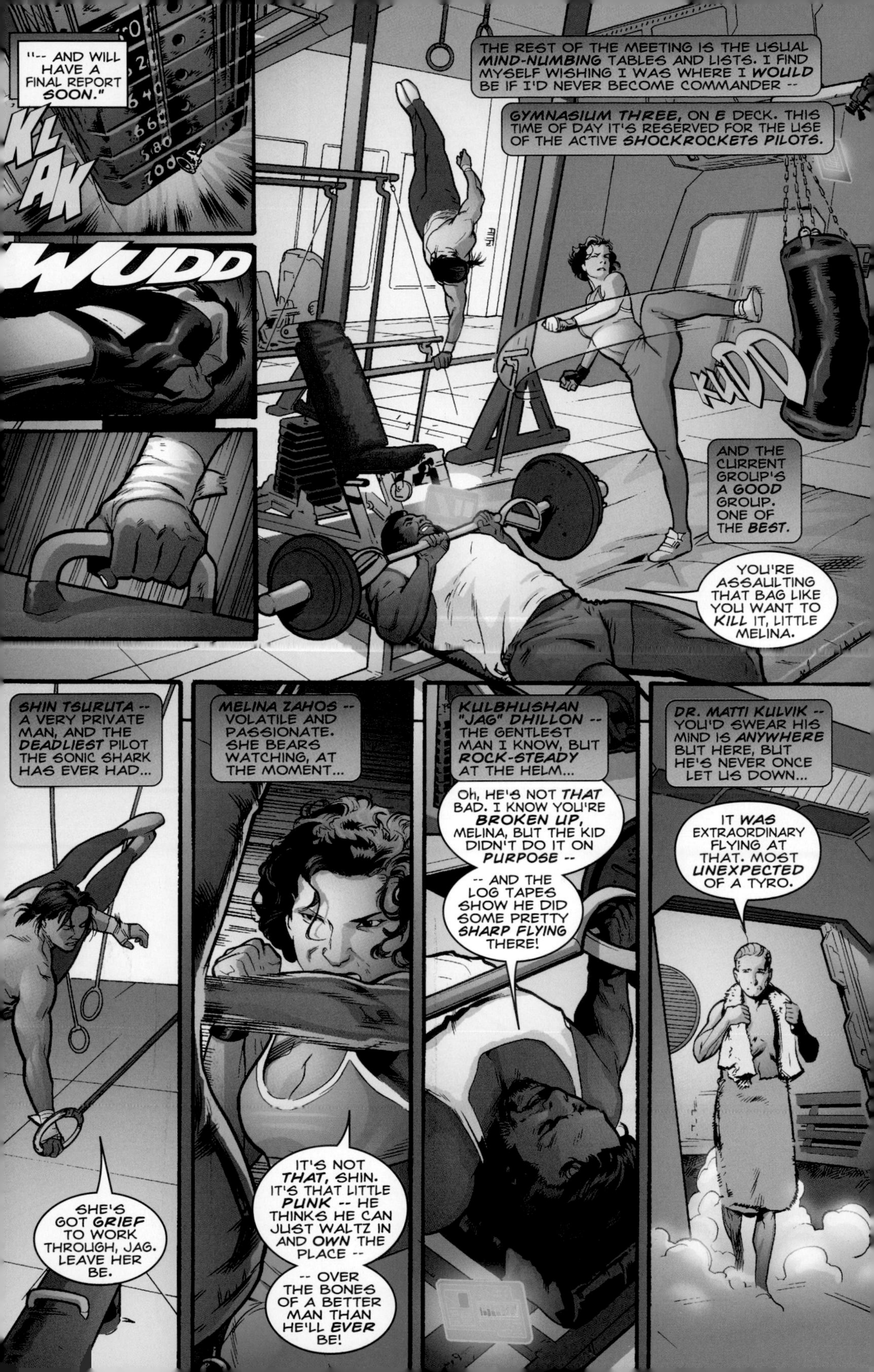
"-- AND WILL HAVE A FINAL REPORT SOON."
KLAK
WUDD
THE REST OF THE MEETING IS THE USUAL MIND-NUMBING TABLES AND LISTS. I FIND MYSELF WISHING I WAS WHERE I WOULD BE IF I'D NEVER BECOME COMMANDER --
GYMNASIUM THREE, ON E DECK. THIS TIME OF DAY IT'S RESERVED FOR THE USE OF THE ACTIVE SHOCKROCKETS PILOTS.
KUDD
AND THE CURRENT GROUP'S A GOOD GROUP. ONE OF THE BEST.
YOU'RE ASSAULTING THAT BAG LIKE YOU WANT TO KILL IT, LITTLE MELINA.
SHIN TSURUTA -- A VERY PRIVATE MAN, AND THE DEADLIEST PILOT THE SONIC SHARK HAS EVER HAD...
SHE'S GOT GRIEF TO WORK THROUGH, JAG. LEAVE HER BE.
MELINA ZAHOS -- VOLATILE AND PASSIONATE. SHE BEARS WATCHING, AT THE MOMENT...
IT'S NOT THAT, SHIN. IT'S THAT LITTLE PUNK -- HE THINKS HE CAN JUST WALTZ IN AND OWN THE PLACE --
-- OVER THE BONES OF A BETTER MAN THAN HE'LL EVER BE!
KULBHUSHAN "JAG" DHILLON -- THE GENTLEST MAN I KNOW, BUT ROCK-STEADY AT THE HELM...
Oh, HE'S NOT THAT BAD. I KNOW YOU'RE BROKEN UP, MELINA, BUT THE KID DIDN'T DO IT ON PURPOSE --
-- AND THE LOG TAPES SHOW HE DID SOME PRETTY SHARP FLYING THERE!
DR. MATTI KULVIK -- YOU'D SWEAR HIS MIND IS ANYWHERE BUT HERE, BUT HE'S NEVER ONCE LET US DOWN...
IT WAS EXTRAORDINARY FLYING AT THAT. MOST UNEXPECTED OF A TYRO.

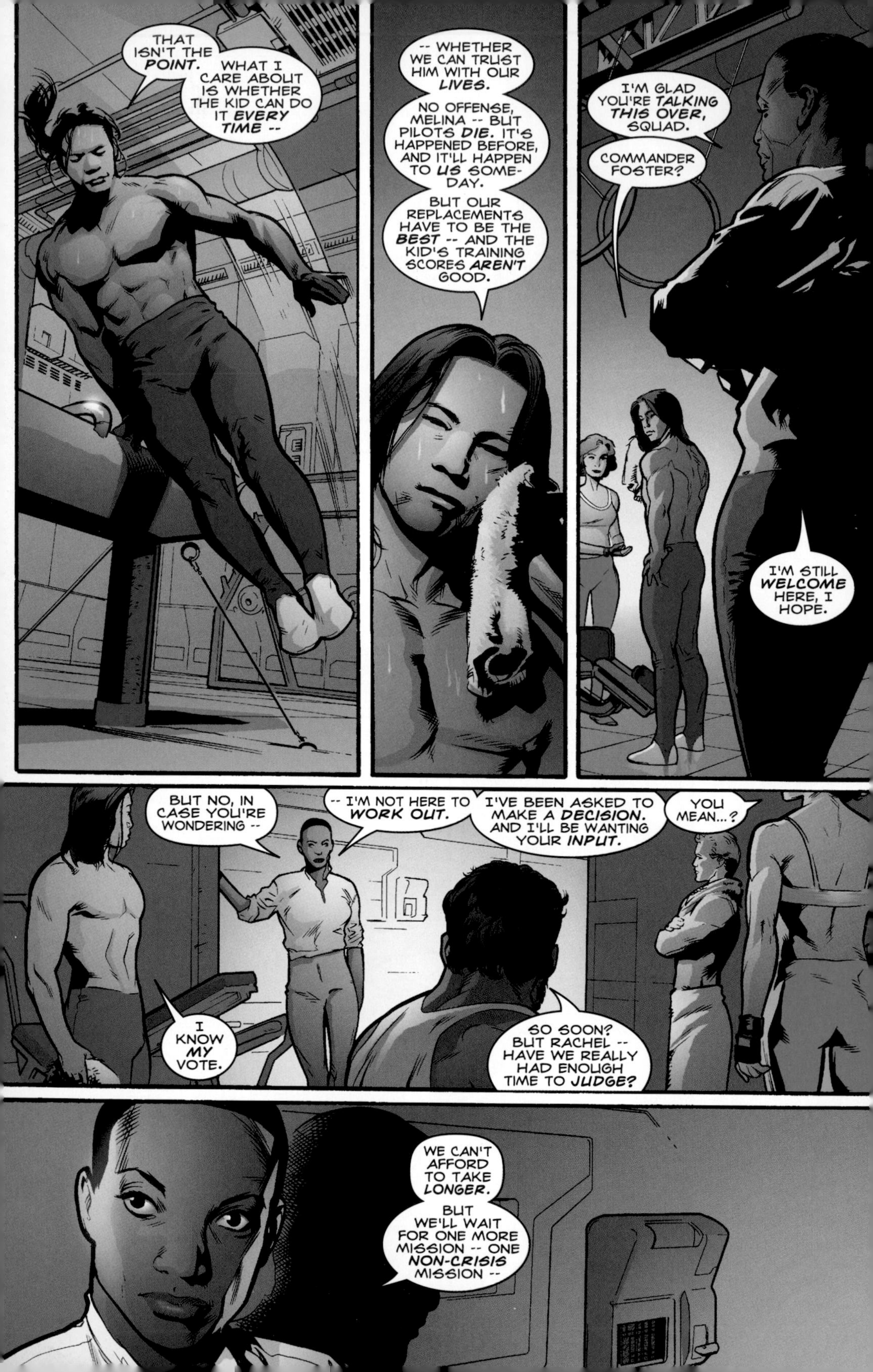
THAT ISN'T THE POINT.
WHAT I CARE ABOUT IS WHETHER THE KID CAN DO IT EVERY TIME --
-- WHETHER WE CAN TRUST HIM WITH OUR LIVES.
NO OFFENSE, MELINA -- BUT PILOTS DIE. IT'S HAPPENED BEFORE, AND IT'LL HAPPEN TO US SOME-DAY.
BUT OUR REPLACEMENTS HAVE TO BE THE BEST -- AND THE KID'S TRAINING SCORES AREN'T GOOD.
I'M GLAD YOU'RE TALKING THIS OVER, SQUAD.
COMMANDER FOSTER?
I'M STILL WELCOME HERE, I HOPE.
BUT NO, IN CASE YOU'RE WONDERING --
-- I'M NOT HERE TO WORK OUT.
I'VE BEEN ASKED TO MAKE A DECISION. AND I'LL BE WANTING YOUR INPUT.
YOU MEAN...?
I KNOW MY VOTE.
SO SOON? BUT RACHEL -- HAVE WE REALLY HAD ENOUGH TIME TO JUDGE?
WE CAN'T AFFORD TO TAKE LONGER.
BUT WE'LL WAIT FOR ONE MORE MISSION -- ONE NON-CRISIS MISSION --

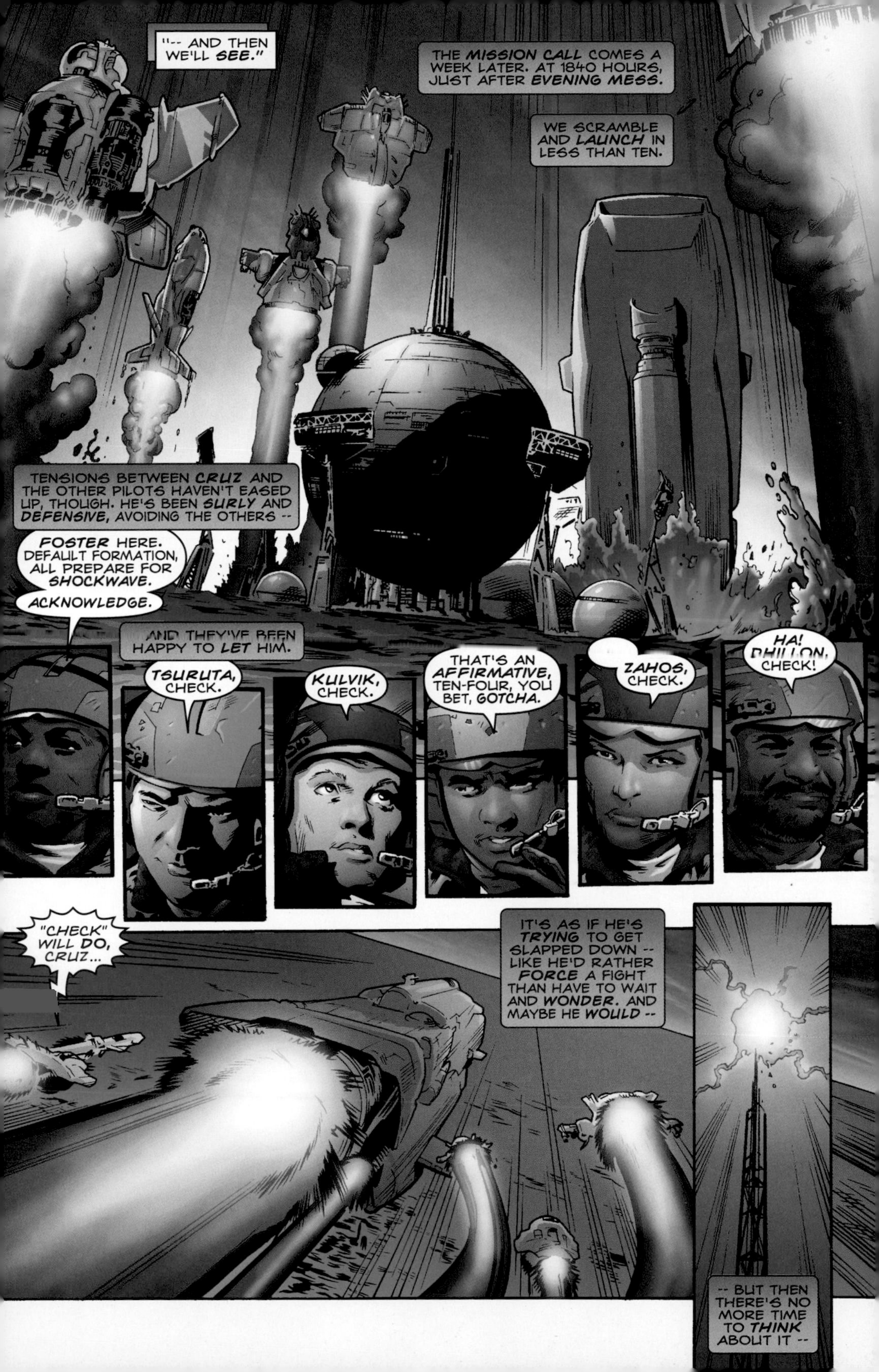
"-- AND THEN WE'LL SEE."
THE MISSION CALL COMES A WEEK LATER. AT 1840 HOURS, JUST AFTER EVENING MESS.
WE SCRAMBLE AND LAUNCH IN LESS THAN TEN.
TENSIONS BETWEEN CRUZ AND THE OTHER PILOTS HAVEN'T EASED UP, THOUGH. HE'S BEEN SURLY AND DEFENSIVE, AVOIDING THE OTHERS --
FOSTER HERE. DEFAULT FORMATION, ALL PREPARE FOR SHOCKWAVE.
ACKNOWLEDGE.
AND THEY'VE BEEN HAPPY TO LET HIM.
TSURUTA, CHECK.
KULVIK, CHECK.
THAT'S AN AFFIRMATIVE, TEN-FOUR, YOU BET, GOTCHA.
ZAHOS, CHECK.
HA! DHILLON, CHECK!
"CHECK" WILL DO, CRUZ...
IT'S AS IF HE'S TRYING TO GET SLAPPED DOWN -- LIKE HE'D RATHER FORCE A FIGHT THAN HAVE TO WAIT AND WONDER. AND MAYBE HE WOULD --
-- BUT THEN THERE'S NO MORE TIME TO THINK ABOUT IT --

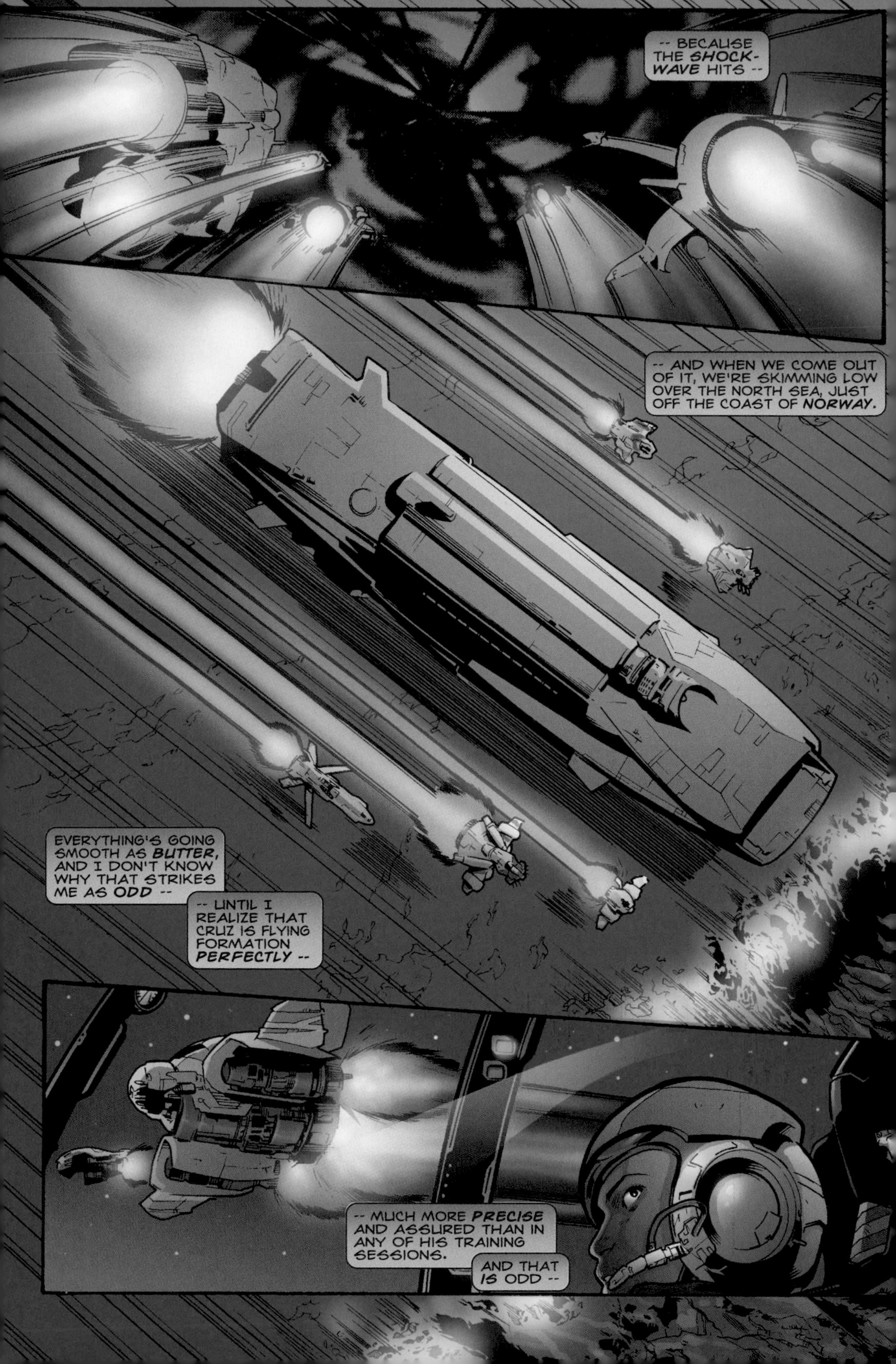
-- BECAUSE THE SHOCK-WAVE HITS --
-- AND WHEN WE COME OUT OF IT, WE'RE SKIMMING LOW OVER THE NORTH SEA, JUST OFF THE COAST OF NORWAY.
EVERYTHING'S GOING SMOOTH AS BUTTER, AND I DON'T KNOW WHY THAT STRIKES ME AS ODD --
-- UNTIL I REALIZE THAT CRUZ IS FLYING FORMATION PERFECTLY --
-- MUCH MORE PRECISE AND ASSURED THAN IN ANY OF HIS TRAINING SESSIONS.
AND THAT IS ODD --

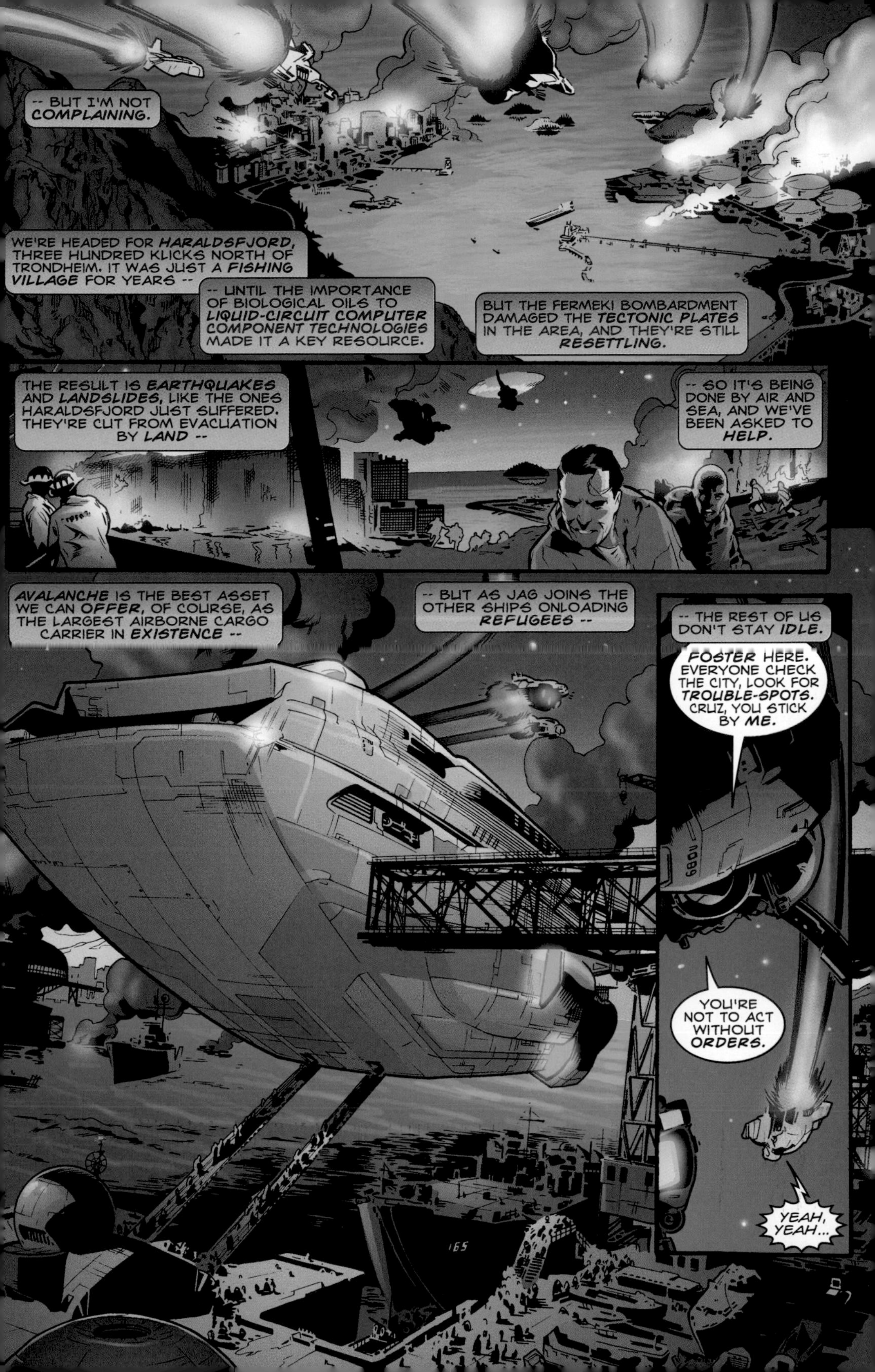
-- BUT I'M NOT COMPLAINING.
WE'RE HEADED FOR HARALDSFJORD, THREE HUNDRED KLICKS NORTH OF TRONDHEIM. IT WAS JUST A FISHING VILLAGE FOR YEARS --
-- UNTIL THE IMPORTANCE OF BIOLOGICAL OILS TO LIQUID-CIRCUIT COMPUTER COMPONENT TECHNOLOGIES MADE IT A KEY RESOURCE.
BUT THE FERMEKI BOMBARDMENT DAMAGED THE TECTONIC PLATES IN THE AREA, AND THEY'RE STILL RESETTLING.
THE RESULT IS EARTHQUAKES AND LANDSLIDES, LIKE THE ONES HARALDSFJORD JUST SUFFERED. THEY'RE CUT FROM EVACUATION BY LAND --
-- SO IT'S BEING DONE BY AIR AND SEA, AND WE'VE BEEN ASKED TO HELP.
AVALANCHE IS THE BEST ASSET WE CAN OFFER, OF COURSE, AS THE LARGEST AIRBORNE CARGO CARRIER IN EXISTENCE --
-- BUT AS JAG JOINS THE OTHER SHIPS ONLOADING REFUGEES --
-- THE REST OF US DON'T STAY IDLE.
FOSTER HERE. EVERYONE CHECK THE CITY, LOOK FOR TROUBLE-SPOTS. CRUZ, YOU STICK BY ME.
YOU'RE NOT TO ACT WITHOUT ORDERS.
YEAH, YEAH...

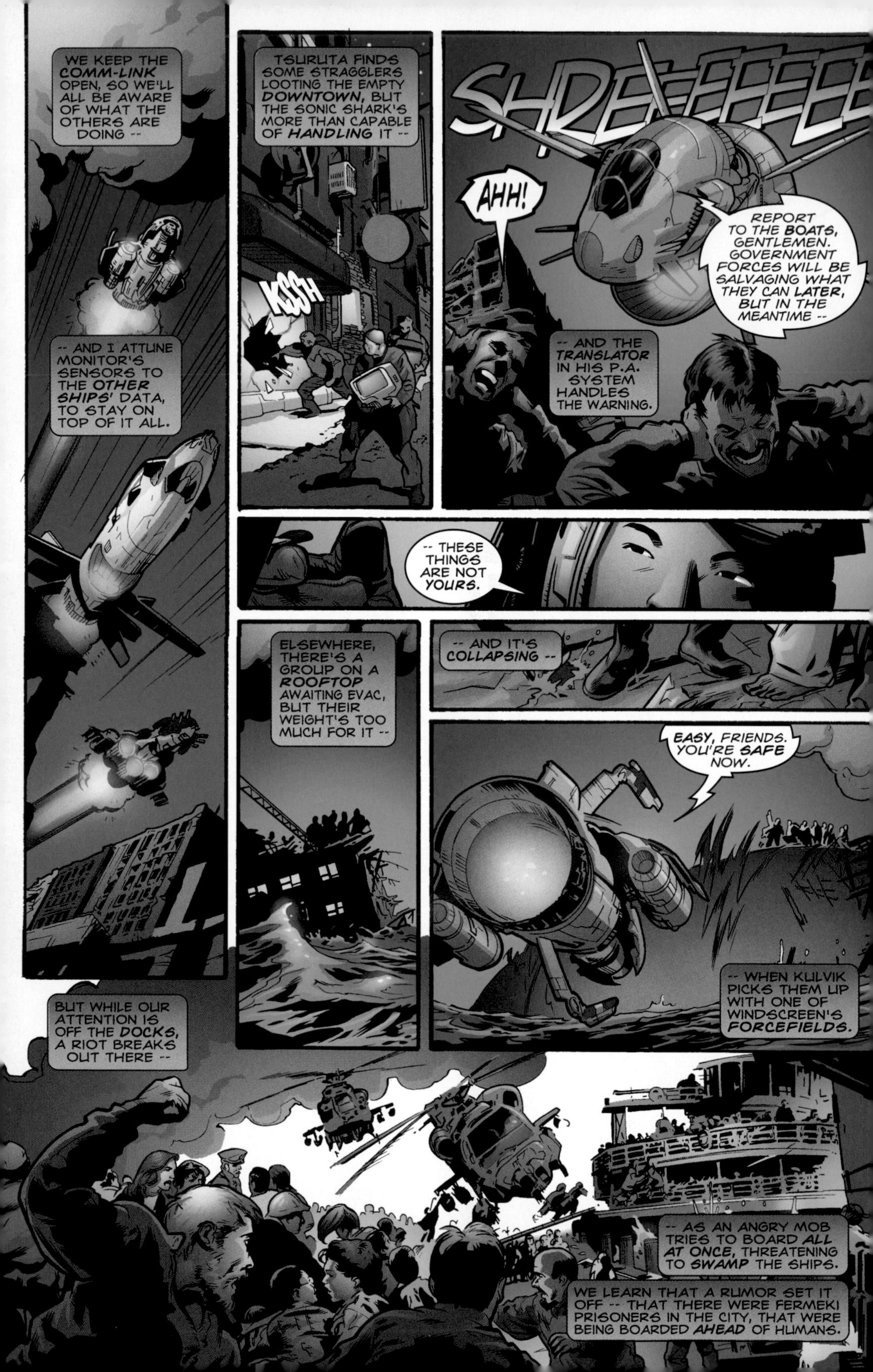
WE KEEP THE COMM-LINK OPEN, SO WE'LL ALL BE AWARE OF WHAT THE OTHERS ARE DOING --
-- AND I ATTUNE MONITOR'S SENSORS TO THE OTHER SHIPS' DATA, TO STAY ON TOP OF IT ALL.
TSURUTA FINDS SOME STRAGGLERS LOOTING THE EMPTY DOWNTOWN, BUT THE SONIC SHARK'S MORE THAN CAPABLE OF HANDLING IT --
KSSH
SHREEEEEEEE
AHH!
REPORT TO THE BOATS, GENTLEMEN. GOVERNMENT FORCES WILL BE SALVAGING WHAT THEY CAN LATER, BUT IN THE MEANTIME --
-- AND THE TRANSLATOR IN HIS P.A. SYSTEM HANDLES THE WARNING.
-- THESE THINGS ARE NOT YOURS.
ELSEWHERE, THERE'S A GROUP ON A ROOFTOP AWAITING EVAC, BUT THEIR WEIGHT'S TOO MUCH FOR IT --
-- AND IT'S COLLAPSING --
EASY, FRIENDS. YOU'RE SAFE NOW.
-- WHEN KULVIK PICKS THEM UP WITH ONE OF WINDSCREEN'S FORCEFIELDS.
BUT WHILE OUR ATTENTION IS OFF THE DOCKS, A RIOT BREAKS OUT THERE --
-- AS AN ANGRY MOB TRIES TO BOARD ALL AT ONCE, THREATENING TO SWAMP THE SHIPS.
WE LEARN THAT A RUMOR SET IT OFF -- THAT THERE WERE FERMEKI PRISONERS IN THE CITY, THAT WERE BEING BOARDED AHEAD OF HUMANS.

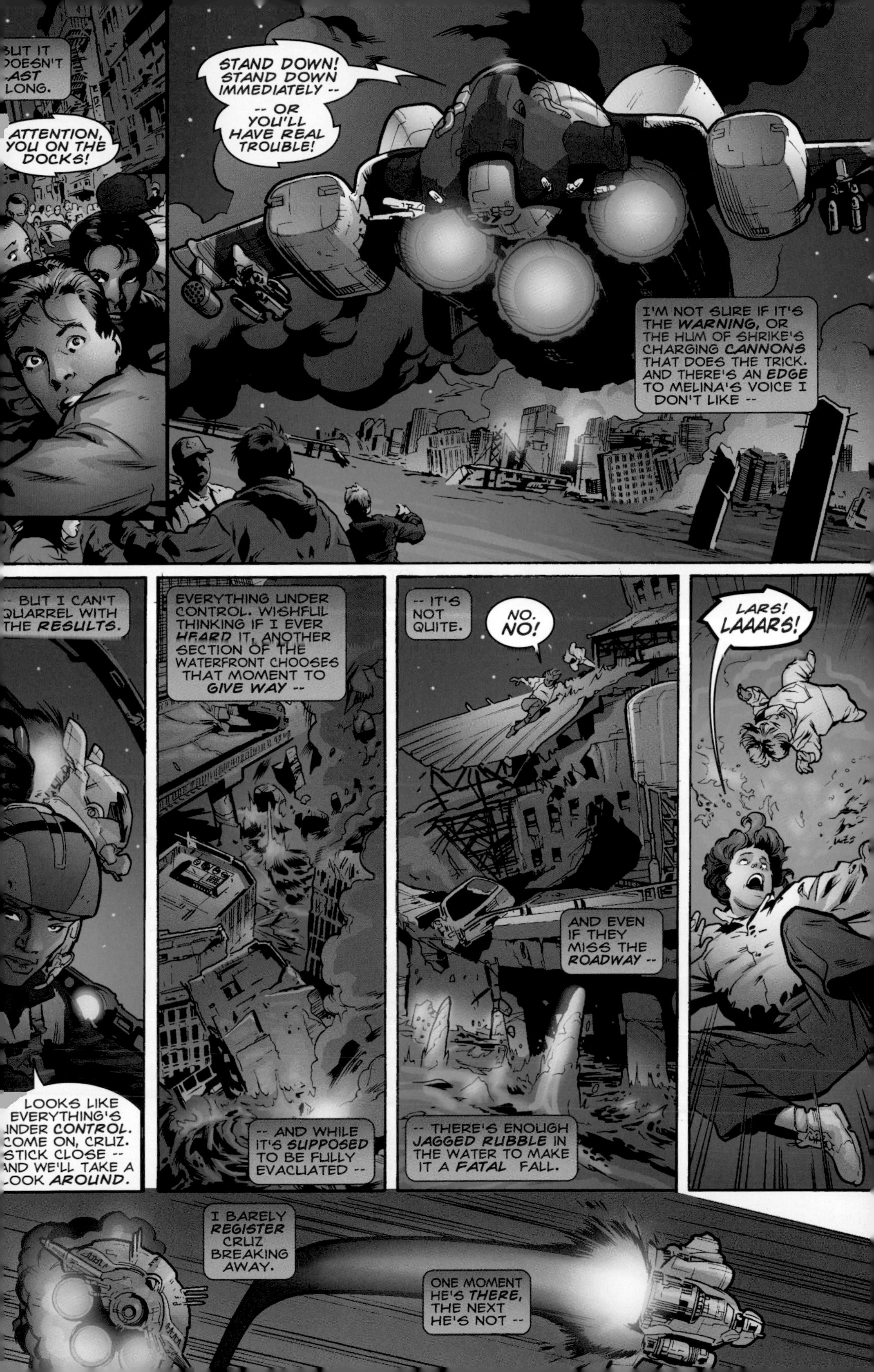
BUT IT DOESN'T LAST LONG.
ATTENTION, YOU ON THE DOCKS!
STAND DOWN! STAND DOWN IMMEDIATELY --
-- OR YOU'LL HAVE REAL TROUBLE!
I'M NOT SURE IF IT'S THE WARNING, OR THE HUM OF SHRIKE'S CHARGING CANNONS THAT DOES THE TRICK. AND THERE'S AN EDGE TO MELINA'S VOICE I DON'T LIKE --
-- BUT I CAN'T QUARREL WITH THE RESULTS.
LOOKS LIKE EVERYTHING'S UNDER CONTROL. COME ON, CRUZ. STICK CLOSE -- AND WE'LL TAKE A LOOK AROUND.
EVERYTHING UNDER CONTROL. WISHFUL THINKING IF I EVER HEARD IT. ANOTHER SECTION OF THE WATERFRONT CHOOSES THAT MOMENT TO GIVE WAY --
-- AND WHILE IT'S SUPPOSED TO BE FULLY EVACUATED --
-- IT'S NOT QUITE.
NO. NO!
AND EVEN IF THEY MISS THE ROADWAY --
-- THERE'S ENOUGH JAGGED RUBBLE IN THE WATER TO MAKE IT A FATAL FALL.
LARS! LAAARS!
I BARELY REGISTER CRUZ BREAKING AWAY.
ONE MOMENT HE'S THERE, THE NEXT HE'S NOT --

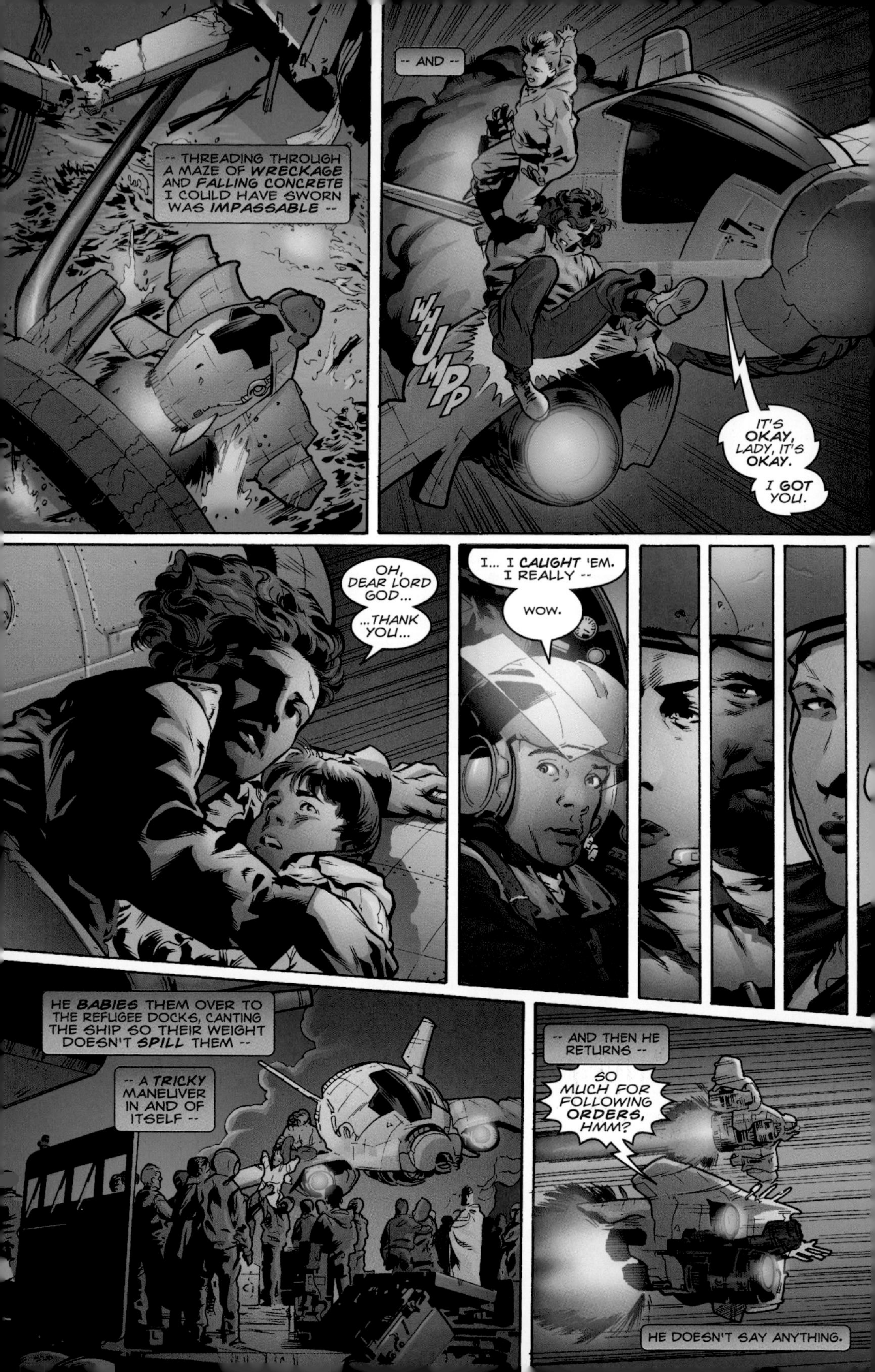
-- THREADING THROUGH A MAZE OF WRECKAGE AND FALLING CONCRETE I COULD HAVE SWORN WAS IMPASSABLE --
-- AND --
WHUMPP
IT'S OKAY, LADY, IT'S OKAY.
I GOT YOU.
OH, DEAR LORD GOD...
...THANK YOU...
I... I CAUGHT 'EM. I REALLY --
WOW.
HE BABIES THEM OVER TO THE REFUGEE DOCKS, CANTING THE SHIP SO THEIR WEIGHT DOESN'T SPILL THEM --
-- A TRICKY MANEUVER IN AND OF ITSELF --
-- AND THEN HE RETURNS --
SO MUCH FOR FOLLOWING ORDERS, HMM?
HE DOESN'T SAY ANYTHING.

IT TAKES ANOTHER *SEVEN HOURS* TO COMPLETE OUR PART OF THE EVAC --

-- SO BY THE TIME WE HIT THE *SHOCK-RECALL* TO THE BASE --

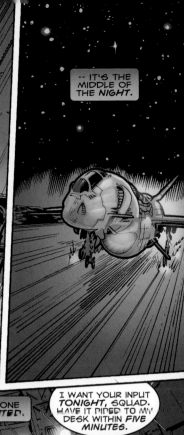

-- IT'S THE MIDDLE OF THE *NIGHT.*

EVERYONE'S *TIRED* AND *HUNGRY.* CRUZ FOLDS BACK INTO HIMSELF BEFORE ANYONE HAS A CHANCE TO *REJECT* HIM, SO BY THE TIME I HIT THE HANGAR, MY SQUAD IS *TWO GROUPS* AGAIN --

-- ONE SOLITARY --

-- ONE *UNITED.*

I WANT YOUR INPUT *TONIGHT,* SQUAD. HAVE IT PIPED TO MY DESK WITHIN *FIVE* MINUTES.

AND CRUZ -- I'D LIKE TO SEE YOU IN MY *OFFICE,* NOW.

THAT WAS SOME *PRETTY FANCY* FLYING BACK THERE, WITH THE WOMAN AND HER SON.

DO YOU HAVE AN *EXPLANATION?*

I'M... *SORRY* I DISOBEYED *ORDERS.* BUT I SAW 'EM *FALLING,* SAW A *PATH* TO 'EM -- AN' KNEW I COULD REACH 'EM WHEN *NO ONE ELSE* COULD.

THERE WASN'T *TIME* TO ASK PERMISSION.

NOTED.

BUT THE THING IS -- YOUR *TEST SCORES* DON'T INDICATE THAT YOU CAN *FLY* THAT WELL.

SO WHAT ARE YOU *SAYIN'?* THAT I *SHOULDN'TA* RISKED STINGER ON A MOVE I WASN'T *GOOD ENOUGH* TO *MAKE?!*

I SAVED THEIR *LIVES,* LADY!

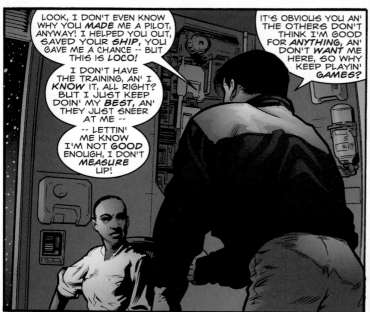

LOOK, I DON'T EVEN KNOW WHY YOU *MADE* ME A PILOT, ANYWAY! I HELPED YOU *OUT,* SAVED YOUR *SHIP,* YOU GAVE ME A CHANCE -- BUT THIS IS *LOCO!*

I DON'T HAVE THE TRAINING, AN' I *KNOW* IT, ALL RIGHT? BUT I JUST KEEP DOIN' MY *BEST,* AN' THEY JUST SNEER AT ME --

-- LETTIN' ME KNOW I'M NOT *GOOD* ENOUGH, I DON'T *MEASURE UP!*

IT'S OBVIOUS YOU AN' THE OTHERS DON'T THINK I'M GOOD FOR *ANYTHING,* AN' DON'T *WANT* ME HERE, SO WHY KEEP PLAYIN' *GAMES?*

JUST REPLACE ME WITH THAT *WILDE* CHICK THAT SHOULDA GOTTEN THE JOB --

-- AN' SEND ME BACK TO THE *GUTTERS* WHERE YOU THINK I *BELONG!*

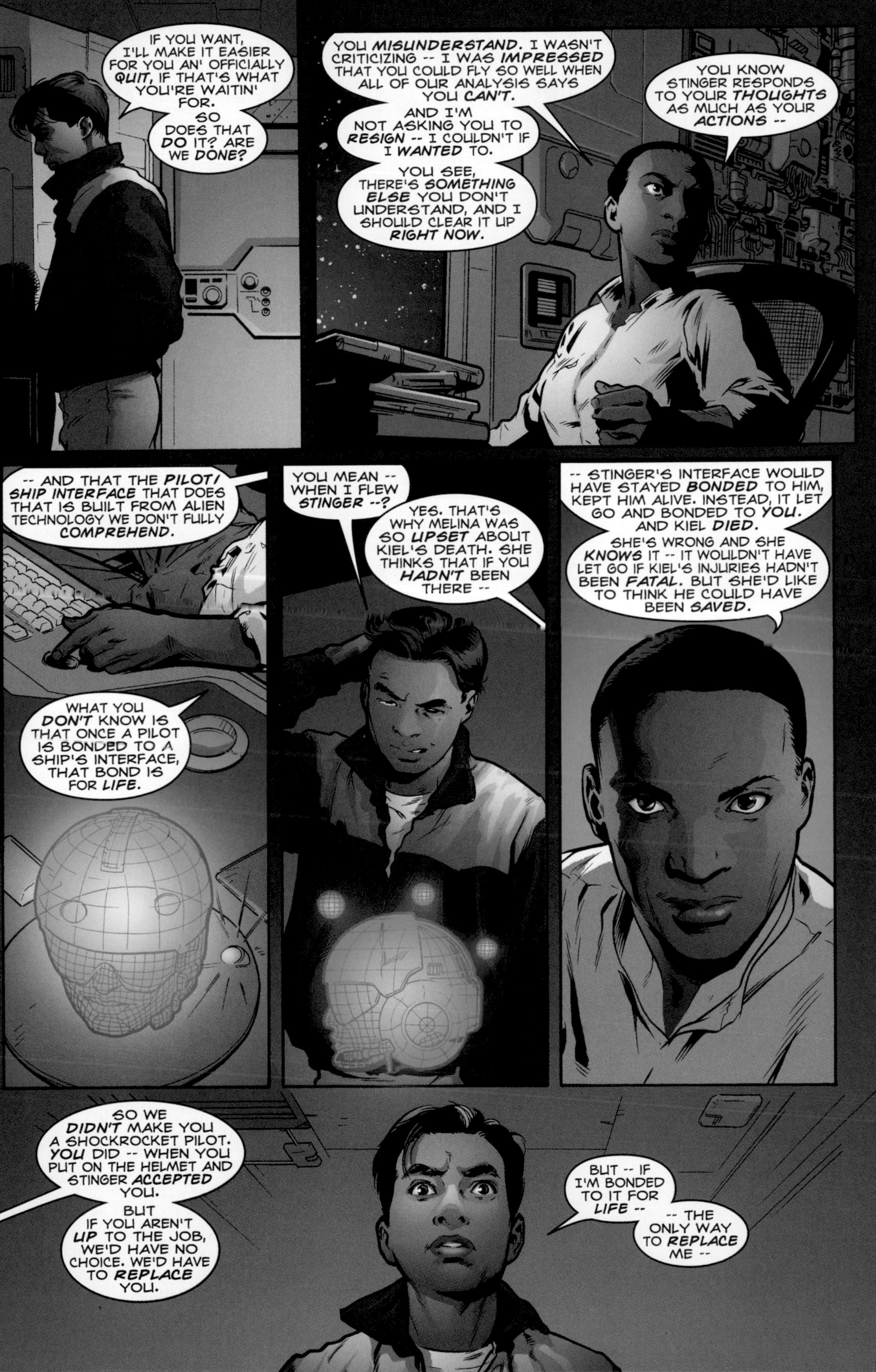
IF YOU WANT, I'LL MAKE IT EASIER FOR YOU AN' OFFICIALLY QUIT, IF THAT'S WHAT YOU'RE WAITIN' FOR.
SO DOES THAT DO IT? ARE WE DONE?
YOU MISUNDERSTAND. I WASN'T CRITICIZING -- I WAS IMPRESSED THAT YOU COULD FLY SO WELL WHEN ALL OF OUR ANALYSIS SAYS YOU CAN'T.
AND I'M NOT ASKING YOU TO RESIGN -- I COULDN'T IF I WANTED TO.
YOU SEE, THERE'S SOMETHING ELSE YOU DON'T UNDERSTAND, AND I SHOULD CLEAR IT UP RIGHT NOW.
YOU KNOW STINGER RESPONDS TO YOUR THOUGHTS AS MUCH AS YOUR ACTIONS --
-- AND THAT THE PILOT/SHIP INTERFACE THAT DOES THAT IS BUILT FROM ALIEN TECHNOLOGY WE DON'T FULLY COMPREHEND.
WHAT YOU DON'T KNOW IS THAT ONCE A PILOT IS BONDED TO A SHIP'S INTERFACE, THAT BOND IS FOR LIFE.
YOU MEAN -- WHEN I FLEW STINGER --?
YES. THAT'S WHY MELINA WAS SO UPSET ABOUT KIEL'S DEATH. SHE THINKS THAT IF YOU HADN'T BEEN THERE --
-- STINGER'S INTERFACE WOULD HAVE STAYED BONDED TO HIM, KEPT HIM ALIVE. INSTEAD, IT LET GO AND BONDED TO YOU. AND KIEL DIED.
SHE'S WRONG AND SHE KNOWS IT -- IT WOULDN'T HAVE LET GO IF KIEL'S INJURIES HADN'T BEEN FATAL. BUT SHE'D LIKE TO THINK HE COULD HAVE BEEN SAVED.
SO WE DIDN'T MAKE YOU A SHOCKROCKET PILOT. YOU DID -- WHEN YOU PUT ON THE HELMET AND STINGER ACCEPTED YOU.
BUT IF YOU AREN'T UP TO THE JOB, WE'D HAVE NO CHOICE. WE'D HAVE TO REPLACE YOU.
BUT -- IF I'M BONDED TO IT FOR LIFE --
-- THE ONLY WAY TO REPLACE ME --

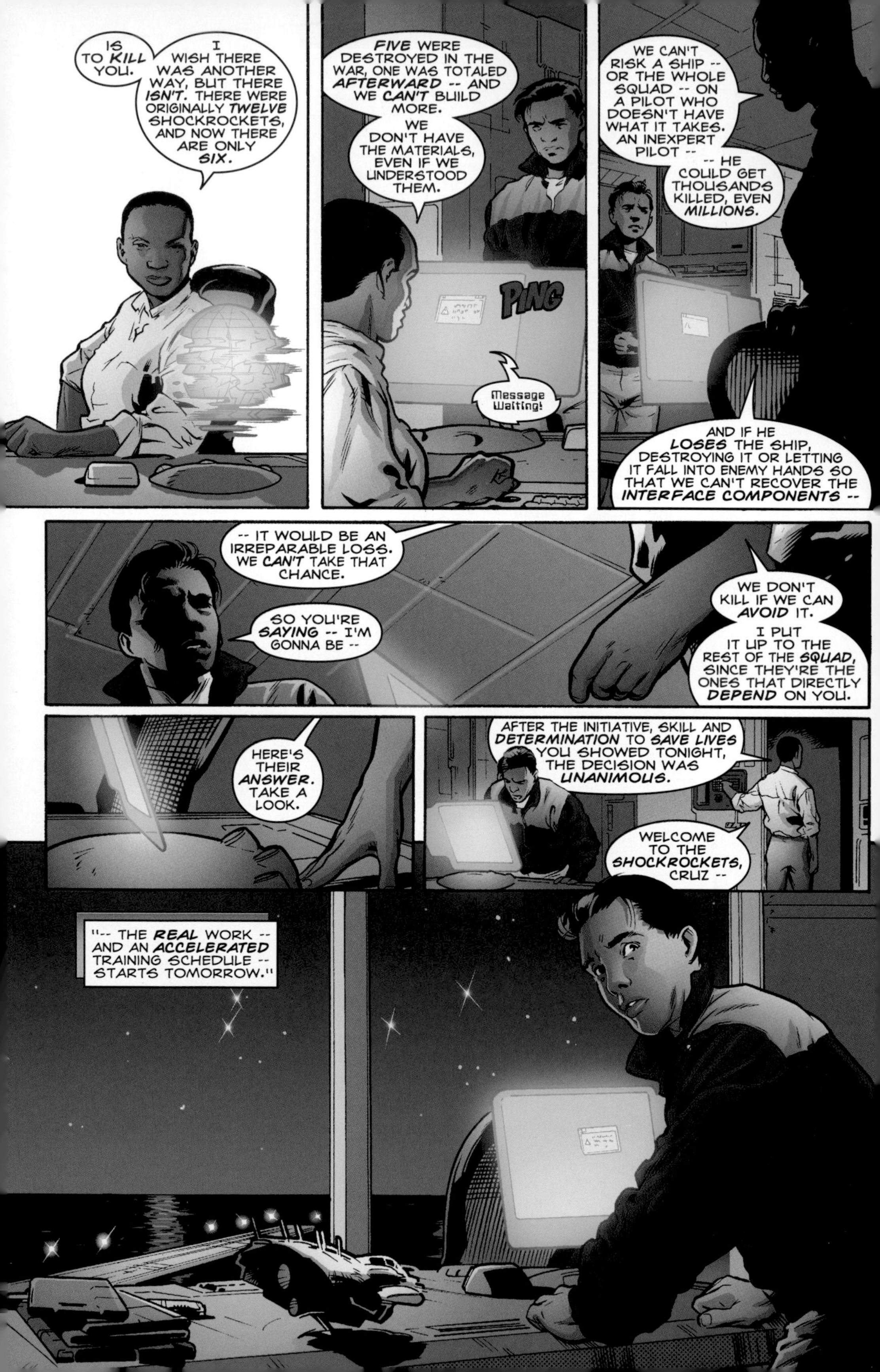

IS TO KILL YOU.
I WISH THERE WAS ANOTHER WAY, BUT THERE ISN'T. THERE WERE ORIGINALLY TWELVE SHOCKROCKETS, AND NOW THERE ARE ONLY SIX.
FIVE WERE DESTROYED IN THE WAR, ONE WAS TOTALED AFTERWARD -- AND WE CAN'T BUILD MORE.
WE DON'T HAVE THE MATERIALS, EVEN IF WE UNDERSTOOD THEM.
PING
Message Waiting!
WE CAN'T RISK A SHIP -- OR THE WHOLE SQUAD -- ON A PILOT WHO DOESN'T HAVE WHAT IT TAKES. AN INEXPERT PILOT --
-- HE COULD GET THOUSANDS KILLED, EVEN MILLIONS.
AND IF HE LOSES THE SHIP, DESTROYING IT OR LETTING IT FALL INTO ENEMY HANDS SO THAT WE CAN'T RECOVER THE INTERFACE COMPONENTS --
-- IT WOULD BE AN IRREPARABLE LOSS. WE CAN'T TAKE THAT CHANCE.
SO YOU'RE SAYING -- I'M GONNA BE --
WE DON'T KILL IF WE CAN AVOID IT.
I PUT IT UP TO THE REST OF THE SQUAD, SINCE THEY'RE THE ONES THAT DIRECTLY DEPEND ON YOU.
HERE'S THEIR ANSWER. TAKE A LOOK.
AFTER THE INITIATIVE, SKILL AND DETERMINATION TO SAVE LIVES YOU SHOWED TONIGHT, THE DECISION WAS UNANIMOUS.
WELCOME TO THE SHOCKROCKETS, CRUZ --
"-- THE REAL WORK -- AND AN ACCELERATED TRAINING SCHEDULE -- STARTS TOMORROW."

CHAPTER THREE

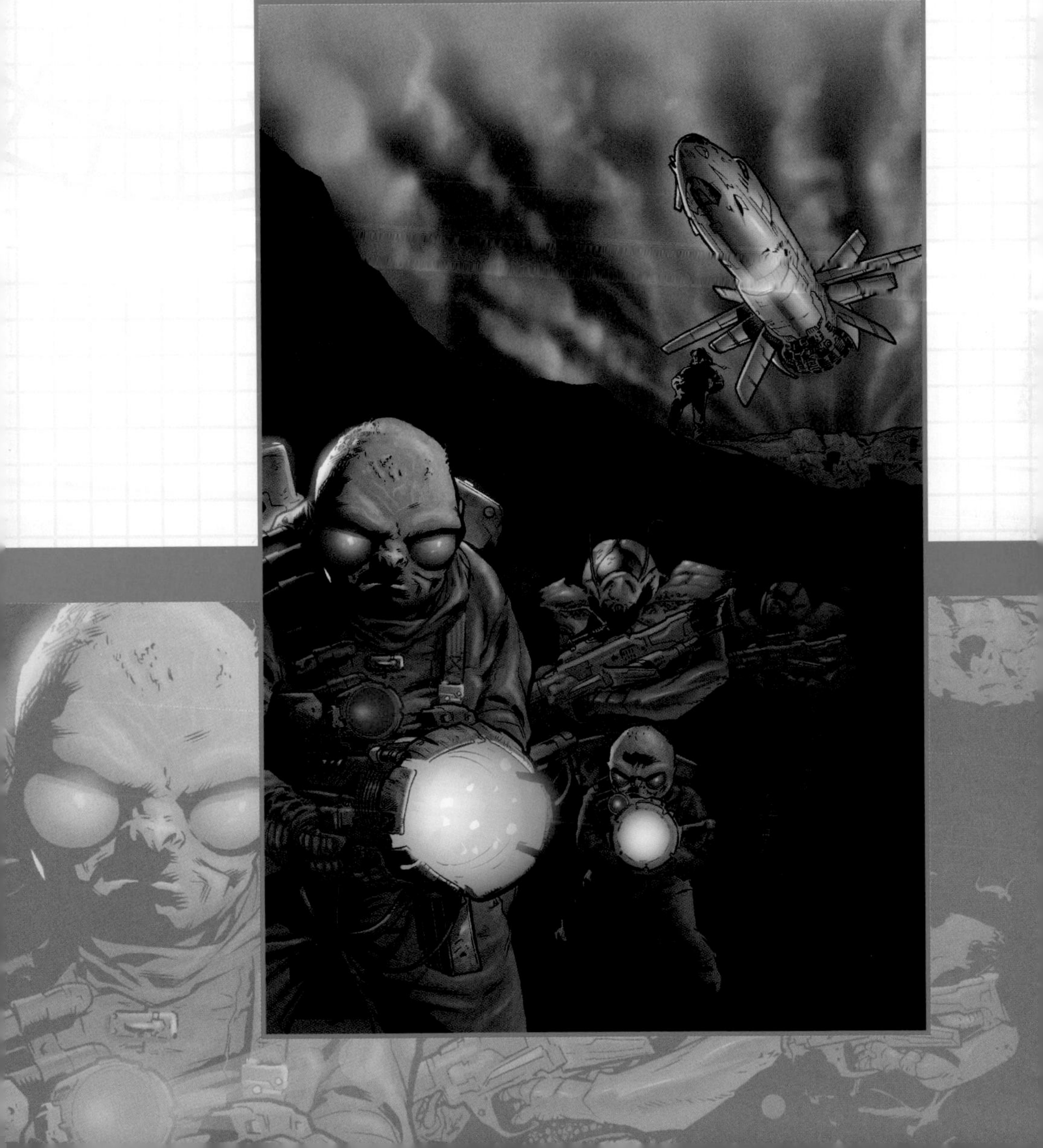

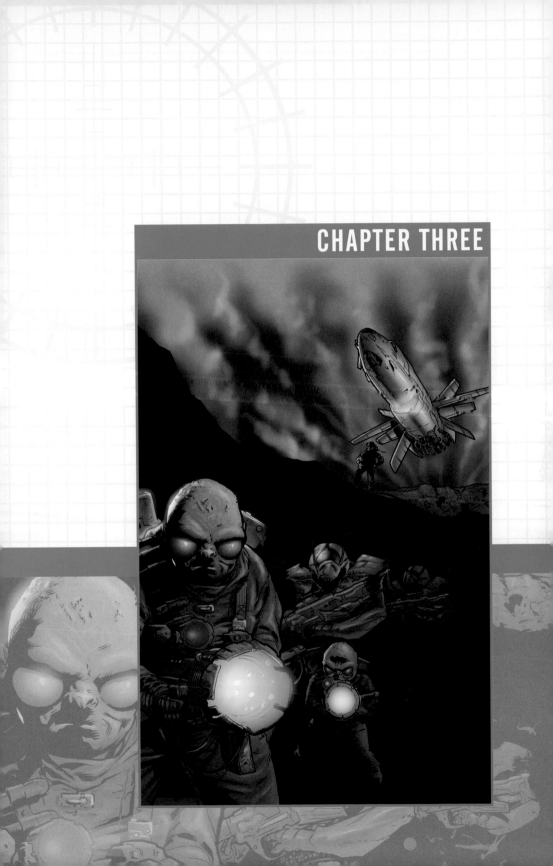

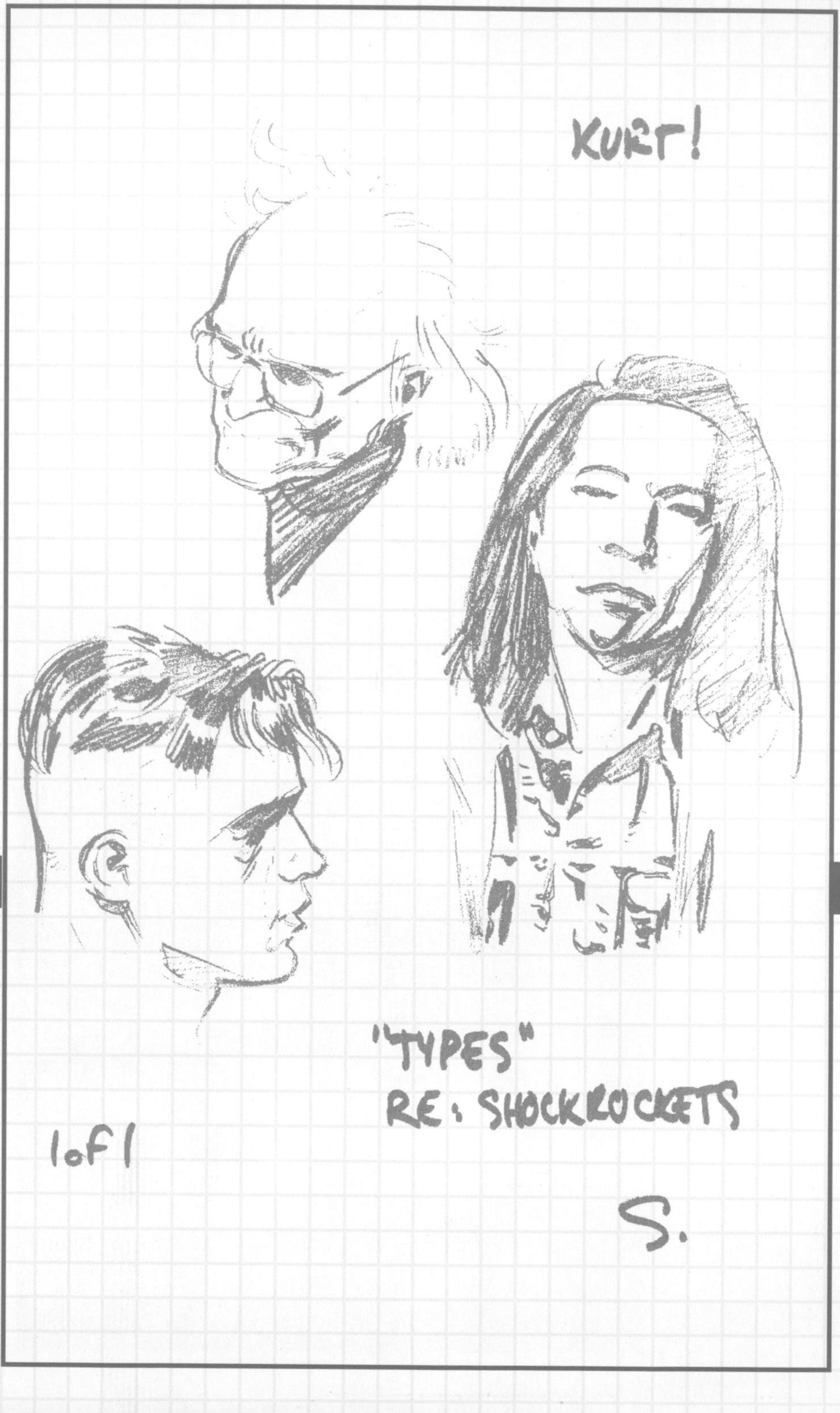
KURT!
"TYPES"
RE: SHOCKROCKETS
1 of 1
S.

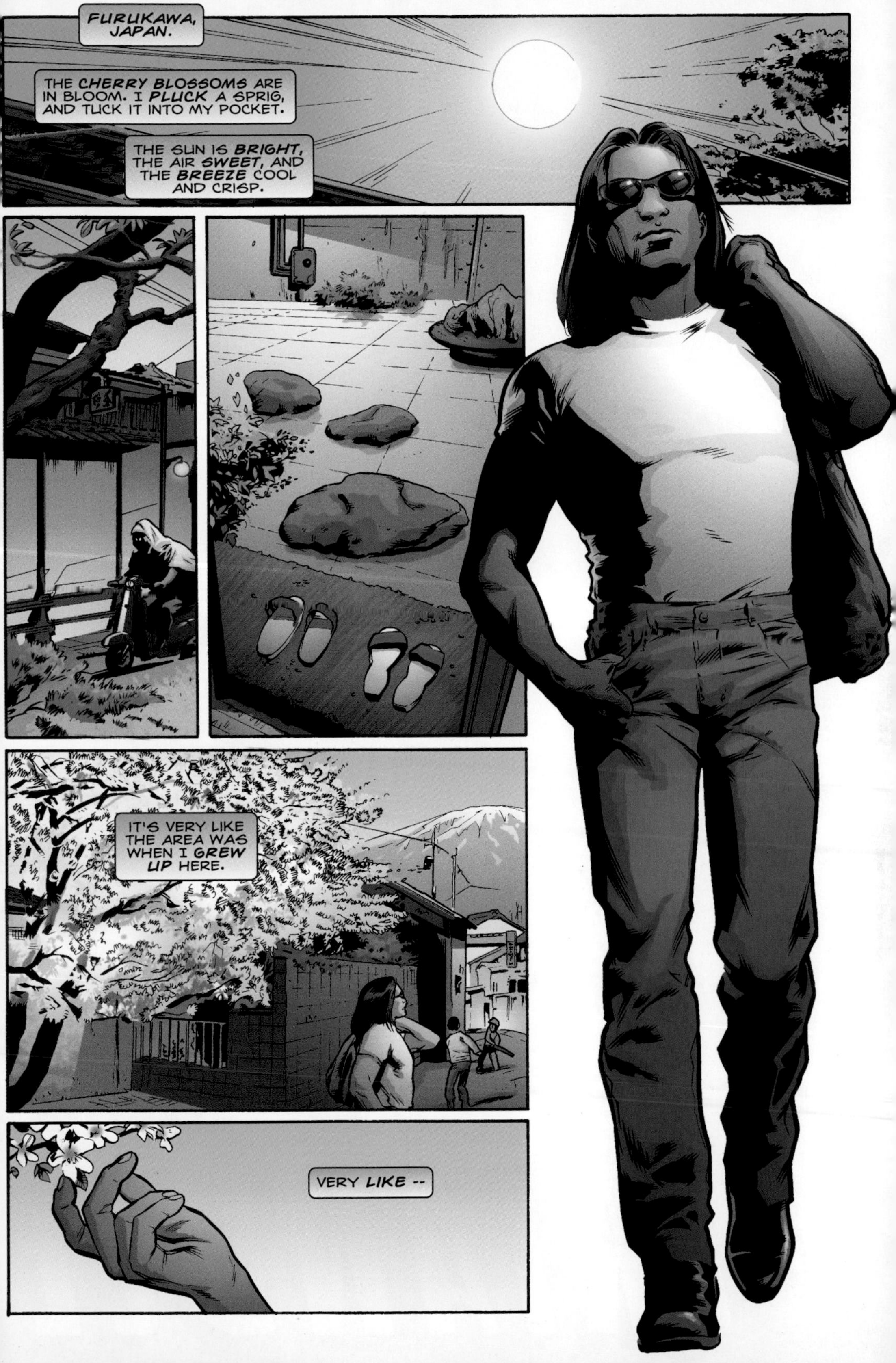
FURUKAWA, JAPAN.
THE CHERRY BLOSSOMS ARE IN BLOOM. I PLUCK A SPRIG, AND TUCK IT INTO MY POCKET.
THE SUN IS BRIGHT, THE AIR SWEET, AND THE BREEZE COOL AND CRISP.
IT'S VERY LIKE THE AREA WAS WHEN I GREW UP HERE.
VERY LIKE --

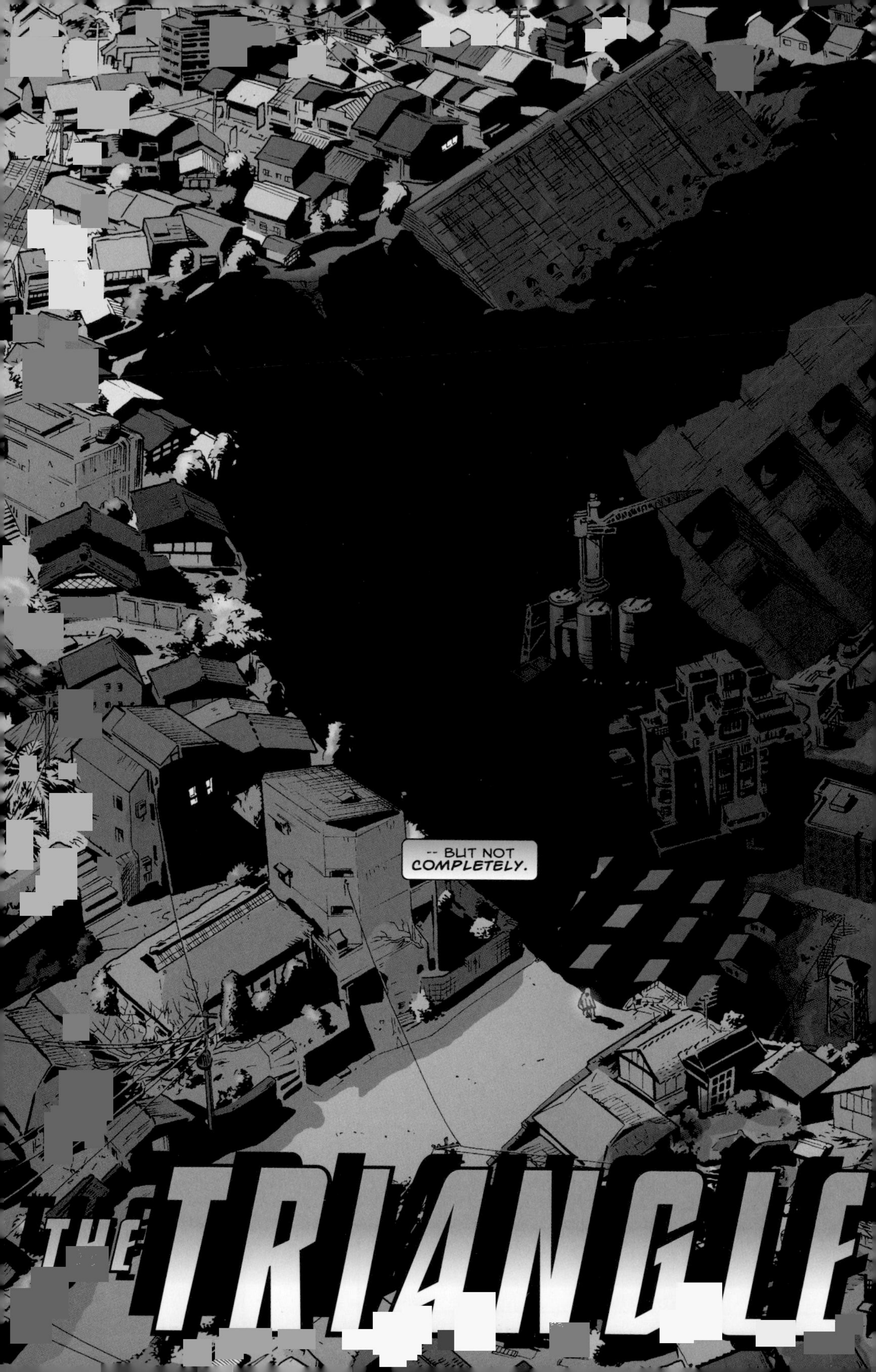
-- BUT NOT COMPLETELY.
THE TRIANGLE

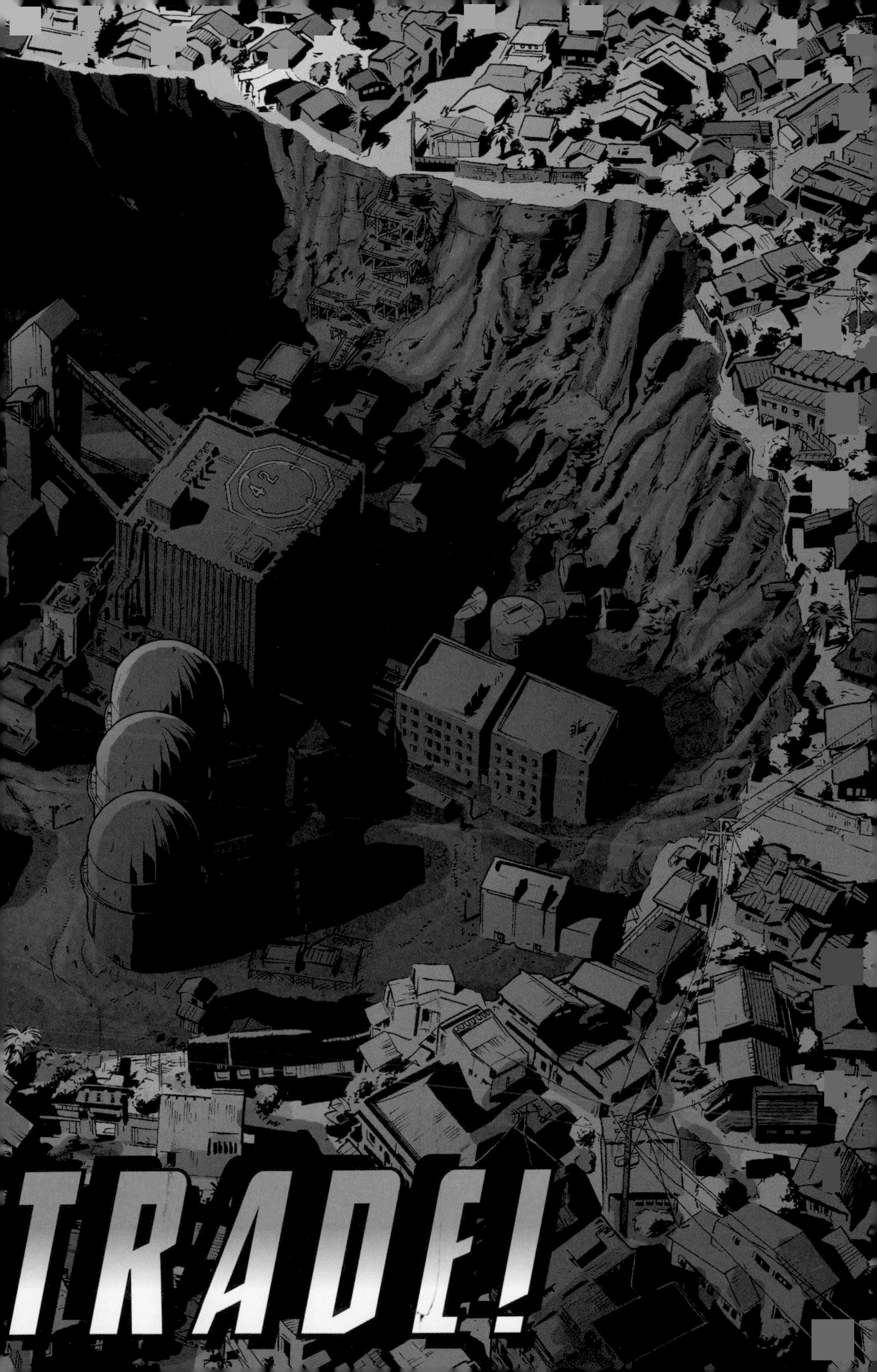
42
TRADE!

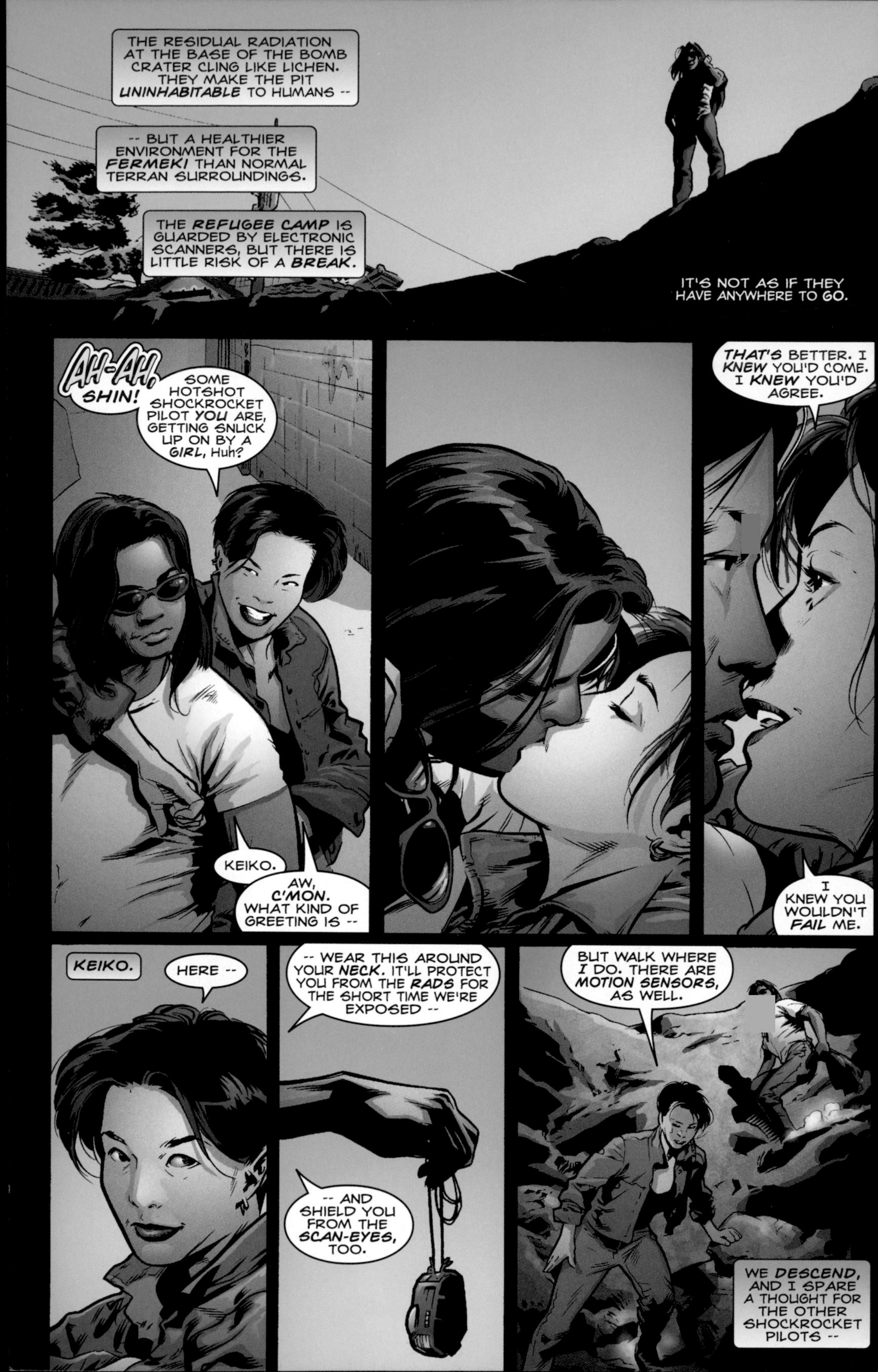
THE RESIDUAL RADIATION AT THE BASE OF THE BOMB CRATER CLING LIKE LICHEN. THEY MAKE THE PIT UNINHABITABLE TO HUMANS --
-- BUT A HEALTHIER ENVIRONMENT FOR THE FERMEKI THAN NORMAL TERRAN SURROUNDINGS.
THE REFUGEE CAMP IS GUARDED BY ELECTRONIC SCANNERS, BUT THERE IS LITTLE RISK OF A BREAK.
IT'S NOT AS IF THEY HAVE ANYWHERE TO GO.
AH-AH, SHIN!
SOME HOTSHOT SHOCKROCKET PILOT YOU ARE, GETTING SNUCK UP ON BY A GIRL, Huh?
KEIKO.
AW, C'MON. WHAT KIND OF GREETING IS --
THAT'S BETTER. I KNEW YOU'D COME. I KNEW YOU'D AGREE.
I KNEW YOU WOULDN'T FAIL ME.
KEIKO.
HERE --
-- WEAR THIS AROUND YOUR NECK. IT'LL PROTECT YOU FROM THE RADS FOR THE SHORT TIME WE'RE EXPOSED --
-- AND SHIELD YOU FROM THE SCAN-EYES, TOO.
BUT WALK WHERE I DO. THERE ARE MOTION SENSORS, AS WELL.
WE DESCEND, AND I SPARE A THOUGHT FOR THE OTHER SHOCKROCKET PILOTS --

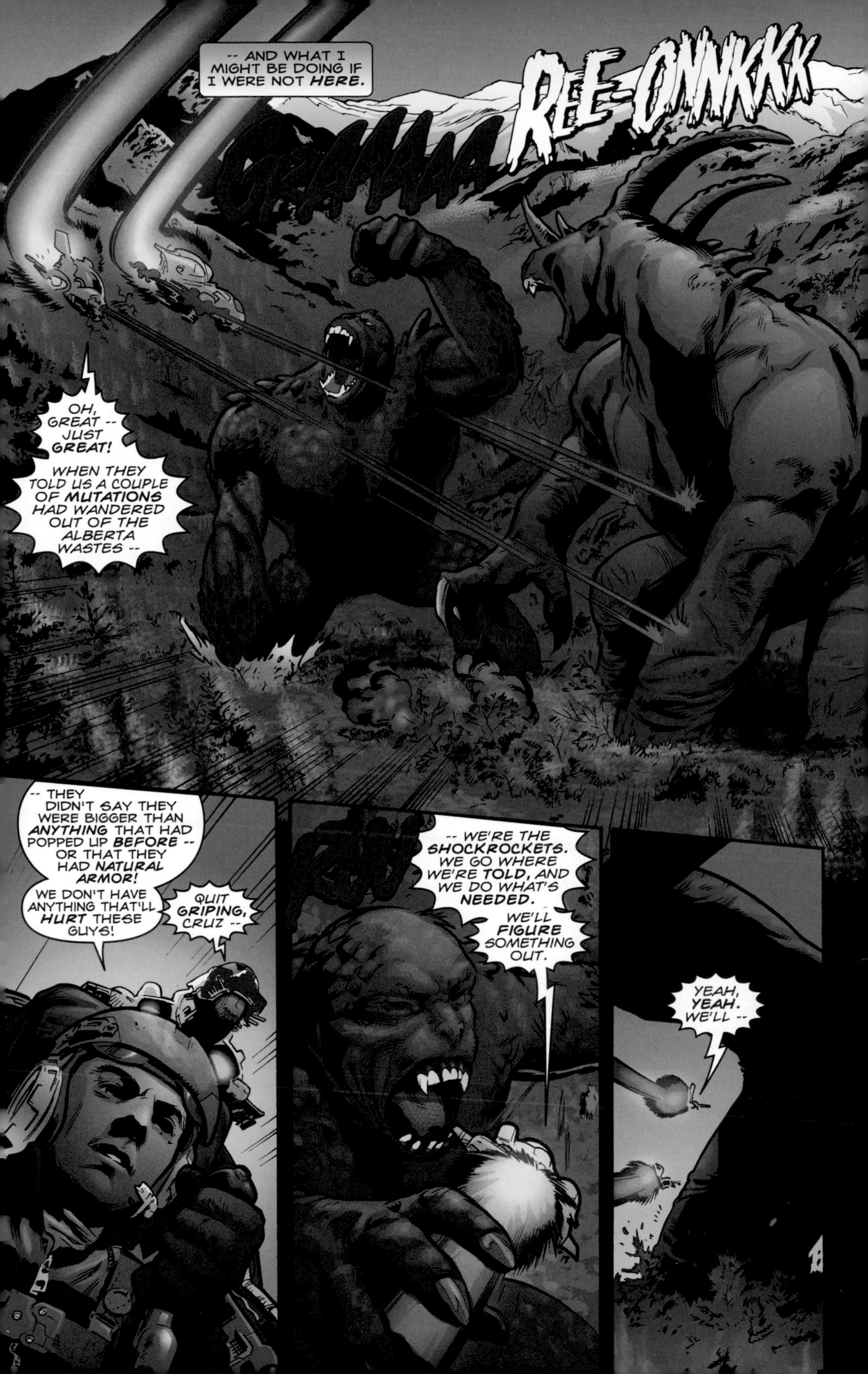
-- AND WHAT I MIGHT BE DOING IF I WERE NOT HERE.
GRAAAAA
REE-ONNKKK
OH, GREAT -- JUST GREAT!
WHEN THEY TOLD US A COUPLE OF MUTATIONS HAD WANDERED OUT OF THE ALBERTA WASTES --
-- THEY DIDN'T SAY THEY WERE BIGGER THAN ANYTHING THAT HAD POPPED UP BEFORE -- OR THAT THEY HAD NATURAL ARMOR!
WE DON'T HAVE ANYTHING THAT'LL HURT THESE GUYS!
QUIT GRIPING, CRUZ --
-- WE'RE THE SHOCKROCKETS. WE GO WHERE WE'RE TOLD, AND WE DO WHAT'S NEEDED.
WE'LL FIGURE SOMETHING OUT.
YEAH, YEAH. WE'LL --

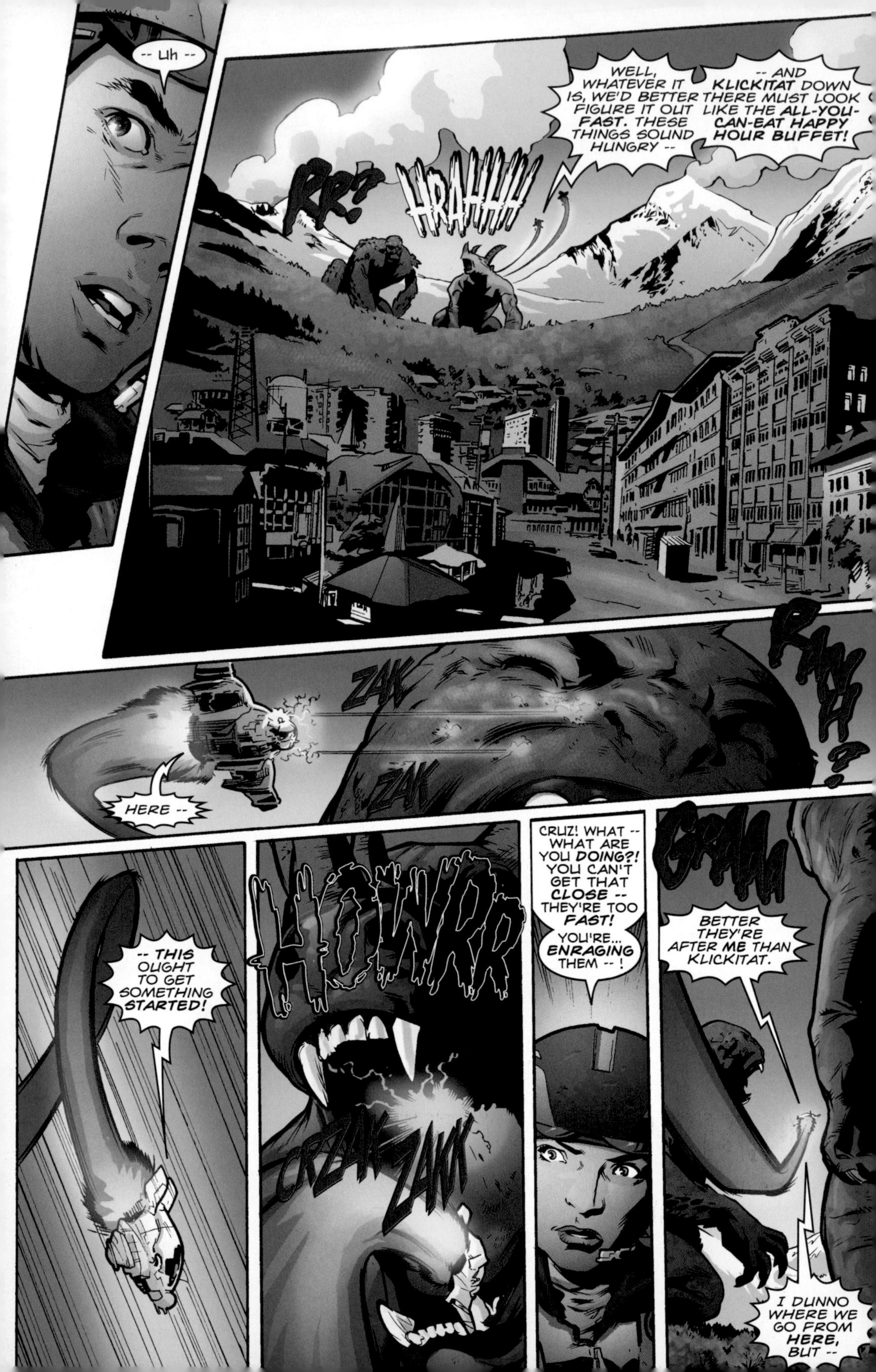
-- Uh --
WELL, WHATEVER IT IS, WE'D BETTER FIGURE IT OUT FAST. THESE THINGS SOUND HUNGRY --
-- AND KLICKITAT DOWN THERE MUST LOOK LIKE THE ALL-YOU-CAN-EAT HAPPY HOUR BUFFET!
RR?
HRAHHH
ZAK
ZAK
RAAHH?
HERE --
-- THIS OUGHT TO GET SOMETHING STARTED!
CRZAK
ZAKK
CRUZ! WHAT -- WHAT ARE YOU DOING?! YOU CAN'T GET THAT CLOSE -- THEY'RE TOO FAST! YOU'RE... ENRAGING THEM -- !
BETTER THEY'RE AFTER ME THAN KLICKITAT.
I DUNNO WHERE WE GO FROM HERE, BUT --

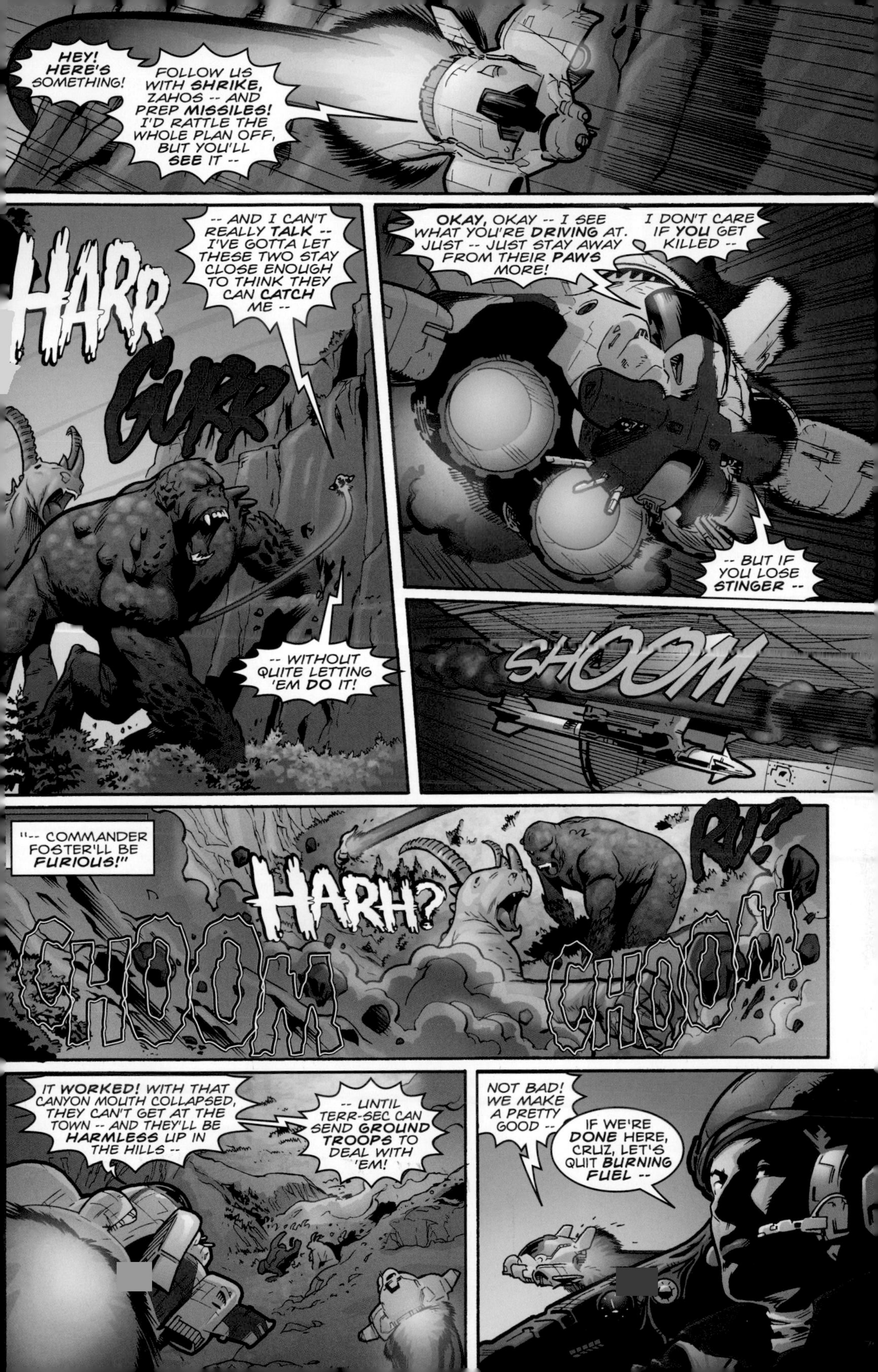
HEY! HERE'S SOMETHING!
FOLLOW US WITH SHRIKE, ZAHOS -- AND PREP MISSILES! I'D RATTLE THE WHOLE PLAN OFF, BUT YOU'LL SEE IT --
HARR
-- AND I CAN'T REALLY TALK -- I'VE GOTTA LET THESE TWO STAY CLOSE ENOUGH TO THINK THEY CAN CATCH ME --
GURR
-- WITHOUT QUITE LETTING 'EM DO IT!
OKAY, OKAY -- I SEE WHAT YOU'RE DRIVING AT. JUST -- JUST STAY AWAY FROM THEIR PAWS MORE!
I DON'T CARE IF YOU GET KILLED --
-- BUT IF YOU LOSE STINGER --
SHOOM
"-- COMMANDER FOSTER'LL BE FURIOUS!"
HARH?
RU?
CHOOM
CHOOM
IT WORKED! WITH THAT CANYON MOUTH COLLAPSED, THEY CAN'T GET AT THE TOWN -- AND THEY'LL BE HARMLESS UP IN THE HILLS --
-- UNTIL TERR-SEC CAN SEND GROUND TROOPS TO DEAL WITH 'EM!
NOT BAD! WE MAKE A PRETTY GOOD --
IF WE'RE DONE HERE, CRUZ, LET'S QUIT BURNING FUEL --

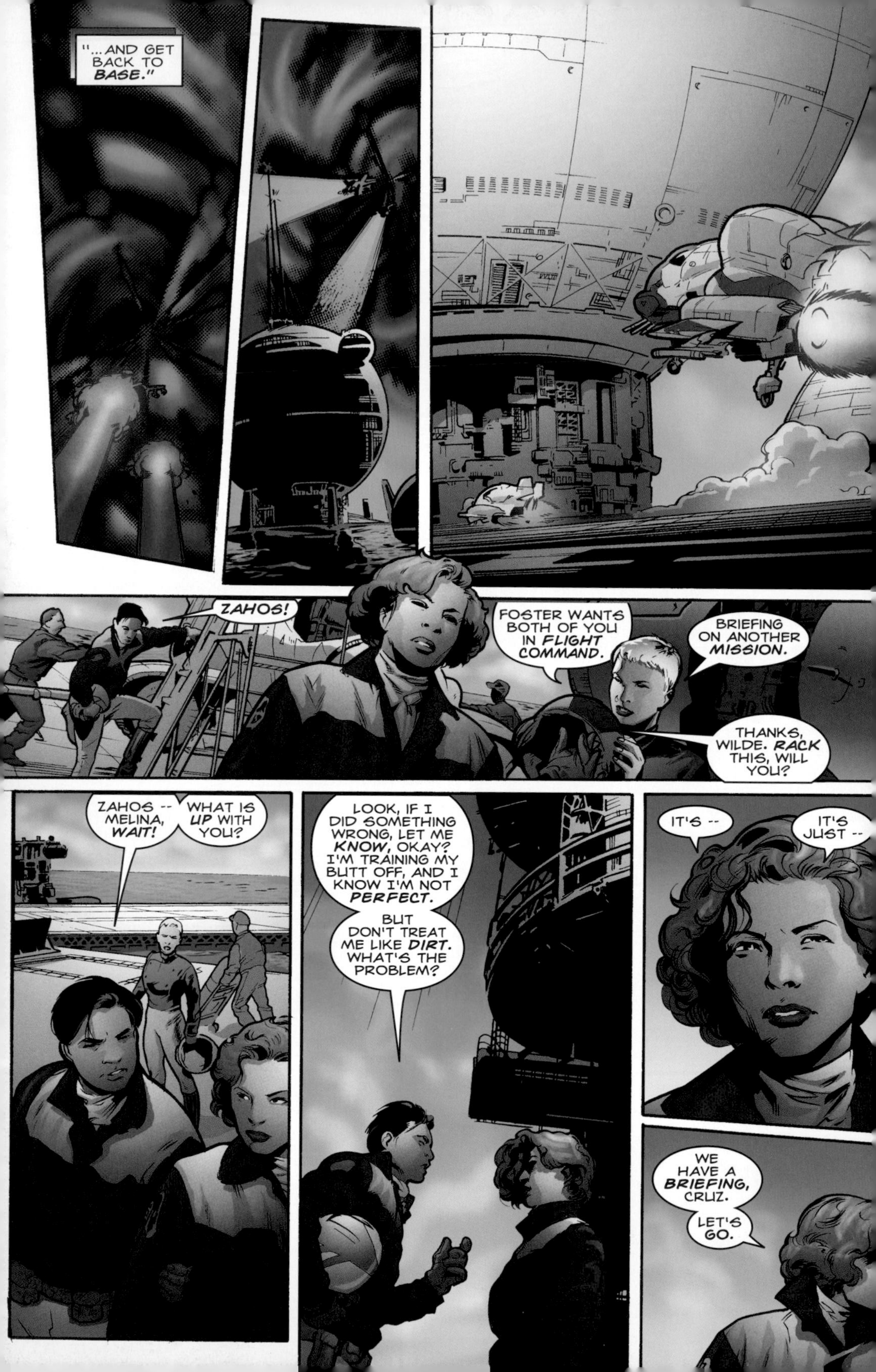
"...AND GET BACK TO BASE."
ZAHOS!
FOSTER WANTS BOTH OF YOU IN FLIGHT COMMAND.
BRIEFING ON ANOTHER MISSION.
THANKS, WILDE. RACK THIS, WILL YOU?
ZAHOS -- MELINA, WAIT!
WHAT IS UP WITH YOU?
LOOK, IF I DID SOMETHING WRONG, LET ME KNOW, OKAY? I'M TRAINING MY BUTT OFF, AND I KNOW I'M NOT PERFECT.
BUT DON'T TREAT ME LIKE DIRT. WHAT'S THE PROBLEM?
IT'S --
IT'S JUST --
WE HAVE A BRIEFING, CRUZ.
LET'S GO.

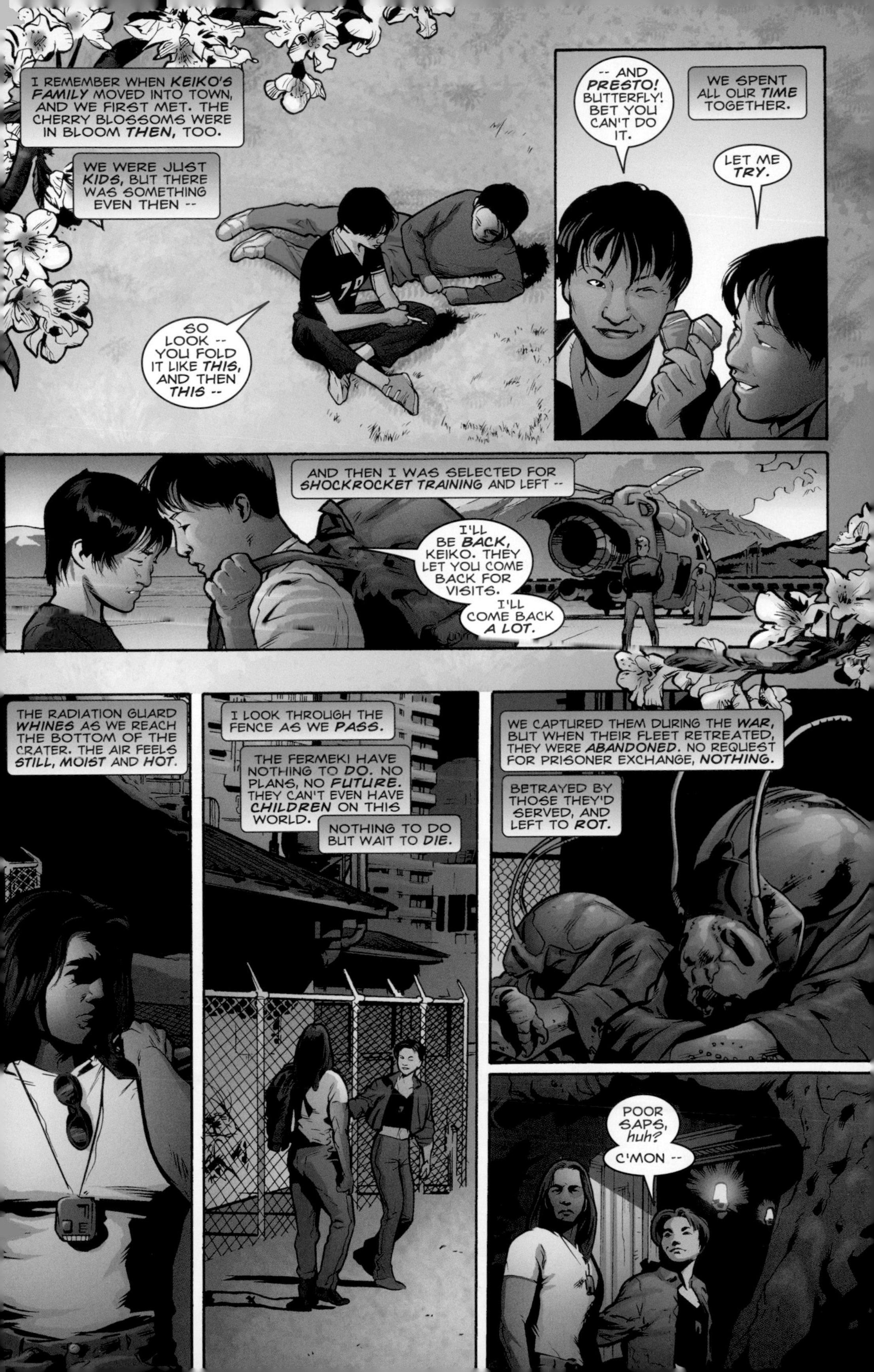
I REMEMBER WHEN KEIKO'S FAMILY MOVED INTO TOWN, AND WE FIRST MET. THE CHERRY BLOSSOMS WERE IN BLOOM THEN, TOO.
WE WERE JUST KIDS, BUT THERE WAS SOMETHING EVEN THEN --
SO LOOK -- YOU FOLD IT LIKE THIS, AND THEN THIS --
-- AND PRESTO! BUTTERFLY! BET YOU CAN'T DO IT.
WE SPENT ALL OUR TIME TOGETHER.
LET ME TRY.
AND THEN I WAS SELECTED FOR SHOCKROCKET TRAINING AND LEFT --
I'LL BE BACK, KEIKO. THEY LET YOU COME BACK FOR VISITS.
I'LL COME BACK A LOT.
THE RADIATION GUARD WHINES AS WE REACH THE BOTTOM OF THE CRATER. THE AIR FEELS STILL, MOIST AND HOT.
I LOOK THROUGH THE FENCE AS WE PASS.
THE FERMEKI HAVE NOTHING TO DO. NO PLANS, NO FUTURE. THEY CAN'T EVEN HAVE CHILDREN ON THIS WORLD.
NOTHING TO DO BUT WAIT TO DIE.
WE CAPTURED THEM DURING THE WAR, BUT WHEN THEIR FLEET RETREATED, THEY WERE ABANDONED. NO REQUEST FOR PRISONER EXCHANGE, NOTHING.
BETRAYED BY THOSE THEY'D SERVED, AND LEFT TO ROT.
POOR SAPS, huh?
C'MON --

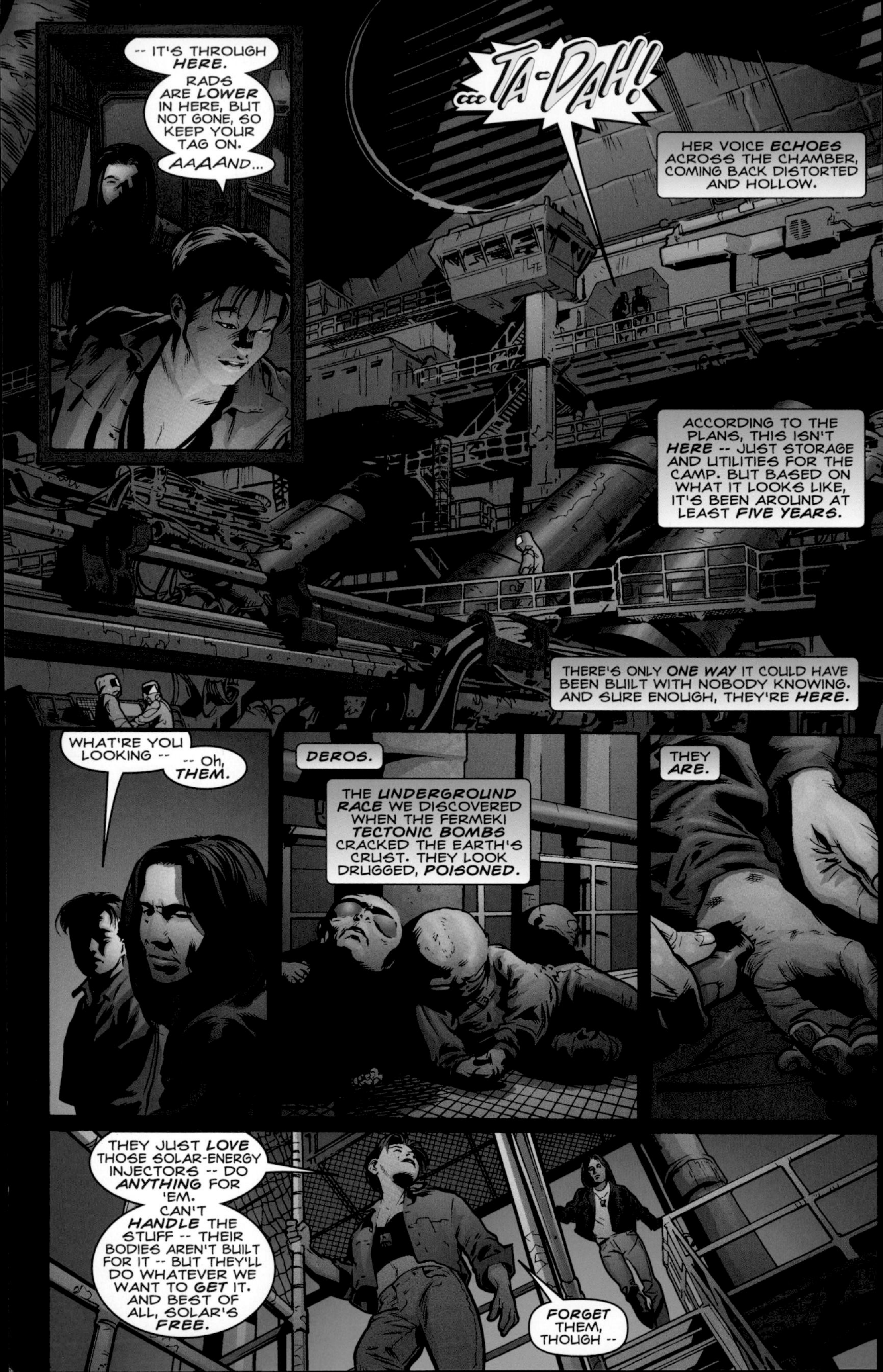

-- IT'S THROUGH HERE. RADS ARE LOWER IN HERE, BUT NOT GONE, SO KEEP YOUR TAG ON. AAAAND...
...TA-DAH!
HER VOICE ECHOES ACROSS THE CHAMBER, COMING BACK DISTORTED AND HOLLOW.
ACCORDING TO THE PLANS, THIS ISN'T HERE -- JUST STORAGE AND UTILITIES FOR THE CAMP. BUT BASED ON WHAT IT LOOKS LIKE, IT'S BEEN AROUND AT LEAST FIVE YEARS.
THERE'S ONLY ONE WAY IT COULD HAVE BEEN BUILT WITH NOBODY KNOWING. AND SURE ENOUGH, THEY'RE HERE.
WHAT'RE YOU LOOKING --
-- Oh, THEM.
DEROS.
THE UNDERGROUND RACE WE DISCOVERED WHEN THE FERMEKI TECTONIC BOMBS CRACKED THE EARTH'S CRUST. THEY LOOK DRUGGED, POISONED.
THEY ARE.
THEY JUST LOVE THOSE SOLAR-ENERGY INJECTORS -- DO ANYTHING FOR 'EM.
CAN'T HANDLE THE STUFF -- THEIR BODIES AREN'T BUILT FOR IT -- BUT THEY'LL DO WHATEVER WE WANT TO GET IT. AND BEST OF ALL, SOLAR'S FREE.
FORGET THEM, THOUGH --

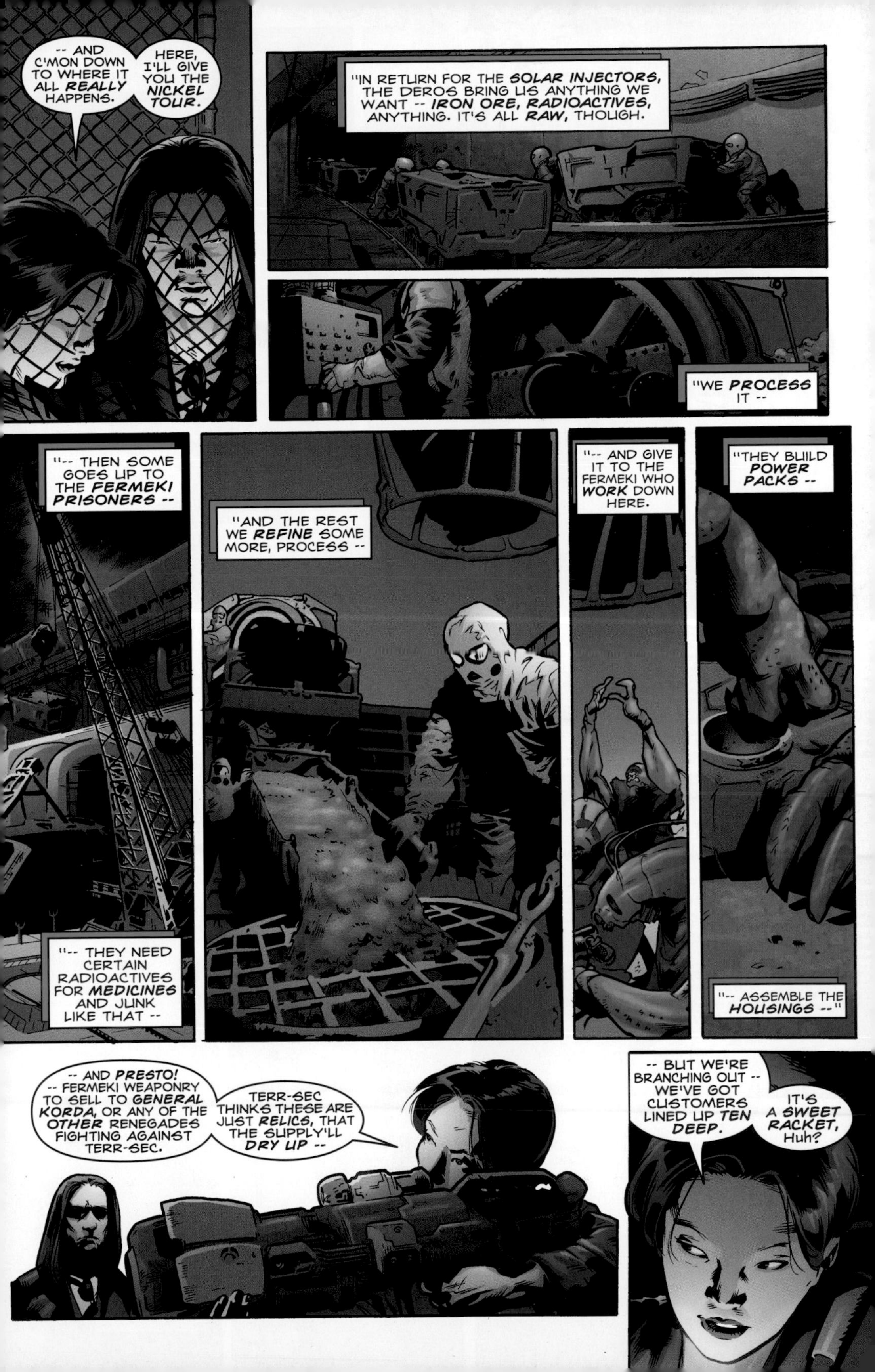
-- AND C'MON DOWN TO WHERE IT ALL REALLY HAPPENS.
HERE, I'LL GIVE YOU THE NICKEL TOUR.
"IN RETURN FOR THE SOLAR INJECTORS, THE DEROS BRING US ANYTHING WE WANT -- IRON ORE, RADIOACTIVES, ANYTHING. IT'S ALL RAW, THOUGH.
"WE PROCESS IT --
"-- THEN SOME GOES UP TO THE FERMEKI PRISONERS --
"-- THEY NEED CERTAIN RADIOACTIVES FOR MEDICINES AND JUNK LIKE THAT --
"AND THE REST WE REFINE SOME MORE, PROCESS --
"-- AND GIVE IT TO THE FERMEKI WHO WORK DOWN HERE.
"THEY BUILD POWER PACKS --
"-- ASSEMBLE THE HOUSINGS --"
-- AND PRESTO! -- FERMEKI WEAPONRY TO SELL TO GENERAL KORDA, OR ANY OF THE OTHER RENEGADES FIGHTING AGAINST TERR-SEC.
TERR-SEC THINKS THESE ARE JUST RELICS, THAT THE SUPPLY'LL DRY UP --
-- BUT WE'RE BRANCHING OUT -- WE'VE GOT CUSTOMERS LINED UP TEN DEEP.
IT'S A SWEET RACKET, Huh?

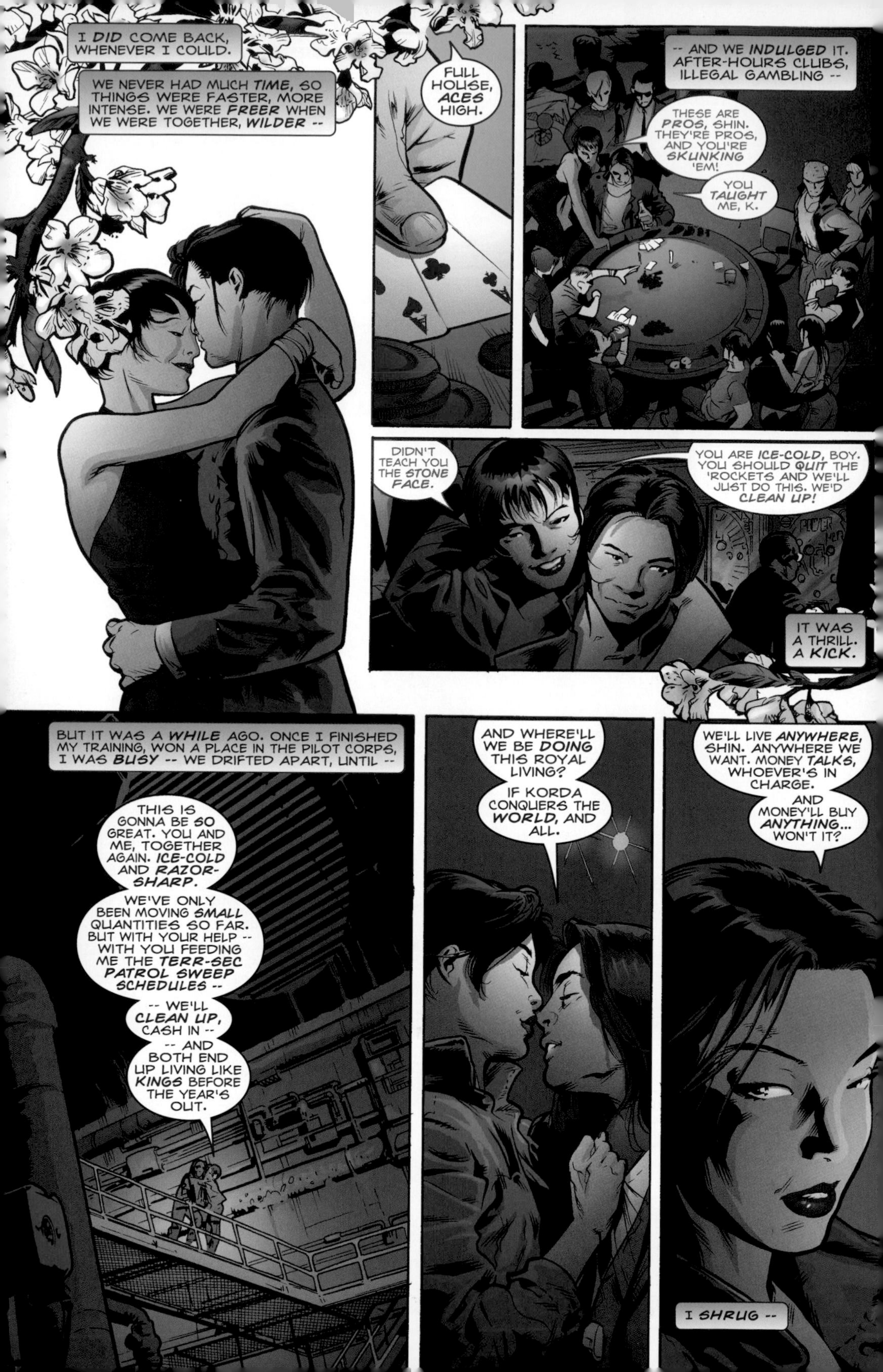
I DID COME BACK, WHENEVER I COULD.
WE NEVER HAD MUCH TIME, SO THINGS WERE FASTER, MORE INTENSE. WE WERE FREER WHEN WE WERE TOGETHER, WILDER --
FULL HOUSE, ACES HIGH.
-- AND WE INDULGED IT. AFTER-HOURS CLUBS, ILLEGAL GAMBLING --
THESE ARE PROS, SHIN. THEY'RE PROS, AND YOU'RE SKUNKING 'EM!
YOU TAUGHT ME, K.
DIDN'T TEACH YOU THE STONE FACE.
YOU ARE ICE-COLD, BOY. YOU SHOULD QUIT THE 'ROCKETS AND WE'LL JUST DO THIS. WE'D CLEAN UP!
IT WAS A THRILL. A KICK.
BUT IT WAS A WHILE AGO. ONCE I FINISHED MY TRAINING, WON A PLACE IN THE PILOT CORPS, I WAS BUSY -- WE DRIFTED APART, UNTIL --
THIS IS GONNA BE SO GREAT. YOU AND ME, TOGETHER AGAIN. ICE-COLD AND RAZOR-SHARP.
WE'VE ONLY BEEN MOVING SMALL QUANTITIES SO FAR. BUT WITH YOUR HELP -- WITH YOU FEEDING ME THE TERR-SEC PATROL SWEEP SCHEDULES --
-- WE'LL CLEAN UP, CASH IN --
-- AND BOTH END UP LIVING LIKE KINGS BEFORE THE YEAR'S OUT.
AND WHERE'LL WE BE DOING THIS ROYAL LIVING?
IF KORDA CONQUERS THE WORLD, AND ALL.
WE'LL LIVE ANYWHERE, SHIN. ANYWHERE WE WANT. MONEY TALKS, WHOEVER'S IN CHARGE.
AND MONEY'LL BUY ANYTHING... WON'T IT?
I SHRUG --

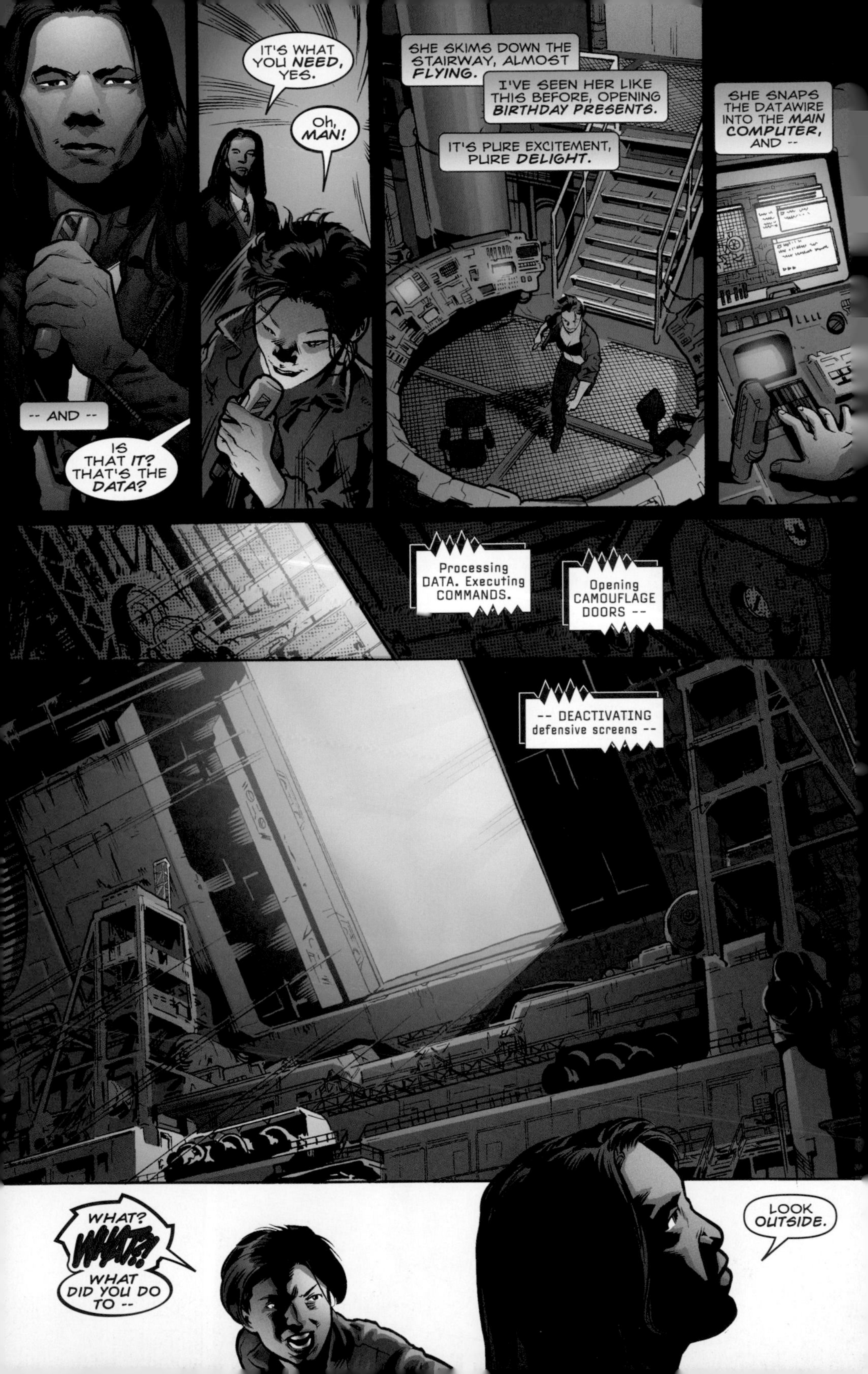
IT'S WHAT YOU NEED, YES.
Oh, MAN!
-- AND --
IS THAT IT? THAT'S THE DATA?
SHE SKIMS DOWN THE STAIRWAY, ALMOST FLYING.
I'VE SEEN HER LIKE THIS BEFORE, OPENING BIRTHDAY PRESENTS.
IT'S PURE EXCITEMENT, PURE DELIGHT.
SHE SNAPS THE DATAWIRE INTO THE MAIN COMPUTER, AND --
Processing DATA. Executing COMMANDS.
Opening CAMOUFLAGE DOORS --
-- DEACTIVATING defensive screens --
WHAT? WHAT?! WHAT DID YOU DO TO --
LOOK OUTSIDE.

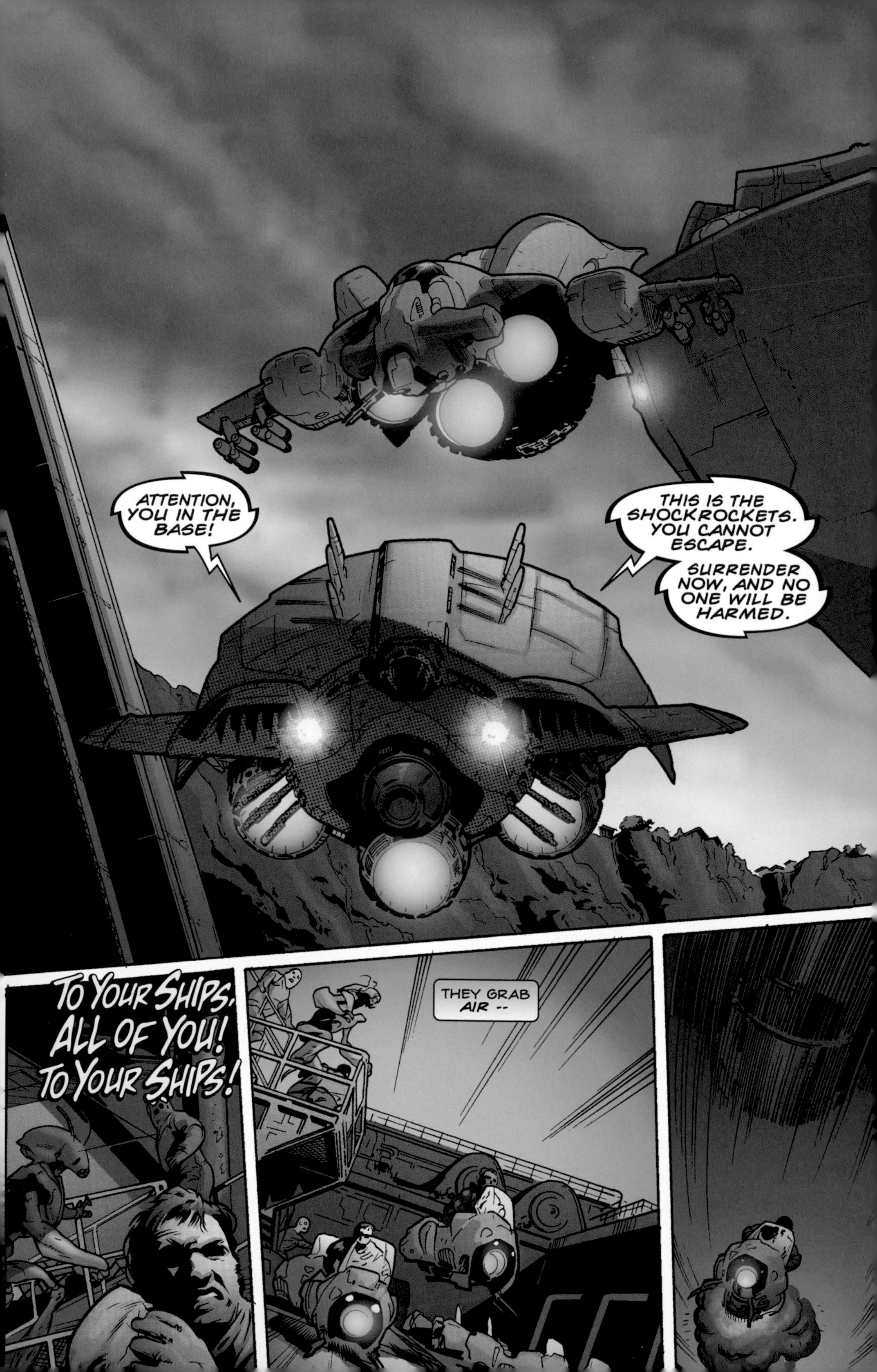
ATTENTION, YOU IN THE BASE!
THIS IS THE SHOCKROCKETS. YOU CANNOT ESCAPE.
SURRENDER NOW, AND NO ONE WILL BE HARMED.
TO YOUR SHIPS, ALL OF YOU! TO YOUR SHIPS!
THEY GRAB AIR --

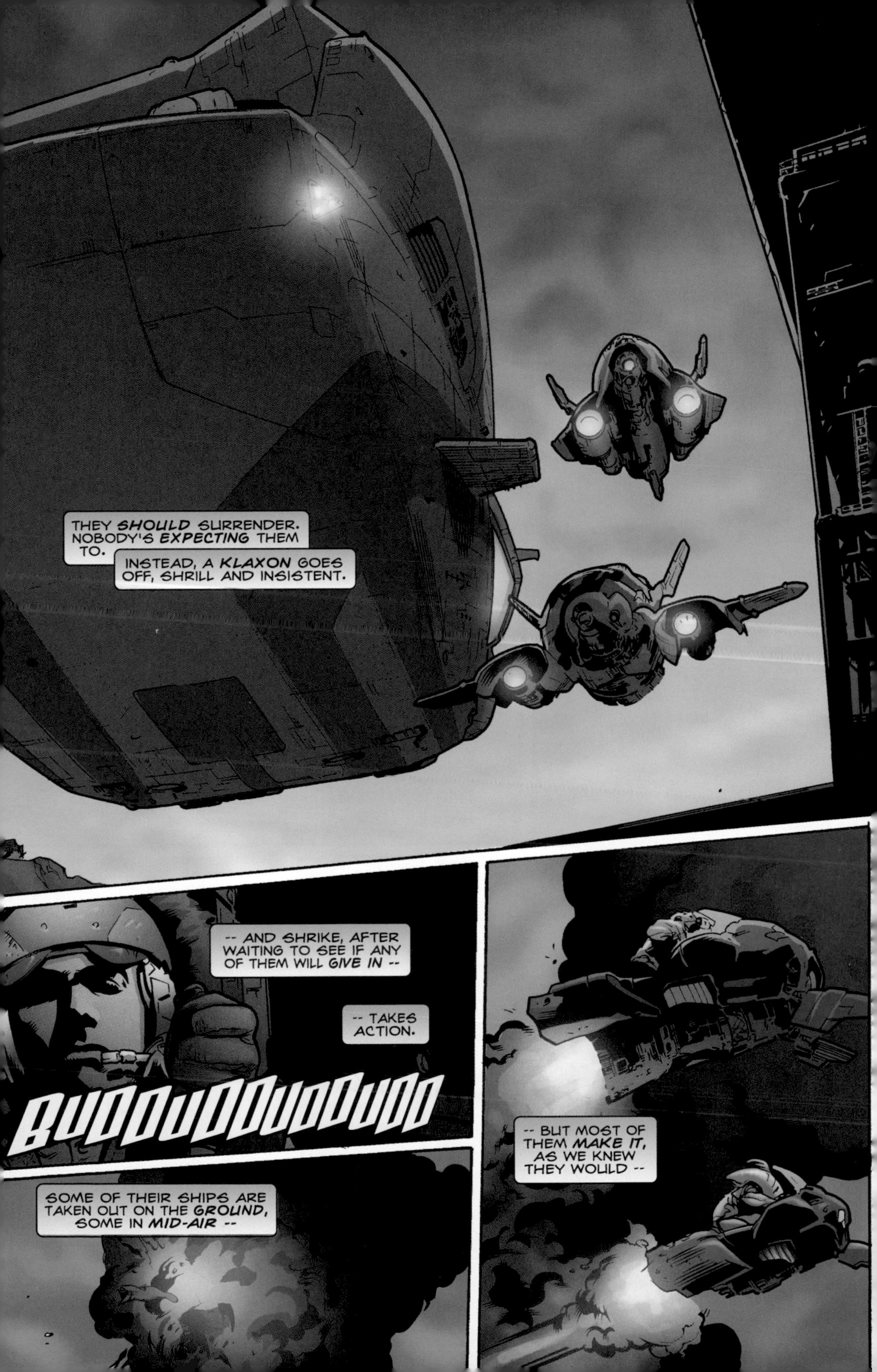

THEY *SHOULD* SURRENDER. NOBODY'S *EXPECTING* THEM TO.
INSTEAD, A *KLAXON* GOES OFF, SHRILL AND INSISTENT.
-- AND SHRIKE, AFTER WAITING TO SEE IF ANY OF THEM WILL *GIVE IN* --
-- TAKES ACTION.
BUDDUDDUDDUDD
SOME OF THEIR SHIPS ARE TAKEN OUT ON THE *GROUND,* SOME IN *MID-AIR* --
-- BUT MOST OF THEM *MAKE IT,* AS WE KNEW THEY WOULD --

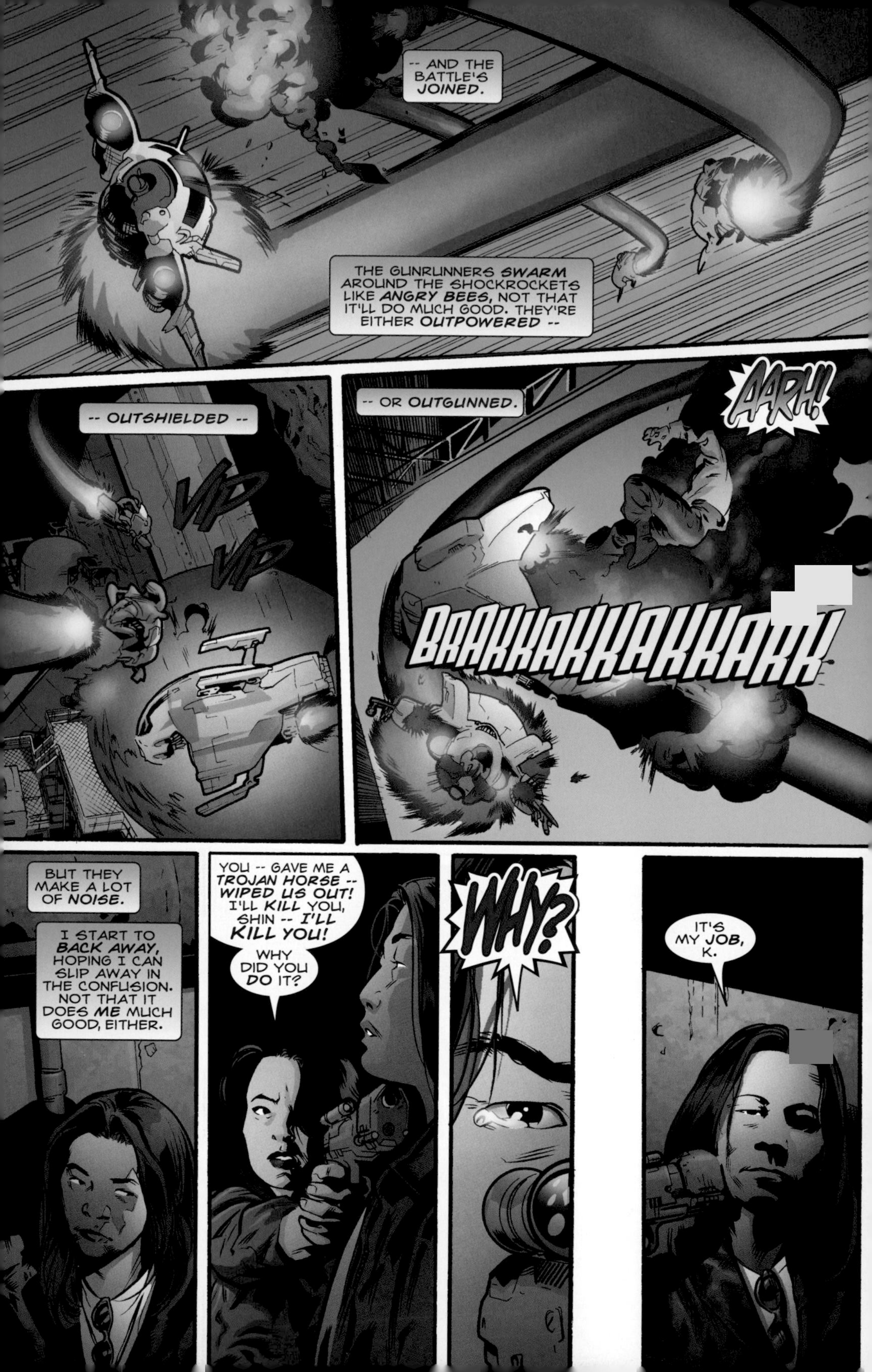

-- AND THE BATTLE'S JOINED.
THE GUNRUNNERS SWARM AROUND THE SHOCKROCKETS LIKE ANGRY BEES, NOT THAT IT'LL DO MUCH GOOD. THEY'RE EITHER OUTPOWERED --
-- OUTSHIELDED --
VIP
VIP
-- OR OUTGUNNED.
AARH!
BRAKKAKKAKKAKK!
BUT THEY MAKE A LOT OF NOISE.
I START TO BACK AWAY, HOPING I CAN SLIP AWAY IN THE CONFUSION. NOT THAT IT DOES ME MUCH GOOD, EITHER.
YOU -- GAVE ME A TROJAN HORSE -- WIPED US OUT! I'LL KILL YOU, SHIN -- I'LL KILL YOU!
WHY DID YOU DO IT?
WHY?
IT'S MY JOB, K.

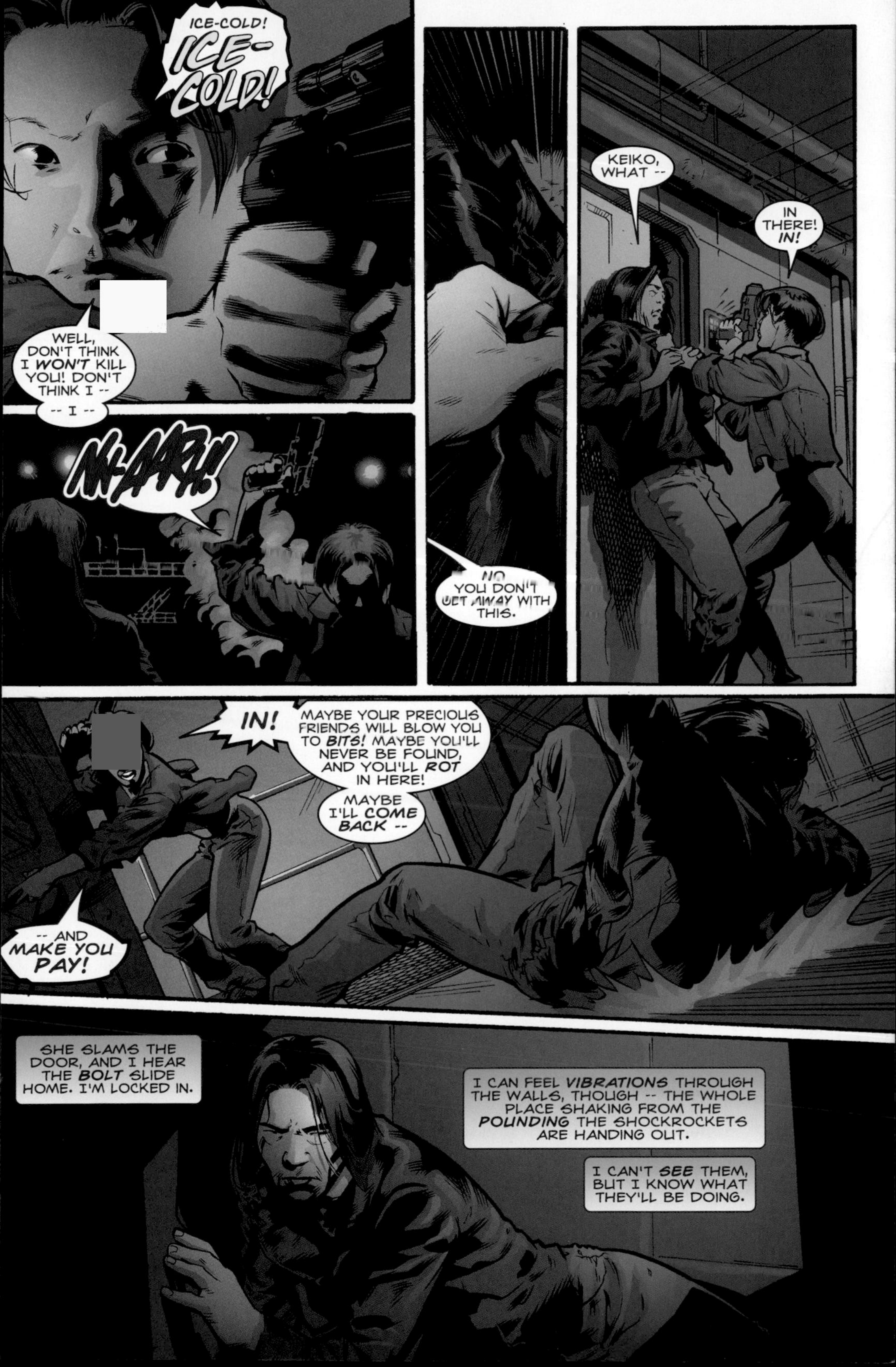
ICE-COLD! ICE-COLD!
WELL, DON'T THINK I WON'T KILL YOU! DON'T THINK I --
-- I --
NN-AARH!!
NO YOU DON'T GET AWAY WITH THIS.
KEIKO, WHAT --
IN THERE! IN!
IN!
MAYBE YOUR PRECIOUS FRIENDS WILL BLOW YOU TO BITS! MAYBE YOU'LL NEVER BE FOUND, AND YOU'LL ROT IN HERE!
MAYBE I'LL COME BACK --
-- AND MAKE YOU PAY!
SHE SLAMS THE DOOR, AND I HEAR THE BOLT SLIDE HOME. I'M LOCKED IN.
I CAN FEEL VIBRATIONS THROUGH THE WALLS, THOUGH -- THE WHOLE PLACE SHAKING FROM THE POUNDING THE SHOCKROCKETS ARE HANDING OUT.
I CAN'T SEE THEM, BUT I KNOW WHAT THEY'LL BE DOING.

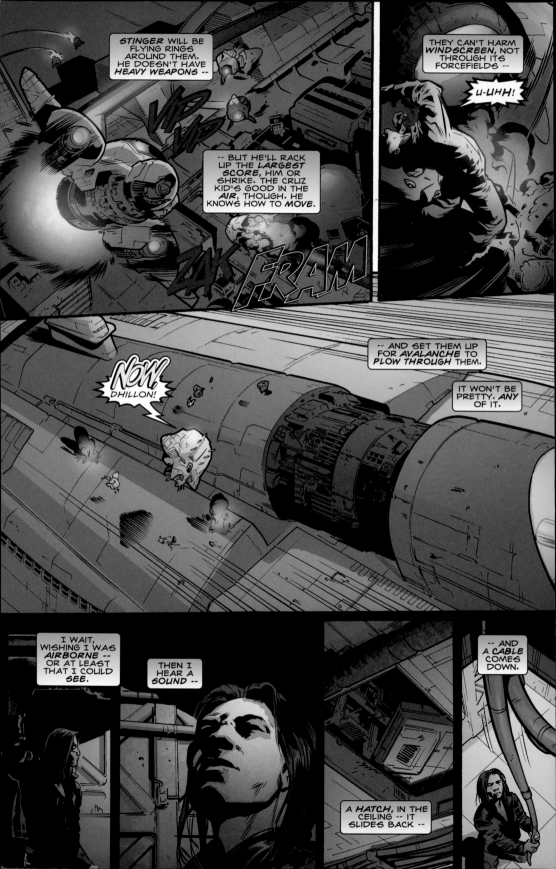

STINGER WILL BE FLYING RINGS AROUND THEM. HE DOESN'T HAVE HEAVY WEAPONS --

THEY CAN'T HARM *WINDSCREEN*, NOT THROUGH ITS FORCEFIELDS --

U-UHH!

-- BUT HE'LL RACK UP THE *LARGEST SCORE*, HIM OR SHRIKE. THE CRUZ KID'S GOOD IN THE *AIR*, THOUGH. HE KNOWS HOW TO *MOVE*.

VIP VIP

ZAK FRAM

NOW, DHILLON!

-- AND SET THEM UP FOR *AVALANCHE* TO *PLOW THROUGH* THEM.

IT WON'T BE PRETTY. *ANY* OF IT.

I WAIT, WISHING I WAS *AIRBORNE* -- OR AT LEAST THAT I COULD *SEE*.

THEN I HEAR A *SOUND* --

-- AND A *CABLE* COMES DOWN.

A *HATCH*, IN THE CEILING -- IT SLIDES BACK --

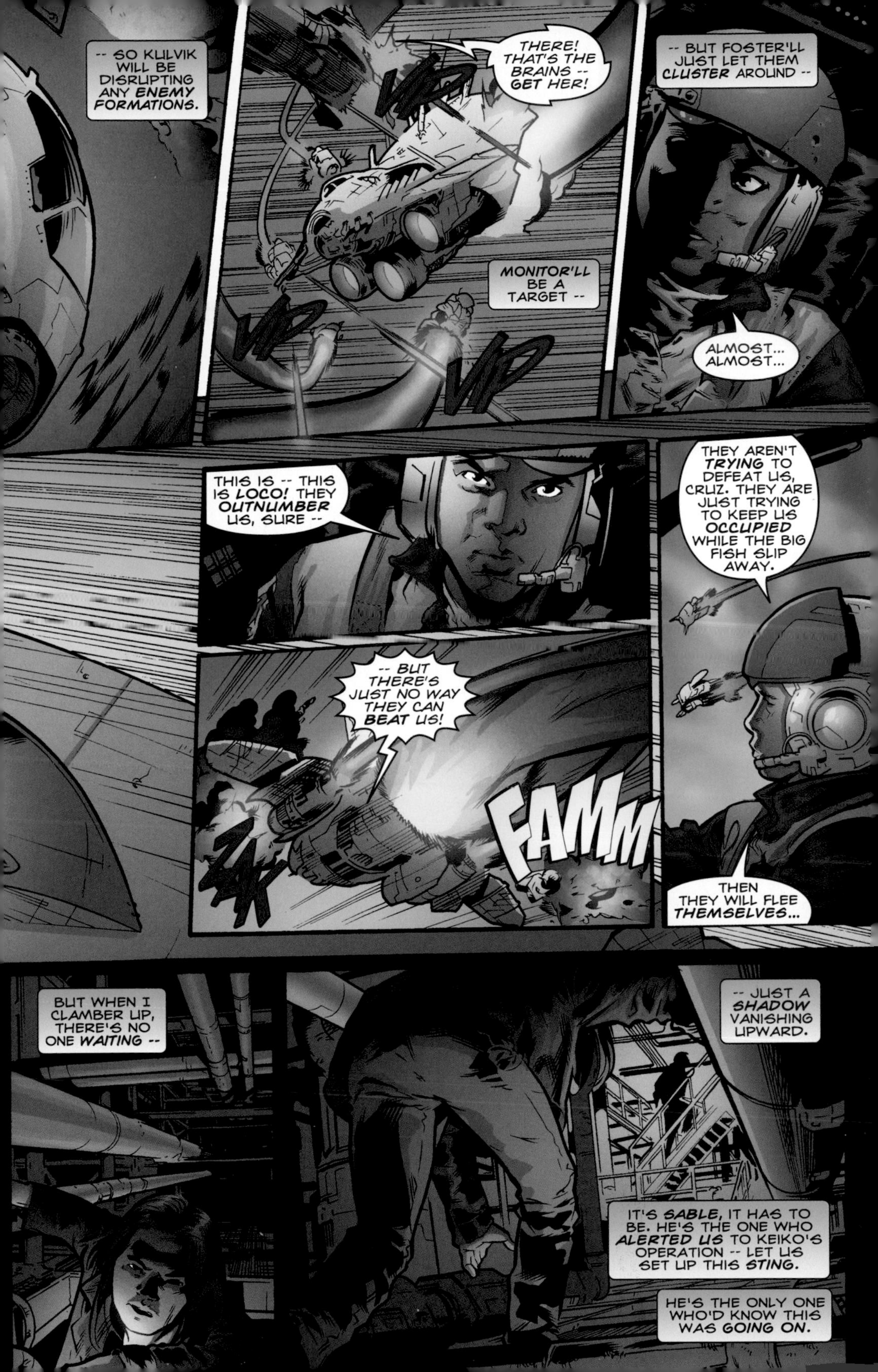
-- SO KULVIK WILL BE DISRUPTING ANY ENEMY FORMATIONS.
THERE! THAT'S THE BRAINS -- GET HER!
VIP
MONITOR'LL BE A TARGET --
VIP
VIP
-- BUT FOSTER'LL JUST LET THEM CLUSTER AROUND --
ALMOST... ALMOST...
THIS IS -- THIS IS LOCO! THEY OUTNUMBER US, SURE --
-- BUT THERE'S JUST NO WAY THEY CAN BEAT US!
FAMM
ZAK
THEY AREN'T TRYING TO DEFEAT US, CRUZ. THEY ARE JUST TRYING TO KEEP US OCCUPIED WHILE THE BIG FISH SLIP AWAY.
THEN THEY WILL FLEE THEMSELVES...
BUT WHEN I CLAMBER UP, THERE'S NO ONE WAITING --
-- JUST A SHADOW VANISHING UPWARD.
IT'S SABLE, IT HAS TO BE. HE'S THE ONE WHO ALERTED US TO KEIKO'S OPERATION -- LET US SET UP THIS STING.
HE'S THE ONLY ONE WHO'D KNOW THIS WAS GOING ON.

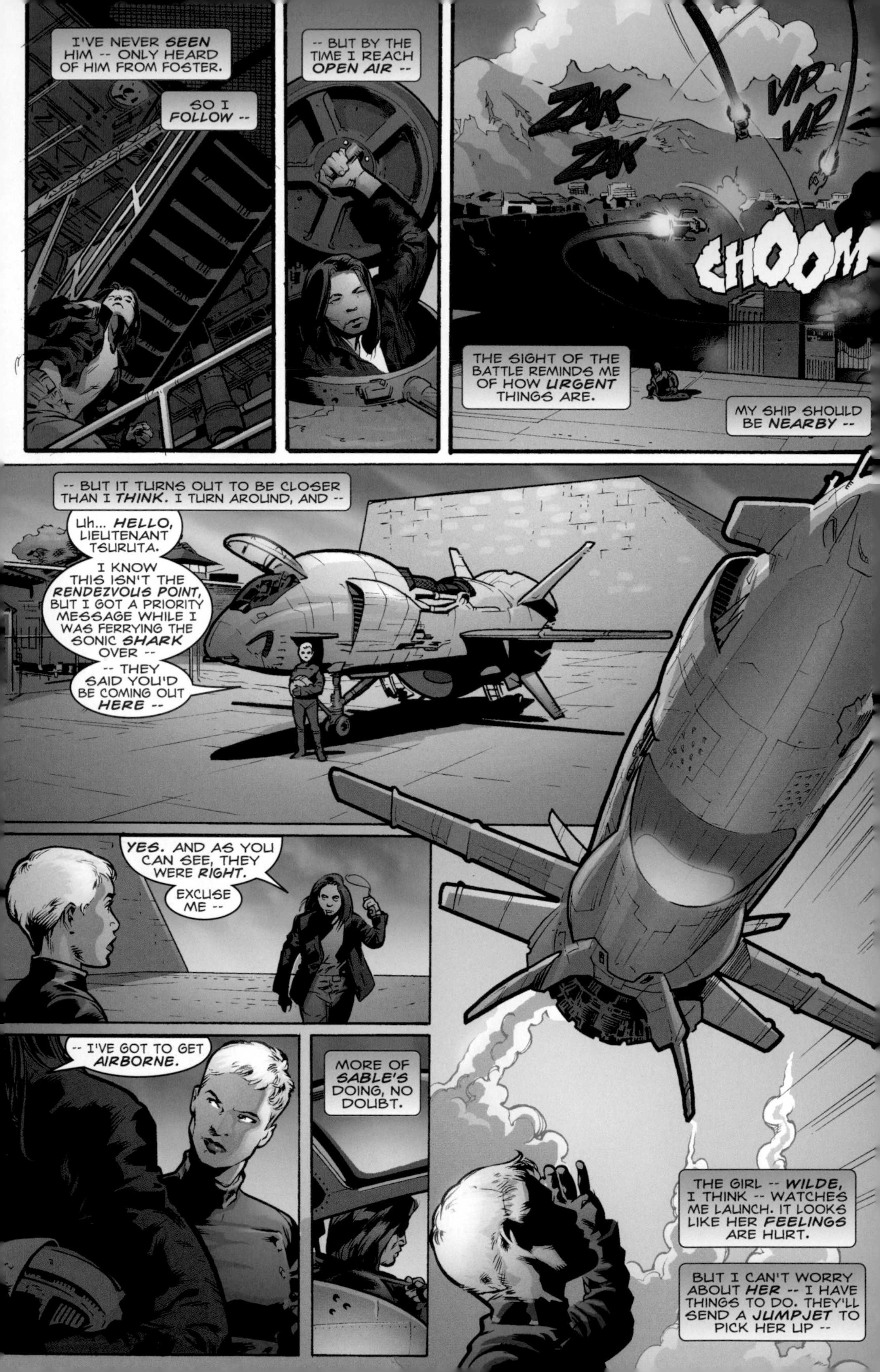
I'VE NEVER SEEN HIM -- ONLY HEARD OF HIM FROM FOSTER.
SO I FOLLOW --
-- BUT BY THE TIME I REACH OPEN AIR --
ZAK ZAK
VIP VIP
CHOOM
THE SIGHT OF THE BATTLE REMINDS ME OF HOW URGENT THINGS ARE.
MY SHIP SHOULD BE NEARBY --
-- BUT IT TURNS OUT TO BE CLOSER THAN I THINK. I TURN AROUND, AND --
Uh... HELLO, LIEUTENANT TSURUTA.
I KNOW THIS ISN'T THE RENDEZVOUS POINT, BUT I GOT A PRIORITY MESSAGE WHILE I WAS FERRYING THE SONIC SHARK OVER --
-- THEY SAID YOU'D BE COMING OUT HERE --
YES. AND AS YOU CAN SEE, THEY WERE RIGHT.
EXCUSE ME --
-- I'VE GOT TO GET AIRBORNE.
MORE OF SABLE'S DOING, NO DOUBT.
THE GIRL -- WILDE, I THINK -- WATCHES ME LAUNCH. IT LOOKS LIKE HER FEELINGS ARE HURT.
BUT I CAN'T WORRY ABOUT HER -- I HAVE THINGS TO DO. THEY'LL SEND A JUMPJET TO PICK HER UP --

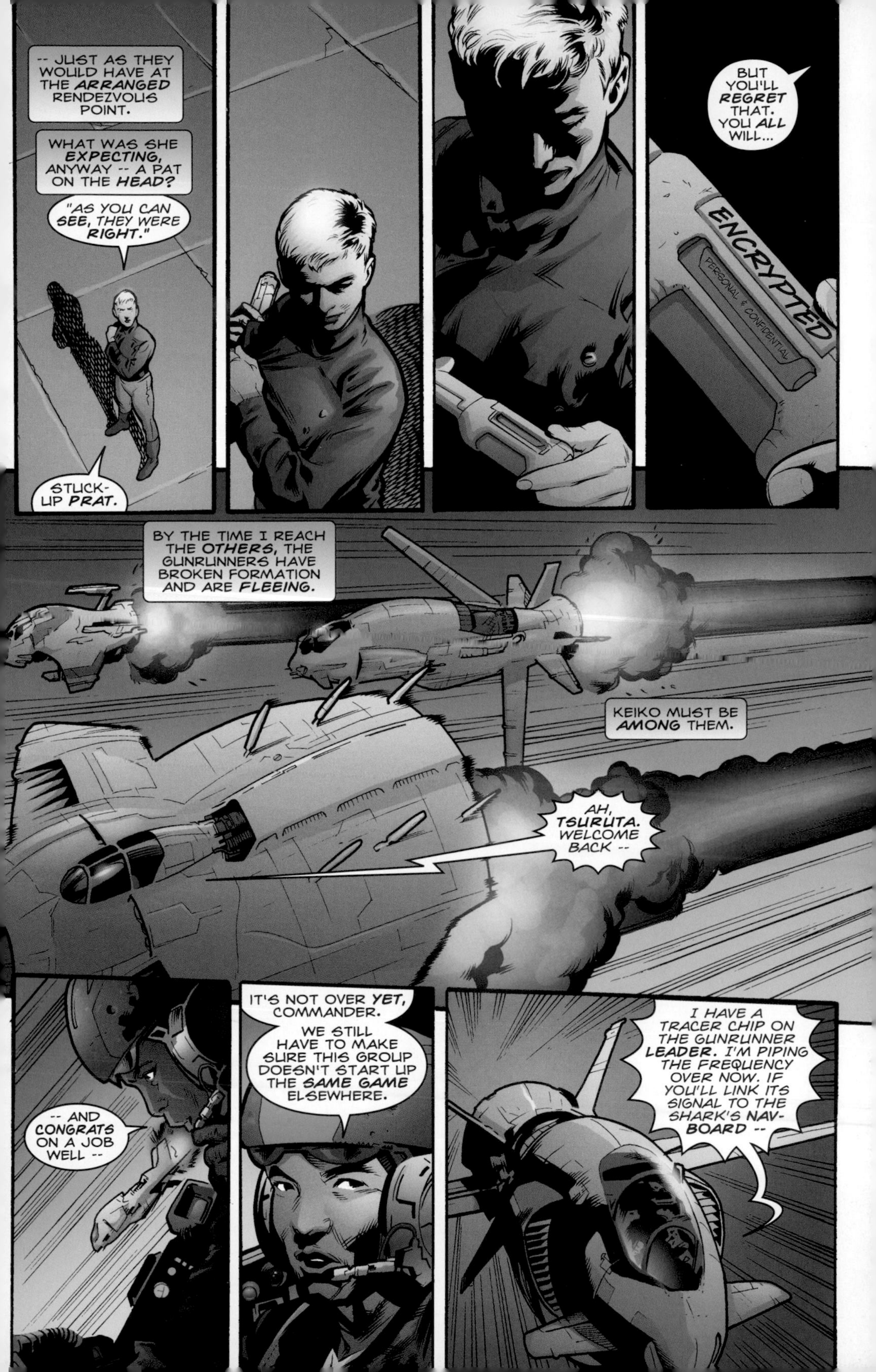

-- JUST AS THEY WOULD HAVE AT THE ARRANGED RENDEZVOUS POINT.
WHAT WAS SHE EXPECTING, ANYWAY -- A PAT ON THE HEAD?
"AS YOU CAN SEE, THEY WERE RIGHT."
STUCK-UP PRAT.
BUT YOU'LL REGRET THAT. YOU ALL WILL...
ENCRYPTED
PERSONAL & CONFIDENTIAL
BY THE TIME I REACH THE OTHERS, THE GUNRUNNERS HAVE BROKEN FORMATION AND ARE FLEEING.
KEIKO MUST BE AMONG THEM.
AH, TSURUTA. WELCOME BACK --
-- AND CONGRATS ON A JOB WELL --
IT'S NOT OVER YET, COMMANDER.
WE STILL HAVE TO MAKE SURE THIS GROUP DOESN'T START UP THE SAME GAME ELSEWHERE.
I HAVE A TRACER CHIP ON THE GUNRUNNER LEADER. I'M PIPING THE FREQUENCY OVER NOW. IF YOU'LL LINK ITS SIGNAL TO THE SHARK'S NAV-BOARD --

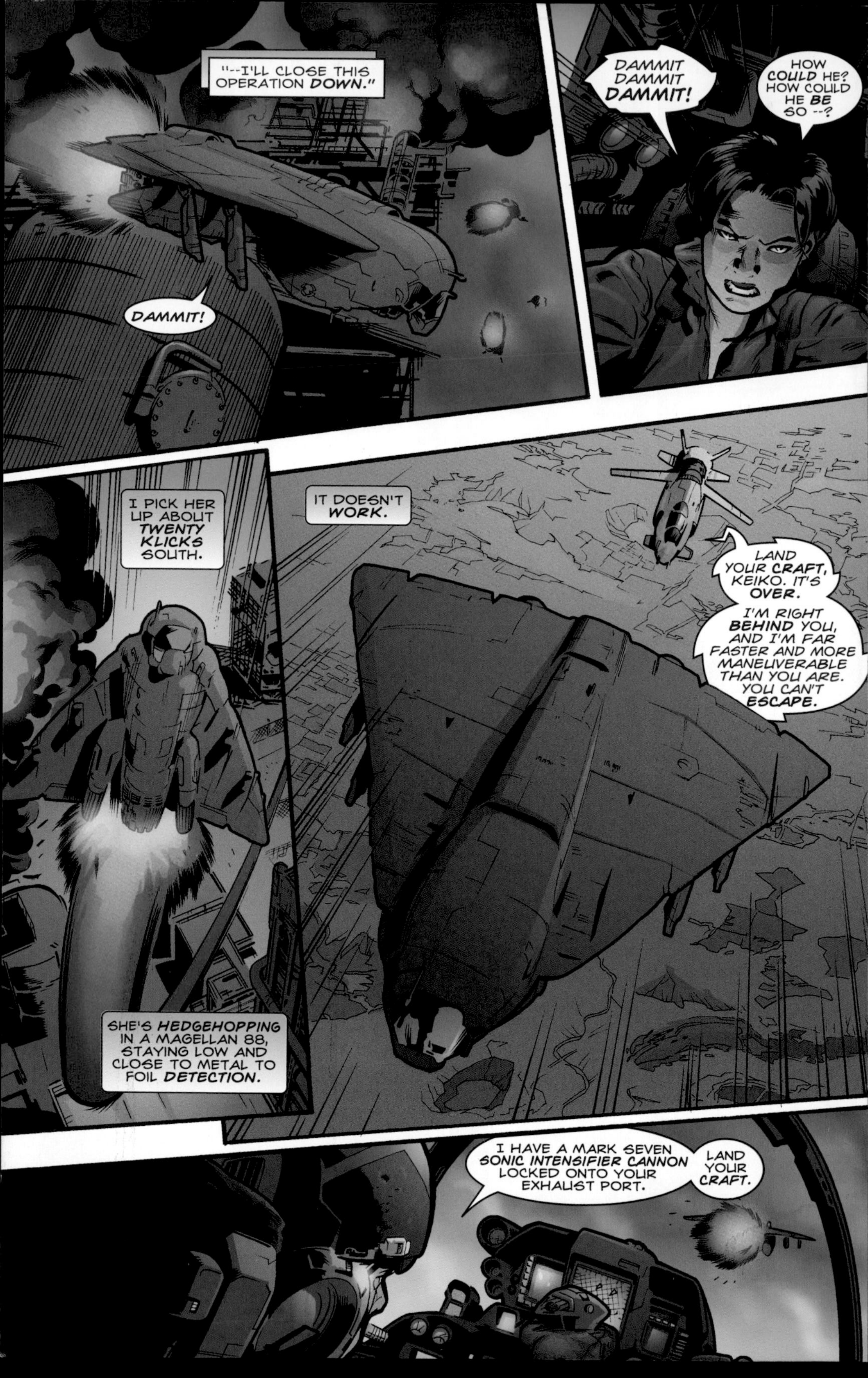
"--I'LL CLOSE THIS OPERATION DOWN."
DAMMIT!
DAMMIT DAMMIT DAMMIT!
HOW COULD HE? HOW COULD HE BE SO --?
I PICK HER UP ABOUT TWENTY KLICKS SOUTH.
SHE'S HEDGEHOPPING IN A MAGELLAN 88, STAYING LOW AND CLOSE TO METAL TO FOIL DETECTION.
IT DOESN'T WORK.
LAND YOUR CRAFT, KEIKO. IT'S OVER.
I'M RIGHT BEHIND YOU, AND I'M FAR FASTER AND MORE MANEUVERABLE THAN YOU ARE. YOU CAN'T ESCAPE.
I HAVE A MARK SEVEN SONIC INTENSIFIER CANNON LOCKED ONTO YOUR EXHAUST PORT.
LAND YOUR CRAFT.

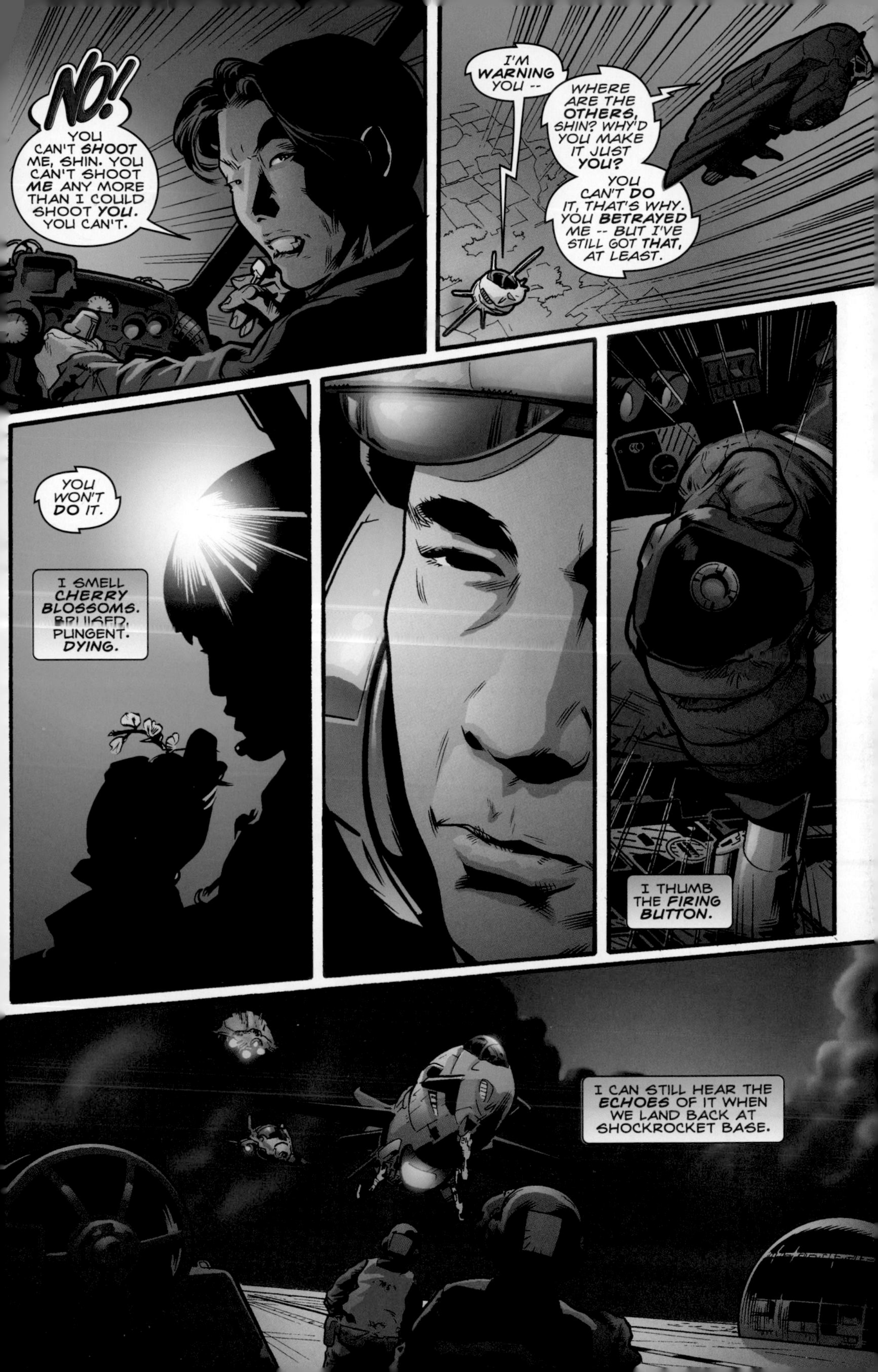
NO!
YOU CAN'T SHOOT ME, SHIN. YOU CAN'T SHOOT ME ANY MORE THAN I COULD SHOOT YOU. YOU CAN'T.
I'M WARNING YOU --
WHERE ARE THE OTHERS, SHIN? WHY'D YOU MAKE IT JUST YOU?
YOU CAN'T DO IT, THAT'S WHY. YOU BETRAYED ME -- BUT I'VE STILL GOT THAT, AT LEAST.
YOU WON'T DO IT.
I SMELL CHERRY BLOSSOMS. BRUISED. PUNGENT. DYING.
I THUMB THE FIRING BUTTON.
I CAN STILL HEAR THE ECHOES OF IT WHEN WE LAND BACK AT SHOCKROCKET BASE.

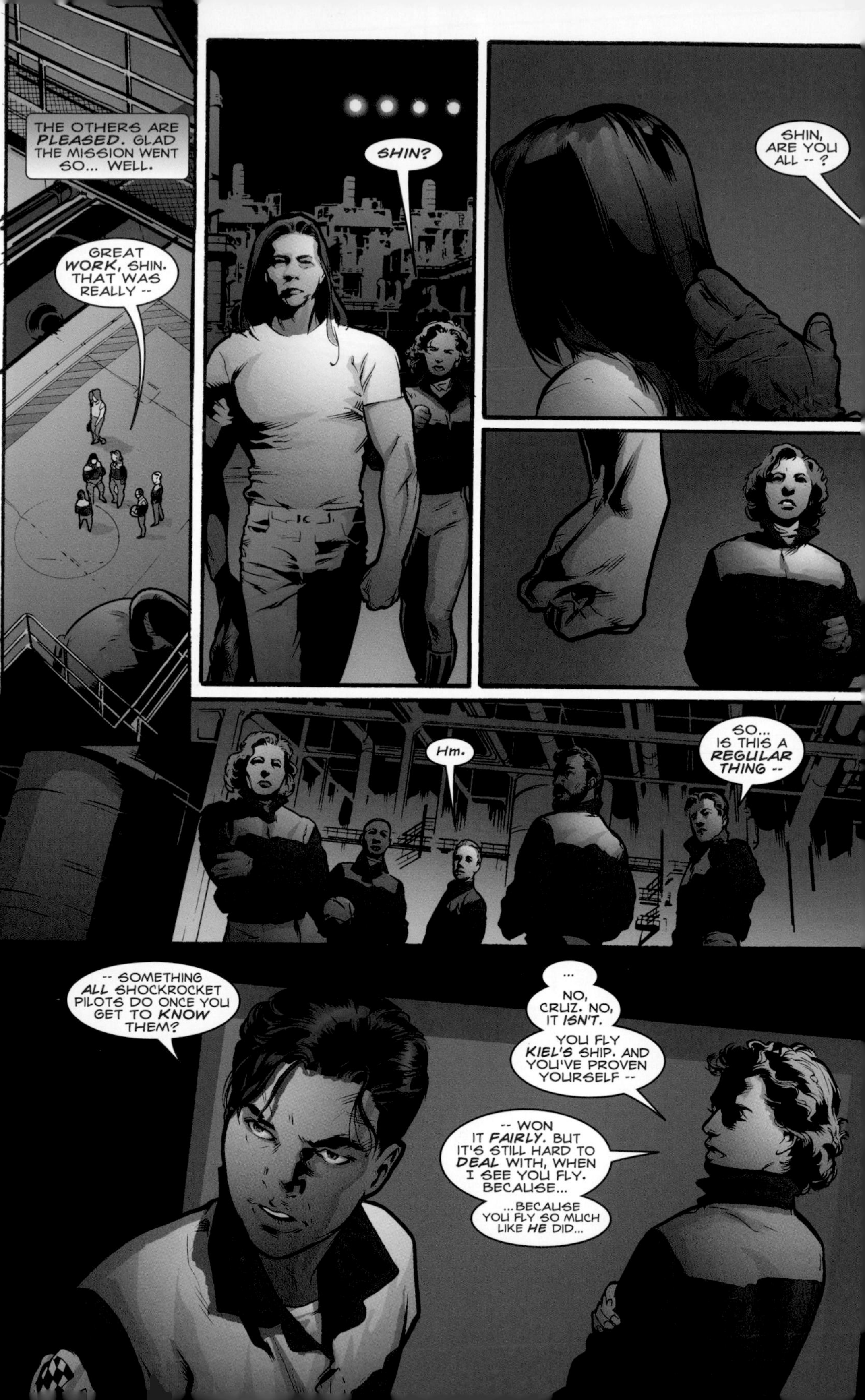
THE OTHERS ARE PLEASED. GLAD THE MISSION WENT SO... WELL.
GREAT WORK, SHIN. THAT WAS REALLY --
SHIN?
SHIN, ARE YOU ALL -- ?
Hm.
SO... IS THIS A REGULAR THING --
-- SOMETHING ALL SHOCKROCKET PILOTS DO ONCE YOU GET TO KNOW THEM?
...
NO, CRUZ. NO, IT ISN'T.
YOU FLY KIEL'S SHIP. AND YOU'VE PROVEN YOURSELF --
-- WON IT FAIRLY. BUT IT'S STILL HARD TO DEAL WITH, WHEN I SEE YOU FLY. BECAUSE...
...BECAUSE YOU FLY SO MUCH LIKE HE DID...

CHAPTER FOUR

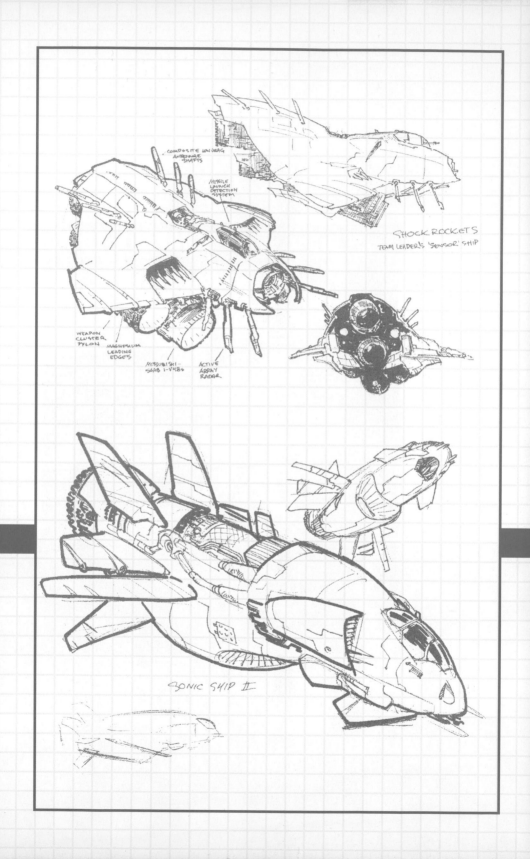

COMPOSITE LOW DRAG
ANTENNAE SHAFTS

MISSILE
LAUNCH
DETECTION
SYSTEM

SHOCK ROCKETS
TEAM LEADER'S 'SENSOR' SHIP

WEAPON
CLUSTER
PYLON

MAGNESIUM
LEADING
EDGES

MITSUBISHI—
SAAB 1-V48s

ACTIVE
ARRAY
RADAR

SONIC SHIP II

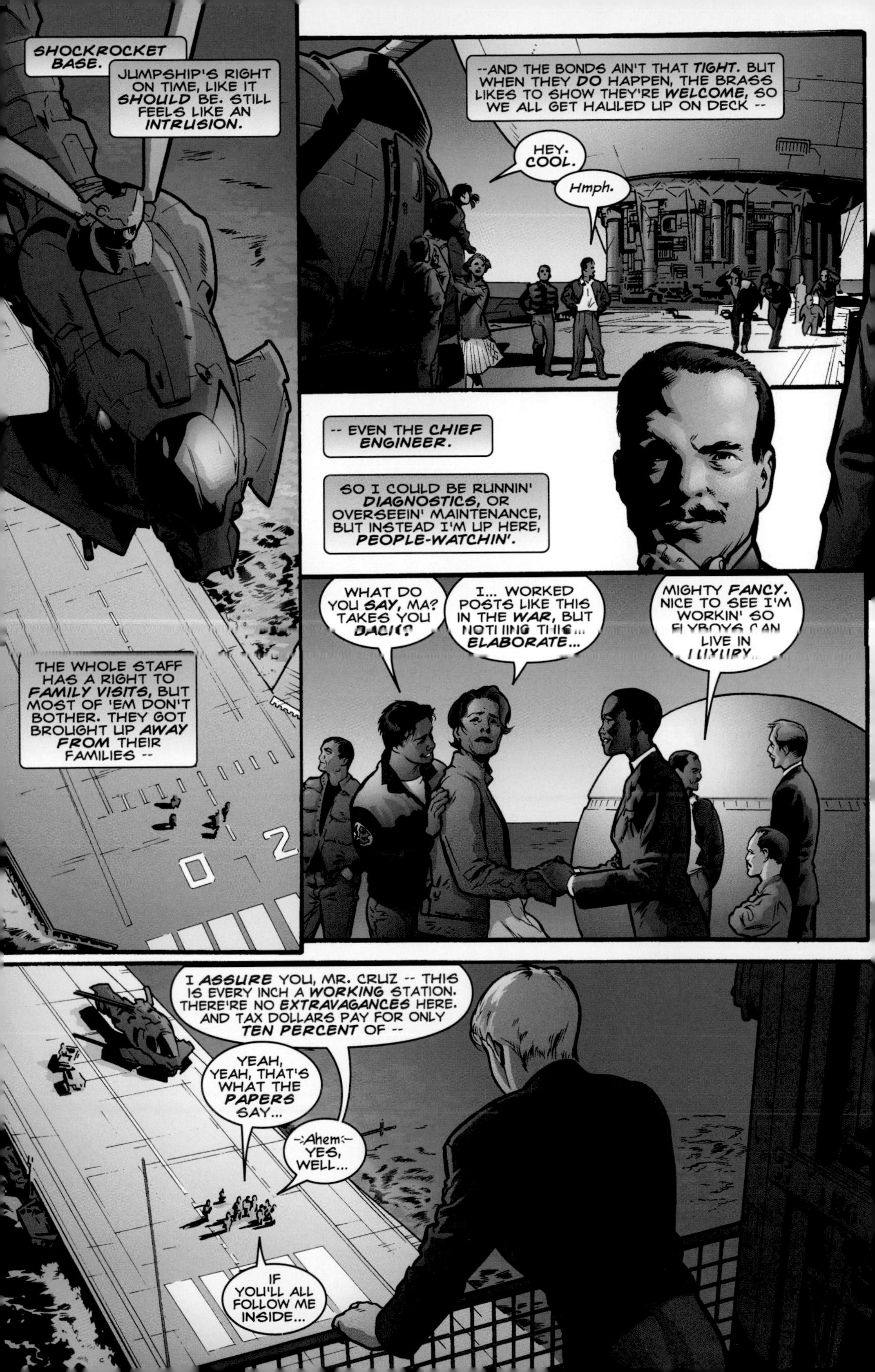
SHOCKROCKET BASE.
JUMPSHIP'S RIGHT ON TIME, LIKE IT SHOULD BE. STILL FEELS LIKE AN INTRUSION.
--AND THE BONDS AIN'T THAT TIGHT. BUT WHEN THEY DO HAPPEN, THE BRASS LIKES TO SHOW THEY'RE WELCOME, SO WE ALL GET HAULED UP ON DECK --
HEY. COOL.
Hmph.
-- EVEN THE CHIEF ENGINEER.
SO I COULD BE RUNNIN' DIAGNOSTICS, OR OVERSEEIN' MAINTENANCE, BUT INSTEAD I'M UP HERE, PEOPLE-WATCHIN'.
THE WHOLE STAFF HAS A RIGHT TO FAMILY VISITS, BUT MOST OF 'EM DON'T BOTHER. THEY GOT BROUGHT UP AWAY FROM THEIR FAMILIES --
WHAT DO YOU SAY, MA? TAKES YOU BACK?
I... WORKED POSTS LIKE THIS IN THE WAR, BUT NOTHING THIS... ELABORATE...
MIGHTY FANCY. NICE TO SEE I'M WORKIN' SO FLYBOYS CAN LIVE IN LUXURY...
I ASSURE YOU, MR. CRUZ -- THIS IS EVERY INCH A WORKING STATION. THERE'RE NO EXTRAVAGANCES HERE. AND TAX DOLLARS PAY FOR ONLY TEN PERCENT OF --
YEAH, YEAH, THAT'S WHAT THE PAPERS SAY...
-:-Ahem-:- YES, WELL...
IF YOU'LL ALL FOLLOW ME INSIDE...

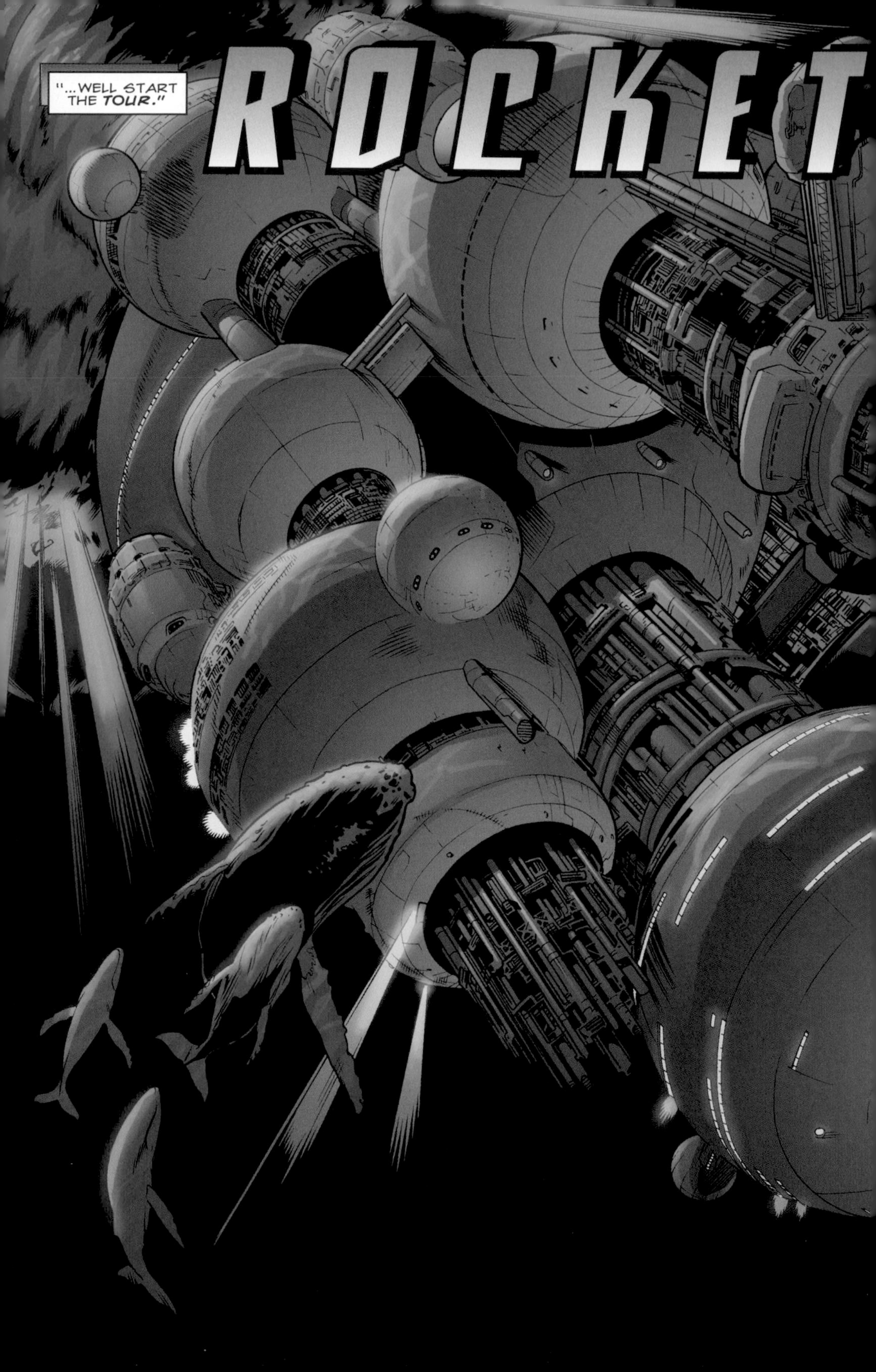
"...WELL START THE *TOUR*."
ROCKET

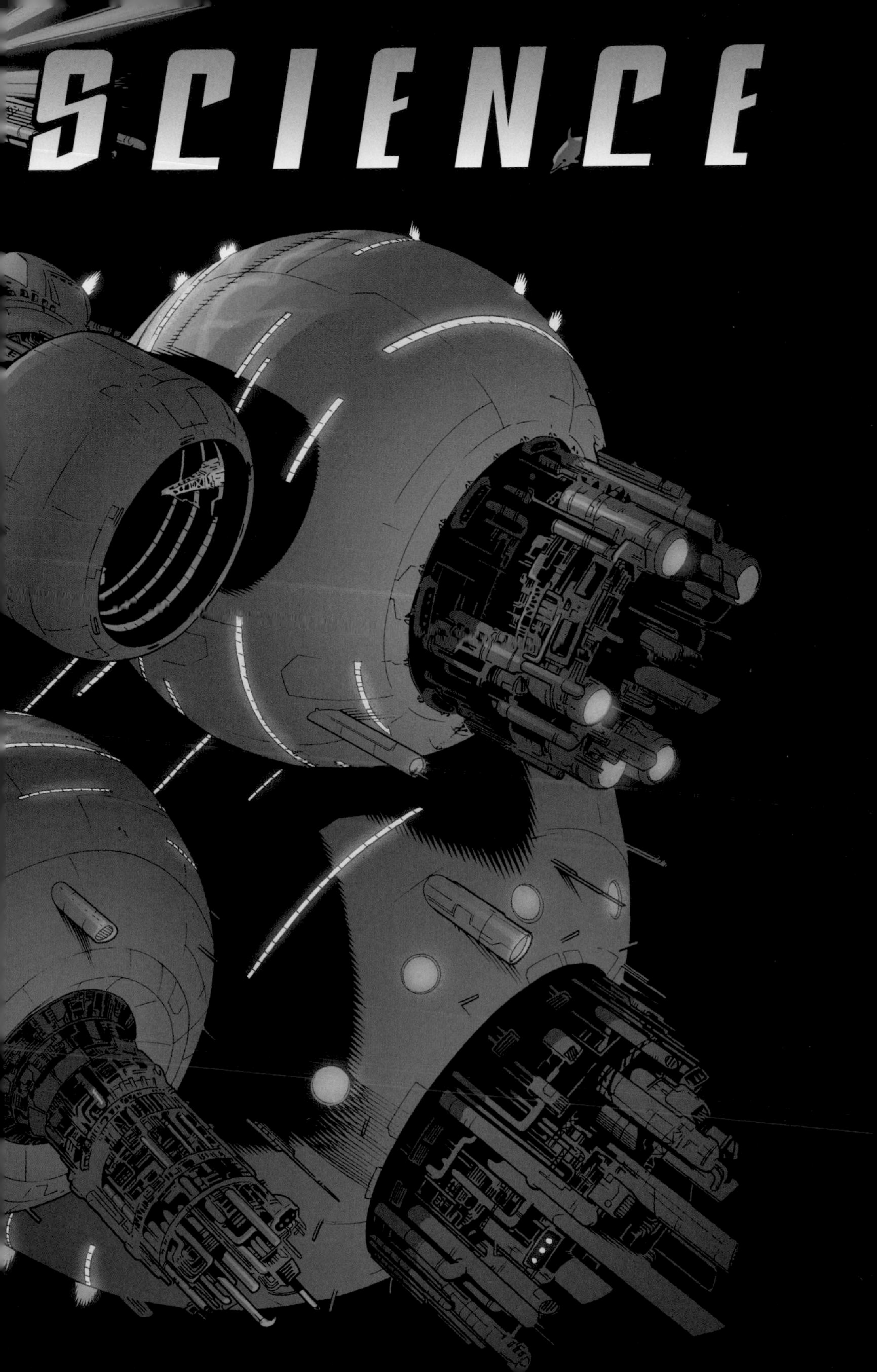
SCIENCE

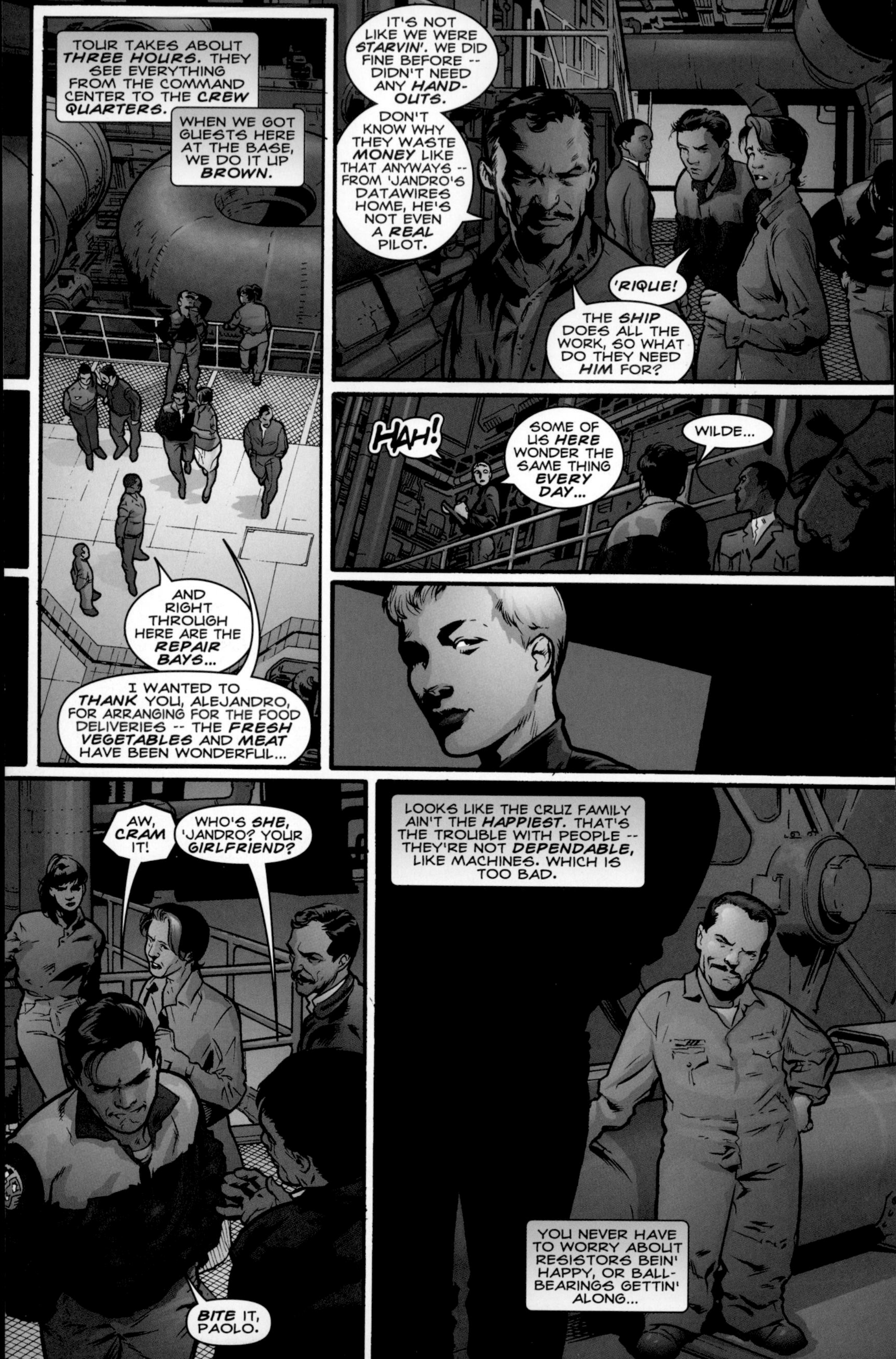
TOUR TAKES ABOUT THREE HOURS. THEY SEE EVERYTHING FROM THE COMMAND CENTER TO THE CREW QUARTERS.
WHEN WE GOT GUESTS HERE AT THE BASE, WE DO IT UP BROWN.
AND RIGHT THROUGH HERE ARE THE REPAIR BAYS...
I WANTED TO THANK YOU, ALEJANDRO, FOR ARRANGING FOR THE FOOD DELIVERIES -- THE FRESH VEGETABLES AND MEAT HAVE BEEN WONDERFUL...
IT'S NOT LIKE WE WERE STARVIN'. WE DID FINE BEFORE -- DIDN'T NEED ANY HAND-OUTS.
DON'T KNOW WHY THEY WASTE MONEY LIKE THAT ANYWAYS -- FROM 'JANDRO'S DATAWIRES HOME, HE'S NOT EVEN A REAL PILOT.
'RIQUE!
THE SHIP DOES ALL THE WORK, SO WHAT DO THEY NEED HIM FOR?
HAH!
SOME OF US HERE WONDER THE SAME THING EVERY DAY...
WILDE...
AW, CRAM IT!
WHO'S SHE, 'JANDRO? YOUR GIRLFRIEND?
BITE IT, PAOLO.
LOOKS LIKE THE CRUZ FAMILY AIN'T THE HAPPIEST. THAT'S THE TROUBLE WITH PEOPLE -- THEY'RE NOT DEPENDABLE, LIKE MACHINES. WHICH IS TOO BAD.
YOU NEVER HAVE TO WORRY ABOUT RESISTORS BEIN' HAPPY, OR BALL-BEARINGS GETTIN' ALONG...

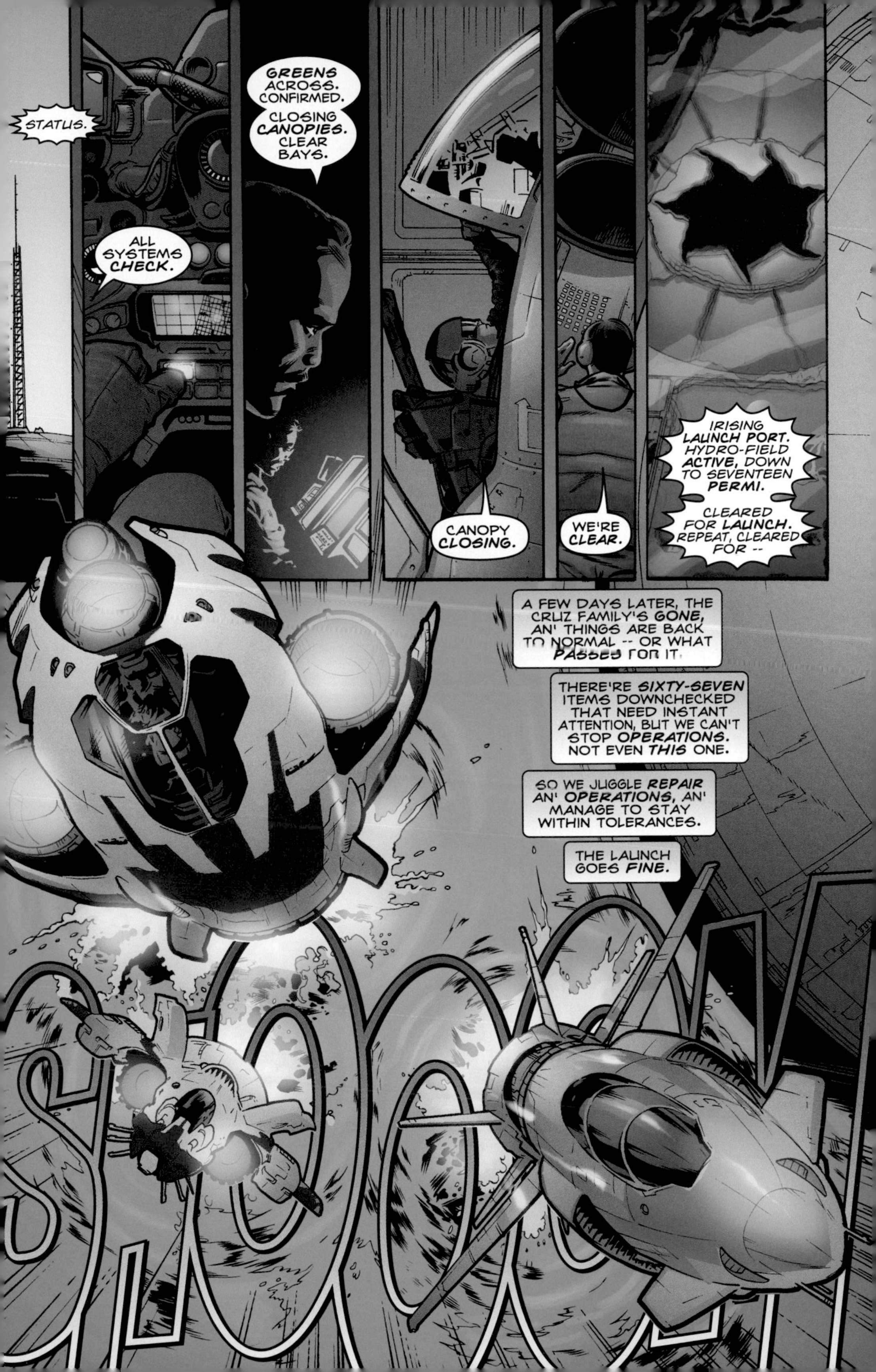
STATUS.
ALL SYSTEMS CHECK.
GREENS ACROSS. CONFIRMED.
CLOSING CANOPIES. CLEAR BAYS.
CANOPY CLOSING.
WE'RE CLEAR.
IRISING LAUNCH PORT. HYDRO-FIELD ACTIVE, DOWN TO SEVENTEEN PERMI.
CLEARED FOR LAUNCH. REPEAT, CLEARED FOR --
A FEW DAYS LATER, THE CRUZ FAMILY'S GONE, AN' THINGS ARE BACK TO NORMAL -- OR WHAT PASSES FOR IT.
THERE'RE SIXTY-SEVEN ITEMS DOWNCHECKED THAT NEED INSTANT ATTENTION, BUT WE CAN'T STOP OPERATIONS. NOT EVEN THIS ONE.
SO WE JUGGLE REPAIR AN' OPERATIONS, AN' MANAGE TO STAY WITHIN TOLERANCES.
THE LAUNCH GOES FINE.

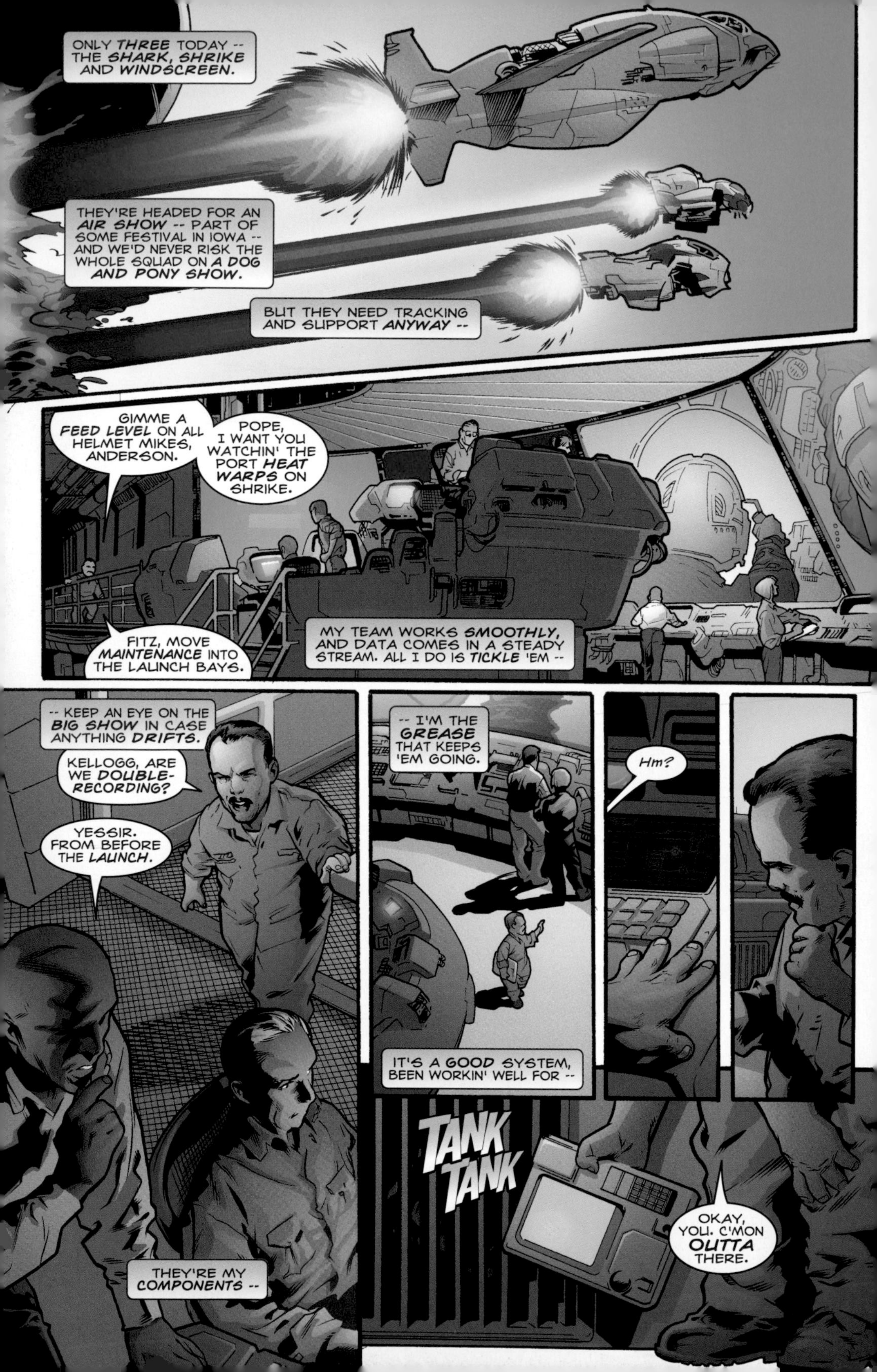
ONLY THREE TODAY -- THE SHARK, SHRIKE AND WINDSCREEN.
THEY'RE HEADED FOR AN AIR SHOW -- PART OF SOME FESTIVAL IN IOWA -- AND WE'D NEVER RISK THE WHOLE SQUAD ON A DOG AND PONY SHOW.
BUT THEY NEED TRACKING AND SUPPORT ANYWAY --
GIMME A FEED LEVEL ON ALL HELMET MIKES, ANDERSON.
POPE, I WANT YOU WATCHIN' THE PORT HEAT WARPS ON SHRIKE.
FITZ, MOVE MAINTENANCE INTO THE LAUNCH BAYS.
MY TEAM WORKS SMOOTHLY, AND DATA COMES IN A STEADY STREAM. ALL I DO IS TICKLE 'EM --
-- KEEP AN EYE ON THE BIG SHOW IN CASE ANYTHING DRIFTS.
KELLOGG, ARE WE DOUBLE-RECORDING?
YESSIR. FROM BEFORE THE LAUNCH.
THEY'RE MY COMPONENTS --
-- I'M THE GREASE THAT KEEPS 'EM GOING.
IT'S A GOOD SYSTEM, BEEN WORKIN' WELL FOR --
Hm?
TANK TANK
OKAY, YOU. C'MON OUTTA THERE.

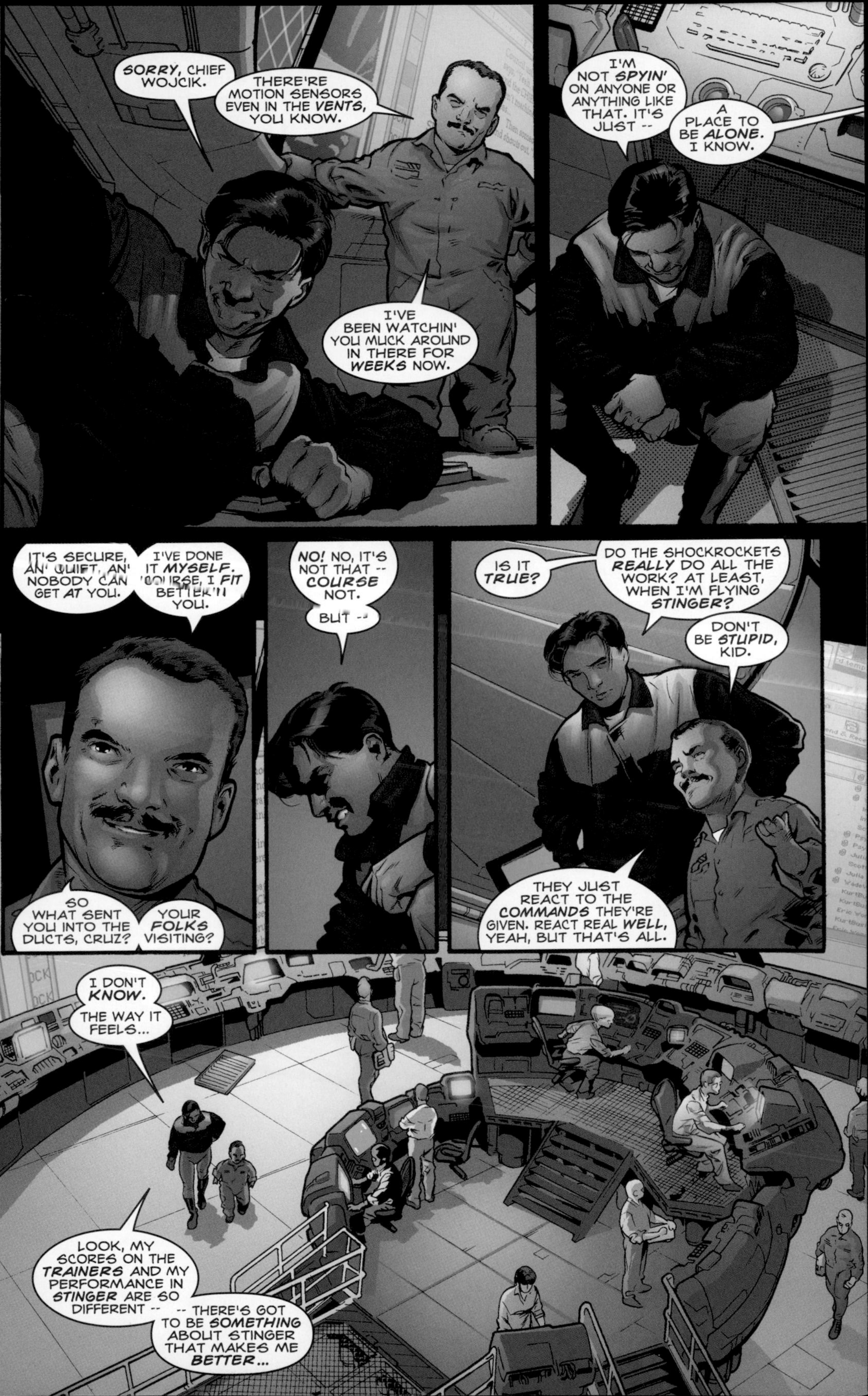
SORRY, CHIEF WOJCIK.
THERE'RE MOTION SENSORS EVEN IN THE VENTS, YOU KNOW.
I'VE BEEN WATCHIN' YOU MUCK AROUND IN THERE FOR WEEKS NOW.
I'M NOT SPYIN' ON ANYONE OR ANYTHING LIKE THAT. IT'S JUST --
A PLACE TO BE ALONE. I KNOW.
IT'S SECURE, AN' QUIET, AN' NOBODY CAN GET AT YOU.
I'VE DONE IT MYSELF. 'COURSE, I FIT BETTER'N YOU.
SO WHAT SENT YOU INTO THE DUCTS, CRUZ?
YOUR FOLKS VISITING?
NO! NO, IT'S NOT THAT -- COURSE NOT.
BUT --
IS IT TRUE?
DO THE SHOCKROCKETS REALLY DO ALL THE WORK? AT LEAST, WHEN I'M FLYING STINGER?
DON'T BE STUPID, KID.
THEY JUST REACT TO THE COMMANDS THEY'RE GIVEN. REACT REAL WELL, YEAH, BUT THAT'S ALL.
I DON'T KNOW.
THE WAY IT FEELS...
LOOK, MY SCORES ON THE TRAINERS AND MY PERFORMANCE IN STINGER ARE SO DIFFERENT --
-- THERE'S GOT TO BE SOMETHING ABOUT STINGER THAT MAKES ME BETTER...

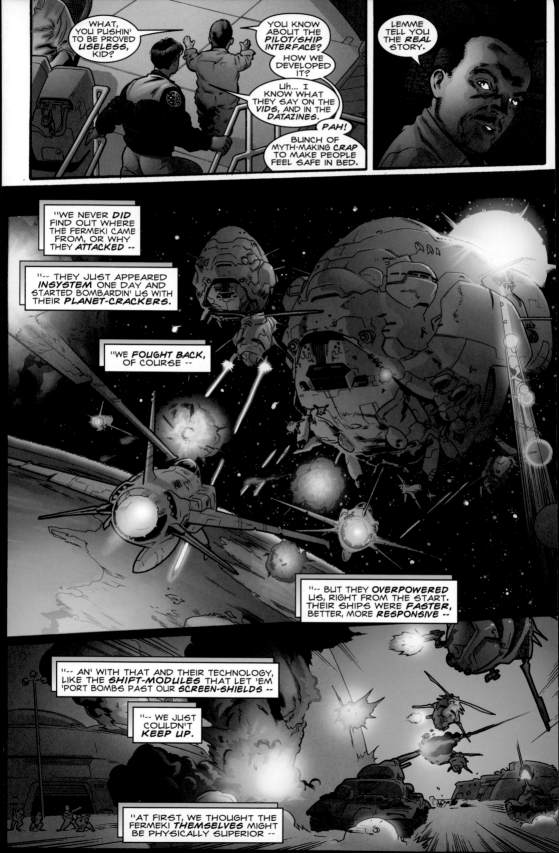

WHAT, YOU PUSHIN' TO BE PROVED *USELESS*, KID?

YOU KNOW ABOUT THE *PILOT/SHIP INTERFACE?* HOW WE DEVELOPED IT?

UH... I KNOW WHAT THEY SAY ON THE *VIDS*, AND IN THE *DATAZINES.*

PAH! BUNCH OF MYTH-MAKING *CRAP* TO MAKE PEOPLE FEEL SAFE IN BED.

LEMME TELL YOU THE *REAL* STORY.

"WE NEVER *DID* FIND OUT WHERE THE FERMEKI CAME FROM, OR WHY THEY *ATTACKED* --

"-- THEY JUST APPEARED *INSYSTEM* ONE DAY AND STARTED BOMBARDIN' US WITH THEIR *PLANET-CRACKERS.*

"WE *FOUGHT BACK,* OF COURSE --

"-- BUT THEY *OVERPOWERED* US, RIGHT FROM THE START. THEIR SHIPS WERE *FASTER,* BETTER, MORE *RESPONSIVE* --

"-- AN' WITH THAT AND THEIR TECHNOLOGY, LIKE THE *SHIFT-MODULES* THAT LET 'EM 'PORT BOMBS PAST OUR *SCREEN-SHIELDS* --

"-- WE JUST COULDN'T *KEEP UP.*

"AT FIRST, WE THOUGHT THE FERMEKI *THEMSELVES* MIGHT BE PHYSICALLY SUPERIOR --

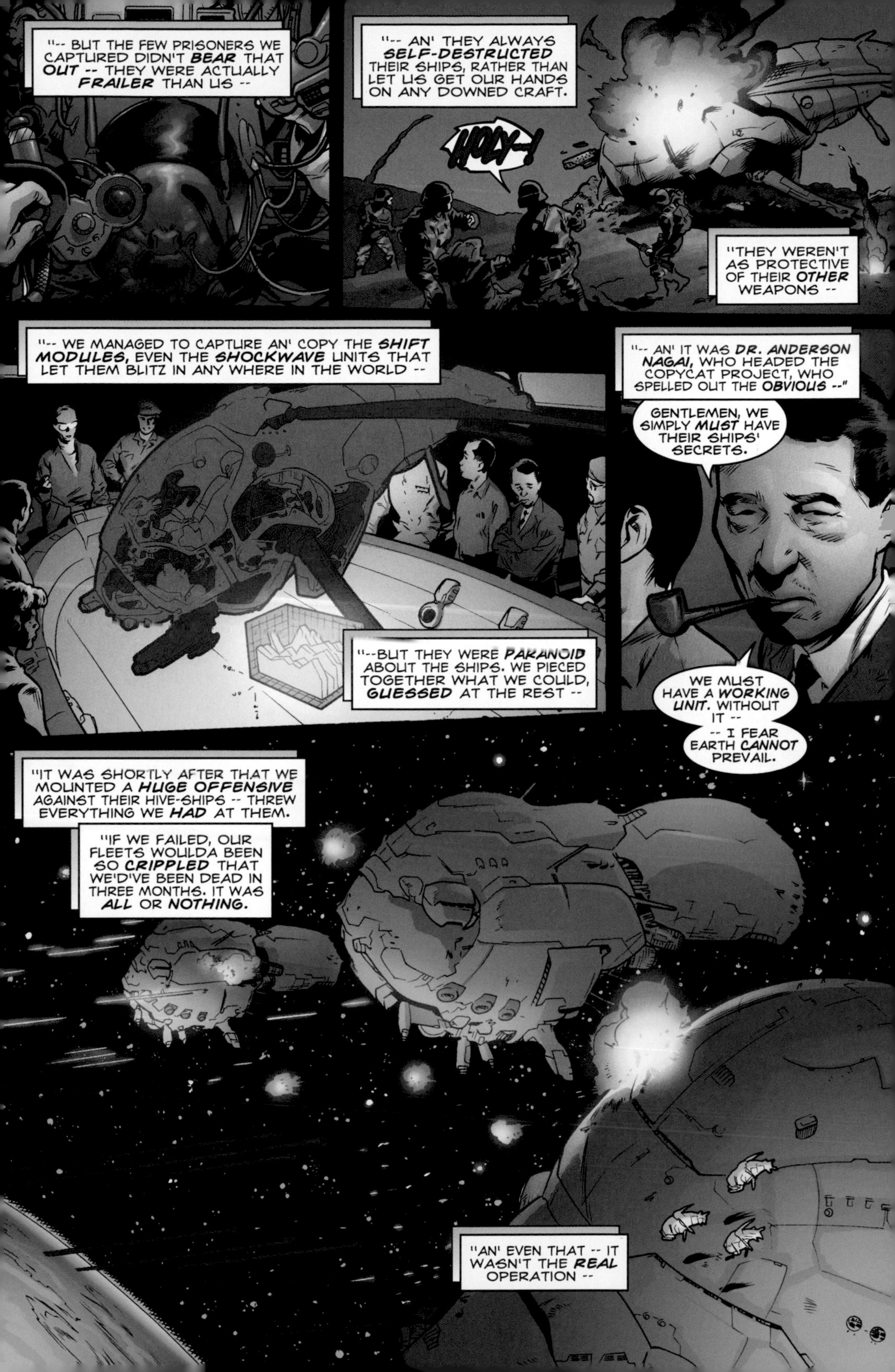
"-- BUT THE FEW PRISONERS WE CAPTURED DIDN'T BEAR THAT OUT -- THEY WERE ACTUALLY FRAILER THAN US --
"-- AN' THEY ALWAYS SELF-DESTRUCTED THEIR SHIPS, RATHER THAN LET US GET OUR HANDS ON ANY DOWNED CRAFT.
HOLY--!
"THEY WEREN'T AS PROTECTIVE OF THEIR OTHER WEAPONS --
"-- WE MANAGED TO CAPTURE AN' COPY THE SHIFT MODULES, EVEN THE SHOCKWAVE UNITS THAT LET THEM BLITZ IN ANY WHERE IN THE WORLD --
"--BUT THEY WERE PARANOID ABOUT THE SHIPS. WE PIECED TOGETHER WHAT WE COULD, GUESSED AT THE REST --
"-- AN' IT WAS DR. ANDERSON NAGAI, WHO HEADED THE COPYCAT PROJECT, WHO SPELLED OUT THE OBVIOUS --"
GENTLEMEN, WE SIMPLY MUST HAVE THEIR SHIPS' SECRETS.
WE MUST HAVE A WORKING UNIT. WITHOUT IT --
-- I FEAR EARTH CANNOT PREVAIL.
"IT WAS SHORTLY AFTER THAT WE MOUNTED A HUGE OFFENSIVE AGAINST THEIR HIVE-SHIPS -- THREW EVERYTHING WE HAD AT THEM.
"IF WE FAILED, OUR FLEETS WOULDA BEEN SO CRIPPLED THAT WE'D'VE BEEN DEAD IN THREE MONTHS. IT WAS ALL OR NOTHING.
"AN' EVEN THAT -- IT WASN'T THE REAL OPERATION --

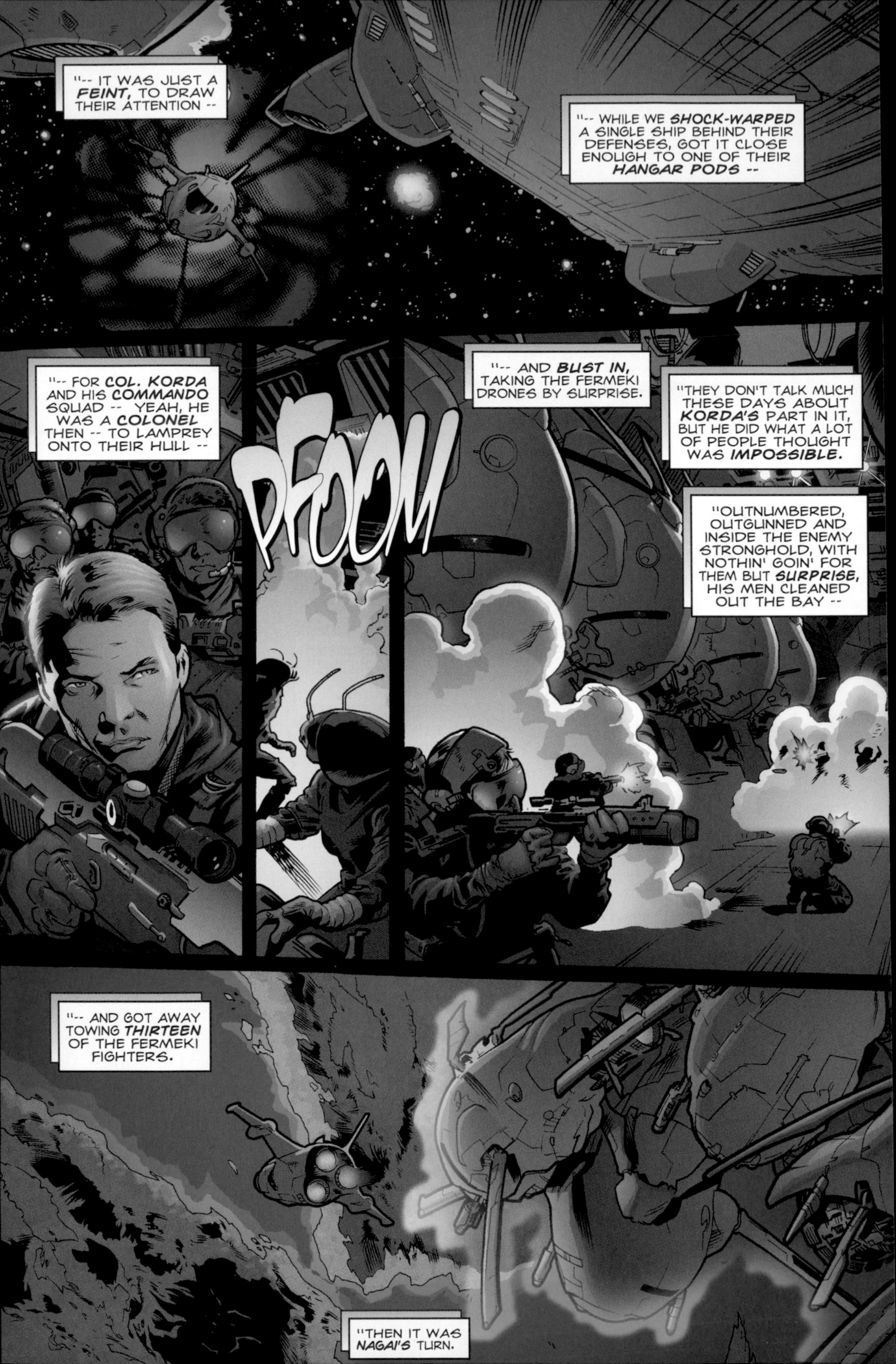
"-- IT WAS JUST A FEINT, TO DRAW THEIR ATTENTION --
"-- WHILE WE SHOCK-WARPED A SINGLE SHIP BEHIND THEIR DEFENSES, GOT IT CLOSE ENOUGH TO ONE OF THEIR HANGAR PODS --
"-- FOR COL. KORDA AND HIS COMMANDO SQUAD -- YEAH, HE WAS A COLONEL THEN -- TO LAMPREY ONTO THEIR HULL --
PFOOM
"-- AND BUST IN, TAKING THE FERMEKI DRONES BY SURPRISE.
"THEY DON'T TALK MUCH THESE DAYS ABOUT KORDA'S PART IN IT, BUT HE DID WHAT A LOT OF PEOPLE THOUGHT WAS IMPOSSIBLE.
"OUTNUMBERED, OUTGUNNED AND INSIDE THE ENEMY STRONGHOLD, WITH NOTHIN' GOIN' FOR THEM BUT SURPRISE, HIS MEN CLEANED OUT THE BAY --
"-- AND GOT AWAY TOWING THIRTEEN OF THE FERMEKI FIGHTERS.
"THEN IT WAS NAGAI'S TURN.

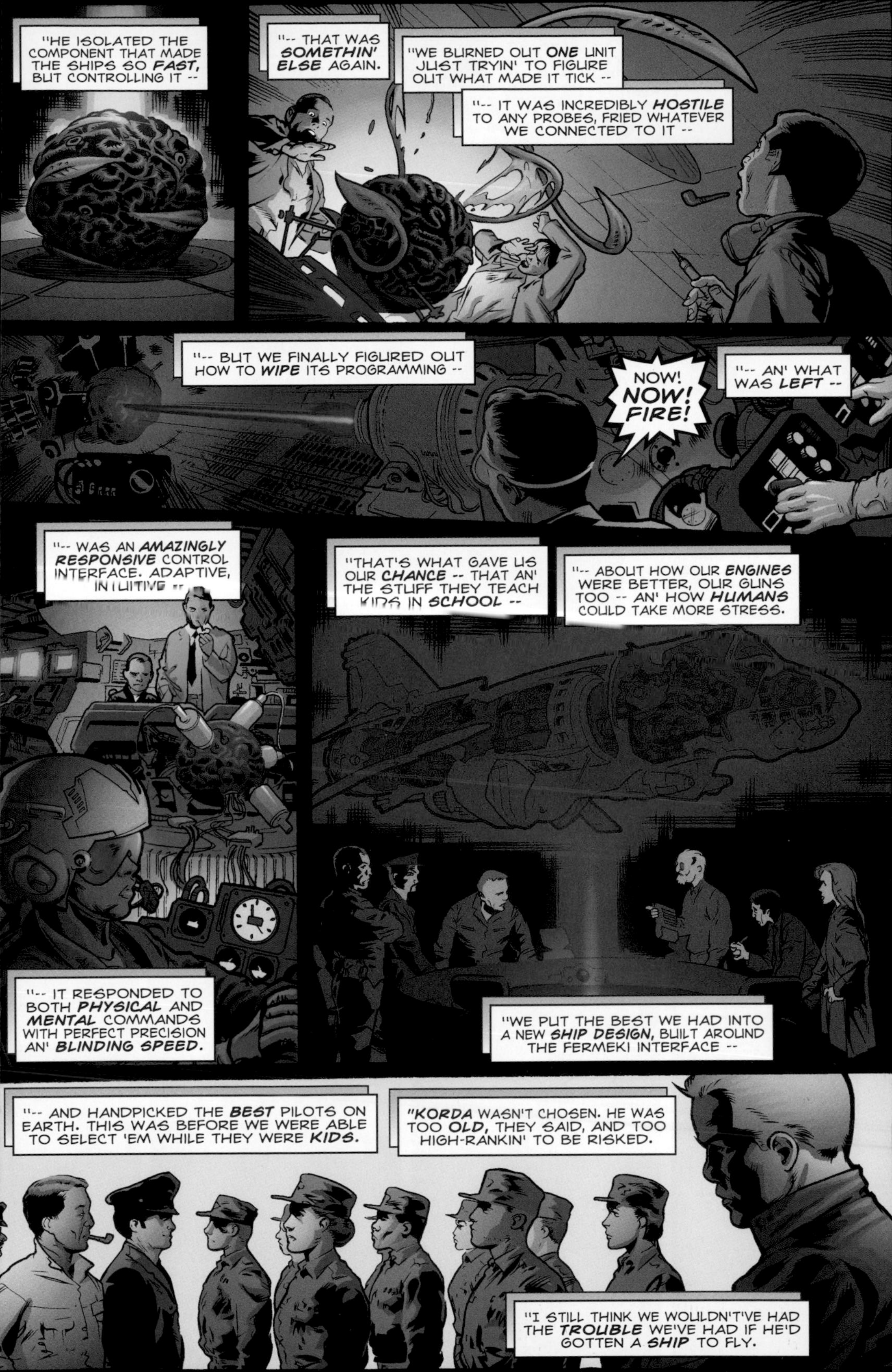
"HE ISOLATED THE COMPONENT THAT MADE THE SHIPS SO FAST, BUT CONTROLLING IT --
"-- THAT WAS SOMETHIN' ELSE AGAIN.
"WE BURNED OUT ONE UNIT JUST TRYIN' TO FIGURE OUT WHAT MADE IT TICK --
"-- IT WAS INCREDIBLY HOSTILE TO ANY PROBES, FRIED WHATEVER WE CONNECTED TO IT --
"-- BUT WE FINALLY FIGURED OUT HOW TO WIPE ITS PROGRAMMING --
NOW! NOW! FIRE!
"-- AN' WHAT WAS LEFT --
"-- WAS AN AMAZINGLY RESPONSIVE CONTROL INTERFACE. ADAPTIVE, INTUITIVE --
"-- IT RESPONDED TO BOTH PHYSICAL AND MENTAL COMMANDS WITH PERFECT PRECISION AN' BLINDING SPEED.
"THAT'S WHAT GAVE US OUR CHANCE -- THAT AN' THE STUFF THEY TEACH KIDS IN SCHOOL --
"-- ABOUT HOW OUR ENGINES WERE BETTER, OUR GUNS TOO -- AN' HOW HUMANS COULD TAKE MORE STRESS.
"WE PUT THE BEST WE HAD INTO A NEW SHIP DESIGN, BUILT AROUND THE FERMEKI INTERFACE --
"-- AND HANDPICKED THE BEST PILOTS ON EARTH. THIS WAS BEFORE WE WERE ABLE TO SELECT 'EM WHILE THEY WERE KIDS.
"KORDA WASN'T CHOSEN. HE WAS TOO OLD, THEY SAID, AND TOO HIGH-RANKIN' TO BE RISKED.
"I STILL THINK WE WOULDN'T'VE HAD THE TROUBLE WE'VE HAD IF HE'D GOTTEN A SHIP TO FLY.

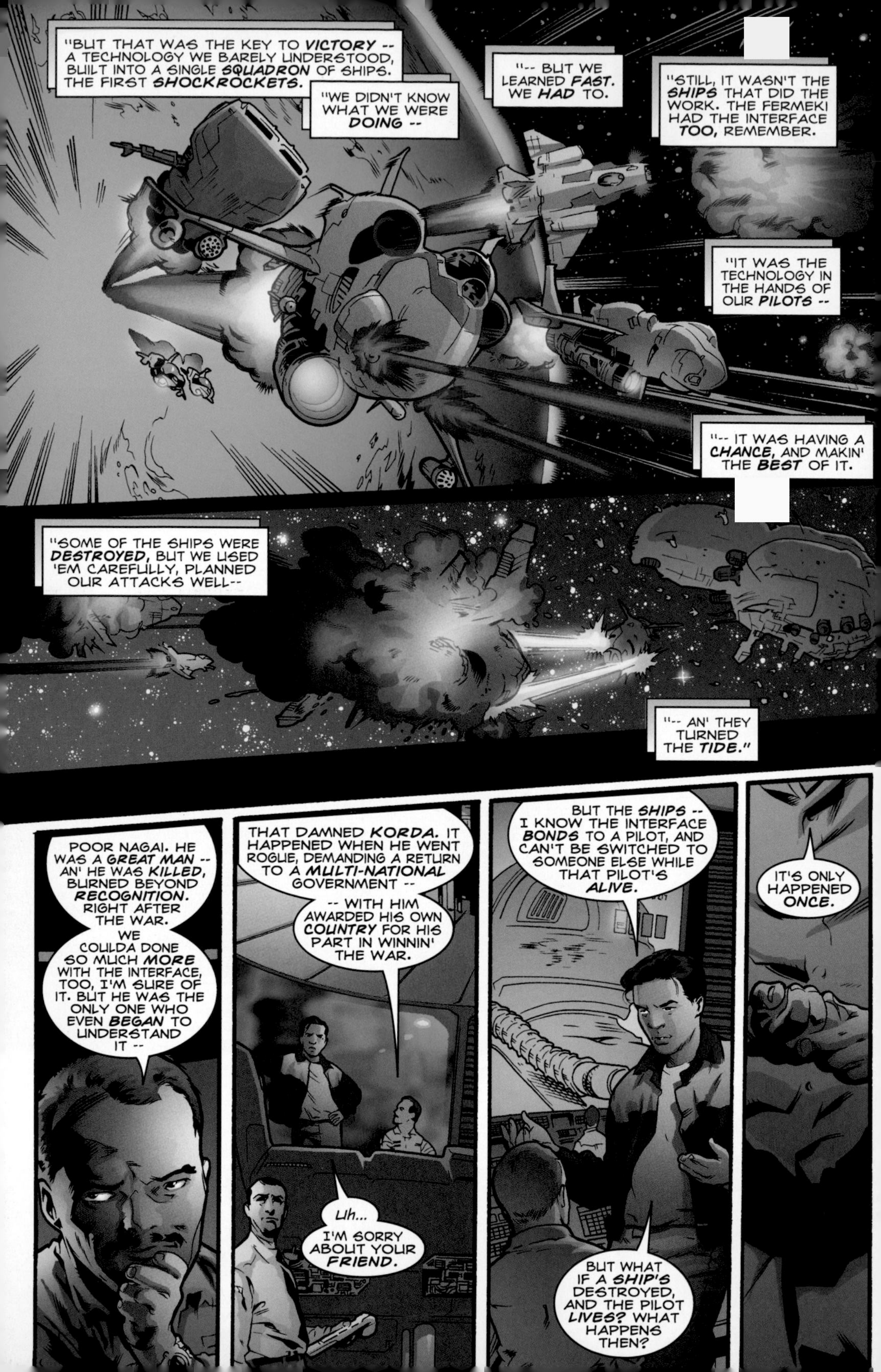
"BUT THAT WAS THE KEY TO VICTORY -- A TECHNOLOGY WE BARELY UNDERSTOOD, BUILT INTO A SINGLE SQUADRON OF SHIPS. THE FIRST SHOCKROCKETS.
"WE DIDN'T KNOW WHAT WE WERE DOING --
"-- BUT WE LEARNED FAST. WE HAD TO.
"STILL, IT WASN'T THE SHIPS THAT DID THE WORK. THE FERMEKI HAD THE INTERFACE TOO, REMEMBER.
"IT WAS THE TECHNOLOGY IN THE HANDS OF OUR PILOTS --
"-- IT WAS HAVING A CHANCE, AND MAKIN' THE BEST OF IT.
"SOME OF THE SHIPS WERE DESTROYED, BUT WE USED 'EM CAREFULLY, PLANNED OUR ATTACKS WELL--
"-- AN' THEY TURNED THE TIDE."
POOR NAGAI. HE WAS A GREAT MAN -- AN' HE WAS KILLED, BURNED BEYOND RECOGNITION. RIGHT AFTER THE WAR.
WE COULDA DONE SO MUCH MORE WITH THE INTERFACE, TOO, I'M SURE OF IT. BUT HE WAS THE ONLY ONE WHO EVEN BEGAN TO UNDERSTAND IT --
THAT DAMNED KORDA. IT HAPPENED WHEN HE WENT ROGUE, DEMANDING A RETURN TO A MULTI-NATIONAL GOVERNMENT --
-- WITH HIM AWARDED HIS OWN COUNTRY FOR HIS PART IN WINNIN' THE WAR.
Uh...
I'M SORRY ABOUT YOUR FRIEND.
BUT THE SHIPS -- I KNOW THE INTERFACE BONDS TO A PILOT, AND CAN'T BE SWITCHED TO SOMEONE ELSE WHILE THAT PILOT'S ALIVE.
BUT WHAT IF A SHIP'S DESTROYED, AND THE PILOT LIVES? WHAT HAPPENS THEN?
IT'S ONLY HAPPENED ONCE.

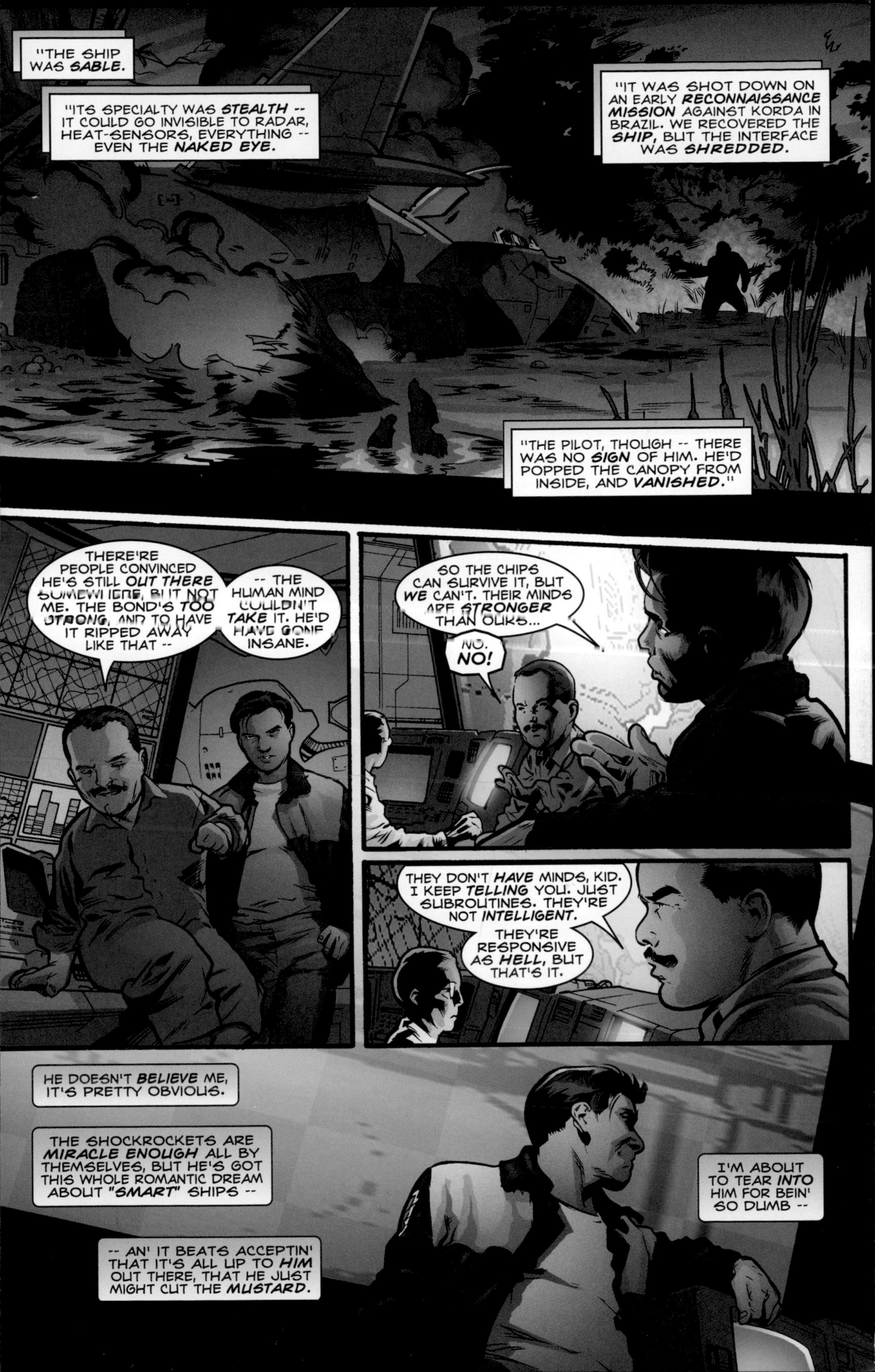
"THE SHIP WAS SABLE.
"ITS SPECIALTY WAS STEALTH -- IT COULD GO INVISIBLE TO RADAR, HEAT-SENSORS, EVERYTHING -- EVEN THE NAKED EYE.
"IT WAS SHOT DOWN ON AN EARLY RECONNAISSANCE MISSION AGAINST KORDA IN BRAZIL. WE RECOVERED THE SHIP, BUT THE INTERFACE WAS SHREDDED.
"THE PILOT, THOUGH -- THERE WAS NO SIGN OF HIM. HE'D POPPED THE CANOPY FROM INSIDE, AND VANISHED."
THERE'RE PEOPLE CONVINCED HE'S STILL OUT THERE SOMEWHERE, BUT NOT ME. THE BOND'S TOO STRONG, AND TO HAVE IT RIPPED AWAY LIKE THAT --
-- THE HUMAN MIND COULDN'T TAKE IT. HE'D HAVE GONE INSANE.
SO THE CHIPS CAN SURVIVE IT, BUT WE CAN'T. THEIR MINDS ARE STRONGER THAN OURS...
NO. NO!
THEY DON'T HAVE MINDS, KID. I KEEP TELLING YOU. JUST SUBROUTINES. THEY'RE NOT INTELLIGENT.
THEY'RE RESPONSIVE AS HELL, BUT THAT'S IT.
HE DOESN'T BELIEVE ME, IT'S PRETTY OBVIOUS.
THE SHOCKROCKETS ARE MIRACLE ENOUGH ALL BY THEMSELVES, BUT HE'S GOT THIS WHOLE ROMANTIC DREAM ABOUT "SMART" SHIPS --
-- AN' IT BEATS ACCEPTIN' THAT IT'S ALL UP TO HIM OUT THERE, THAT HE JUST MIGHT CUT THE MUSTARD.
I'M ABOUT TO TEAR INTO HIM FOR BEIN' SO DUMB --

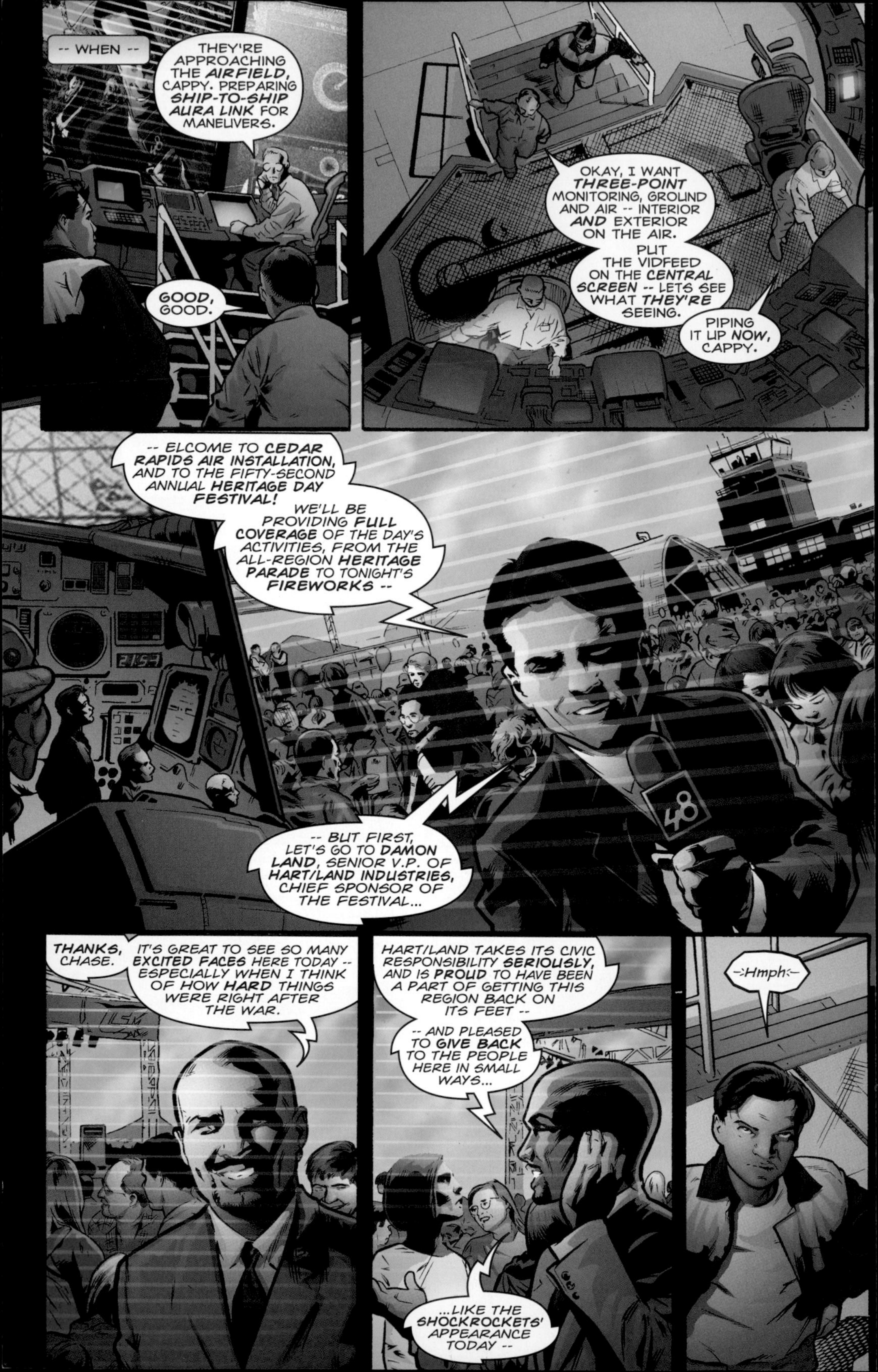
-- WHEN --
THEY'RE APPROACHING THE AIRFIELD, CAPPY. PREPARING SHIP-TO-SHIP AURA LINK FOR MANEUVERS.
GOOD, GOOD.
OKAY, I WANT THREE-POINT MONITORING, GROUND AND AIR -- INTERIOR AND EXTERIOR ON THE AIR.
PUT THE VIDFEED ON THE CENTRAL SCREEN -- LETS SEE WHAT THEY'RE SEEING.
PIPING IT UP NOW, CAPPY.
-- ELCOME TO CEDAR RAPIDS AIR INSTALLATION, AND TO THE FIFTY-SECOND ANNUAL HERITAGE DAY FESTIVAL!
WE'LL BE PROVIDING FULL COVERAGE OF THE DAY'S ACTIVITIES, FROM THE ALL-REGION HERITAGE PARADE TO TONIGHT'S FIREWORKS --
-- BUT FIRST, LET'S GO TO DAMON LAND, SENIOR V.P. OF HART/LAND INDUSTRIES, CHIEF SPONSOR OF THE FESTIVAL...
THANKS, CHASE.
IT'S GREAT TO SEE SO MANY EXCITED FACES HERE TODAY -- ESPECIALLY WHEN I THINK OF HOW HARD THINGS WERE RIGHT AFTER THE WAR.
HART/LAND TAKES ITS CIVIC RESPONSIBILITY SERIOUSLY, AND IS PROUD TO HAVE BEEN A PART OF GETTING THIS REGION BACK ON ITS FEET --
-- AND PLEASED TO GIVE BACK TO THE PEOPLE HERE IN SMALL WAYS...
...LIKE THE SHOCKROCKETS' APPEARANCE TODAY --
Hmph

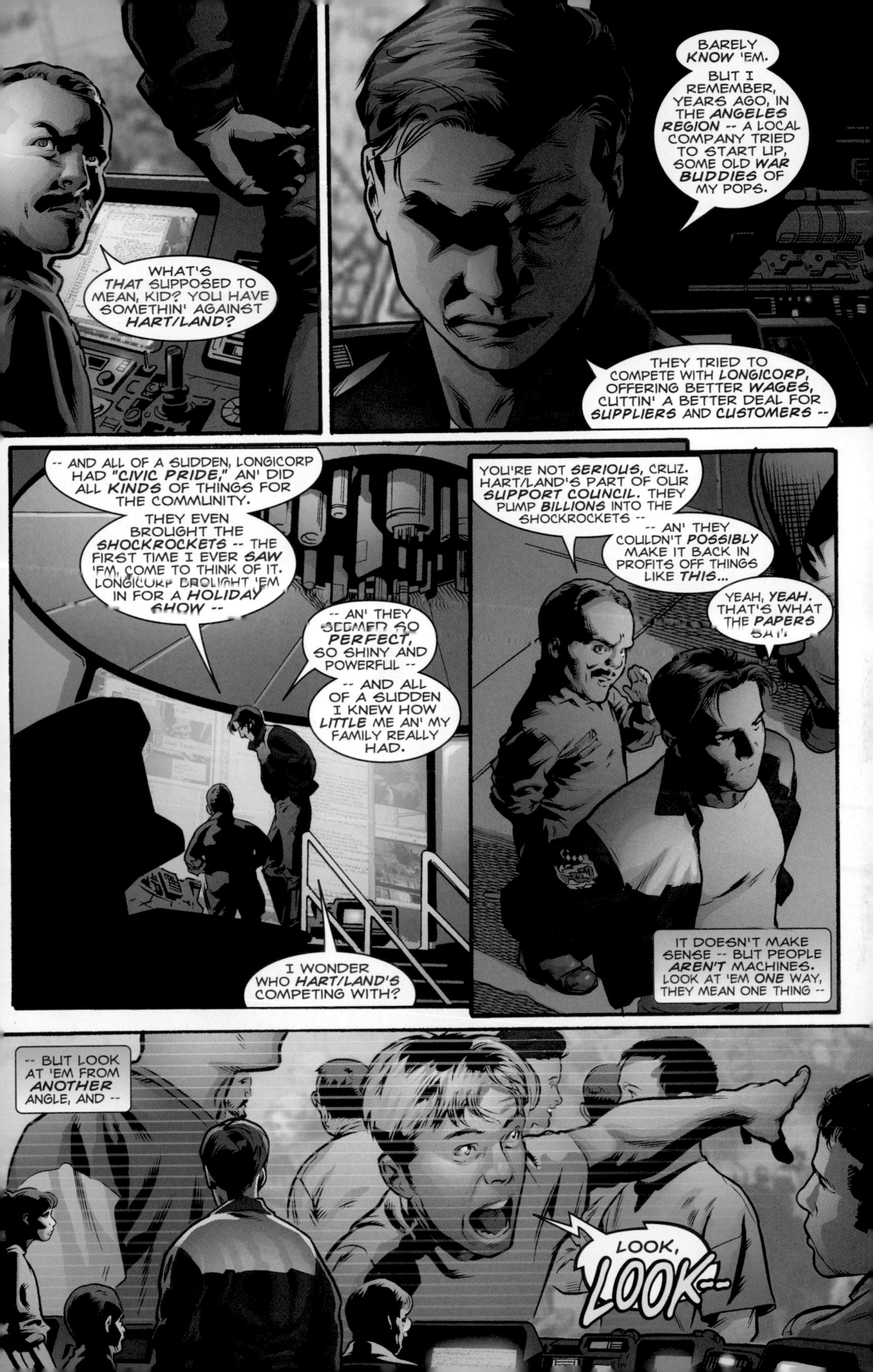
WHAT'S THAT SUPPOSED TO MEAN, KID? YOU HAVE SOMETHIN' AGAINST HART/LAND?
BARELY KNOW 'EM.
BUT I REMEMBER, YEARS AGO, IN THE ANGELES REGION -- A LOCAL COMPANY TRIED TO START UP, SOME OLD WAR BUDDIES OF MY POPS.
THEY TRIED TO COMPETE WITH LONGICORP, OFFERING BETTER WAGES, CUTTIN' A BETTER DEAL FOR SUPPLIERS AND CUSTOMERS --
-- AND ALL OF A SUDDEN, LONGICORP HAD "CIVIC PRIDE," AN' DID ALL KINDS OF THINGS FOR THE COMMUNITY.
THEY EVEN BROUGHT THE SHOCKROCKETS -- THE FIRST TIME I EVER SAW 'EM, COME TO THINK OF IT. LONGICORP BROUGHT 'EM IN FOR A HOLIDAY SHOW --
-- AN' THEY SEEMED SO PERFECT, SO SHINY AND POWERFUL --
-- AND ALL OF A SUDDEN I KNEW HOW LITTLE ME AN' MY FAMILY REALLY HAD.
I WONDER WHO HART/LAND'S COMPETING WITH?
YOU'RE NOT SERIOUS, CRUZ. HART/LAND'S PART OF OUR SUPPORT COUNCIL. THEY PUMP BILLIONS INTO THE SHOCKROCKETS --
-- AN' THEY COULDN'T POSSIBLY MAKE IT BACK IN PROFITS OFF THINGS LIKE THIS...
YEAH, YEAH. THAT'S WHAT THE PAPERS SAY.
IT DOESN'T MAKE SENSE -- BUT PEOPLE AREN'T MACHINES. LOOK AT 'EM ONE WAY, THEY MEAN ONE THING --
-- BUT LOOK AT 'EM FROM ANOTHER ANGLE, AND --
LOOK, LOOK--

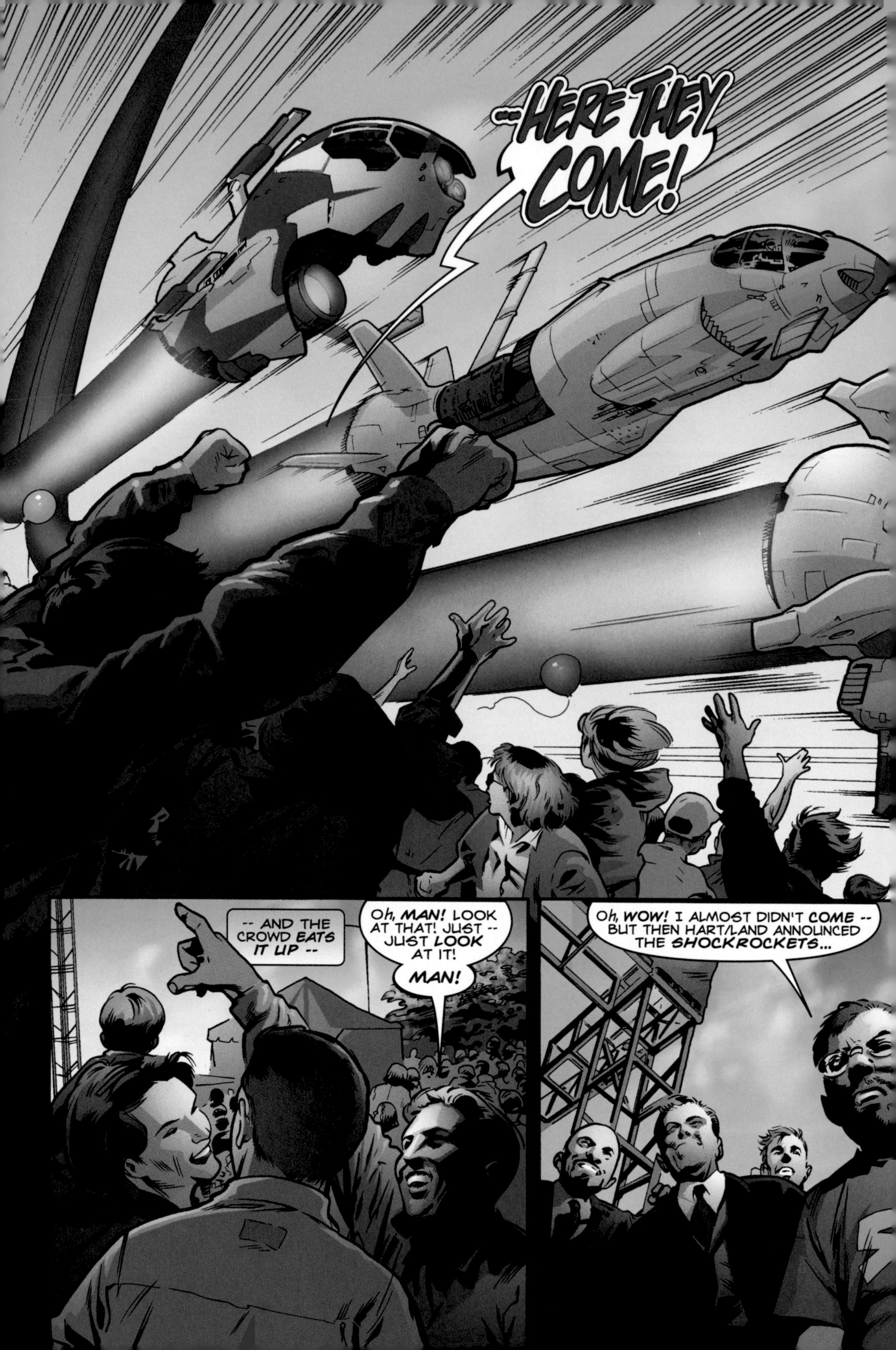
--HERE THEY COME!
-- AND THE CROWD EATS IT UP --
Oh, MAN! LOOK AT THAT! JUST -- JUST LOOK AT IT! MAN!
Oh, WOW! I ALMOST DIDN'T COME -- BUT THEN HART/LAND ANNOUNCED THE SHOCKROCKETS...

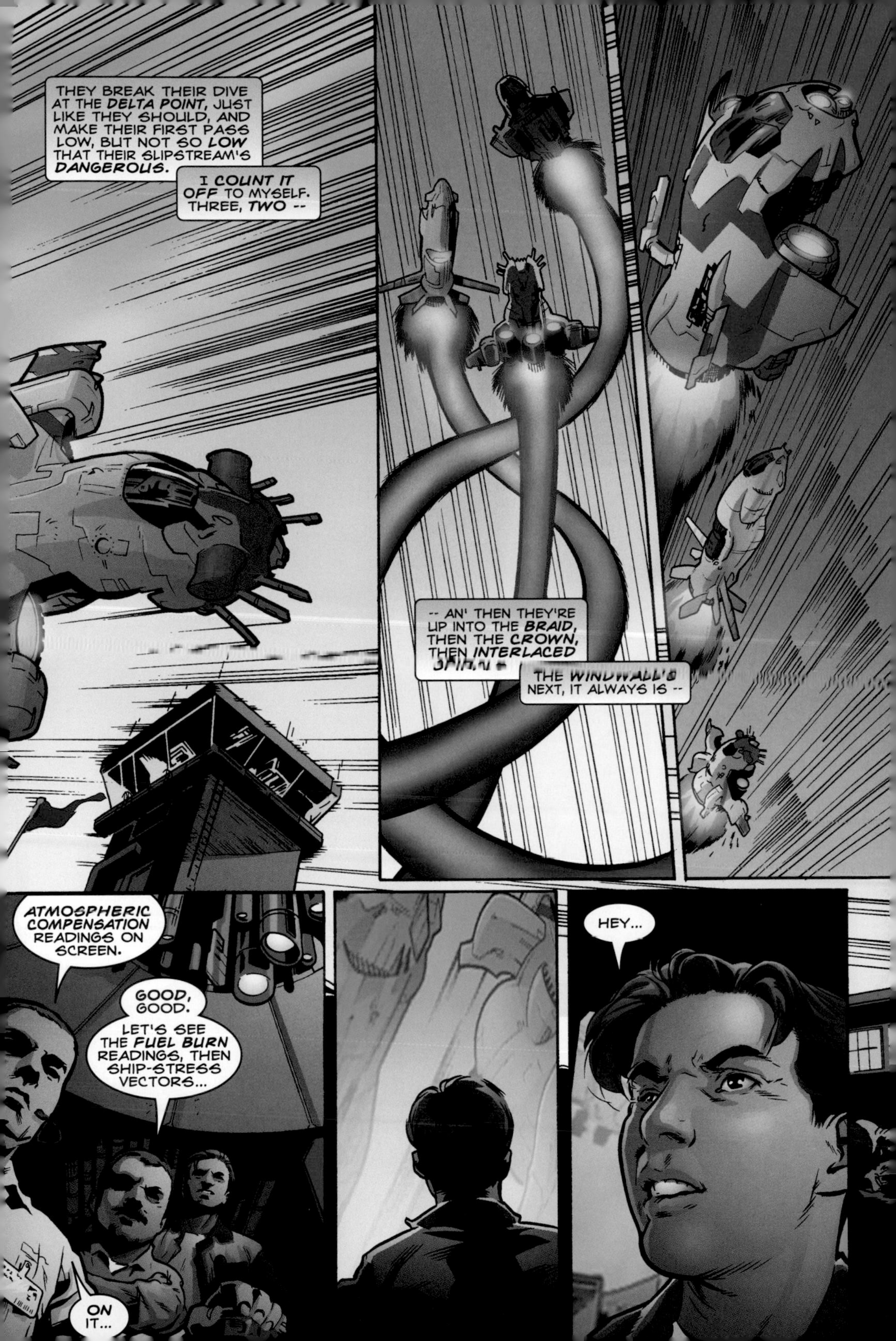
THEY BREAK THEIR DIVE AT THE DELTA POINT, JUST LIKE THEY SHOULD, AND MAKE THEIR FIRST PASS LOW, BUT NOT SO LOW THAT THEIR SLIPSTREAM'S DANGEROUS.
I COUNT IT OFF TO MYSELF. THREE, TWO --
-- AN' THEN THEY'RE UP INTO THE BRAID, THEN THE CROWN, THEN INTERLACED
THE WINDWALL'S NEXT, IT ALWAYS IS --
ATMOSPHERIC COMPENSATION READINGS ON SCREEN.
GOOD, GOOD. LET'S SEE THE FUEL BURN READINGS, THEN SHIP-STRESS VECTORS...
ON IT...
HEY...

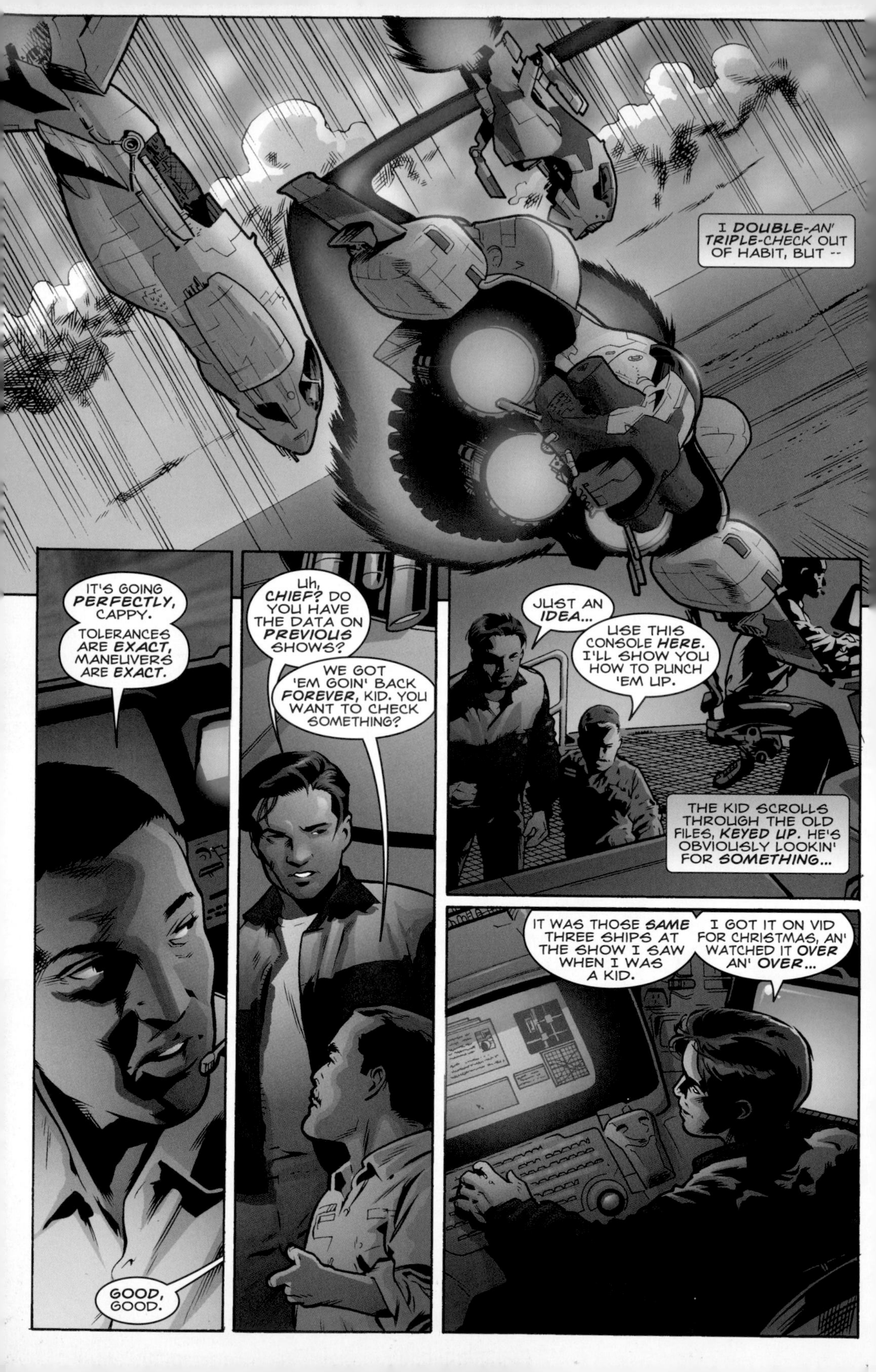
I DOUBLE-AN' TRIPLE-CHECK OUT OF HABIT, BUT --
IT'S GOING PERFECTLY, CAPPY.
TOLERANCES ARE EXACT, MANEUVERS ARE EXACT.
GOOD, GOOD.
UH, CHIEF? DO YOU HAVE THE DATA ON PREVIOUS SHOWS?
WE GOT 'EM GOIN' BACK FOREVER, KID. YOU WANT TO CHECK SOMETHING?
JUST AN IDEA...
USE THIS CONSOLE HERE. I'LL SHOW YOU HOW TO PUNCH 'EM UP.
THE KID SCROLLS THROUGH THE OLD FILES, KEYED UP. HE'S OBVIOUSLY LOOKIN' FOR SOMETHING...
IT WAS THOSE SAME THREE SHIPS AT THE SHOW I SAW WHEN I WAS A KID.
I GOT IT ON VID FOR CHRISTMAS, AN' WATCHED IT OVER AN' OVER...

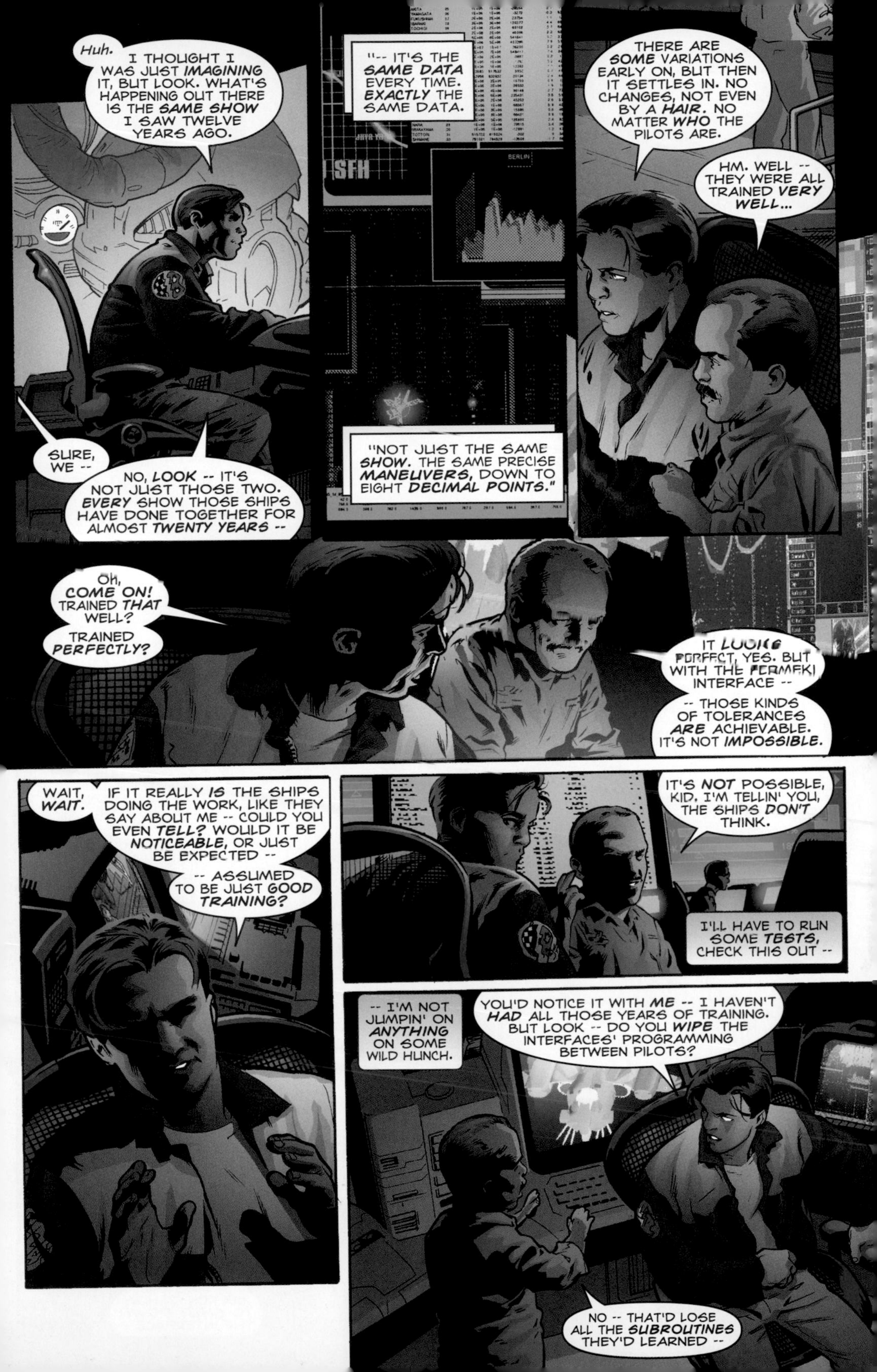
Huh.
I THOUGHT I WAS JUST IMAGINING IT, BUT LOOK. WHAT'S HAPPENING OUT THERE IS THE SAME SHOW I SAW TWELVE YEARS AGO.
SURE, WE --
NO, LOOK -- IT'S NOT JUST THOSE TWO. EVERY SHOW THOSE SHIPS HAVE DONE TOGETHER FOR ALMOST TWENTY YEARS --
"-- IT'S THE SAME DATA EVERY TIME. EXACTLY THE SAME DATA.
BERLIN
"NOT JUST THE SAME SHOW. THE SAME PRECISE MANEUVERS, DOWN TO EIGHT DECIMAL POINTS."
THERE ARE SOME VARIATIONS EARLY ON, BUT THEN IT SETTLES IN. NO CHANGES, NOT EVEN BY A HAIR. NO MATTER WHO THE PILOTS ARE.
HM. WELL -- THEY WERE ALL TRAINED VERY WELL...
Oh, COME ON! TRAINED THAT WELL?
TRAINED PERFECTLY?
IT LOOKS PERFECT, YES. BUT WITH THE FERMEKI INTERFACE --
-- THOSE KINDS OF TOLERANCES ARE ACHIEVABLE. IT'S NOT IMPOSSIBLE.
WAIT, WAIT.
IF IT REALLY IS THE SHIPS DOING THE WORK, LIKE THEY SAY ABOUT ME -- COULD YOU EVEN TELL? WOULD IT BE NOTICEABLE, OR JUST BE EXPECTED --
-- ASSUMED TO BE JUST GOOD TRAINING?
IT'S NOT POSSIBLE, KID. I'M TELLIN' YOU, THE SHIPS DON'T THINK.
I'LL HAVE TO RUN SOME TESTS, CHECK THIS OUT --
-- I'M NOT JUMPIN' ON ANYTHING ON SOME WILD HUNCH.
YOU'D NOTICE IT WITH ME -- I HAVEN'T HAD ALL THOSE YEARS OF TRAINING. BUT LOOK -- DO YOU WIPE THE INTERFACES' PROGRAMMING BETWEEN PILOTS?
NO -- THAT'D LOSE ALL THE SUBROUTINES THEY'D LEARNED --

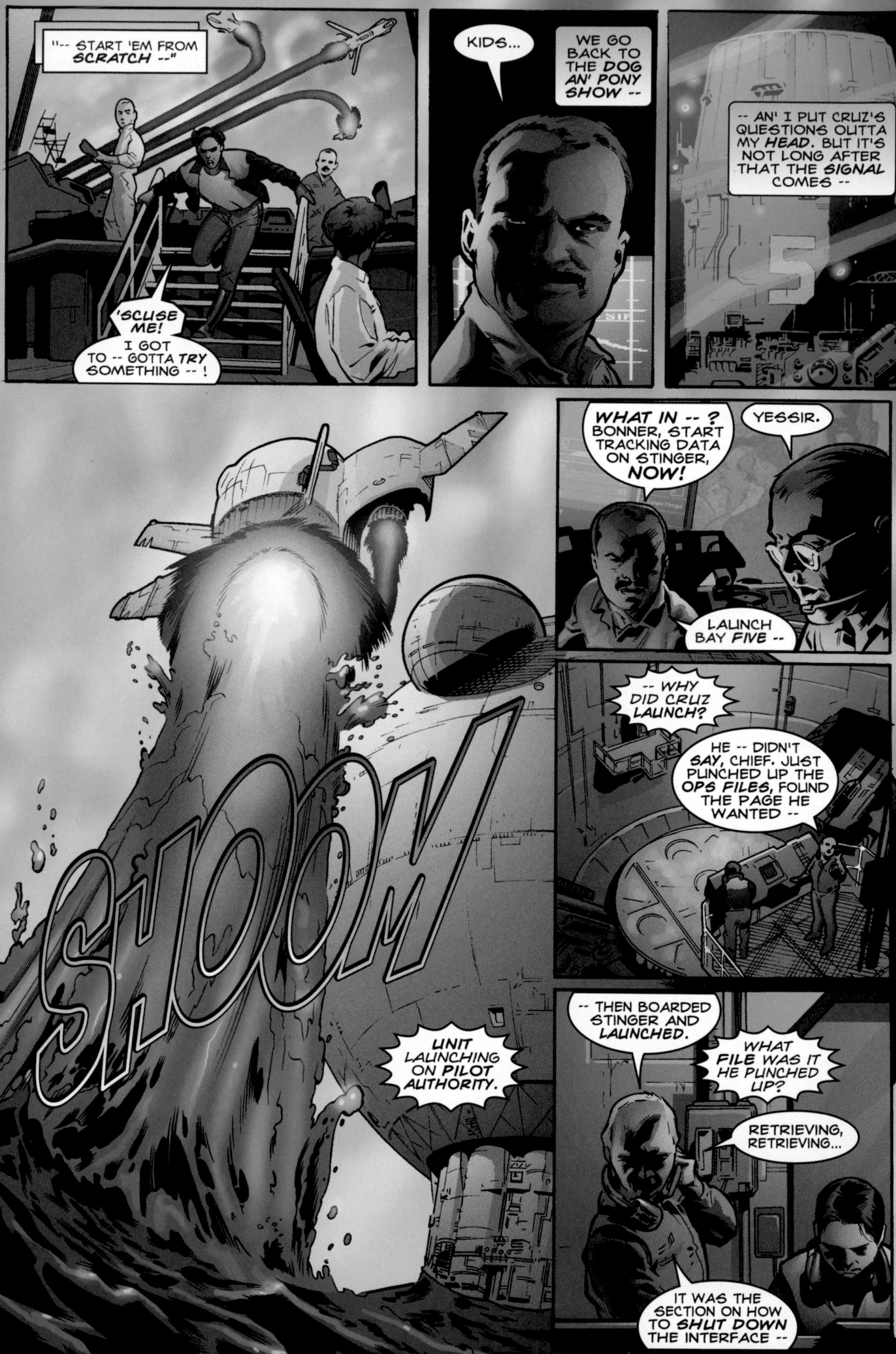
"-- START 'EM FROM SCRATCH --"
'SCUSE ME! I GOT TO -- GOTTA TRY SOMETHING -- !
KIDS...
WE GO BACK TO THE DOG AN' PONY SHOW --
-- AN' I PUT CRUZ'S QUESTIONS OUTTA MY HEAD. BUT IT'S NOT LONG AFTER THAT THE SIGNAL COMES --
WHAT IN -- ? BONNER, START TRACKING DATA ON STINGER, NOW!
YESSIR.
LAUNCH BAY FIVE --
-- WHY DID CRUZ LAUNCH?
HE -- DIDN'T SAY, CHIEF. JUST PUNCHED UP THE OPS FILES, FOUND THE PAGE HE WANTED --
SHOOOM
UNIT LAUNCHING ON PILOT AUTHORITY.
-- THEN BOARDED STINGER AND LAUNCHED.
WHAT FILE WAS IT HE PUNCHED UP?
RETRIEVING, RETRIEVING...
IT WAS THE SECTION ON HOW TO SHUT DOWN THE INTERFACE --

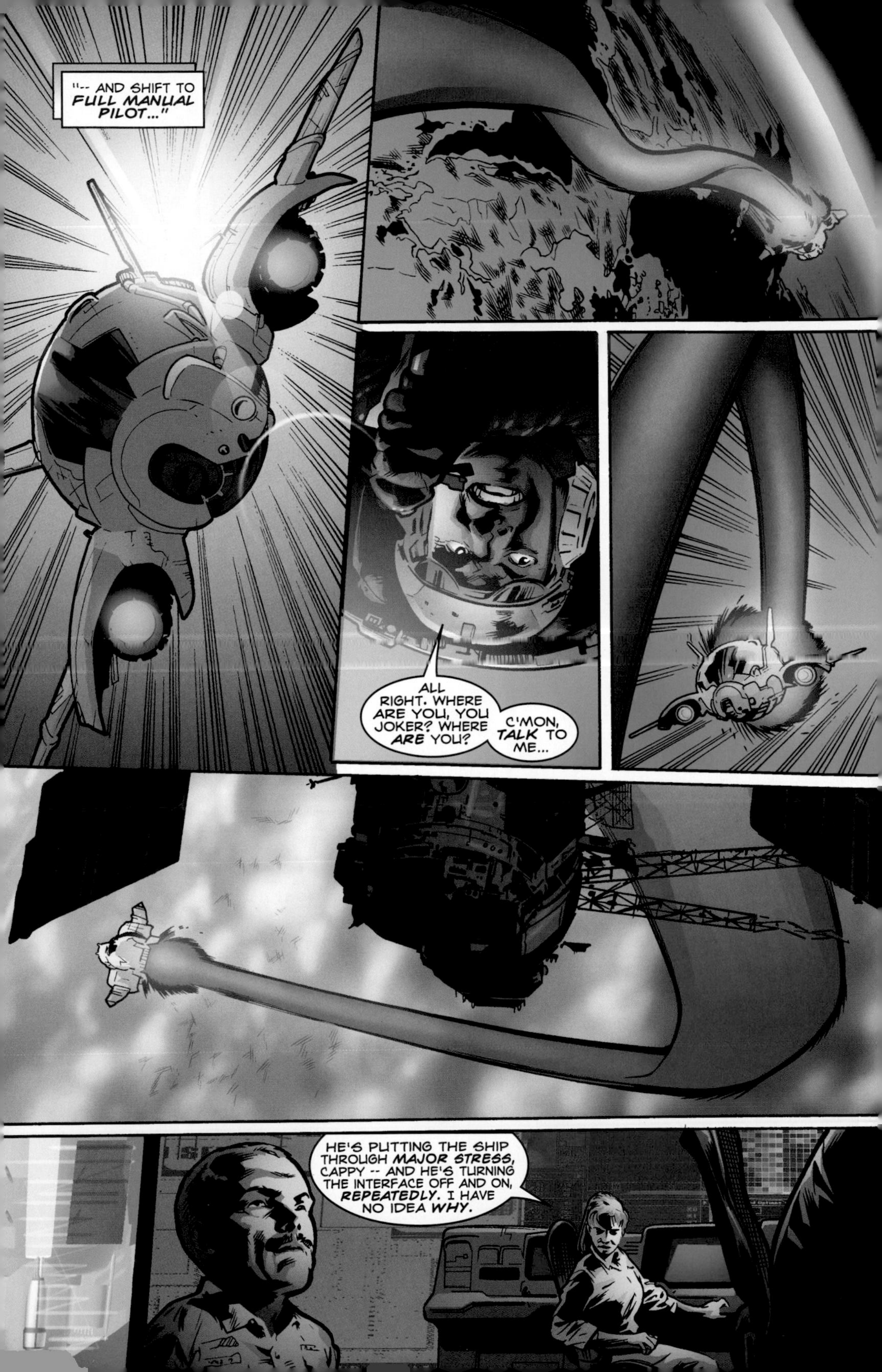
"-- AND SHIFT TO FULL MANUAL PILOT..."
ALL RIGHT. WHERE ARE YOU, YOU JOKER? WHERE ARE YOU?
C'MON, TALK TO ME...
HE'S PUTTING THE SHIP THROUGH MAJOR STRESS, CAPPY -- AND HE'S TURNING THE INTERFACE OFF AND ON, REPEATEDLY. I HAVE NO IDEA WHY.

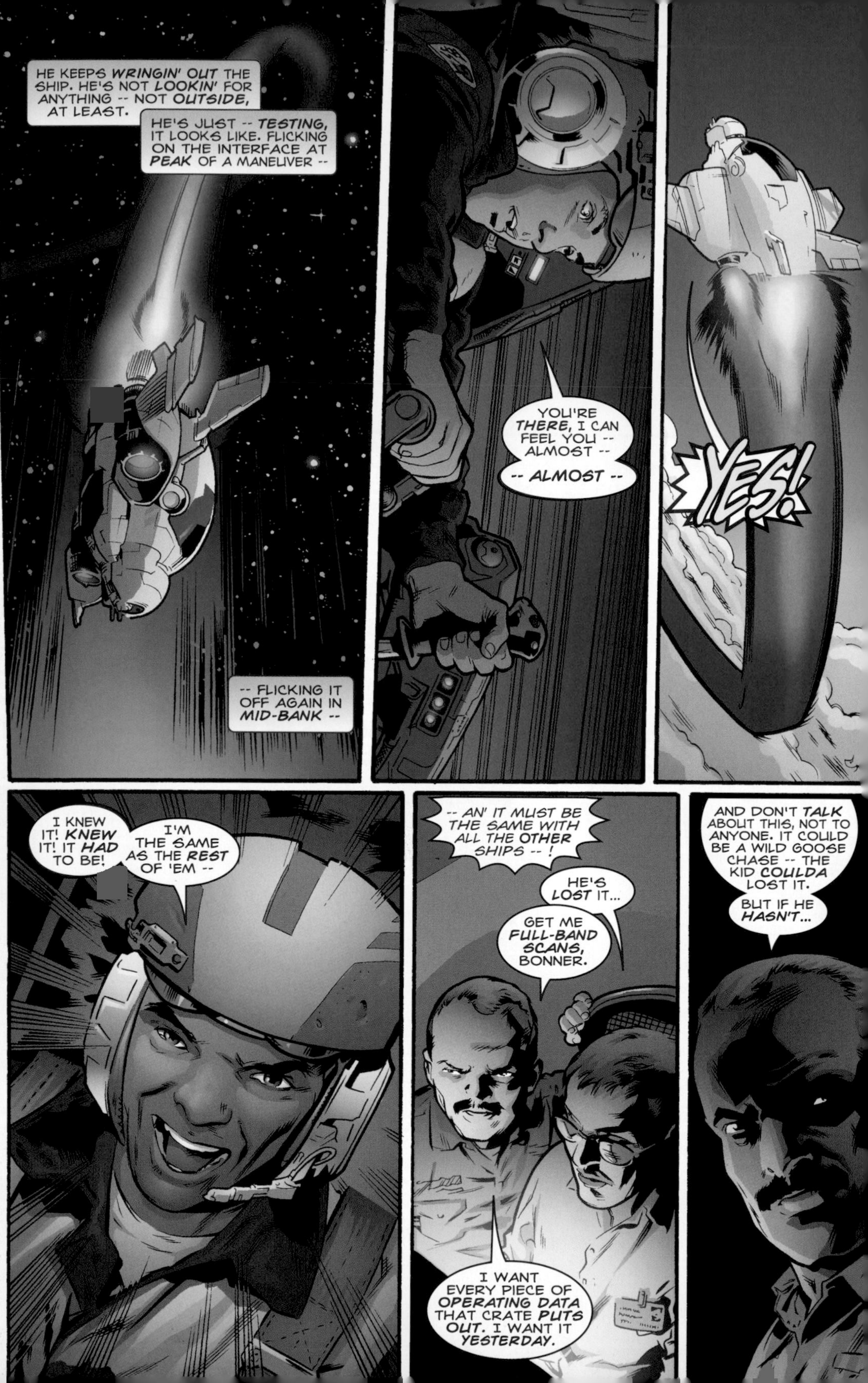
HE KEEPS WRINGIN' OUT THE SHIP. HE'S NOT LOOKIN' FOR ANYTHING -- NOT OUTSIDE, AT LEAST.
HE'S JUST -- TESTING, IT LOOKS LIKE. FLICKING ON THE INTERFACE AT PEAK OF A MANEUVER --
-- FLICKING IT OFF AGAIN IN MID-BANK --
YOU'RE THERE, I CAN FEEL YOU -- ALMOST --
-- ALMOST --
YES!
I KNEW IT! KNEW IT! IT HAD TO BE!
I'M THE SAME AS THE REST OF 'EM --
-- AN' IT MUST BE THE SAME WITH ALL THE OTHER SHIPS -- !
HE'S LOST IT...
GET ME FULL-BAND SCANS, BONNER.
I WANT EVERY PIECE OF OPERATING DATA THAT CRATE PUTS OUT. I WANT IT YESTERDAY.
AND DON'T TALK ABOUT THIS, NOT TO ANYONE. IT COULD BE A WILD GOOSE CHASE -- THE KID COULDA LOST IT.
BUT IF HE HASN'T...

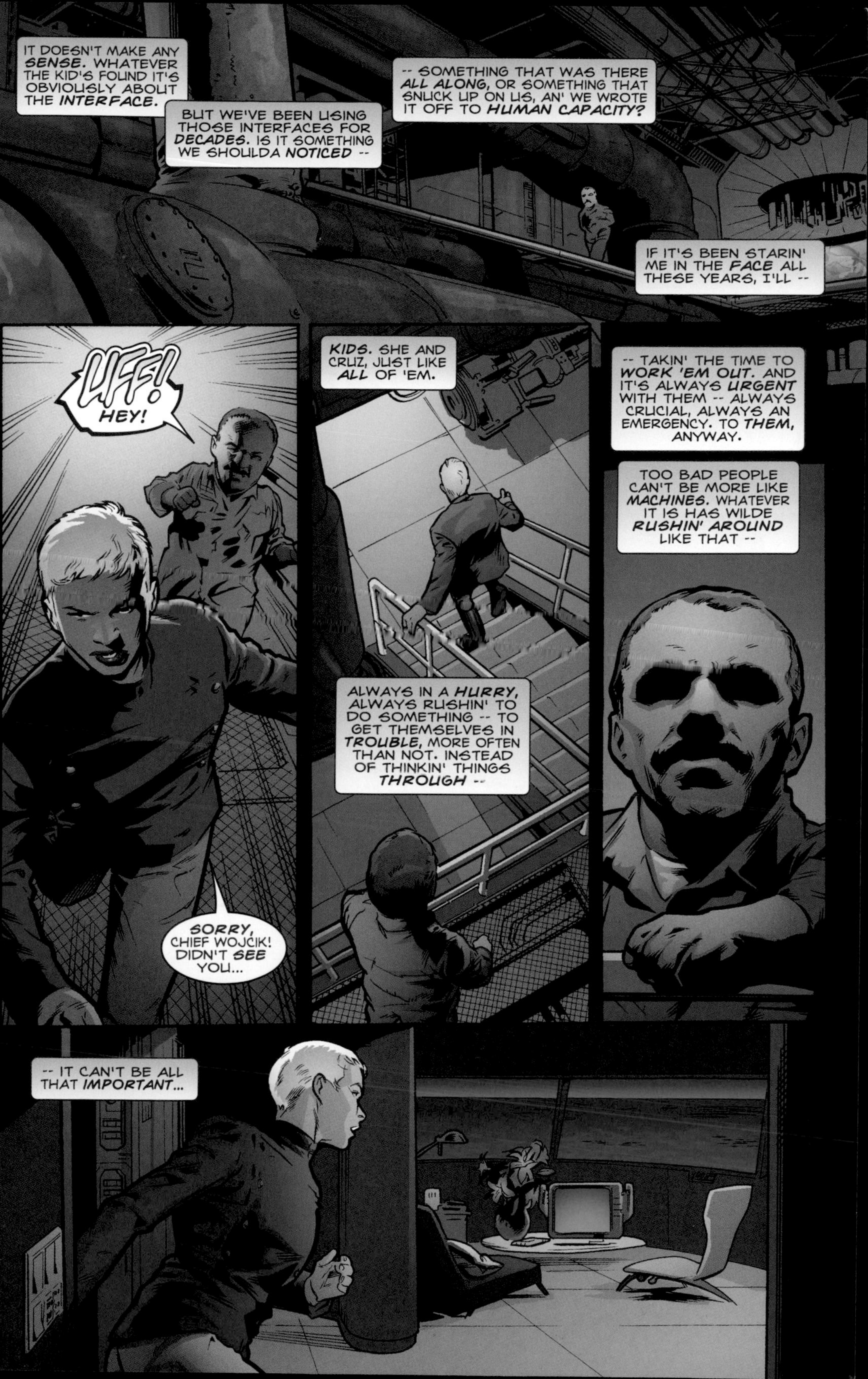
IT DOESN'T MAKE ANY SENSE. WHATEVER THE KID'S FOUND IT'S OBVIOUSLY ABOUT THE INTERFACE.
BUT WE'VE BEEN USING THOSE INTERFACES FOR DECADES. IS IT SOMETHING WE SHOULDA NOTICED --
-- SOMETHING THAT WAS THERE ALL ALONG, OR SOMETHING THAT SNUCK UP ON US, AN' WE WROTE IT OFF TO HUMAN CAPACITY?
IF IT'S BEEN STARIN' ME IN THE FACE ALL THESE YEARS, I'LL --
UFF!
HEY!
SORRY, CHIEF WOJCIK! DIDN'T SEE YOU...
KIDS. SHE AND CRUZ, JUST LIKE ALL OF 'EM.
ALWAYS IN A HURRY, ALWAYS RUSHIN' TO DO SOMETHING -- TO GET THEMSELVES IN TROUBLE, MORE OFTEN THAN NOT. INSTEAD OF THINKIN' THINGS THROUGH --
-- TAKIN' THE TIME TO WORK 'EM OUT. AND IT'S ALWAYS URGENT WITH THEM -- ALWAYS CRUCIAL, ALWAYS AN EMERGENCY. TO THEM, ANYWAY.
TOO BAD PEOPLE CAN'T BE MORE LIKE MACHINES. WHATEVER IT IS HAS WILDE RUSHIN' AROUND LIKE THAT --
-- IT CAN'T BE ALL THAT IMPORTANT...

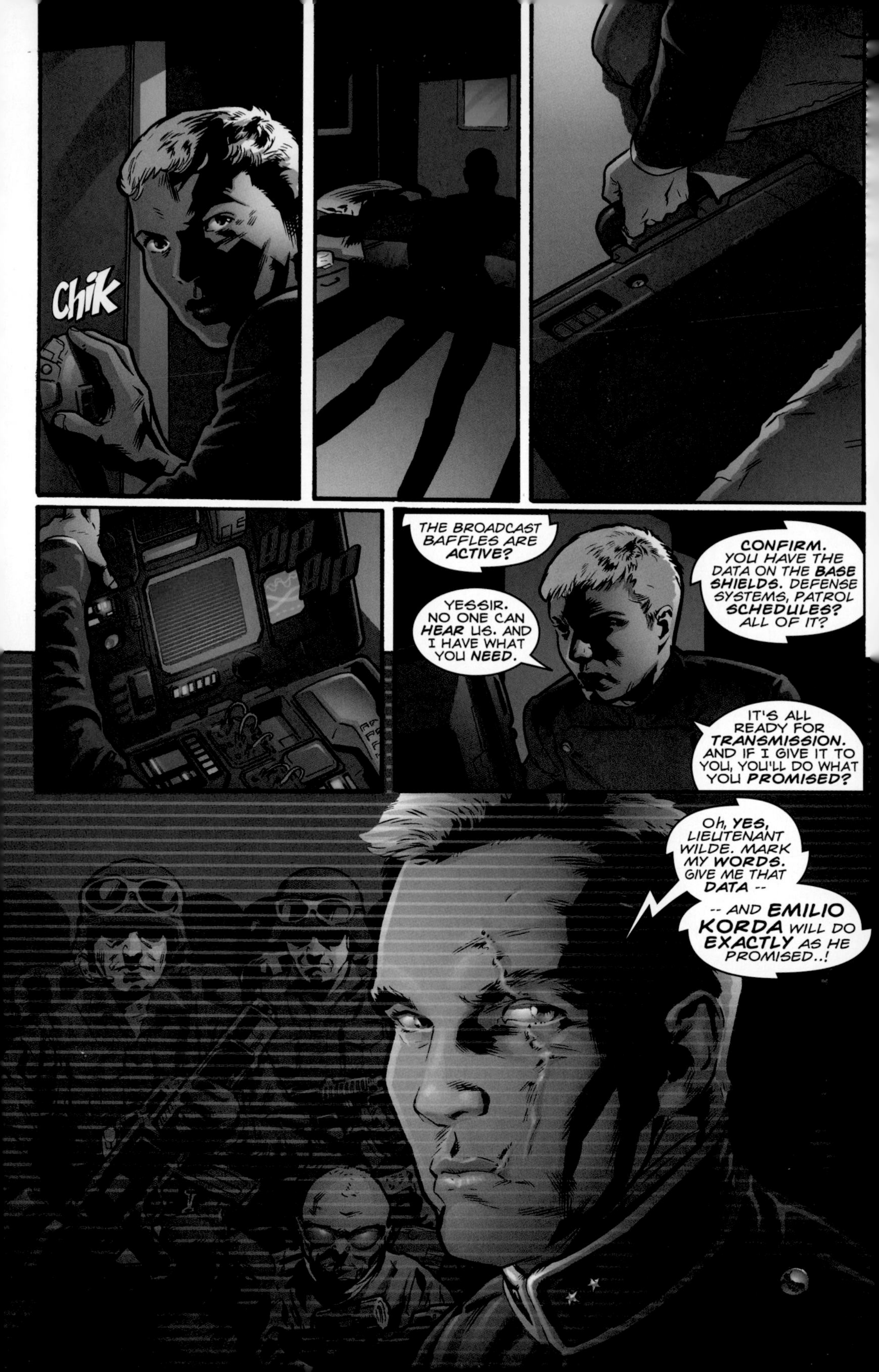
Chik
THE BROADCAST BAFFLES ARE ACTIVE?
YESSIR. NO ONE CAN HEAR US. AND I HAVE WHAT YOU NEED.
CONFIRM. YOU HAVE THE DATA ON THE BASE SHIELDS. DEFENSE SYSTEMS, PATROL SCHEDULES? ALL OF IT?
IT'S ALL READY FOR TRANSMISSION. AND IF I GIVE IT TO YOU, YOU'LL DO WHAT YOU PROMISED?
Oh, YES, LIEUTENANT WILDE. MARK MY WORDS. GIVE ME THAT DATA --
-- AND EMILIO KORDA WILL DO EXACTLY AS HE PROMISED..!

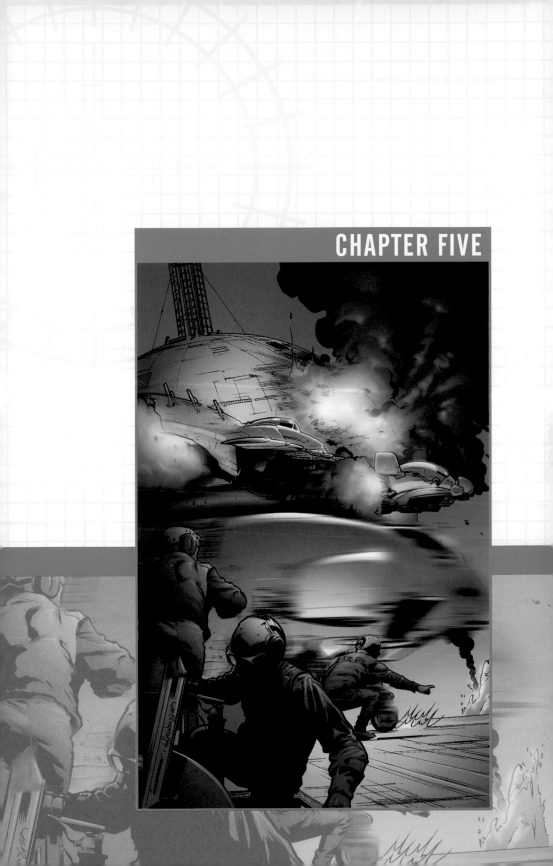

CHAPTER FIVE

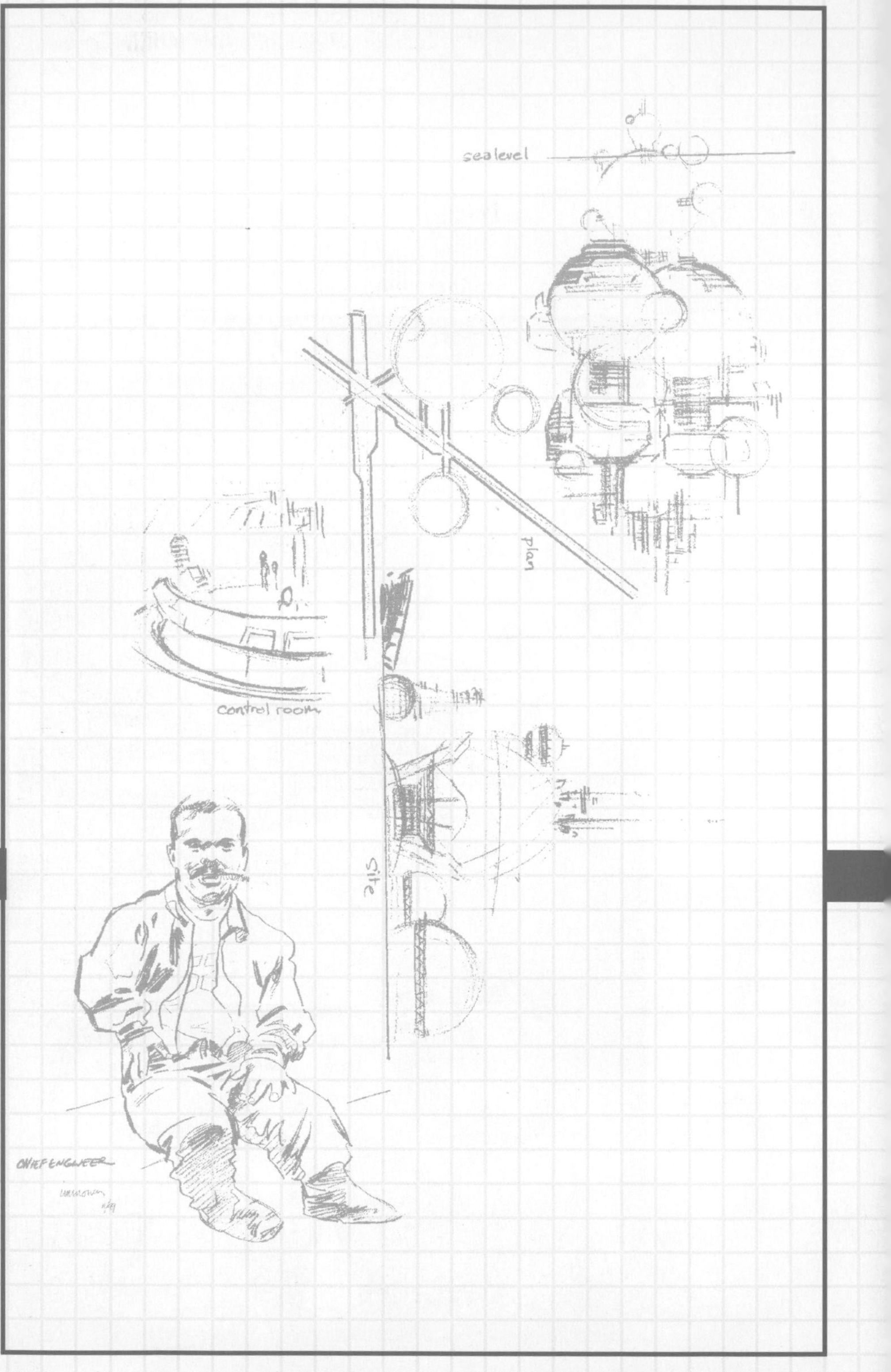
sealevel
plan
control room
site
CHIEF ENGINEER

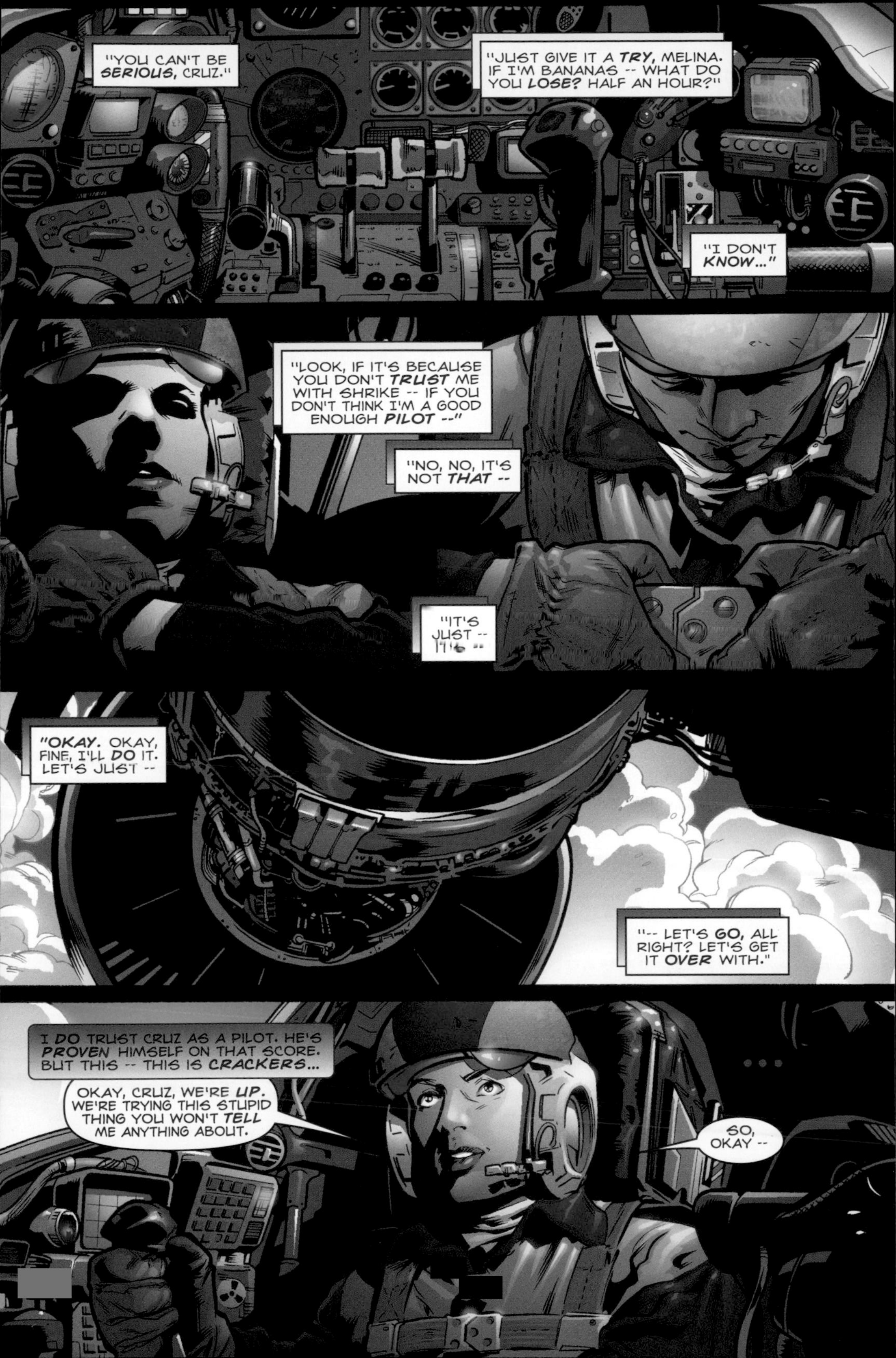
"YOU CAN'T BE SERIOUS, CRUZ."
"JUST GIVE IT A TRY, MELINA. IF I'M BANANAS -- WHAT DO YOU LOSE? HALF AN HOUR?"
"I DON'T KNOW..."
"LOOK, IF IT'S BECAUSE YOU DON'T TRUST ME WITH SHRIKE -- IF YOU DON'T THINK I'M A GOOD ENOUGH PILOT --"
"NO, NO, IT'S NOT THAT --
"IT'S JUST --
"OKAY. OKAY, FINE, I'LL DO IT. LET'S JUST --
"-- LET'S GO, ALL RIGHT? LET'S GET IT OVER WITH."
I DO TRUST CRUZ AS A PILOT. HE'S PROVEN HIMSELF ON THAT SCORE. BUT THIS -- THIS IS CRACKERS...
OKAY, CRUZ, WE'RE UP. WE'RE TRYING THIS STUPID THING YOU WON'T TELL ME ANYTHING ABOUT.
SO, OKAY --

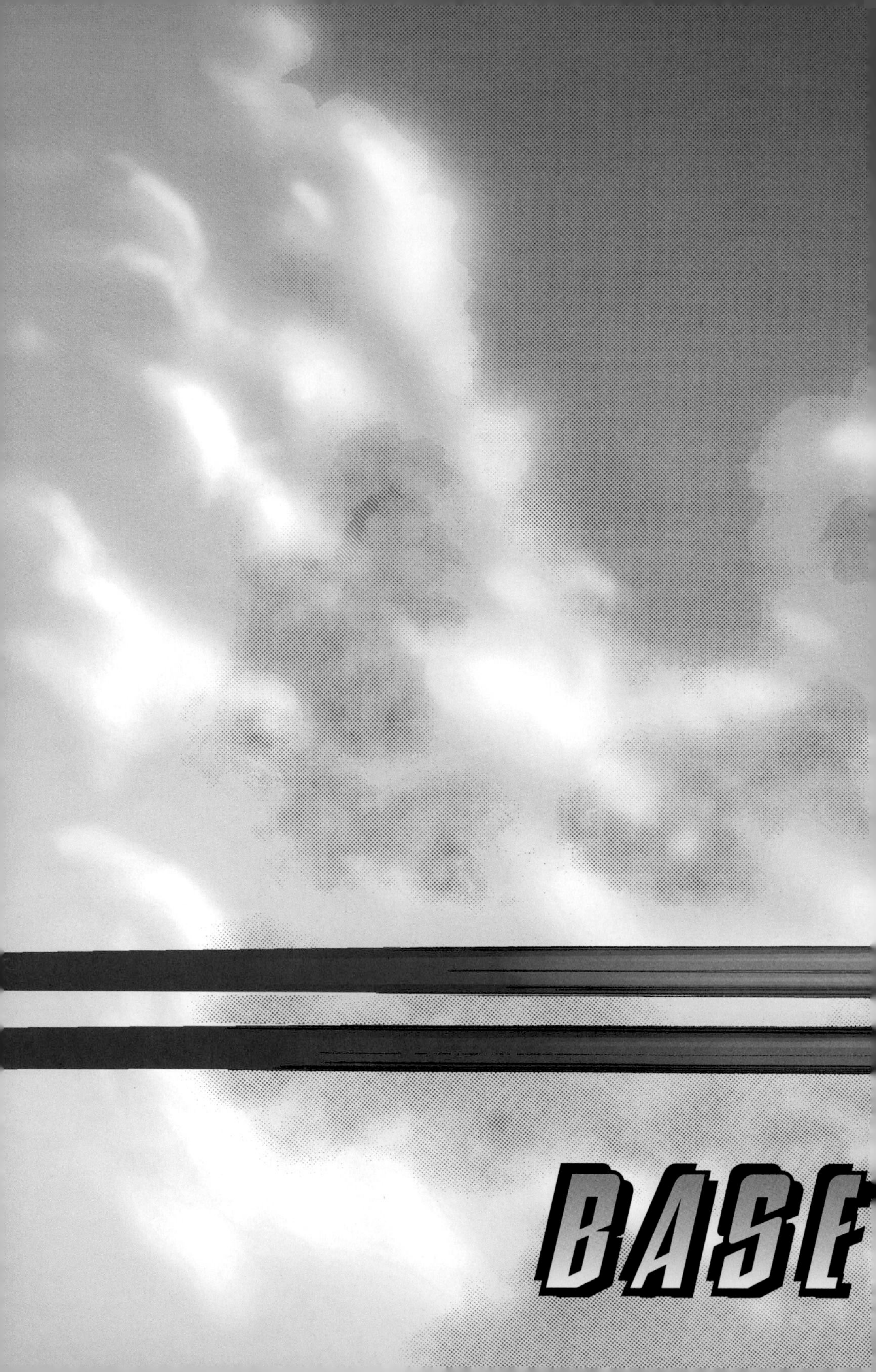
BASE

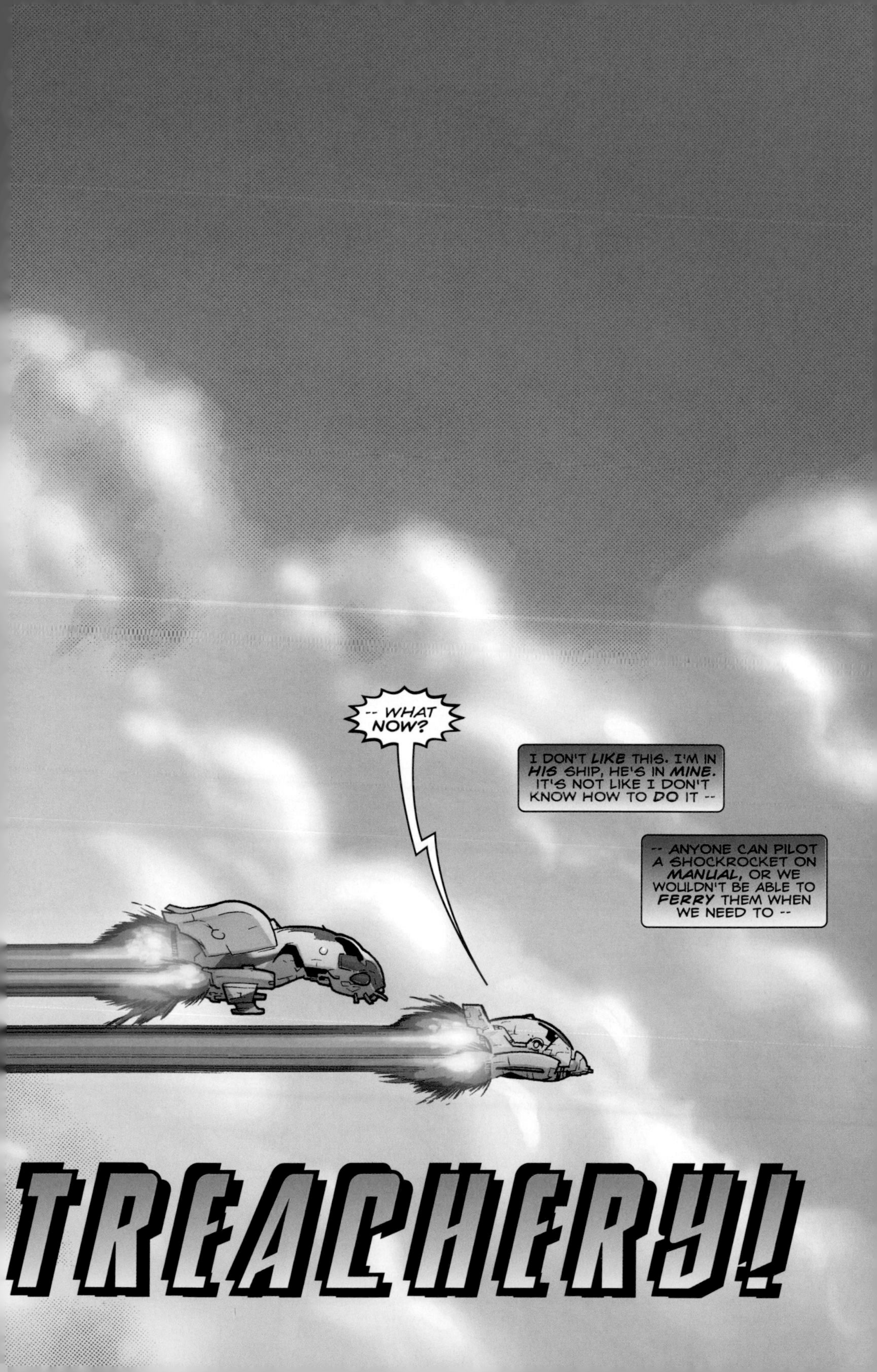
-- WHAT NOW?
I DON'T LIKE THIS. I'M IN HIS SHIP, HE'S IN MINE. IT'S NOT LIKE I DON'T KNOW HOW TO DO IT --
-- ANYONE CAN PILOT A SHOCKROCKET ON MANUAL, OR WE WOULDN'T BE ABLE TO FERRY THEM WHEN WE NEED TO --
TREACHERY!

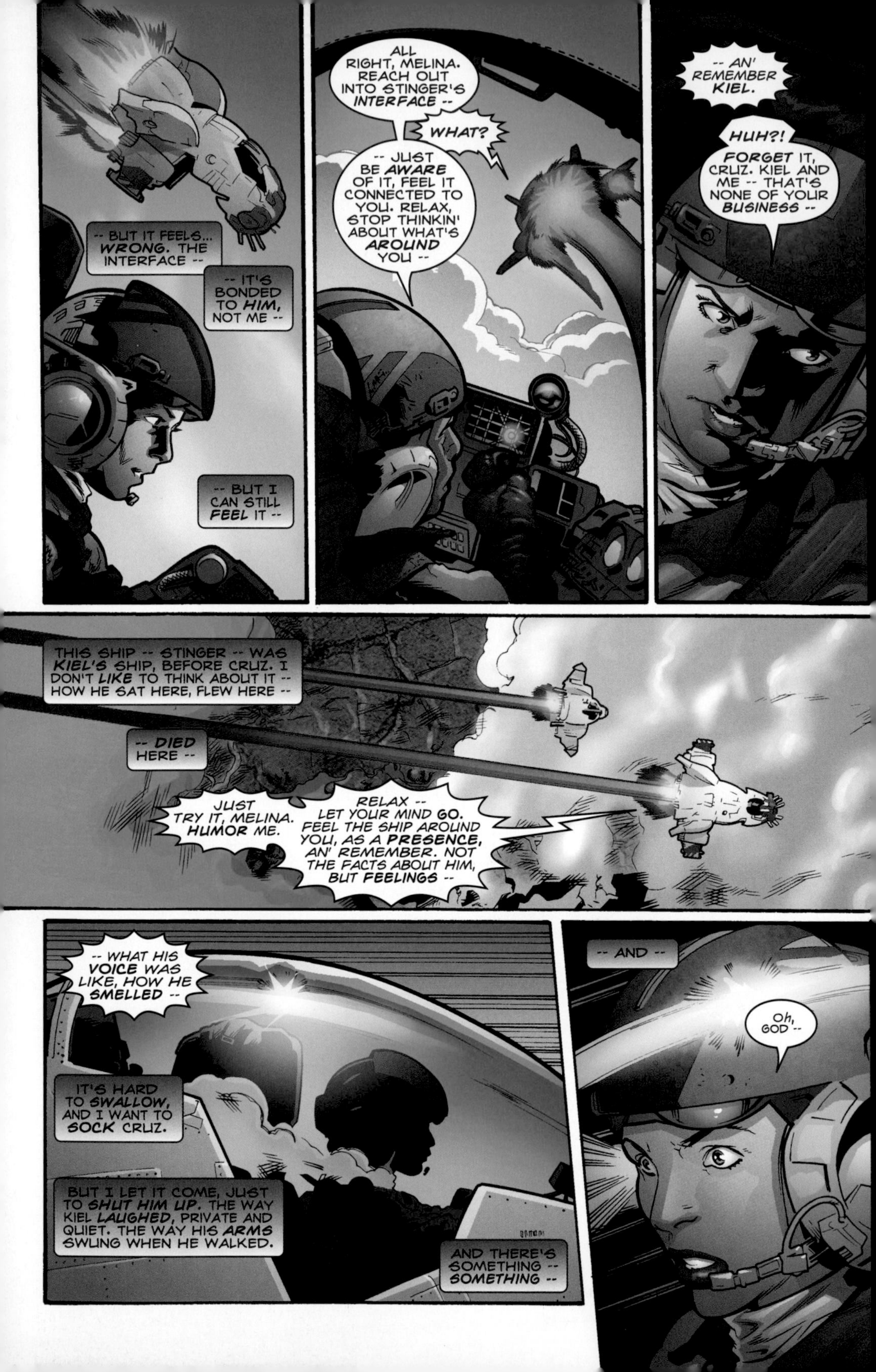
-- BUT IT FEELS... WRONG. THE INTERFACE --
-- IT'S BONDED TO HIM, NOT ME --
-- BUT I CAN STILL FEEL IT --
ALL RIGHT, MELINA. REACH OUT INTO STINGER'S INTERFACE --
WHAT?
-- JUST BE AWARE OF IT, FEEL IT CONNECTED TO YOU. RELAX, STOP THINKIN' ABOUT WHAT'S AROUND YOU --
-- AN' REMEMBER KIEL.
HUH?!
FORGET IT, CRUZ. KIEL AND ME -- THAT'S NONE OF YOUR BUSINESS --
THIS SHIP -- STINGER -- WAS KIEL'S SHIP, BEFORE CRUZ. I DON'T LIKE TO THINK ABOUT IT -- HOW HE SAT HERE, FLEW HERE --
-- DIED HERE --
JUST TRY IT, MELINA. HUMOR ME.
RELAX -- LET YOUR MIND GO. FEEL THE SHIP AROUND YOU, AS A PRESENCE, AN' REMEMBER. NOT THE FACTS ABOUT HIM, BUT FEELINGS --
-- WHAT HIS VOICE WAS LIKE, HOW HE SMELLED --
IT'S HARD TO SWALLOW, AND I WANT TO SOCK CRUZ.
BUT I LET IT COME, JUST TO SHUT HIM UP. THE WAY KIEL LAUGHED, PRIVATE AND QUIET. THE WAY HIS ARMS SWUNG WHEN HE WALKED.
AND THERE'S SOMETHING -- SOMETHING --
-- AND --
Oh, GOD --

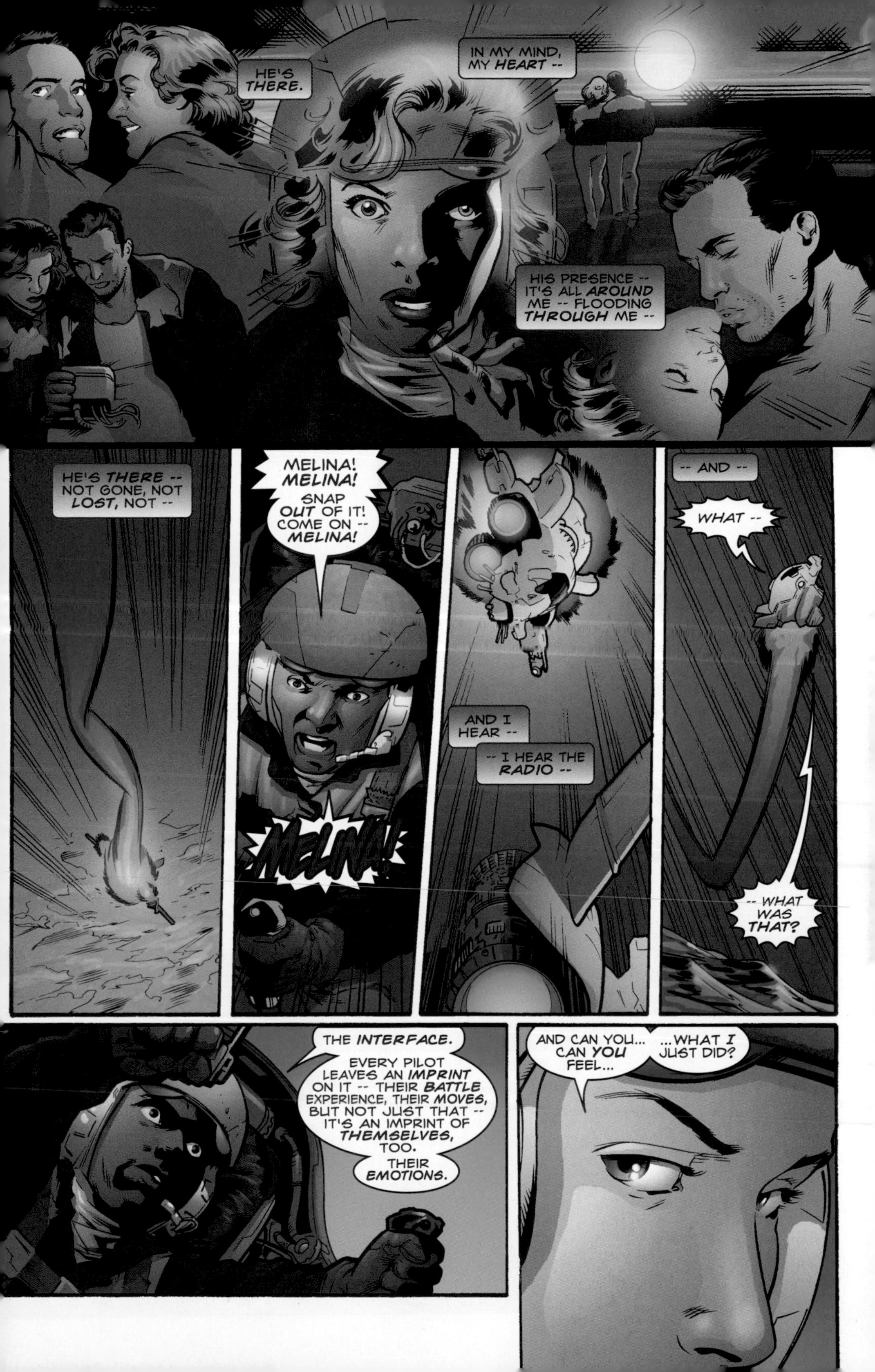
HE'S THERE.
IN MY MIND, MY HEART --
HIS PRESENCE -- IT'S ALL AROUND ME -- FLOODING THROUGH ME --
HE'S THERE -- NOT GONE, NOT LOST, NOT --
MELINA! MELINA! SNAP OUT OF IT! COME ON -- MELINA!
MELINA!
AND I HEAR --
-- I HEAR THE RADIO --
-- AND --
WHAT --
-- WHAT WAS THAT?
THE INTERFACE.
EVERY PILOT LEAVES AN IMPRINT ON IT -- THEIR BATTLE EXPERIENCE, THEIR MOVES, BUT NOT JUST THAT -- IT'S AN IMPRINT OF THEMSELVES, TOO.
THEIR EMOTIONS.
AND CAN YOU... CAN YOU FEEL...
...WHAT I JUST DID?

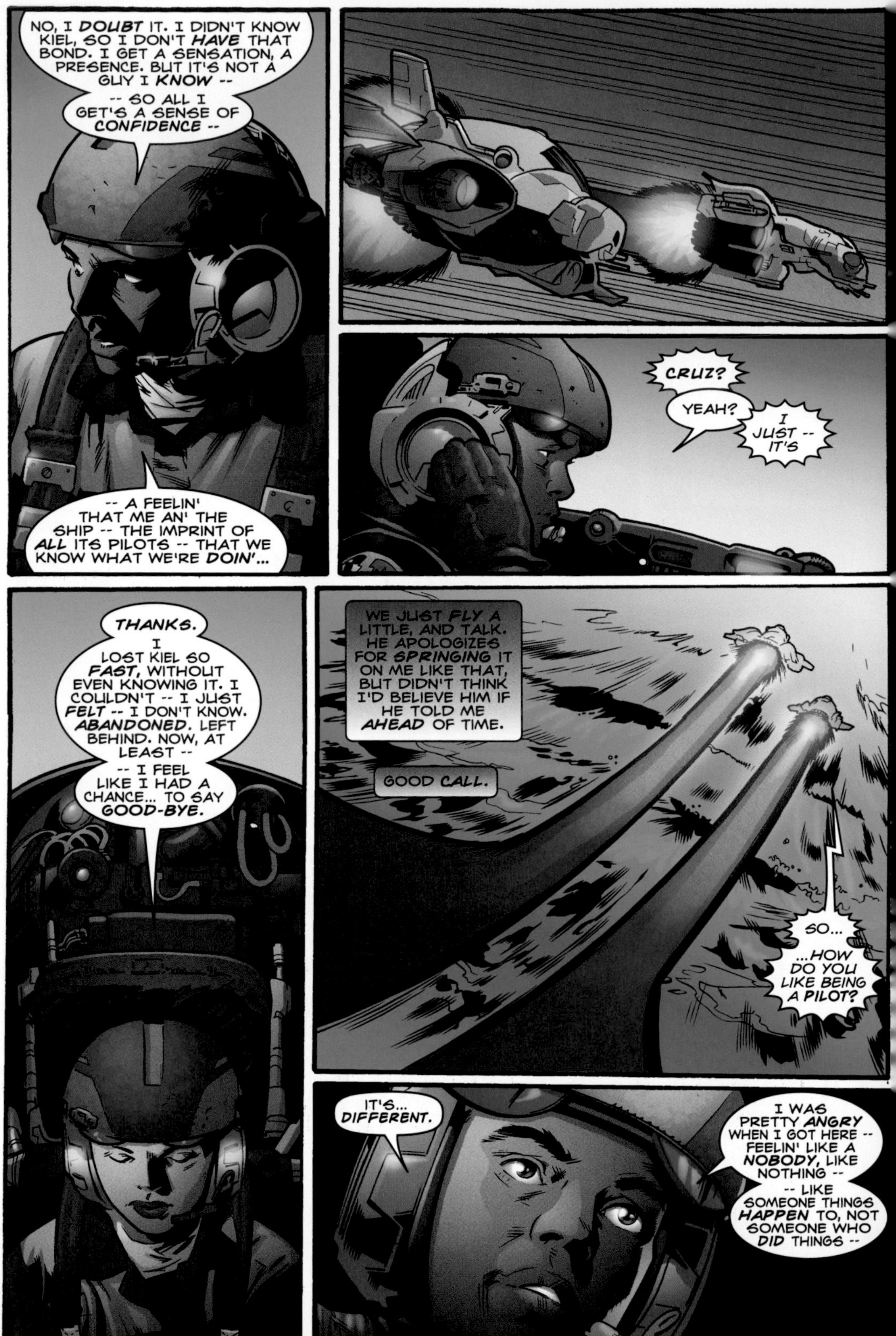
NO, I DOUBT IT. I DIDN'T KNOW KIEL, SO I DON'T HAVE THAT BOND. I GET A SENSATION, A PRESENCE. BUT IT'S NOT A GUY I KNOW --
-- SO ALL I GET'S A SENSE OF CONFIDENCE --
-- A FEELIN' THAT ME AN' THE SHIP -- THE IMPRINT OF ALL ITS PILOTS -- THAT WE KNOW WHAT WE'RE DOIN'...
CRUZ?
YEAH?
I JUST -- IT'S
THANKS.
I LOST KIEL SO FAST, WITHOUT EVEN KNOWING IT. I COULDN'T -- I JUST FELT -- I DON'T KNOW. ABANDONED. LEFT BEHIND. NOW, AT LEAST --
-- I FEEL LIKE I HAD A CHANCE... TO SAY GOOD-BYE.
WE JUST FLY A LITTLE, AND TALK. HE APOLOGIZES FOR SPRINGING IT ON ME LIKE THAT, BUT DIDN'T THINK I'D BELIEVE HIM IF HE TOLD ME AHEAD OF TIME.
GOOD CALL.
SO...
...HOW DO YOU LIKE BEING A PILOT?
IT'S... DIFFERENT.
I WAS PRETTY ANGRY WHEN I GOT HERE -- FEELIN' LIKE A NOBODY, LIKE NOTHING --
-- LIKE SOMEONE THINGS HAPPEN TO, NOT SOMEONE WHO DID THINGS --

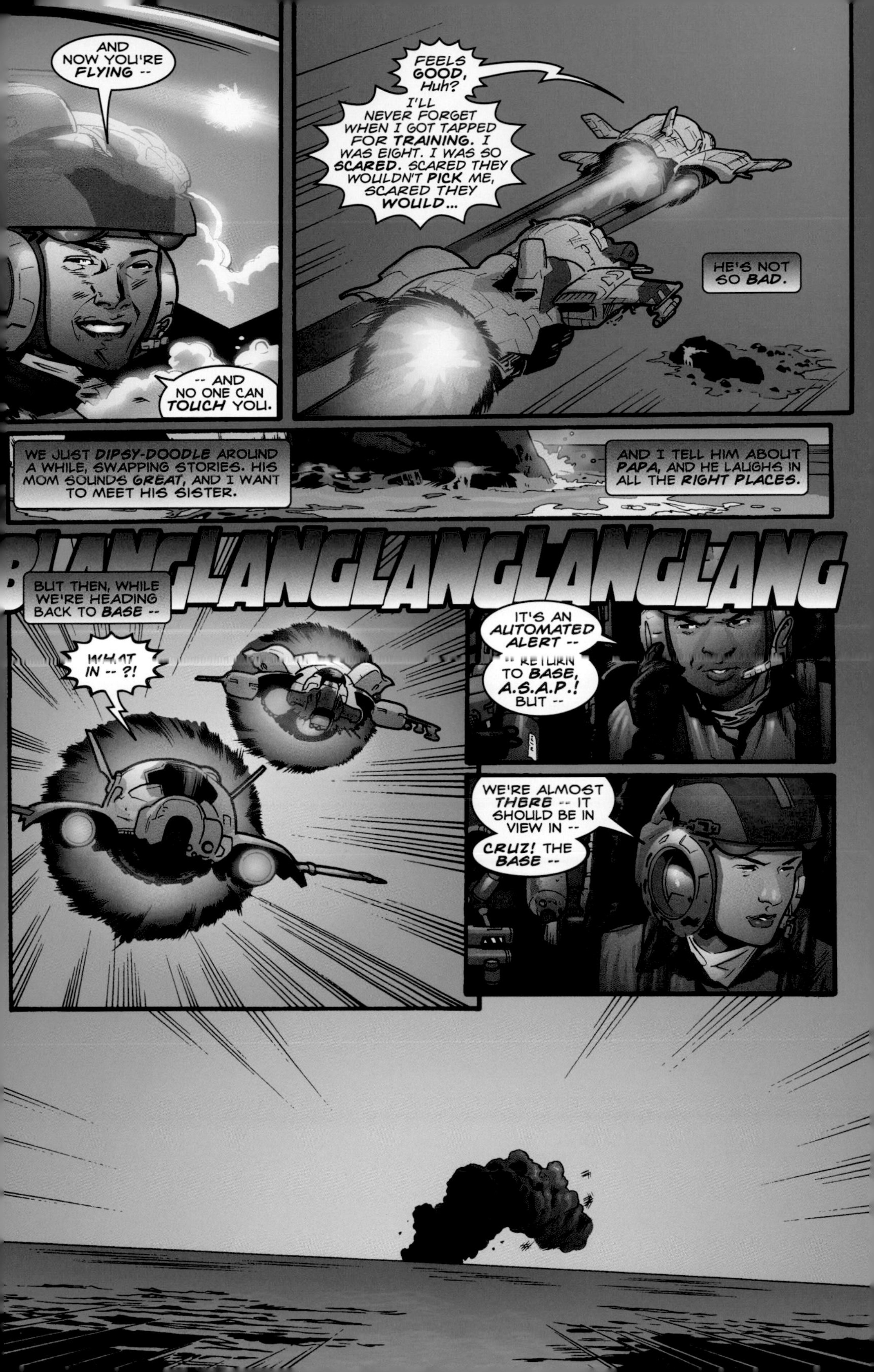
AND NOW YOU'RE FLYING --
-- AND NO ONE CAN TOUCH YOU.
FEELS GOOD, Huh?
I'LL NEVER FORGET WHEN I GOT TAPPED FOR TRAINING. I WAS EIGHT. I WAS SO SCARED. SCARED THEY WOULDN'T PICK ME, SCARED THEY WOULD...
HE'S NOT SO BAD.
WE JUST DIPSY-DOODLE AROUND A WHILE, SWAPPING STORIES. HIS MOM SOUNDS GREAT, AND I WANT TO MEET HIS SISTER.
AND I TELL HIM ABOUT PAPA, AND HE LAUGHS IN ALL THE RIGHT PLACES.
BLANGLANGLANGLANGLANG
BUT THEN, WHILE WE'RE HEADING BACK TO BASE --
WHAT IN -- ?!
IT'S AN AUTOMATED ALERT --
-- RETURN TO BASE, A.S.A.P.! BUT --
WE'RE ALMOST THERE -- IT SHOULD BE IN VIEW IN --
CRUZ! THE BASE --

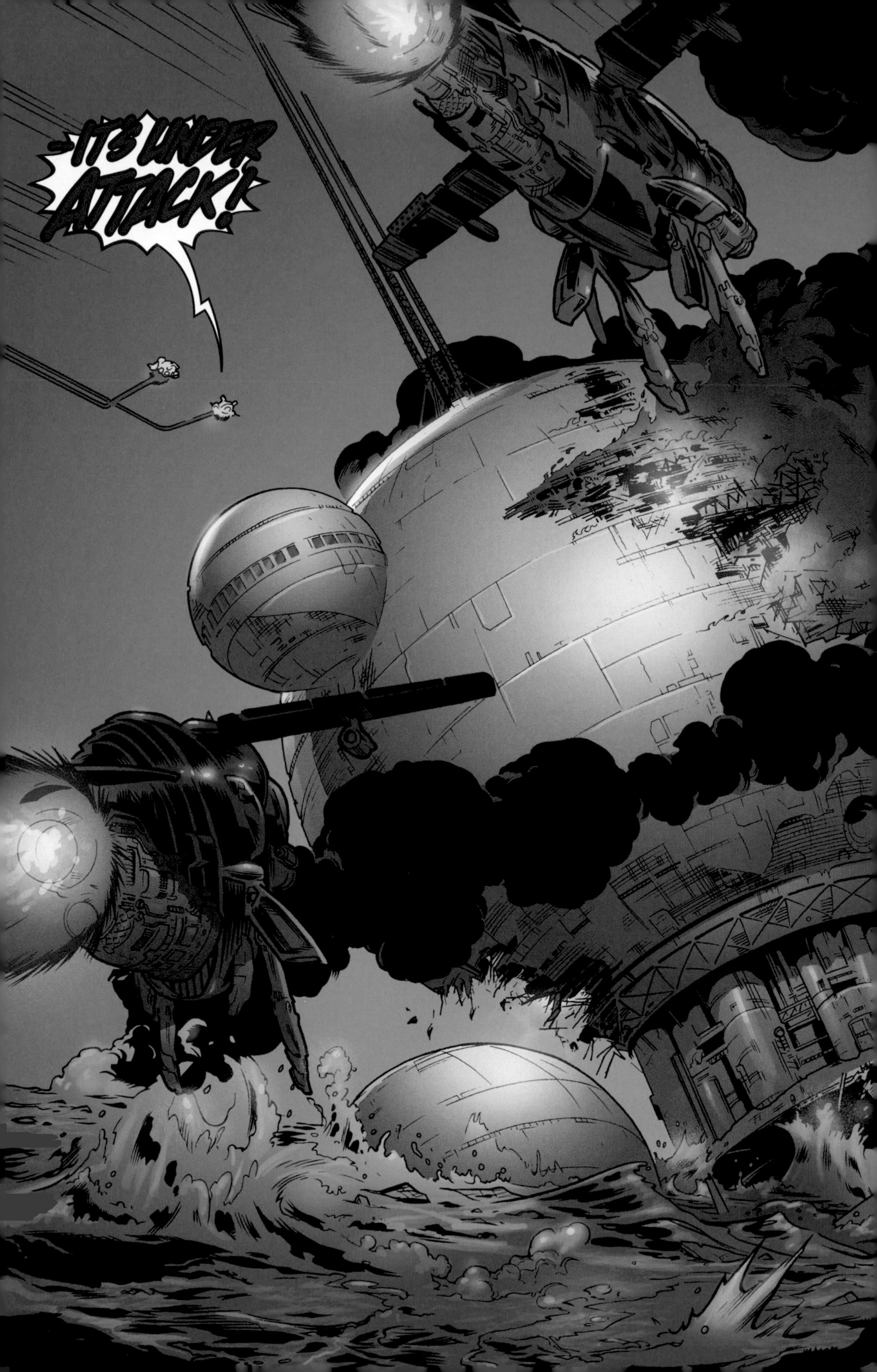
-IT'S UNDER ATTACK!

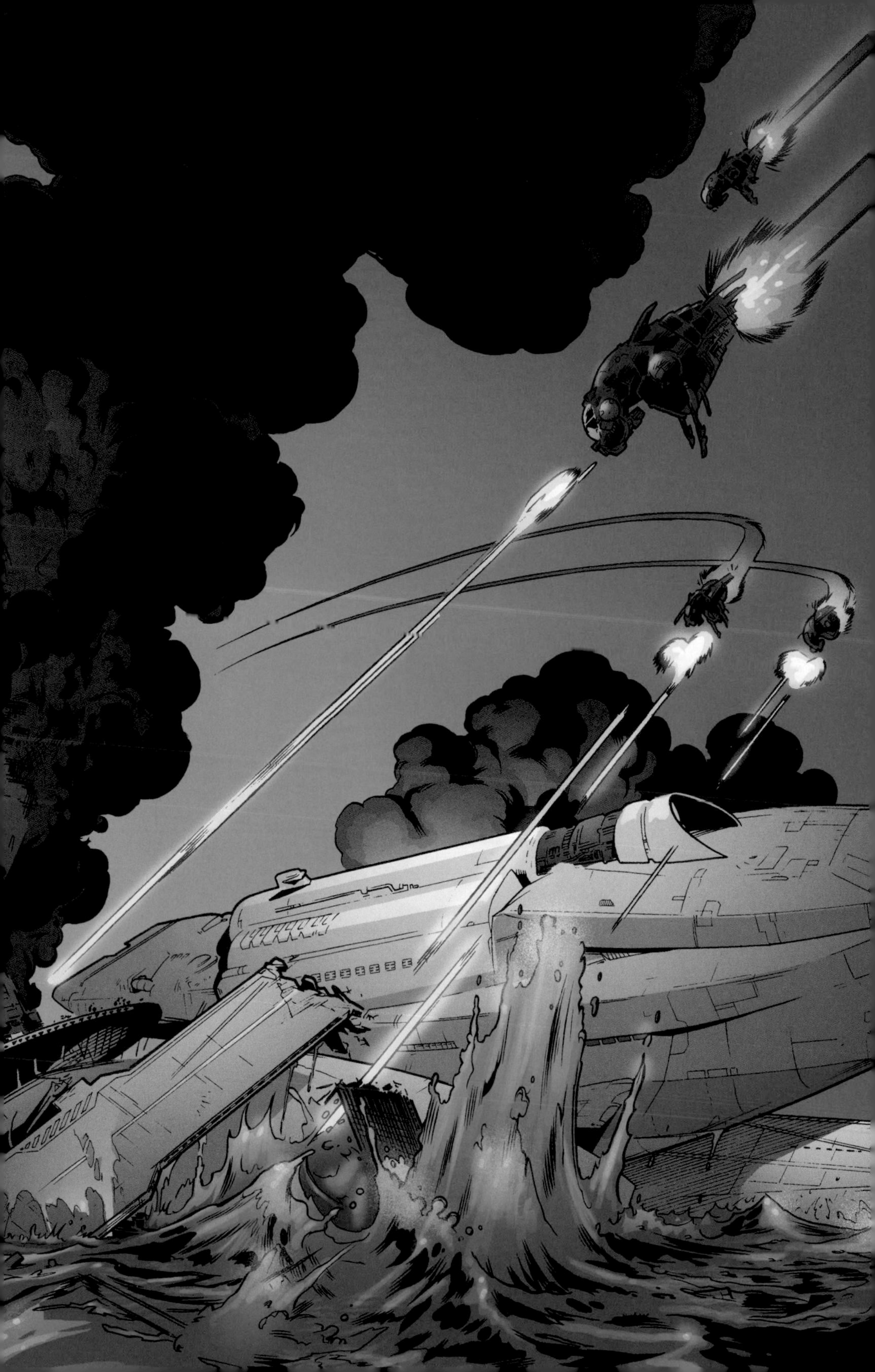

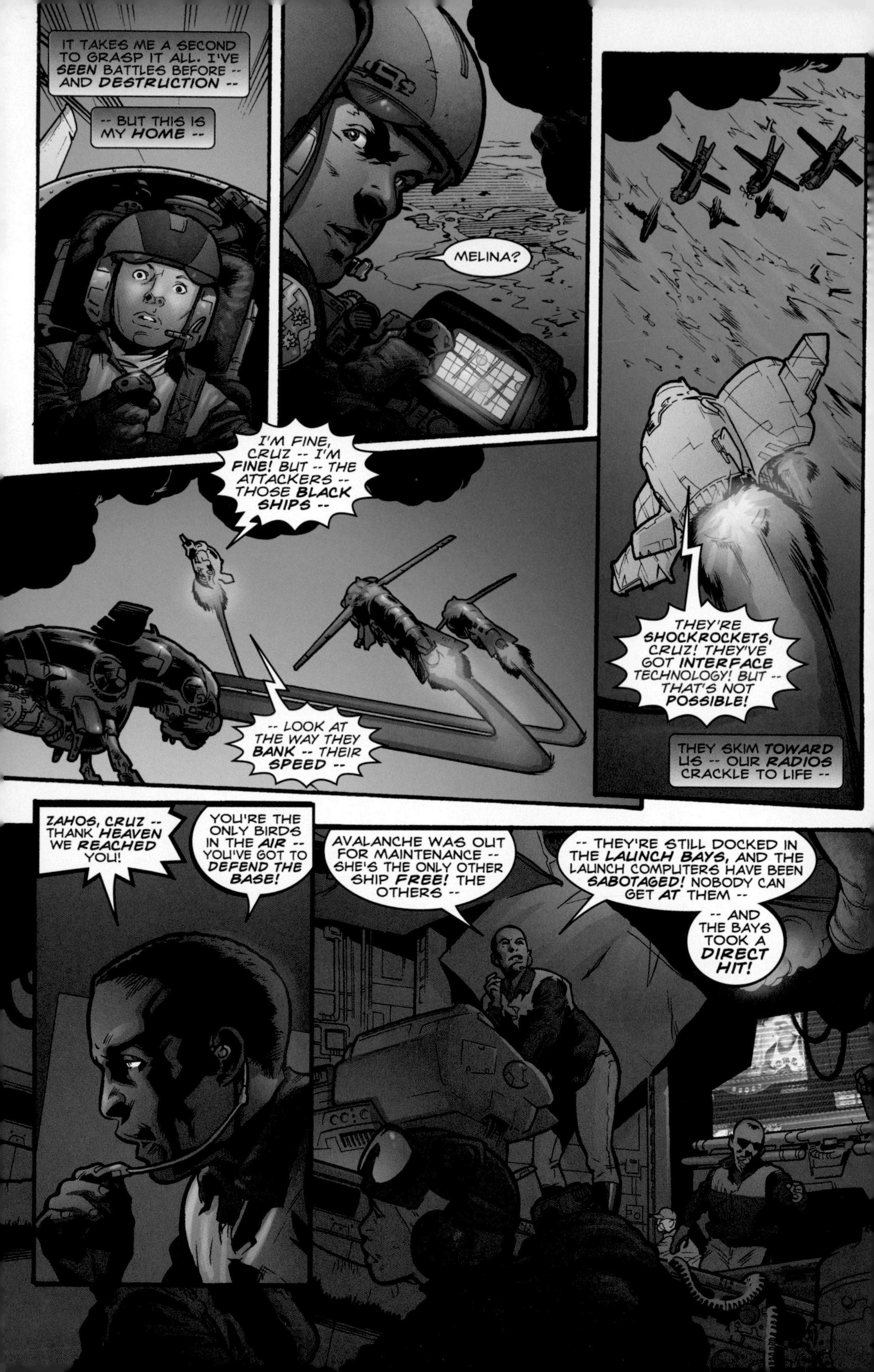
IT TAKES ME A SECOND TO GRASP IT ALL. I'VE SEEN BATTLES BEFORE -- AND DESTRUCTION --
-- BUT THIS IS MY HOME --
MELINA?
I'M FINE, CRUZ -- I'M FINE! BUT -- THE ATTACKERS -- THOSE BLACK SHIPS --
-- LOOK AT THE WAY THEY BANK -- THEIR SPEED --
THEY'RE SHOCKROCKETS, CRUZ! THEY'VE GOT INTERFACE TECHNOLOGY! BUT -- THAT'S NOT POSSIBLE!
THEY SKIM TOWARD US -- OUR RADIOS CRACKLE TO LIFE --
ZAHOS, CRUZ -- THANK HEAVEN WE REACHED YOU!
YOU'RE THE ONLY BIRDS IN THE AIR -- YOU'VE GOT TO DEFEND THE BASE!
AVALANCHE WAS OUT FOR MAINTENANCE -- SHE'S THE ONLY OTHER SHIP FREE! THE OTHERS --
-- THEY'RE STILL DOCKED IN THE LAUNCH BAYS, AND THE LAUNCH COMPUTERS HAVE BEEN SABOTAGED! NOBODY CAN GET AT THEM --
-- AND THE BAYS TOOK A DIRECT HIT!

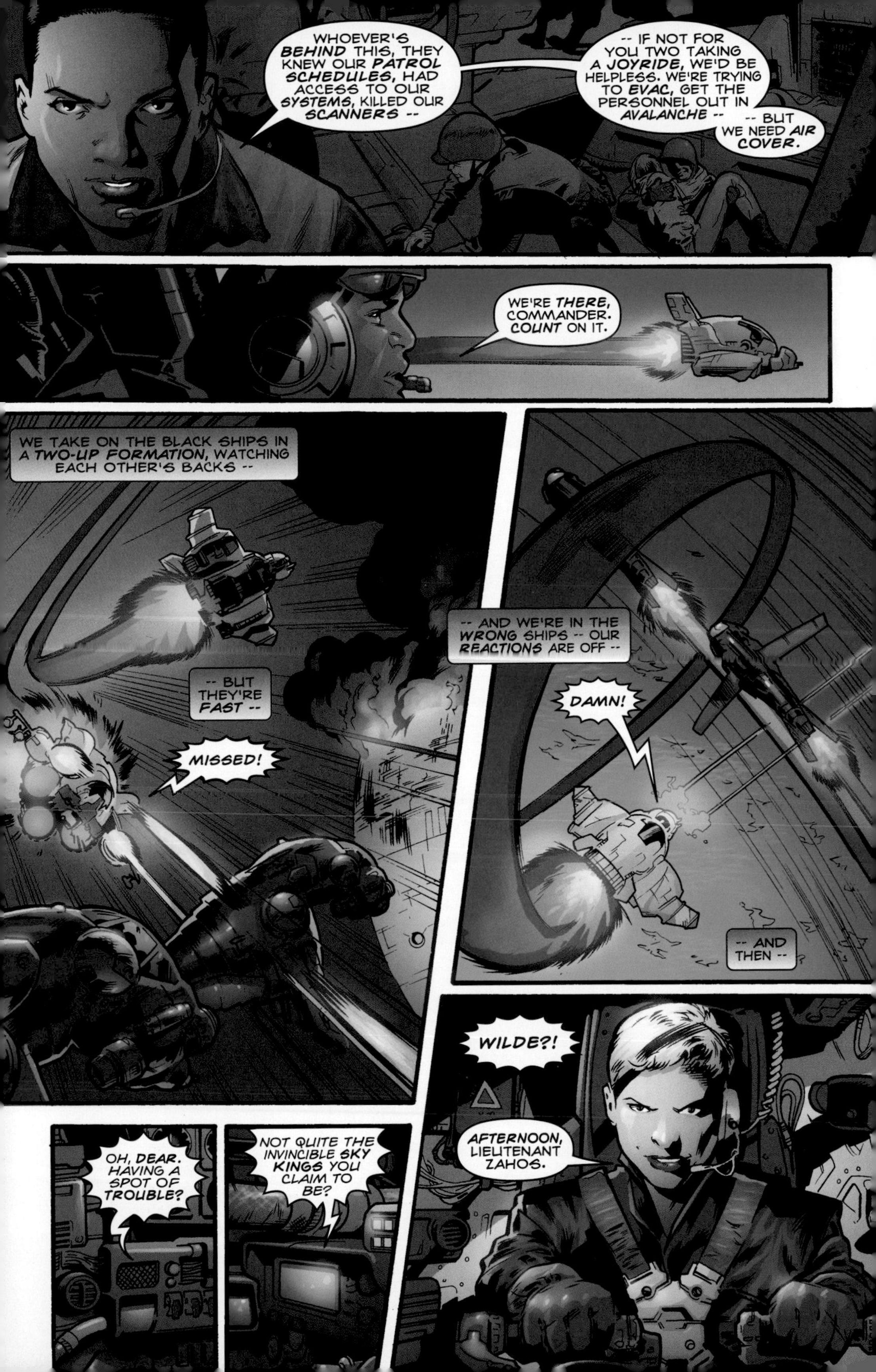
WHOEVER'S BEHIND THIS, THEY KNEW OUR PATROL SCHEDULES, HAD ACCESS TO OUR SYSTEMS, KILLED OUR SCANNERS --
-- IF NOT FOR YOU TWO TAKING A JOYRIDE, WE'D BE HELPLESS. WE'RE TRYING TO EVAC, GET THE PERSONNEL OUT IN AVALANCHE --
-- BUT WE NEED AIR COVER.
WE'RE THERE, COMMANDER. COUNT ON IT.
WE TAKE ON THE BLACK SHIPS IN A TWO-UP FORMATION, WATCHING EACH OTHER'S BACKS --
-- BUT THEY'RE FAST --
MISSED!
-- AND WE'RE IN THE WRONG SHIPS -- OUR REACTIONS ARE OFF --
DAMN!
-- AND THEN --
WILDE?!
OH, DEAR. HAVING A SPOT OF TROUBLE?
NOT QUITE THE INVINCIBLE SKY KINGS YOU CLAIM TO BE?
AFTERNOON, LIEUTENANT ZAHOS.

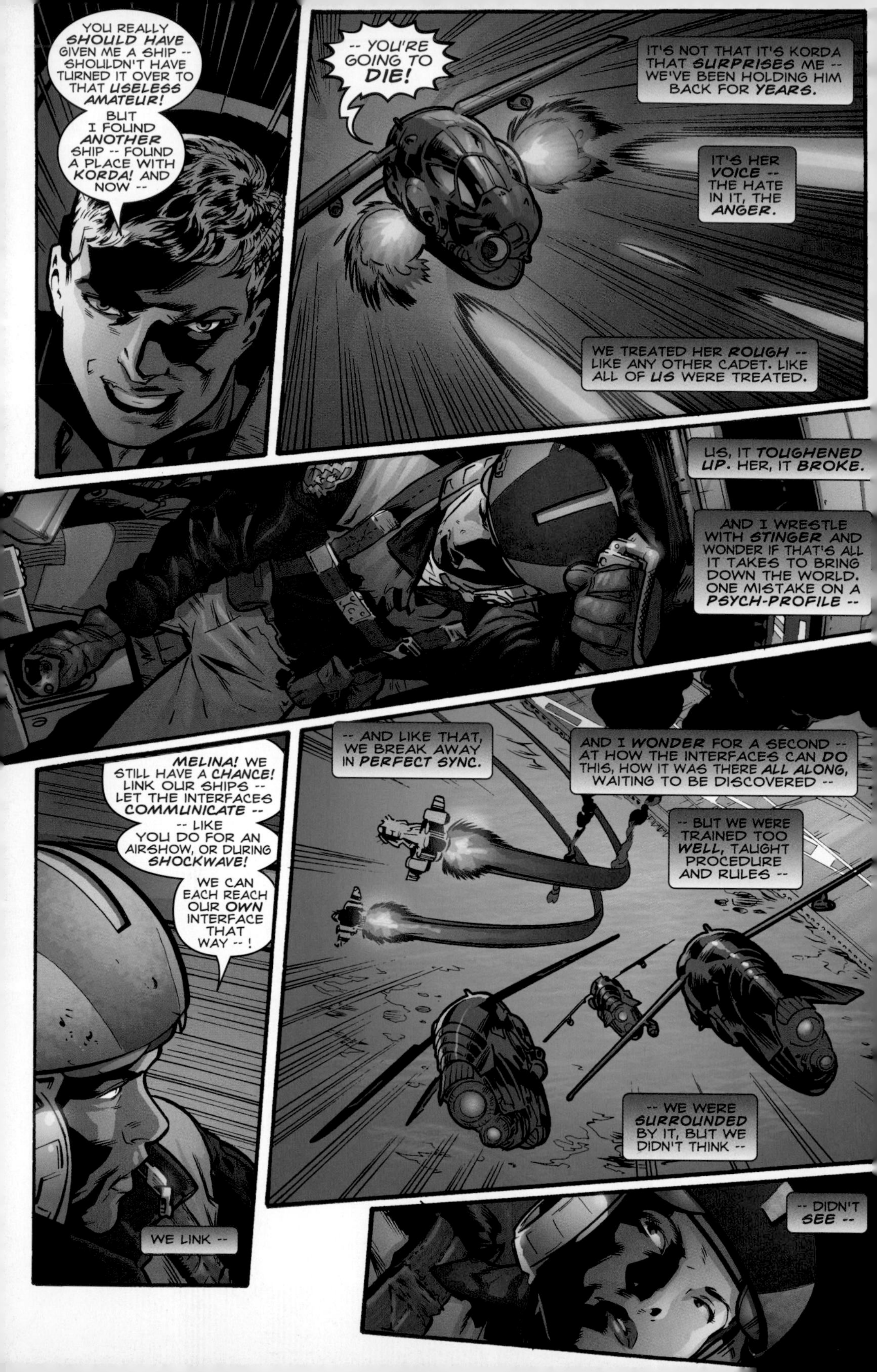
YOU REALLY SHOULD HAVE GIVEN ME A SHIP -- SHOULDN'T HAVE TURNED IT OVER TO THAT USELESS AMATEUR!
BUT I FOUND ANOTHER SHIP -- FOUND A PLACE WITH KORDA! AND NOW --
-- YOU'RE GOING TO DIE!
IT'S NOT THAT IT'S KORDA THAT SURPRISES ME -- WE'VE BEEN HOLDING HIM BACK FOR YEARS.
IT'S HER VOICE -- THE HATE IN IT, THE ANGER.
WE TREATED HER ROUGH -- LIKE ANY OTHER CADET. LIKE ALL OF US WERE TREATED.
US, IT TOUGHENED UP. HER, IT BROKE.
AND I WRESTLE WITH STINGER AND WONDER IF THAT'S ALL IT TAKES TO BRING DOWN THE WORLD. ONE MISTAKE ON A PSYCH-PROFILE --
MELINA! WE STILL HAVE A CHANCE! LINK OUR SHIPS -- LET THE INTERFACES COMMUNICATE --
-- LIKE YOU DO FOR AN AIRSHOW, OR DURING SHOCKWAVE!
WE CAN EACH REACH OUR OWN INTERFACE THAT WAY -- !
WE LINK --
-- AND LIKE THAT, WE BREAK AWAY IN PERFECT SYNC.
AND I WONDER FOR A SECOND -- AT HOW THE INTERFACES CAN DO THIS, HOW IT WAS THERE ALL ALONG, WAITING TO BE DISCOVERED --
-- BUT WE WERE TRAINED TOO WELL, TAUGHT PROCEDURE AND RULES --
-- WE WERE SURROUNDED BY IT, BUT WE DIDN'T THINK --
-- DIDN'T SEE --

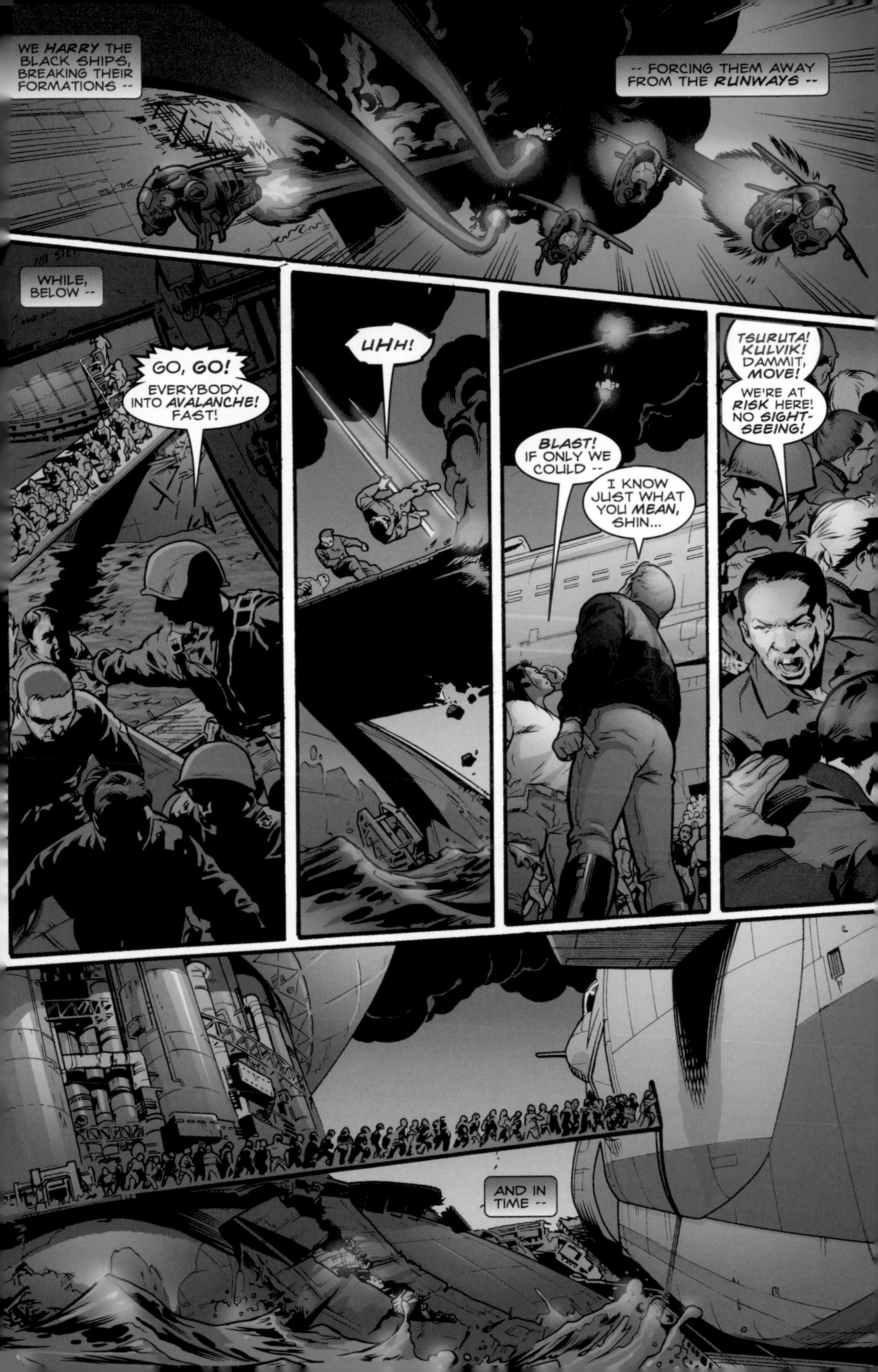
WE HARRY THE BLACK SHIPS, BREAKING THEIR FORMATIONS --
-- FORCING THEM AWAY FROM THE RUNWAYS --
WHILE, BELOW --
GO, GO!
EVERYBODY INTO AVALANCHE! FAST!
UHH!
BLAST! IF ONLY WE COULD --
I KNOW JUST WHAT YOU MEAN, SHIN...
TSURUTA! KULVIK! DAMMIT, MOVE!
WE'RE AT RISK HERE! NO SIGHT-SEEING!
AND IN TIME --

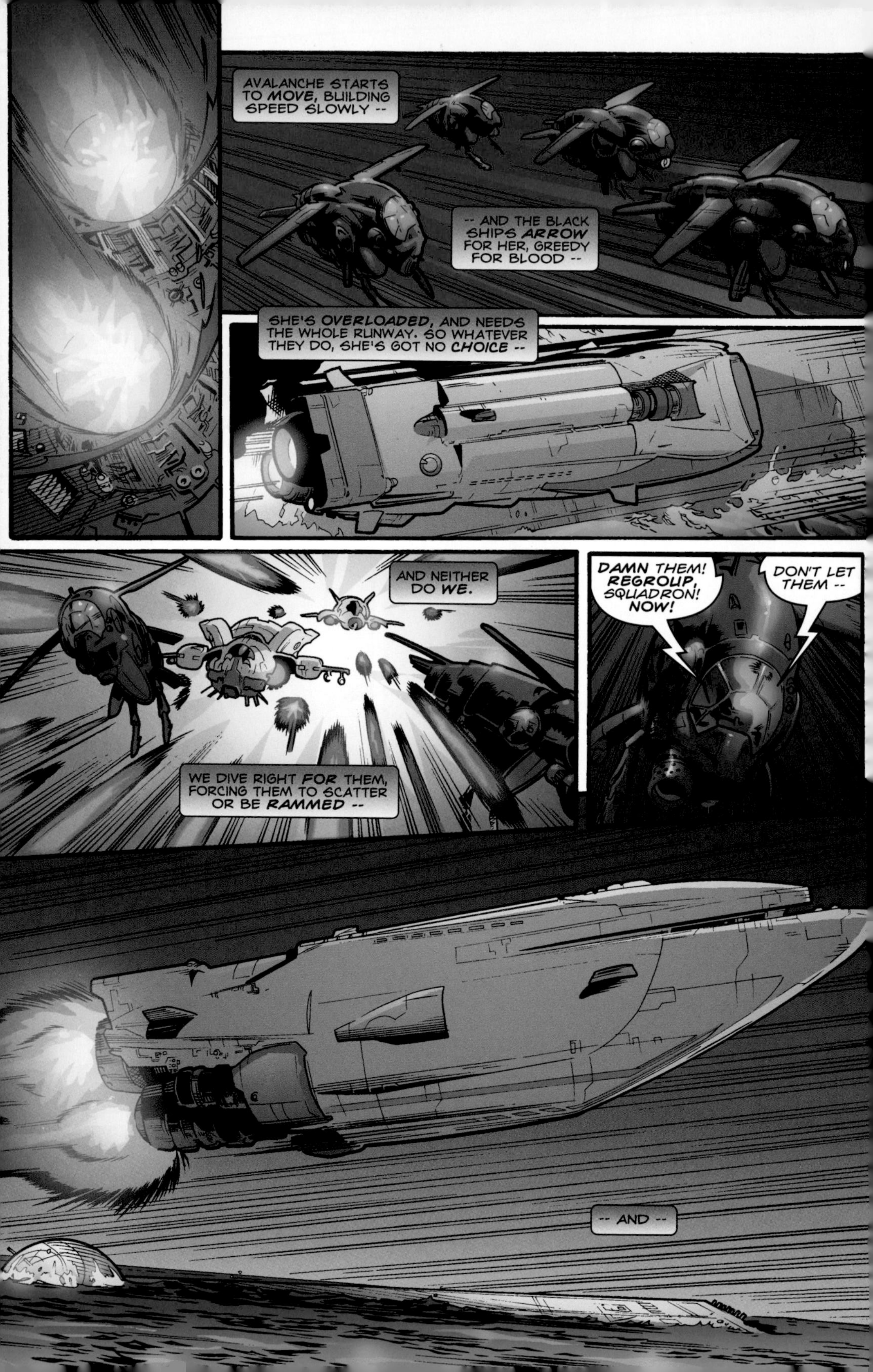
AVALANCHE STARTS TO MOVE, BUILDING SPEED SLOWLY --
-- AND THE BLACK SHIPS ARROW FOR HER, GREEDY FOR BLOOD --
SHE'S OVERLOADED, AND NEEDS THE WHOLE RUNWAY. SO WHATEVER THEY DO, SHE'S GOT NO CHOICE --
AND NEITHER DO WE.
WE DIVE RIGHT FOR THEM, FORCING THEM TO SCATTER OR BE RAMMED --
DAMN THEM! REGROUP, SQUADRON! NOW!
DON'T LET THEM --
-- AND --

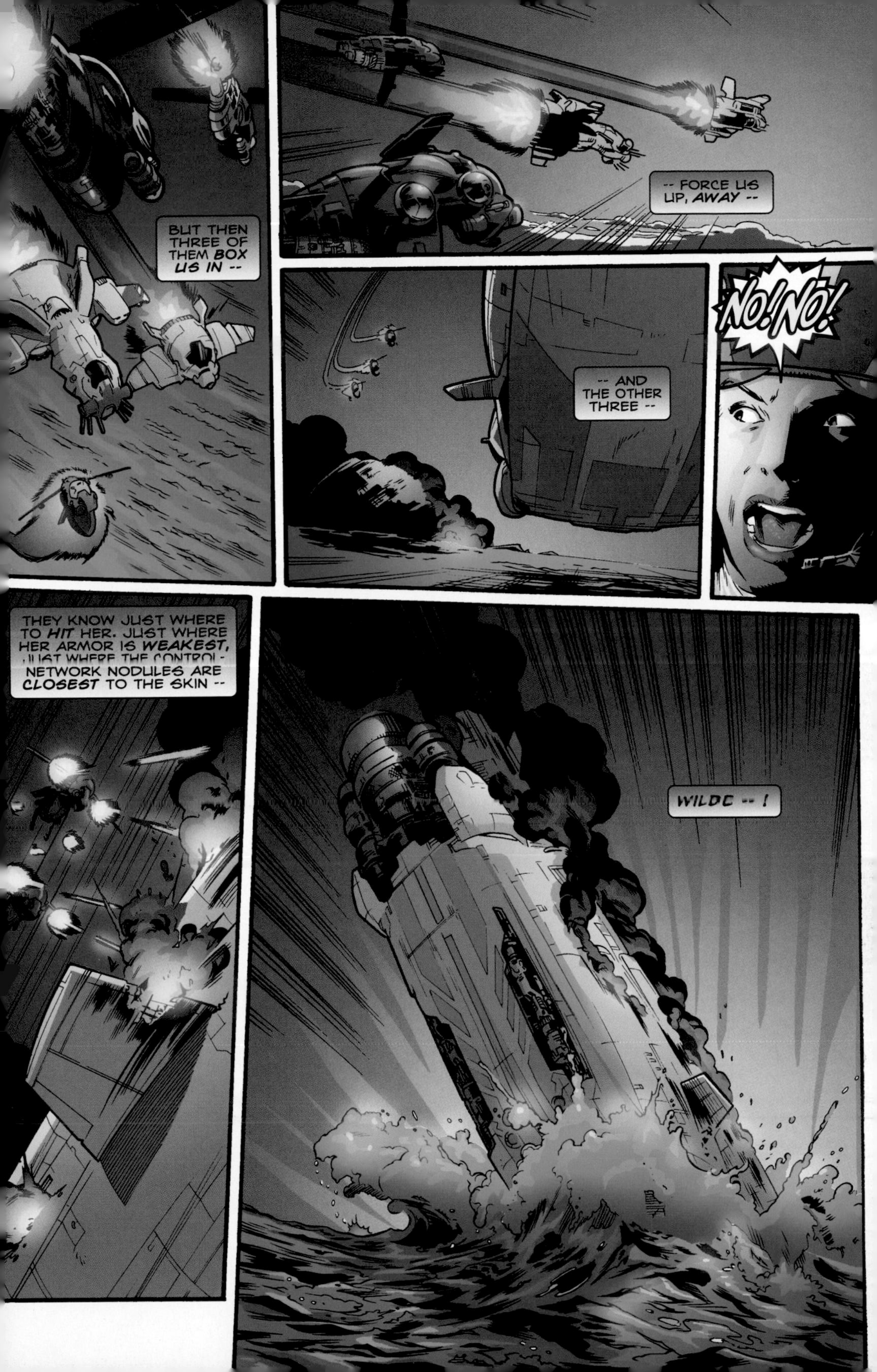
BUT THEN THREE OF THEM BOX US IN --
-- FORCE US UP, AWAY --
-- AND THE OTHER THREE --
NO! NO!
THEY KNOW JUST WHERE TO HIT HER. JUST WHERE HER ARMOR IS WEAKEST, JUST WHERE THE CONTROL-NETWORK NODULES ARE CLOSEST TO THE SKIN --
WILDC -- !

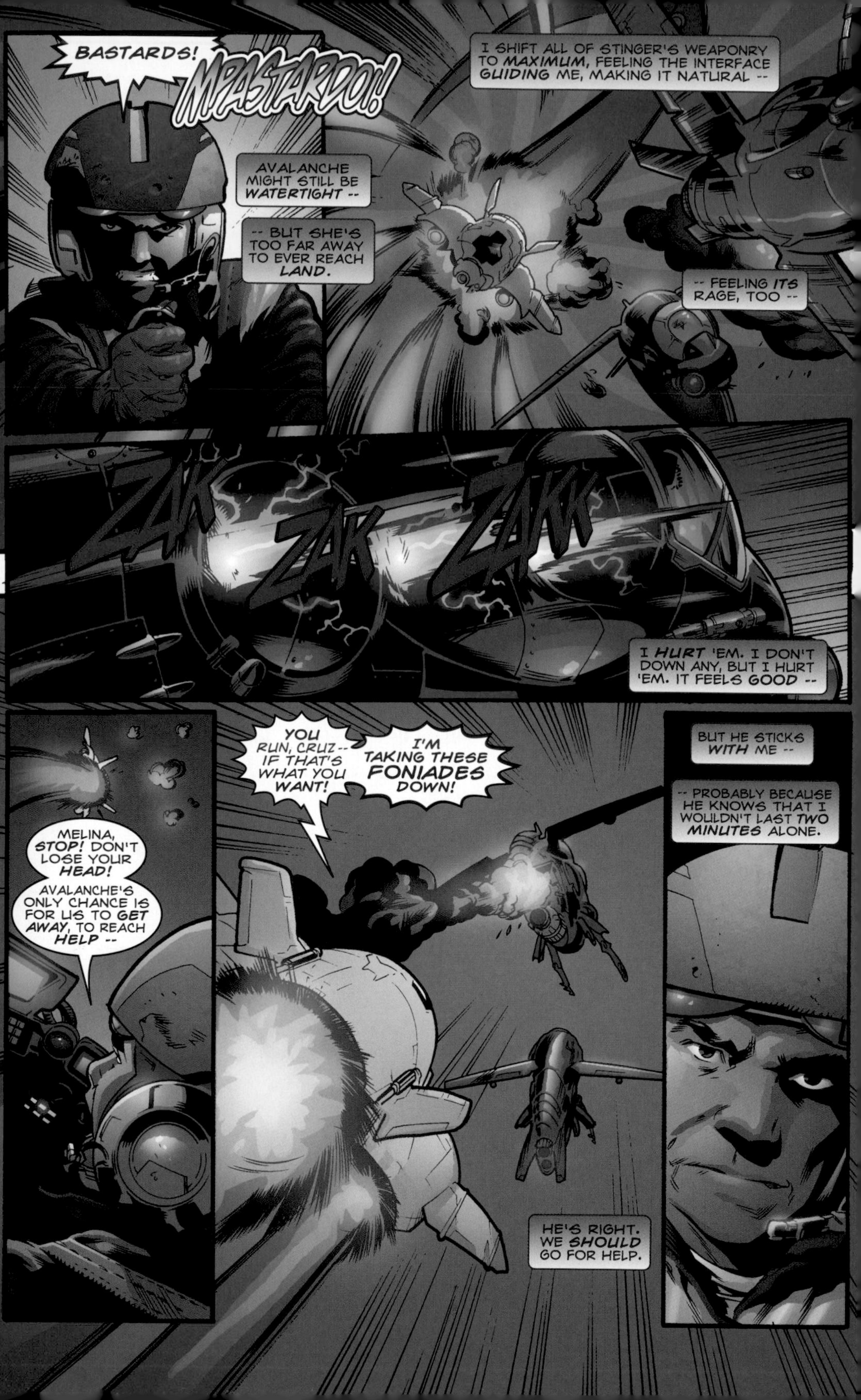
BASTARDS!
MPASTARDO!!
AVALANCHE MIGHT STILL BE WATERTIGHT --
-- BUT SHE'S TOO FAR AWAY TO EVER REACH LAND.
I SHIFT ALL OF STINGER'S WEAPONRY TO MAXIMUM, FEELING THE INTERFACE GUIDING ME, MAKING IT NATURAL --
-- FEELING ITS RAGE, TOO --
ZAK
ZAK
ZAKK
I HURT 'EM. I DON'T DOWN ANY, BUT I HURT 'EM. IT FEELS GOOD --
YOU RUN, CRUZ -- IF THAT'S WHAT YOU WANT!
I'M TAKING THESE FONIADES DOWN!
MELINA, STOP! DON'T LOSE YOUR HEAD!
AVALANCHE'S ONLY CHANCE IS FOR US TO GET AWAY, TO REACH HELP --
BUT HE STICKS WITH ME --
-- PROBABLY BECAUSE HE KNOWS THAT I WOULDN'T LAST TWO MINUTES ALONE.
HE'S RIGHT. WE SHOULD GO FOR HELP.

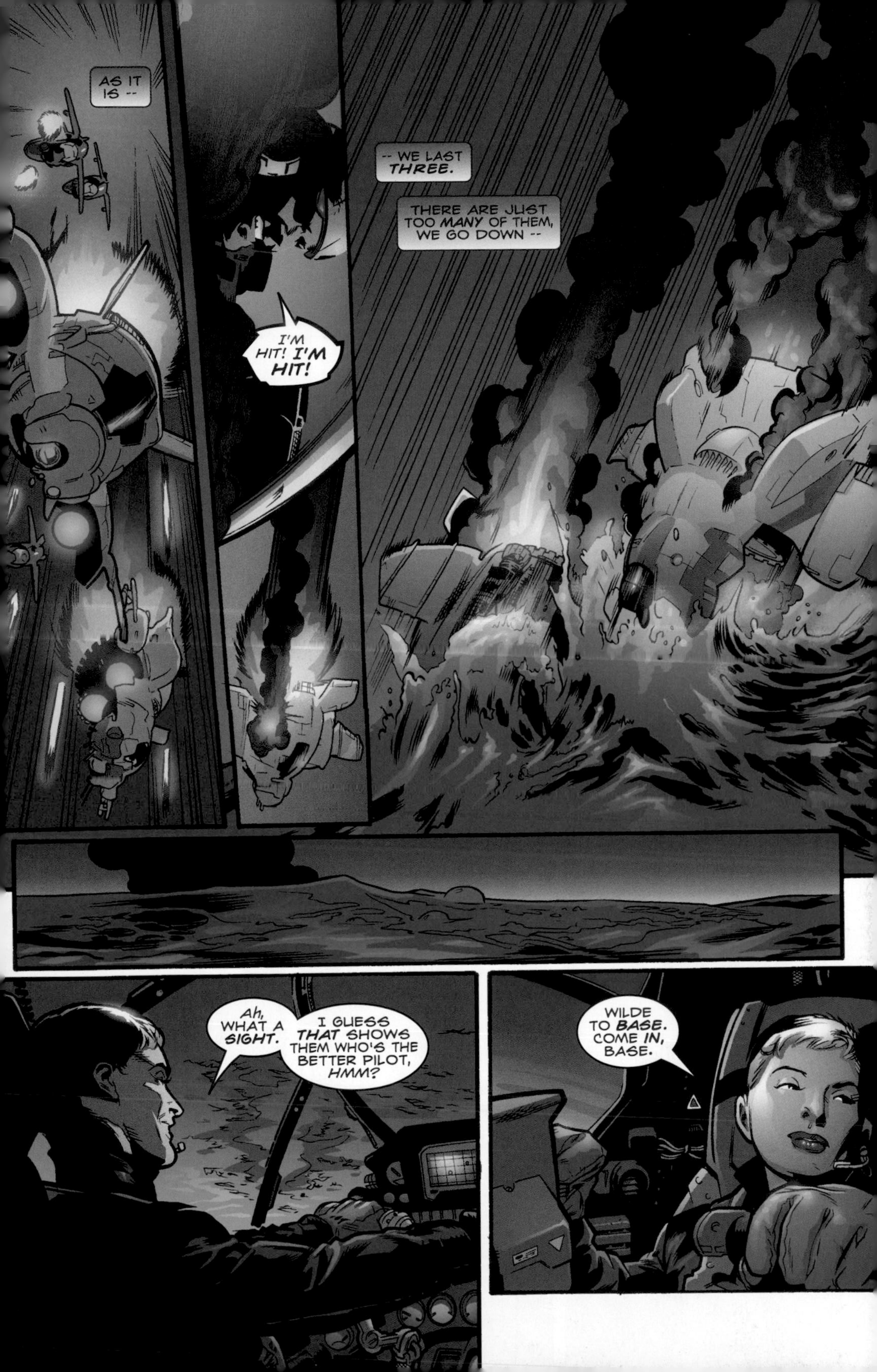
AS IT IS --
I'M HIT! I'M HIT!
-- WE LAST THREE.
THERE ARE JUST TOO MANY OF THEM, WE GO DOWN --
Ah, WHAT A SIGHT.
I GUESS THAT SHOWS THEM WHO'S THE BETTER PILOT, HMM?
WILDE TO BASE. COME IN, BASE.

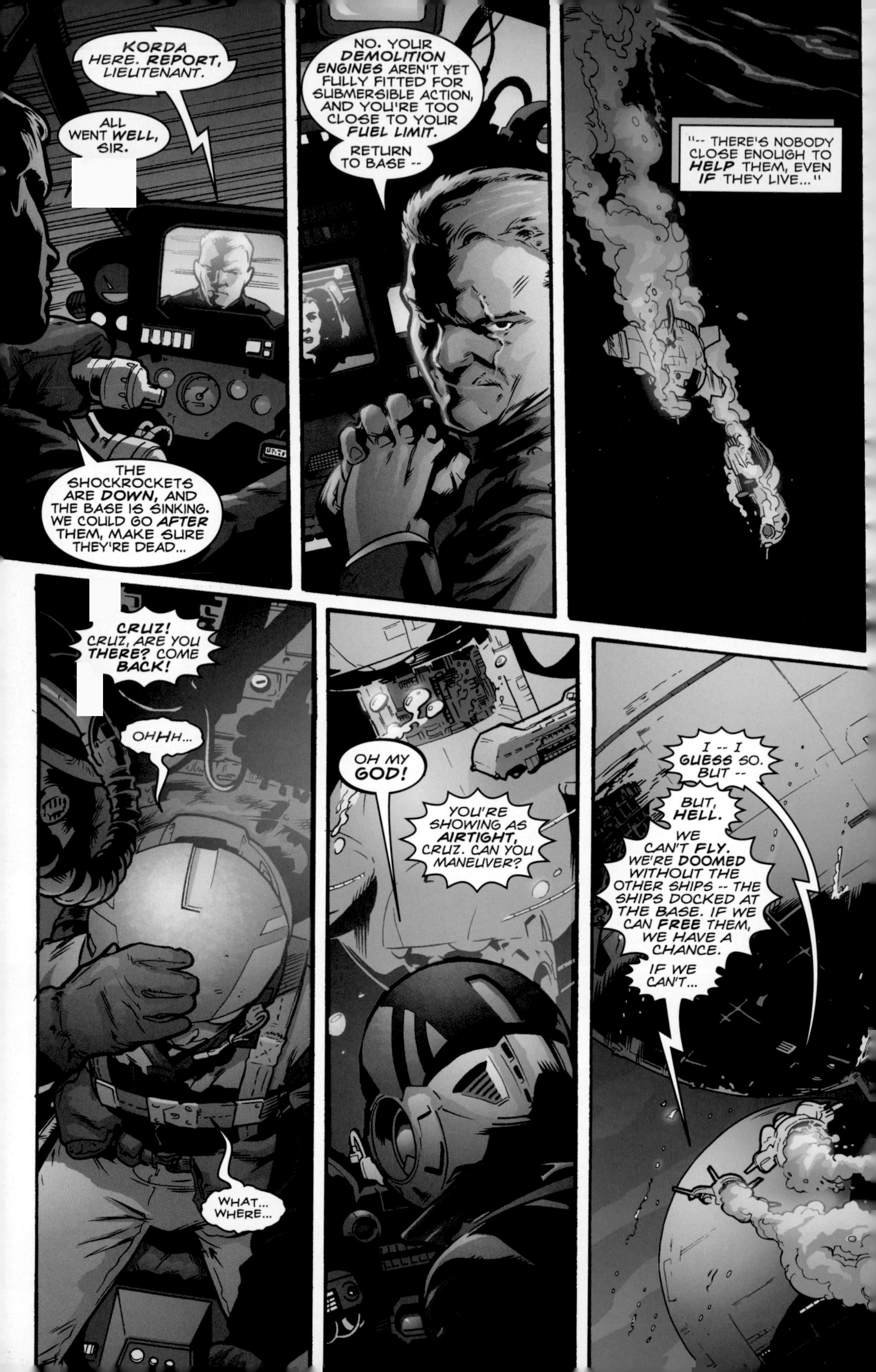

KORDA HERE. REPORT, LIEUTENANT.
ALL WENT WELL, SIR.
THE SHOCKROCKETS ARE DOWN, AND THE BASE IS SINKING. WE COULD GO AFTER THEM, MAKE SURE THEY'RE DEAD...
NO. YOUR DEMOLITION ENGINES AREN'T YET FULLY FITTED FOR SUBMERSIBLE ACTION, AND YOU'RE TOO CLOSE TO YOUR FUEL LIMIT.
RETURN TO BASE --
"-- THERE'S NOBODY CLOSE ENOUGH TO HELP THEM, EVEN IF THEY LIVE..."
CRUZ! CRUZ, ARE YOU THERE? COME BACK!
OHHH...
WHAT... WHERE...
OH MY GOD!
YOU'RE SHOWING AS AIRTIGHT, CRUZ. CAN YOU MANEUVER?
I -- I GUESS SO. BUT --
BUT, HELL.
WE CAN'T FLY. WE'RE DOOMED WITHOUT THE OTHER SHIPS -- THE SHIPS DOCKED AT THE BASE. IF WE CAN FREE THEM, WE HAVE A CHANCE.
IF WE CAN'T...

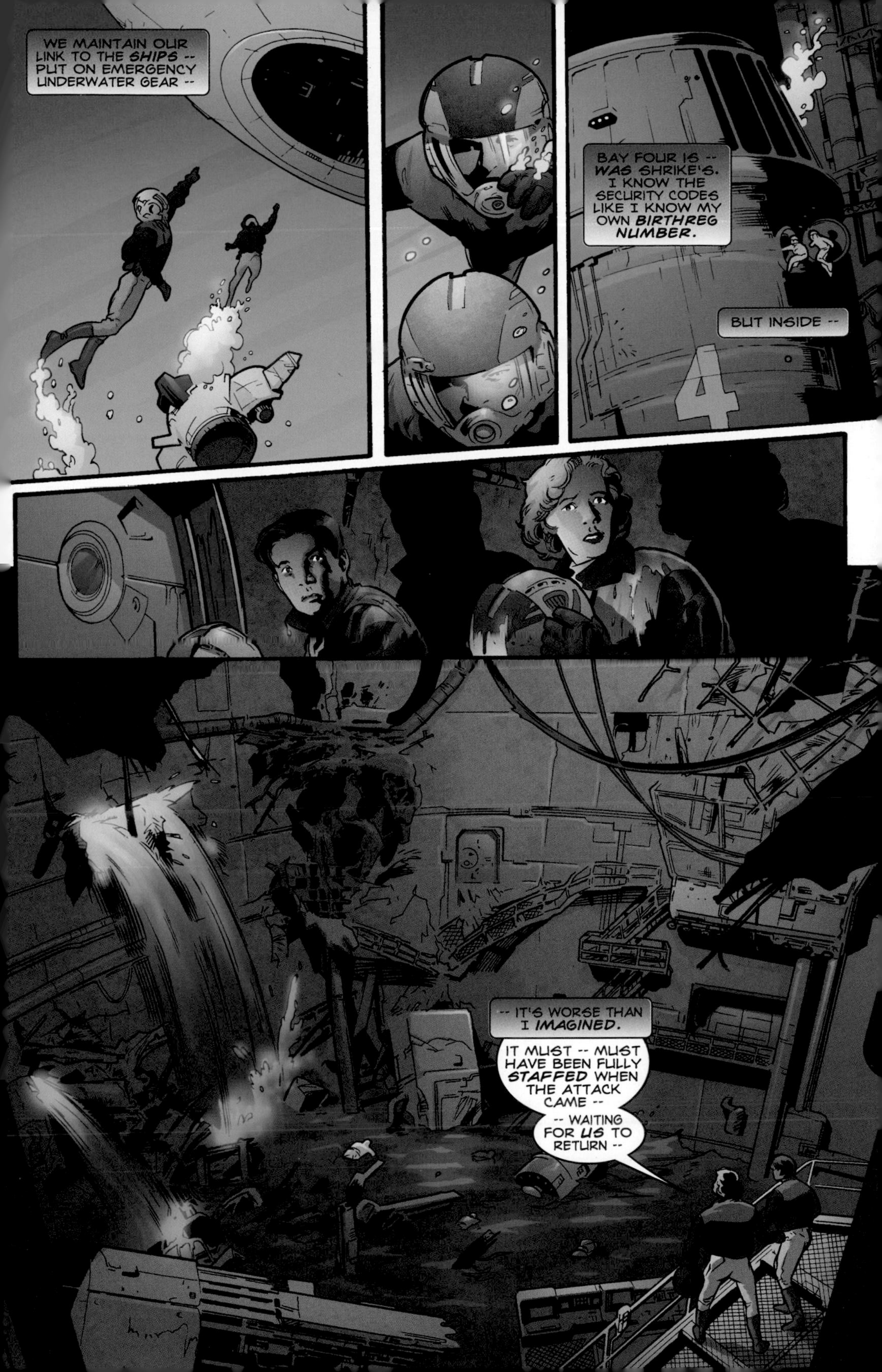
WE MAINTAIN OUR LINK TO THE SHIPS -- PUT ON EMERGENCY UNDERWATER GEAR --
BAY FOUR IS -- WAS SHRIKE'S. I KNOW THE SECURITY CODES LIKE I KNOW MY OWN BIRTHREG NUMBER.
BUT INSIDE --
4
-- IT'S WORSE THAN I IMAGINED.
IT MUST -- MUST HAVE BEEN FULLY STAFFED WHEN THE ATTACK CAME --
-- WAITING FOR US TO RETURN --

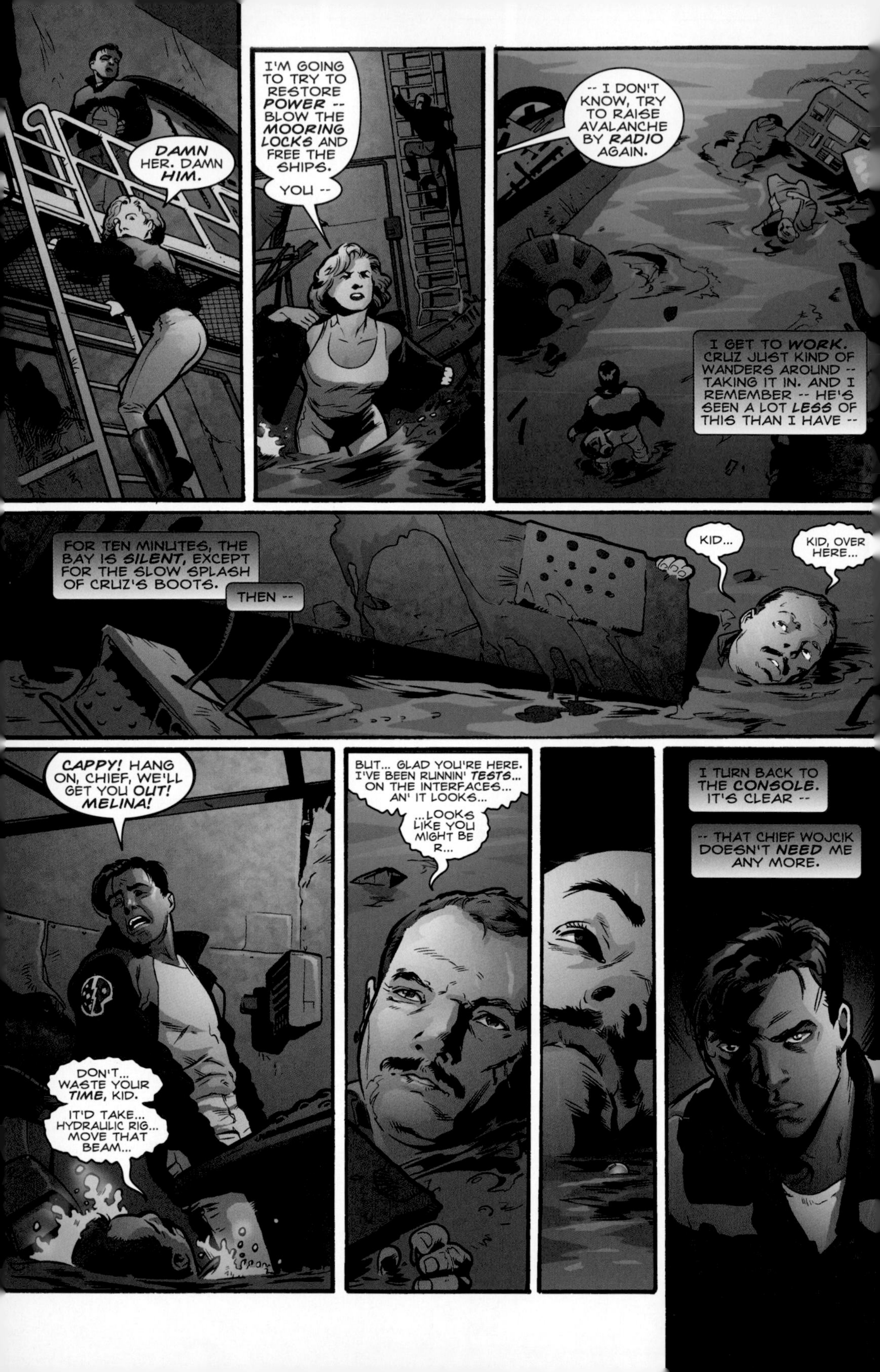
DAMN HER. DAMN HIM.
I'M GOING TO TRY TO RESTORE POWER -- BLOW THE MOORING LOCKS AND FREE THE SHIPS.
YOU --
-- I DON'T KNOW, TRY TO RAISE AVALANCHE BY RADIO AGAIN.
I GET TO WORK. CRUZ JUST KIND OF WANDERS AROUND -- TAKING IT IN. AND I REMEMBER -- HE'S SEEN A LOT LESS OF THIS THAN I HAVE --
FOR TEN MINUTES, THE BAY IS SILENT, EXCEPT FOR THE SLOW SPLASH OF CRUZ'S BOOTS.
THEN --
KID...
KID, OVER HERE...
CAPPY! HANG ON, CHIEF, WE'LL GET YOU OUT! MELINA!
DON'T... WASTE YOUR TIME, KID.
IT'D TAKE... HYDRAULIC RIG... MOVE THAT BEAM...
BUT... GLAD YOU'RE HERE. I'VE BEEN RUNNIN' TESTS... ON THE INTERFACES... AN' IT LOOKS...
...LOOKS LIKE YOU MIGHT BE R...
I TURN BACK TO THE CONSOLE. IT'S CLEAR --
-- THAT CHIEF WOJCIK DOESN'T NEED ME ANY MORE.

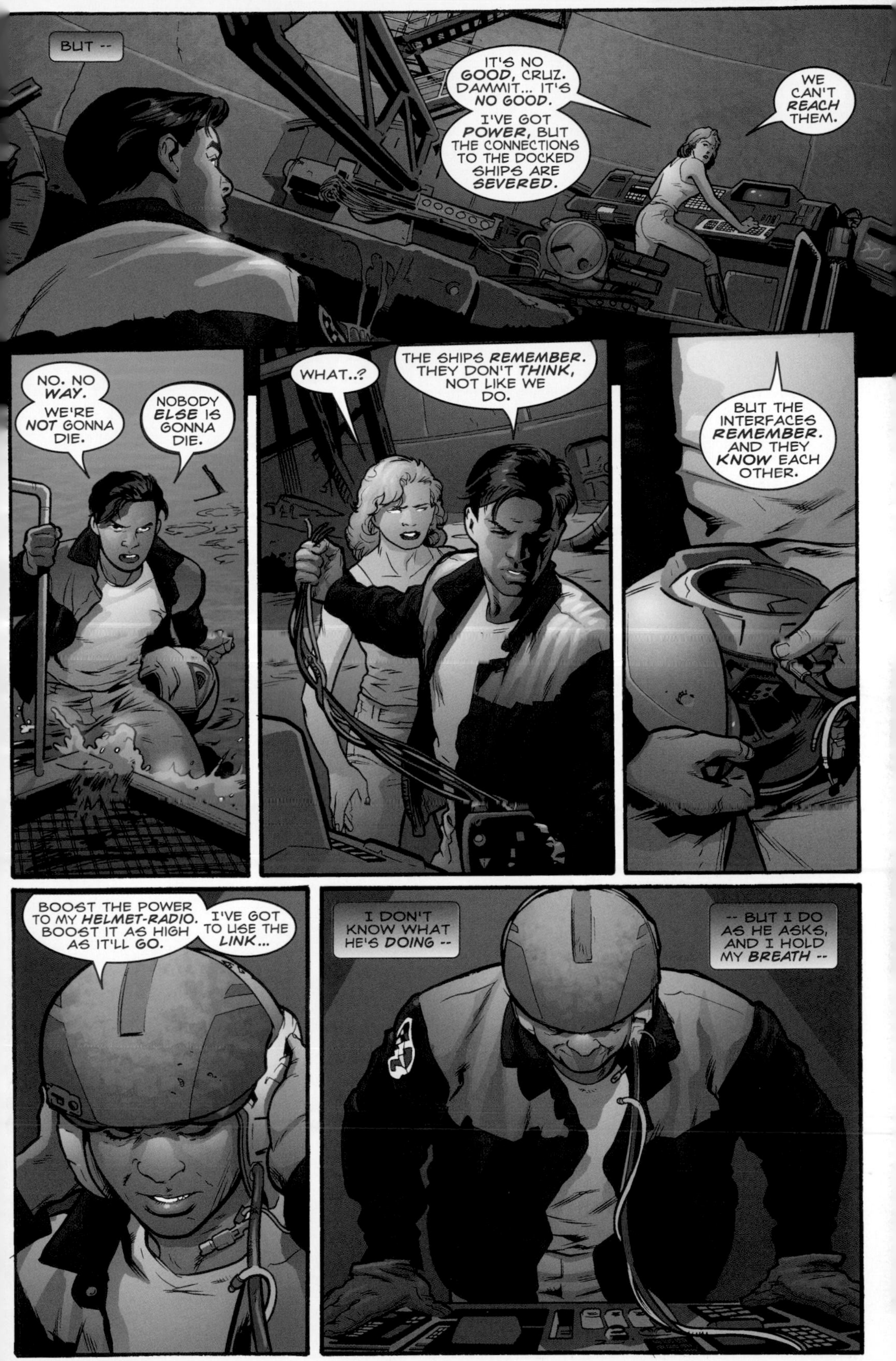
BUT --
IT'S NO GOOD, CRUZ. DAMMIT... IT'S NO GOOD.
I'VE GOT POWER, BUT THE CONNECTIONS TO THE DOCKED SHIPS ARE SEVERED.
WE CAN'T REACH THEM.
NO. NO WAY.
WE'RE NOT GONNA DIE.
NOBODY ELSE IS GONNA DIE.
WHAT..?
THE SHIPS REMEMBER. THEY DON'T THINK, NOT LIKE WE DO.
BUT THE INTERFACES REMEMBER. AND THEY KNOW EACH OTHER.
BOOST THE POWER TO MY HELMET-RADIO. BOOST IT AS HIGH AS IT'LL GO.
I'VE GOT TO USE THE LINK...
I DON'T KNOW WHAT HE'S DOING --
-- BUT I DO AS HE ASKS, AND I HOLD MY BREATH --

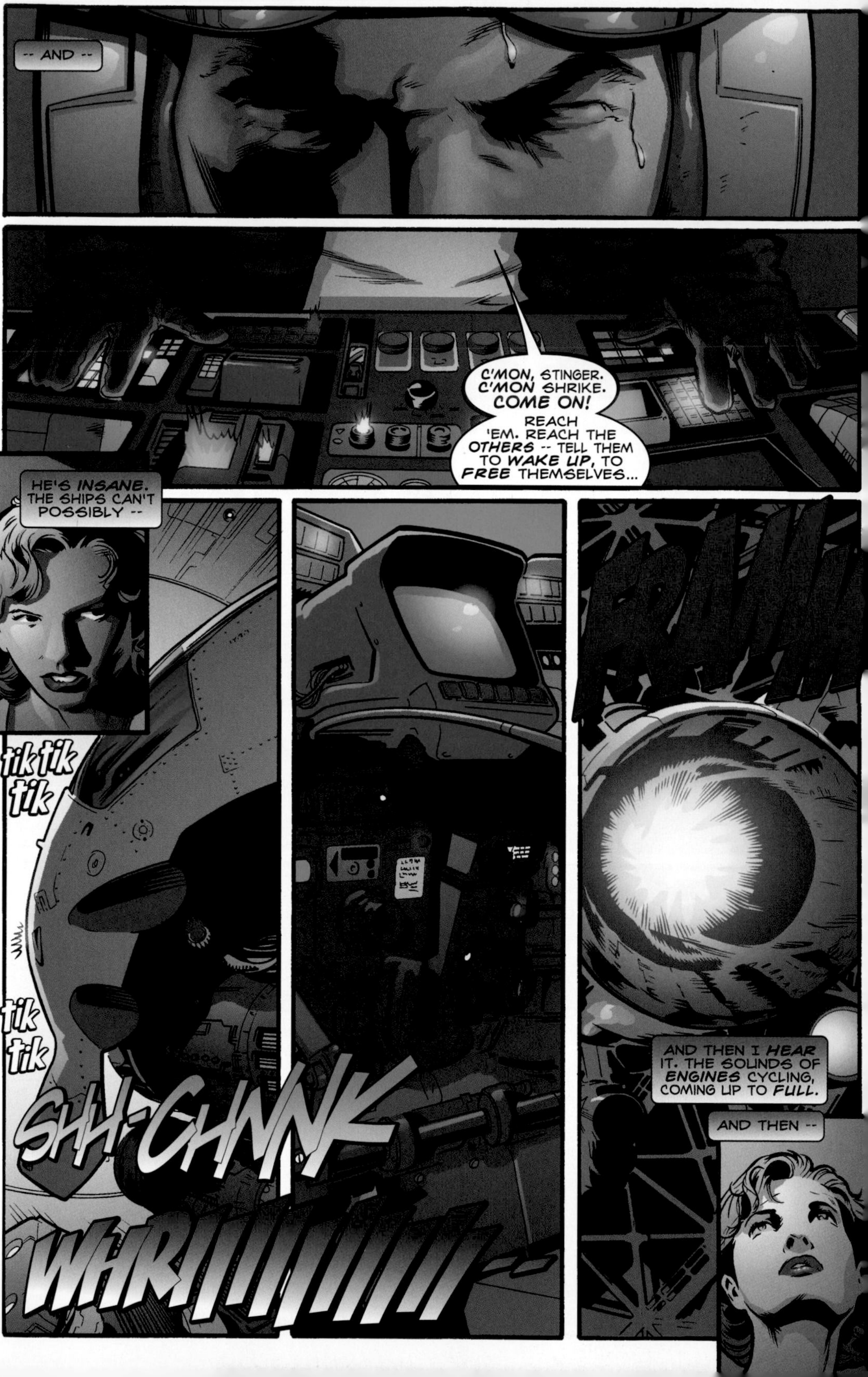
-- AND --
C'MON, STINGER. C'MON SHRIKE. COME ON!
REACH 'EM. REACH THE OTHERS -- TELL THEM TO WAKE UP, TO FREE THEMSELVES...
HE'S INSANE. THE SHIPS CAN'T POSSIBLY --
tik tik tik
tik tik
SHH-CHNNK
WHRIIIIIIIII--
AND THEN I HEAR IT. THE SOUNDS OF ENGINES CYCLING, COMING UP TO FULL.
AND THEN --

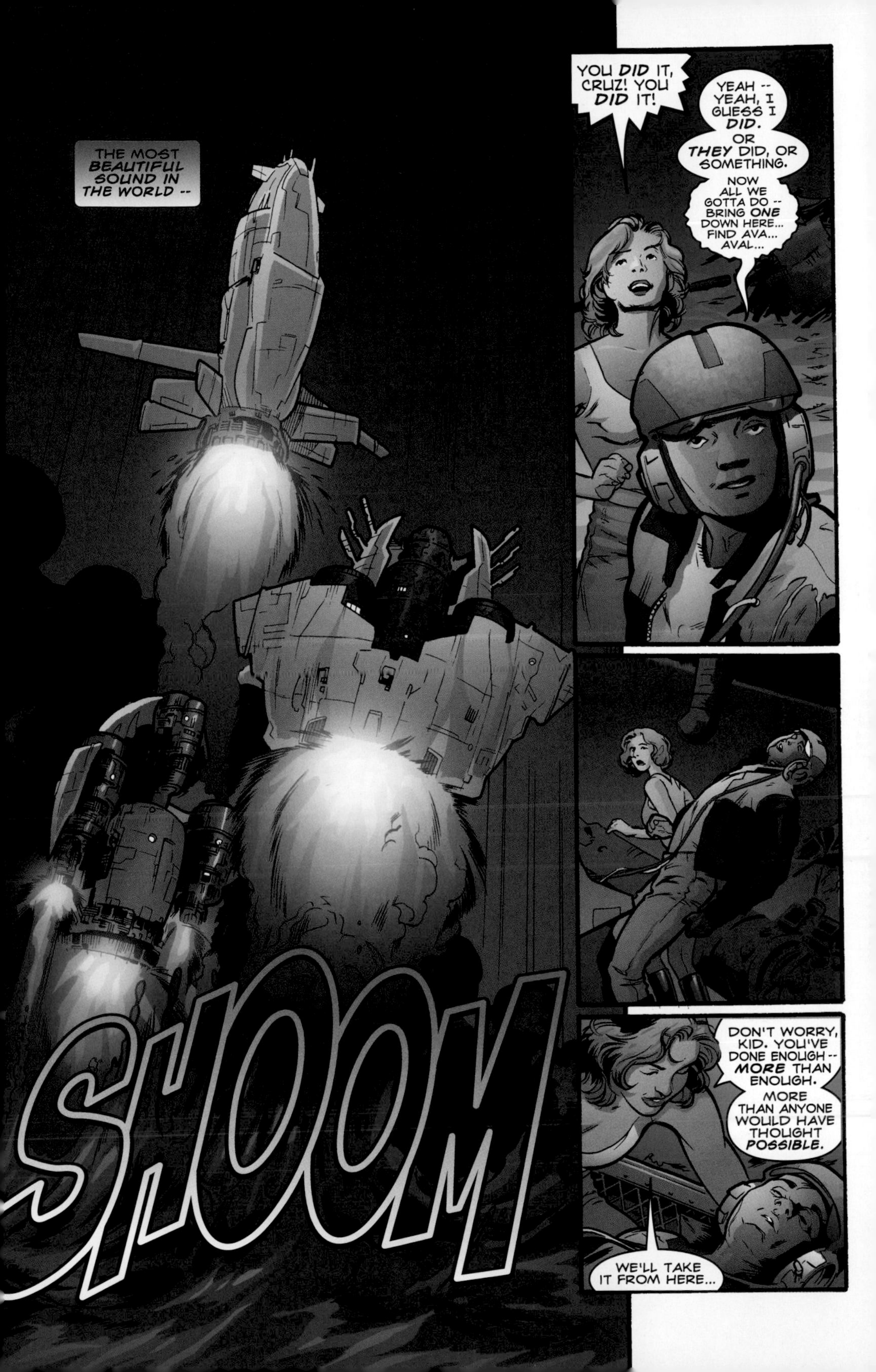

THE MOST BEAUTIFUL SOUND IN THE WORLD --
SHOOOM
YOU DID IT, CRUZ! YOU DID IT!
YEAH -- YEAH, I GUESS I DID. OR THEY DID, OR SOMETHING.
NOW ALL WE GOTTA DO -- BRING ONE DOWN HERE... FIND AVA... AVAL...
DON'T WORRY, KID. YOU'VE DONE ENOUGH -- MORE THAN ENOUGH.
MORE THAN ANYONE WOULD HAVE THOUGHT POSSIBLE.
WE'LL TAKE IT FROM HERE...

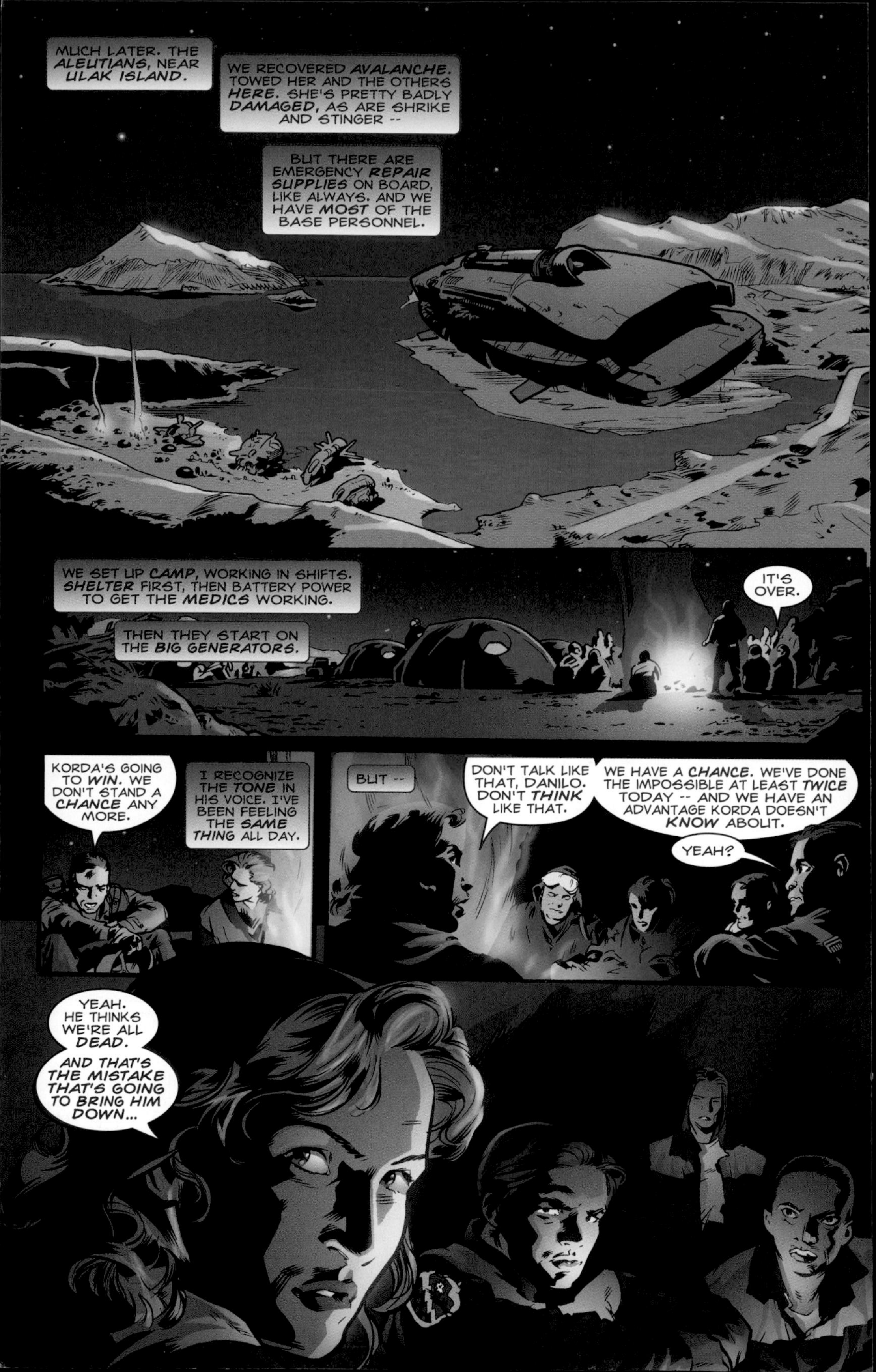
MUCH LATER. THE ALEUTIANS, NEAR ULAK ISLAND.
WE RECOVERED AVALANCHE. TOWED HER AND THE OTHERS HERE. SHE'S PRETTY BADLY DAMAGED, AS ARE SHRIKE AND STINGER --
BUT THERE ARE EMERGENCY REPAIR SUPPLIES ON BOARD, LIKE ALWAYS. AND WE HAVE MOST OF THE BASE PERSONNEL.
WE SET UP CAMP, WORKING IN SHIFTS. SHELTER FIRST, THEN BATTERY POWER TO GET THE MEDICS WORKING.
THEN THEY START ON THE BIG GENERATORS.
IT'S OVER.
KORDA'S GOING TO WIN. WE DON'T STAND A CHANCE ANY MORE.
I RECOGNIZE THE TONE IN HIS VOICE. I'VE BEEN FEELING THE SAME THING ALL DAY.
BUT --
DON'T TALK LIKE THAT, DANILO. DON'T THINK LIKE THAT.
WE HAVE A CHANCE. WE'VE DONE THE IMPOSSIBLE AT LEAST TWICE TODAY -- AND WE HAVE AN ADVANTAGE KORDA DOESN'T KNOW ABOUT.
YEAH?
YEAH. HE THINKS WE'RE ALL DEAD.
AND THAT'S THE MISTAKE THAT'S GOING TO BRING HIM DOWN...

CHAPTER SIX

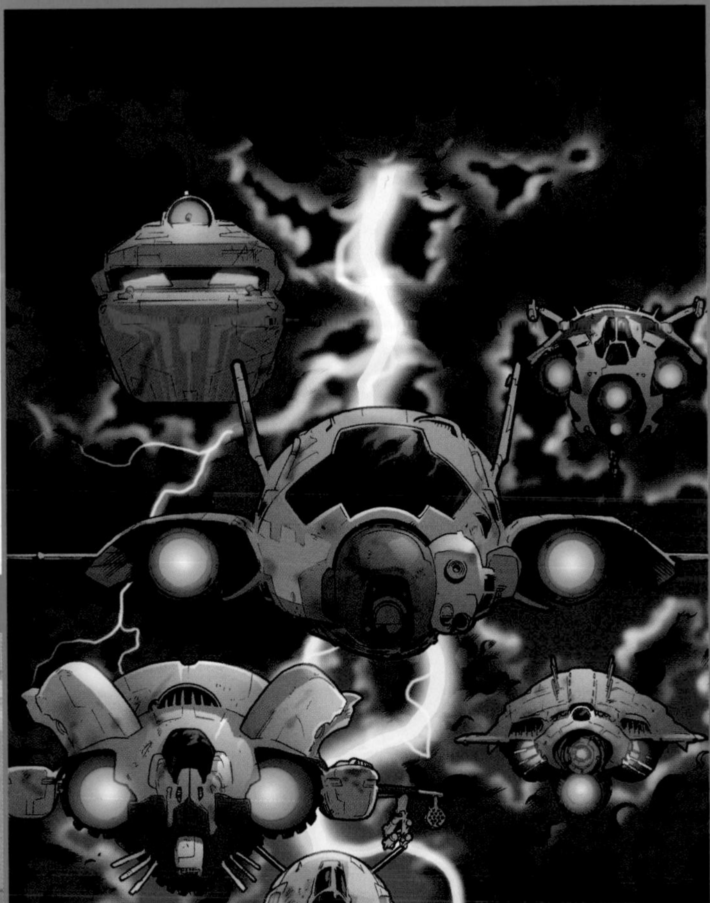

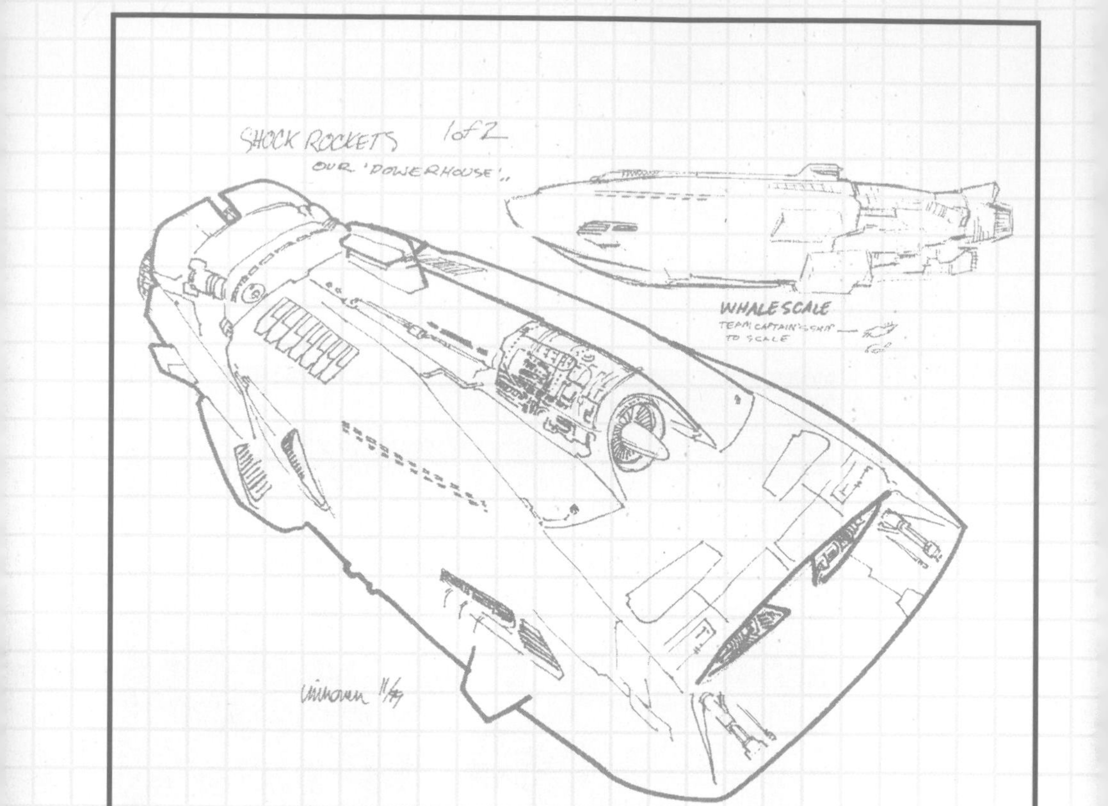
SHOCK ROCKETS 1 of 2
OUR 'POWERHOUSE'
WHALE SCALE
TEAM CAPTAIN'S SHIP
TO SCALE

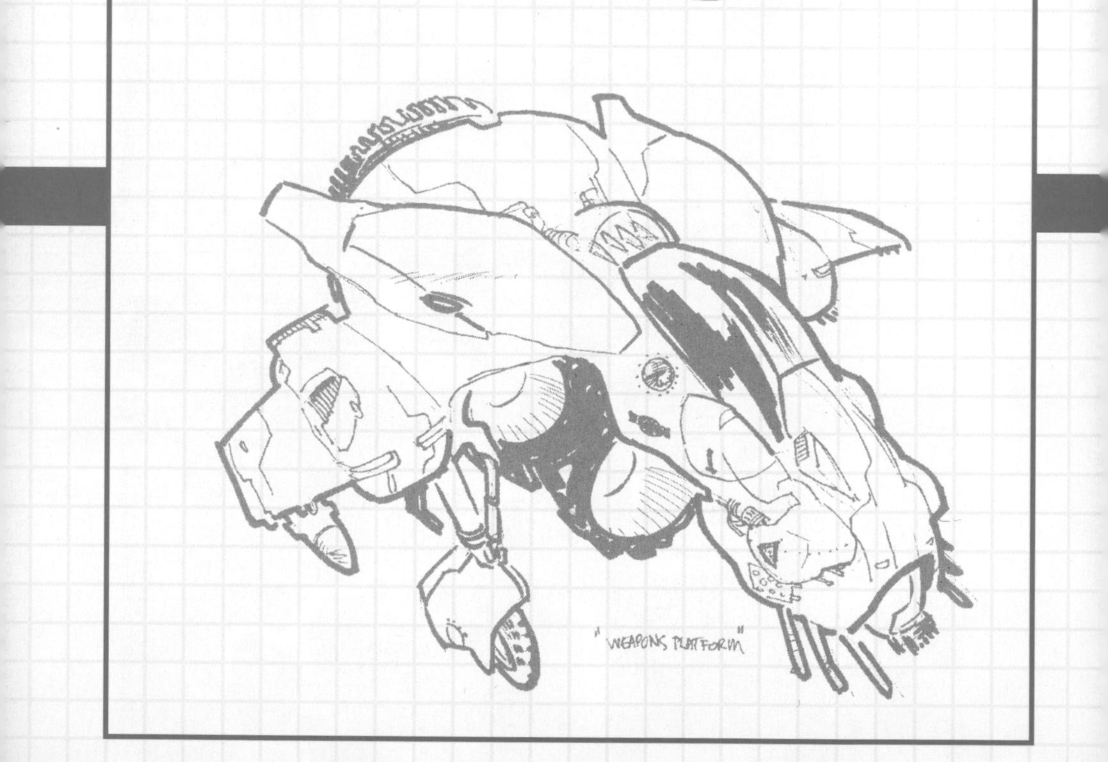
"WEAPONS PLATFORM"

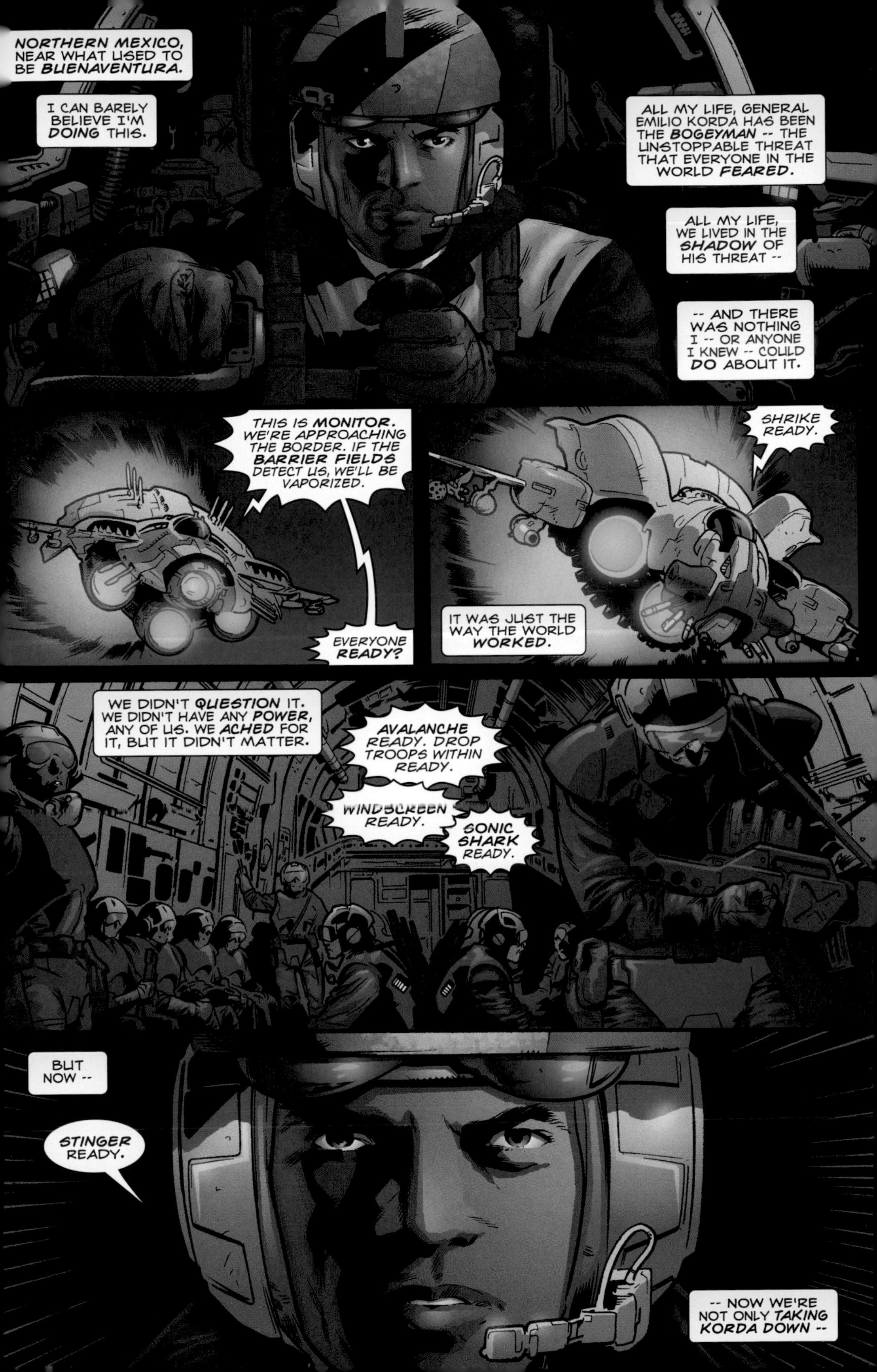
NORTHERN MEXICO, NEAR WHAT USED TO BE BUENAVENTURA.
I CAN BARELY BELIEVE I'M DOING THIS.
ALL MY LIFE, GENERAL EMILIO KORDA HAS BEEN THE BOGEYMAN -- THE UNSTOPPABLE THREAT THAT EVERYONE IN THE WORLD FEARED.
ALL MY LIFE, WE LIVED IN THE SHADOW OF HIS THREAT --
-- AND THERE WAS NOTHING I -- OR ANYONE I KNEW -- COULD DO ABOUT IT.
THIS IS MONITOR. WE'RE APPROACHING THE BORDER. IF THE BARRIER FIELDS DETECT US, WE'LL BE VAPORIZED.
EVERYONE READY?
SHRIKE READY.
IT WAS JUST THE WAY THE WORLD WORKED.
WE DIDN'T QUESTION IT. WE DIDN'T HAVE ANY POWER, ANY OF US. WE ACHED FOR IT, BUT IT DIDN'T MATTER.
AVALANCHE READY. DROP TROOPS WITHIN READY.
WINDSCREEN READY.
SONIC SHARK READY.
BUT NOW --
STINGER READY.
-- NOW WE'RE NOT ONLY TAKING KORDA DOWN --

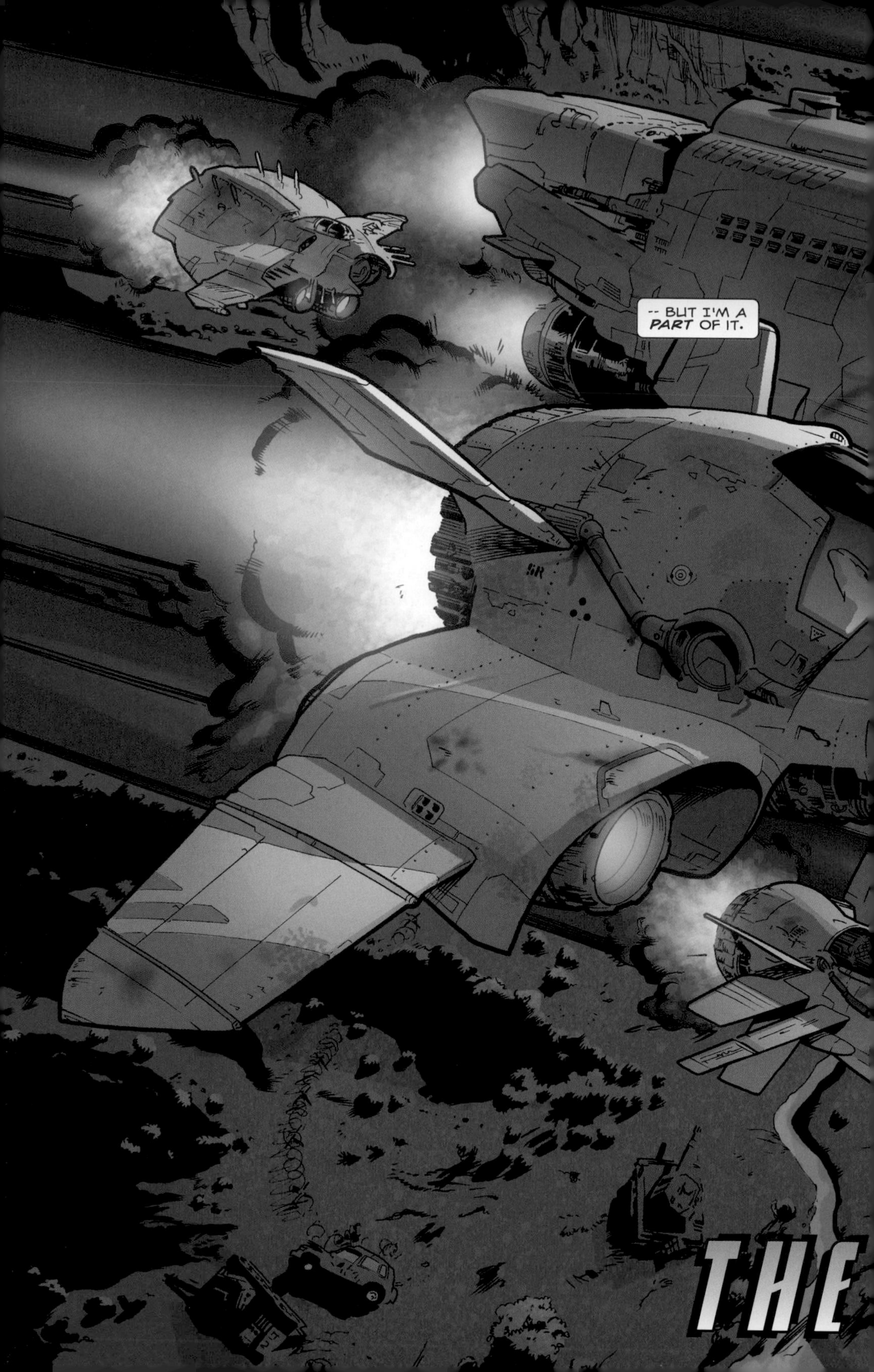
-- BUT I'M A PART OF IT.
THE

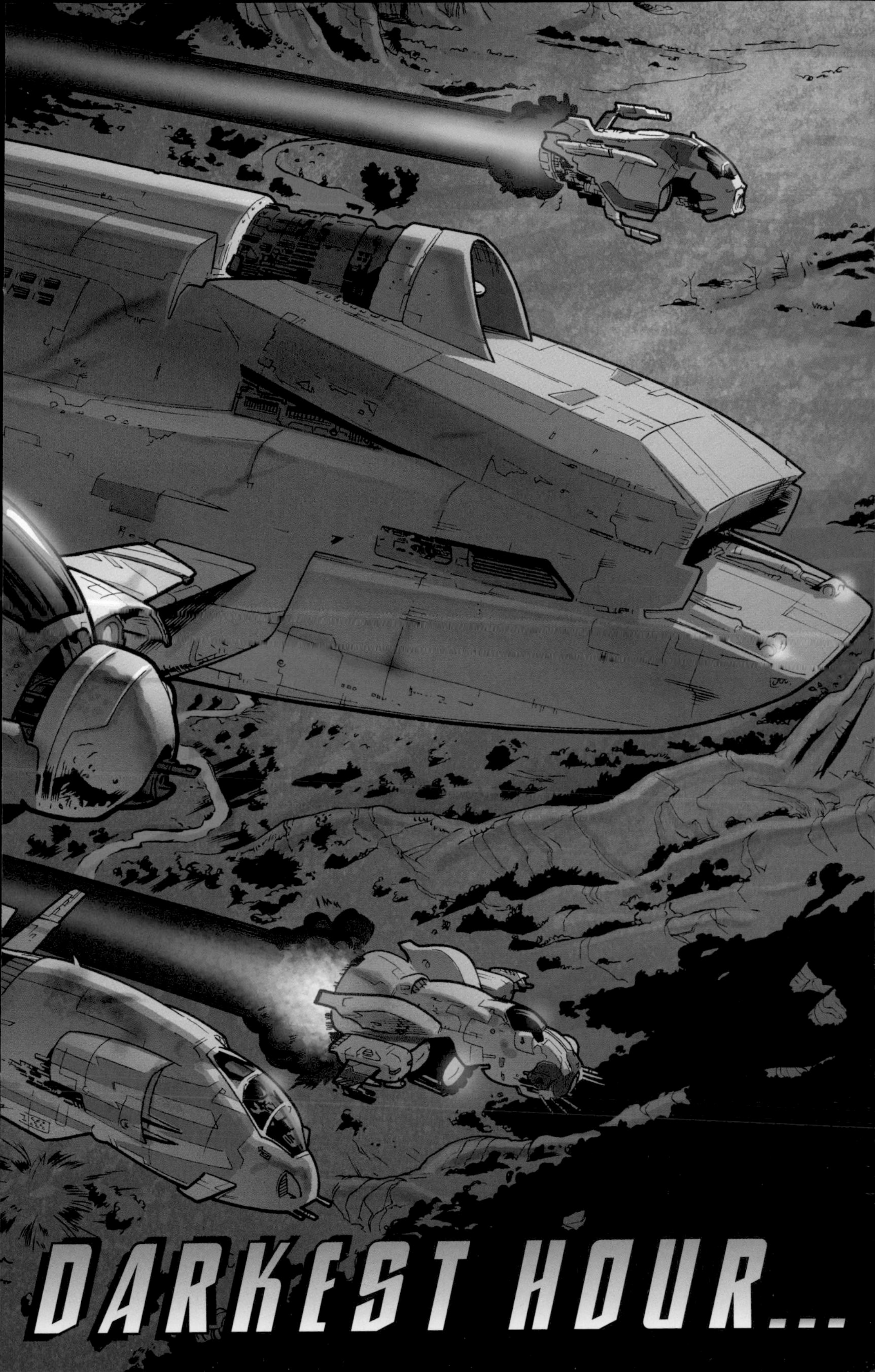
DARKEST HOUR...

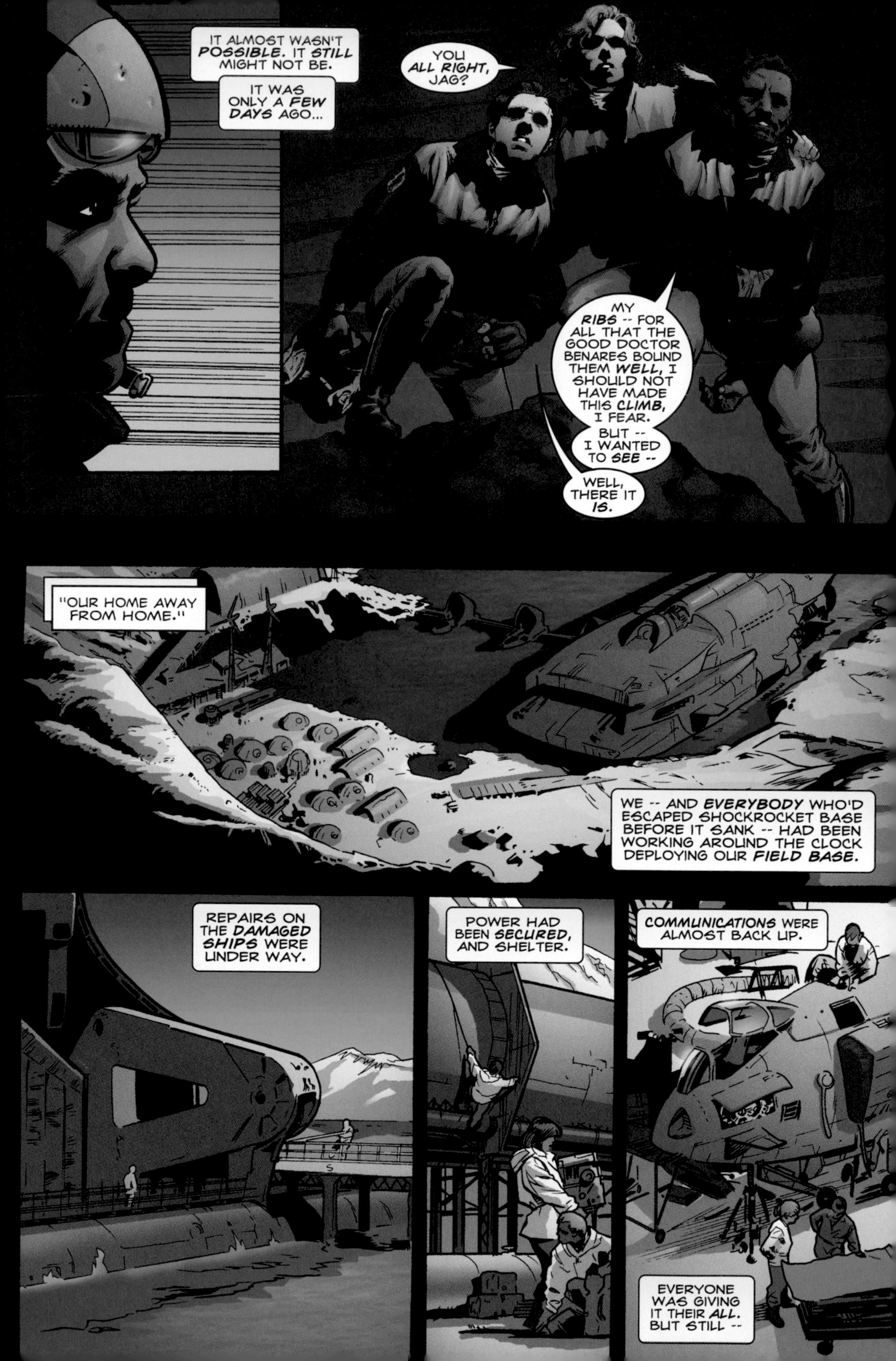

IT ALMOST WASN'T POSSIBLE. IT STILL MIGHT NOT BE.
IT WAS ONLY A FEW DAYS AGO...
YOU ALL RIGHT, JAG?
MY RIBS -- FOR ALL THAT THE GOOD DOCTOR BENARES BOUND THEM WELL, I SHOULD NOT HAVE MADE THIS CLIMB, I FEAR.
BUT -- I WANTED TO SEE --
WELL, THERE IT IS.
"OUR HOME AWAY FROM HOME."
WE -- AND EVERYBODY WHO'D ESCAPED SHOCKROCKET BASE BEFORE IT SANK -- HAD BEEN WORKING AROUND THE CLOCK DEPLOYING OUR FIELD BASE.
REPAIRS ON THE DAMAGED SHIPS WERE UNDER WAY.
POWER HAD BEEN SECURED, AND SHELTER.
COMMUNICATIONS WERE ALMOST BACK UP.
EVERYONE WAS GIVING IT THEIR ALL. BUT STILL --

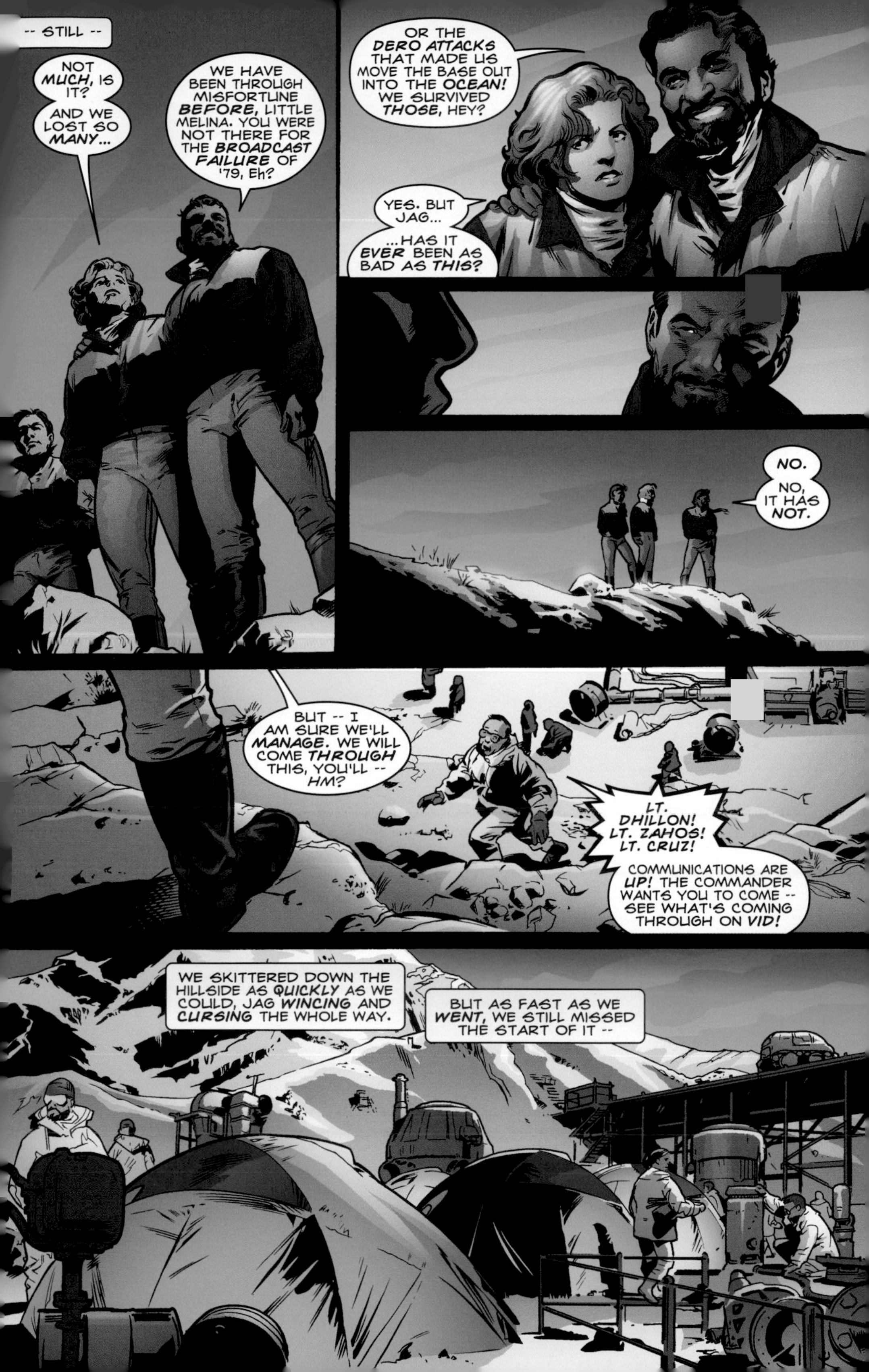
-- STILL --
NOT MUCH, IS IT?
AND WE LOST SO MANY...
WE HAVE BEEN THROUGH MISFORTUNE BEFORE, LITTLE MELINA. YOU WERE NOT THERE FOR THE BROADCAST FAILURE OF '79, EH?
OR THE DERO ATTACKS THAT MADE US MOVE THE BASE OUT INTO THE OCEAN! WE SURVIVED THOSE, HEY?
YES. BUT JAG...
...HAS IT EVER BEEN AS BAD AS THIS?
NO.
NO, IT HAS NOT.
BUT -- I AM SURE WE'LL MANAGE. WE WILL COME THROUGH THIS, YOU'LL -- HM?
LT. DHILLON! LT. ZAHOS! LT. CRUZ!
COMMUNICATIONS ARE UP! THE COMMANDER WANTS YOU TO COME -- SEE WHAT'S COMING THROUGH ON VID!
WE SKITTERED DOWN THE HILLSIDE AS QUICKLY AS WE COULD, JAG WINCING AND CURSING THE WHOLE WAY.
BUT AS FAST AS WE WENT, WE STILL MISSED THE START OF IT --

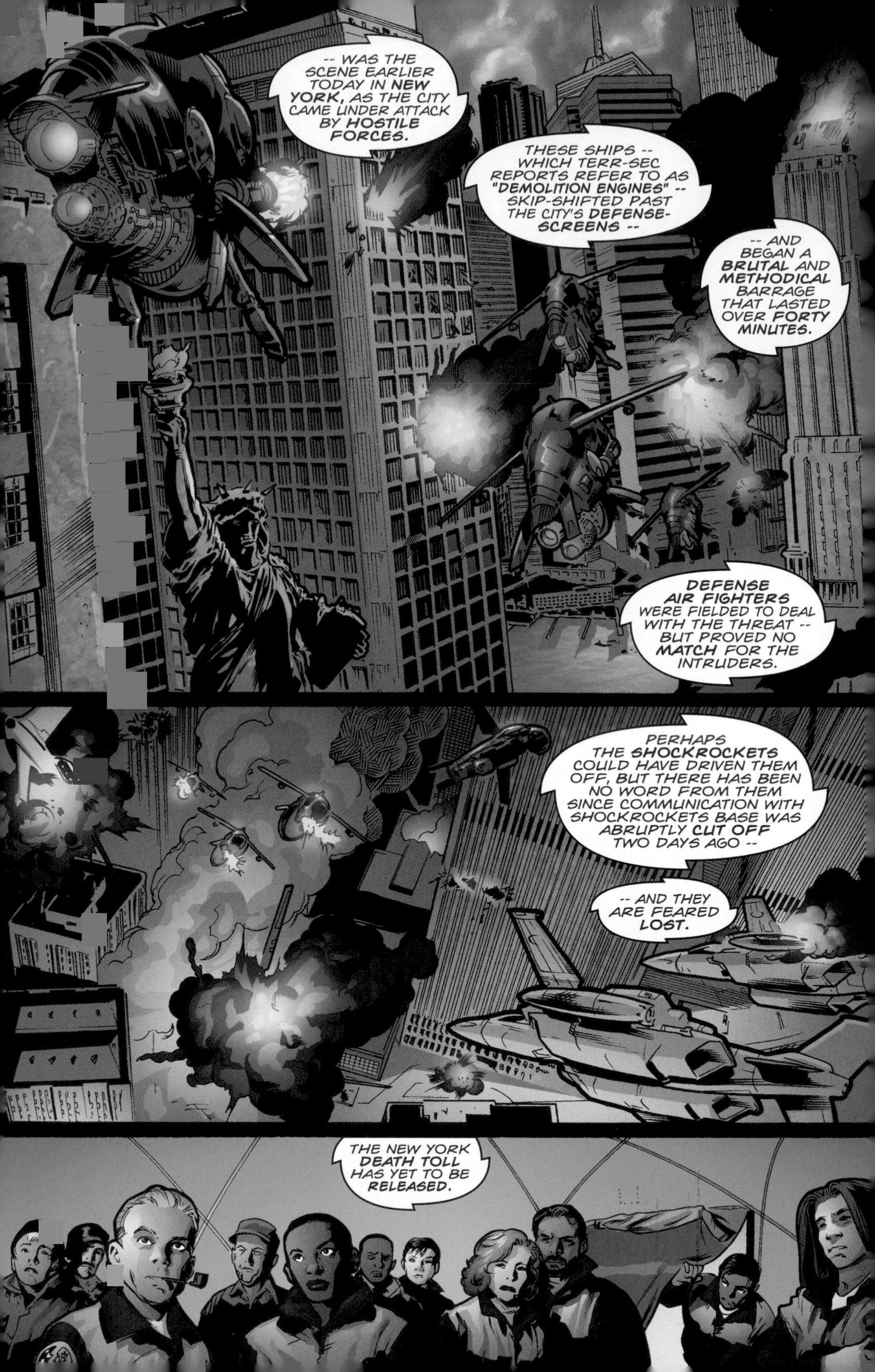
-- WAS THE SCENE EARLIER TODAY IN NEW YORK, AS THE CITY CAME UNDER ATTACK BY HOSTILE FORCES.
THESE SHIPS -- WHICH TERR-SEC REPORTS REFER TO AS "DEMOLITION ENGINES" -- SKIP-SHIFTED PAST THE CITY'S DEFENSE-SCREENS --
-- AND BEGAN A BRUTAL AND METHODICAL BARRAGE THAT LASTED OVER FORTY MINUTES.
DEFENSE AIR FIGHTERS WERE FIELDED TO DEAL WITH THE THREAT -- BUT PROVED NO MATCH FOR THE INTRUDERS.
PERHAPS THE SHOCKROCKETS COULD HAVE DRIVEN THEM OFF, BUT THERE HAS BEEN NO WORD FROM THEM SINCE COMMUNICATION WITH SHOCKROCKETS BASE WAS ABRUPTLY CUT OFF TWO DAYS AGO --
-- AND THEY ARE FEARED LOST.
THE NEW YORK DEATH TOLL HAS YET TO BE RELEASED.

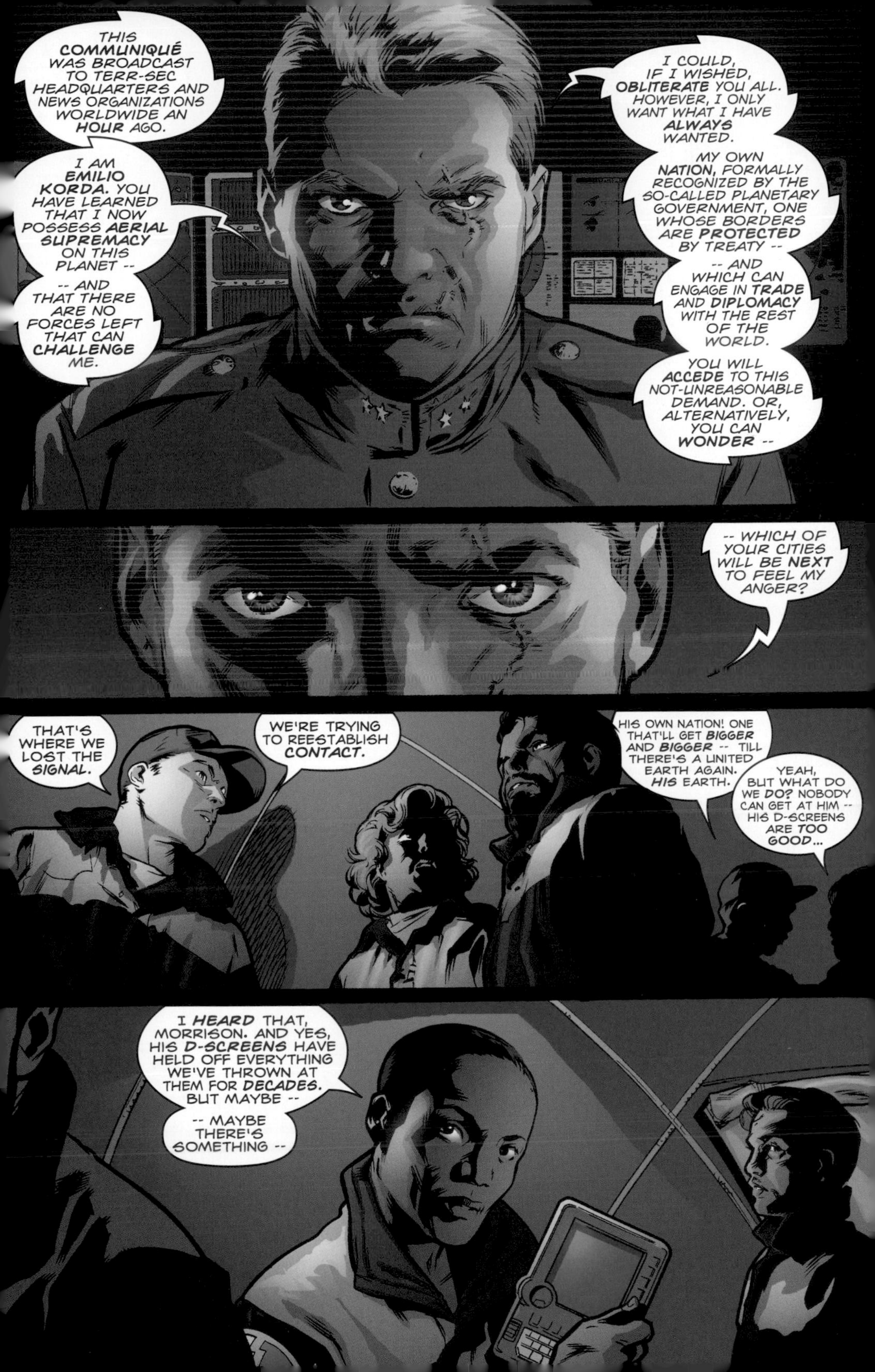

THIS COMMUNIQUÉ WAS BROADCAST TO TERR-SEC HEADQUARTERS AND NEWS ORGANIZATIONS WORLDWIDE AN HOUR AGO.
I AM EMILIO KORDA. YOU HAVE LEARNED THAT I NOW POSSESS AERIAL SUPREMACY ON THIS PLANET --
-- AND THAT THERE ARE NO FORCES LEFT THAT CAN CHALLENGE ME.
I COULD, IF I WISHED, OBLITERATE YOU ALL. HOWEVER, I ONLY WANT WHAT I HAVE ALWAYS WANTED.
MY OWN NATION, FORMALLY RECOGNIZED BY THE SO-CALLED PLANETARY GOVERNMENT, ONE WHOSE BORDERS ARE PROTECTED BY TREATY --
-- AND WHICH CAN ENGAGE IN TRADE AND DIPLOMACY WITH THE REST OF THE WORLD.
YOU WILL ACCEDE TO THIS NOT-UNREASONABLE DEMAND. OR, ALTERNATIVELY, YOU CAN WONDER --
-- WHICH OF YOUR CITIES WILL BE NEXT TO FEEL MY ANGER?
THAT'S WHERE WE LOST THE SIGNAL.
WE'RE TRYING TO REESTABLISH CONTACT.
HIS OWN NATION! ONE THAT'LL GET BIGGER AND BIGGER -- TILL THERE'S A UNITED EARTH AGAIN. HIS EARTH.
YEAH, BUT WHAT DO WE DO? NOBODY CAN GET AT HIM -- HIS D-SCREENS ARE TOO GOOD...
I HEARD THAT, MORRISON. AND YES, HIS D-SCREENS HAVE HELD OFF EVERYTHING WE'VE THROWN AT THEM FOR DECADES. BUT MAYBE --
-- MAYBE THERE'S SOMETHING --

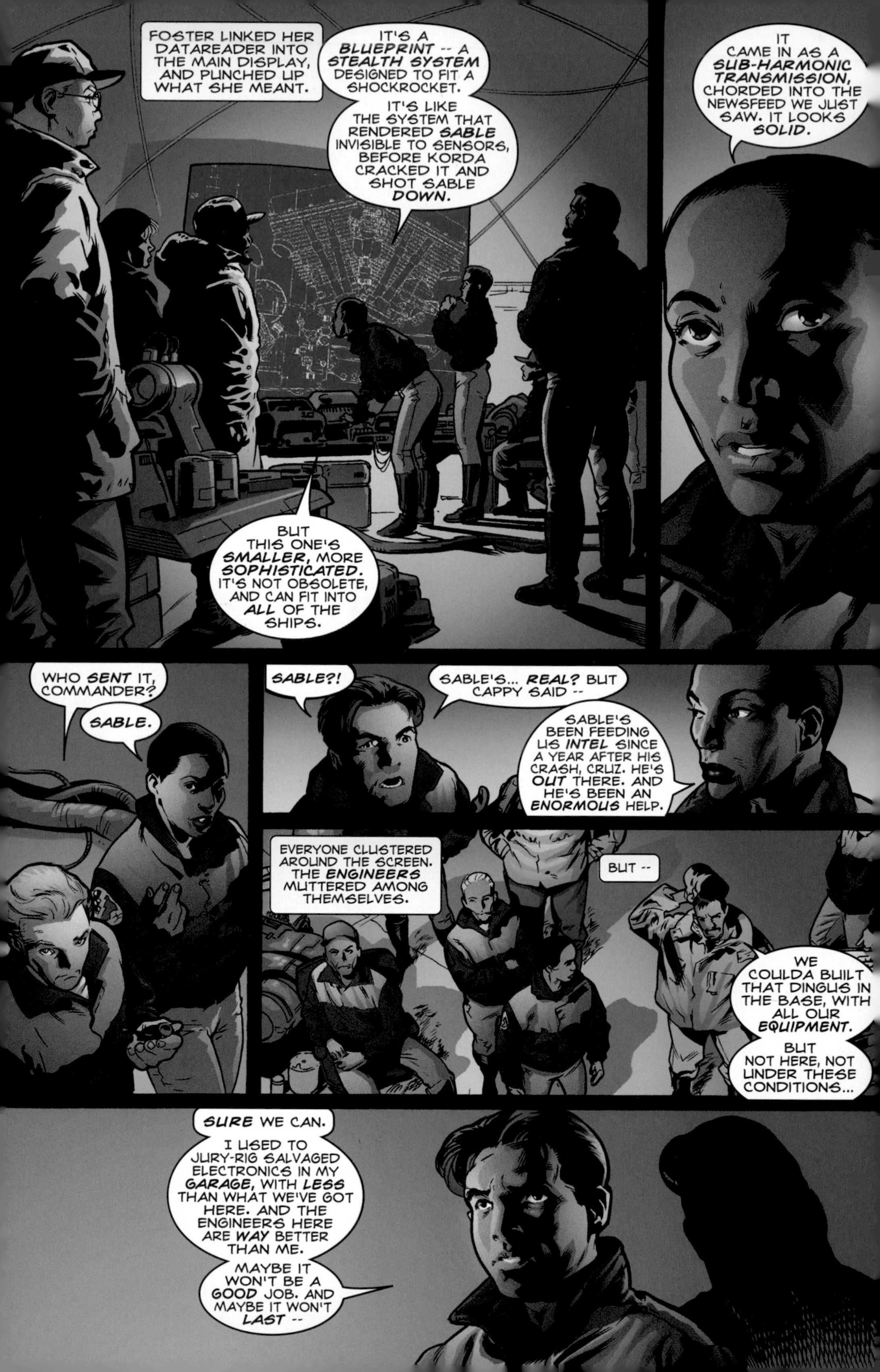
FOSTER LINKED HER DATAREADER INTO THE MAIN DISPLAY, AND PUNCHED UP WHAT SHE MEANT.
IT'S A BLUEPRINT -- A STEALTH SYSTEM DESIGNED TO FIT A SHOCKROCKET.
IT'S LIKE THE SYSTEM THAT RENDERED SABLE INVISIBLE TO SENSORS, BEFORE KORDA CRACKED IT AND SHOT SABLE DOWN.
BUT THIS ONE'S SMALLER, MORE SOPHISTICATED. IT'S NOT OBSOLETE, AND CAN FIT INTO ALL OF THE SHIPS.
IT CAME IN AS A SUB-HARMONIC TRANSMISSION, CHORDED INTO THE NEWSFEED WE JUST SAW. IT LOOKS SOLID.
WHO SENT IT, COMMANDER?
SABLE.
SABLE?!
SABLE'S... REAL? BUT CAPPY SAID --
SABLE'S BEEN FEEDING US INTEL SINCE A YEAR AFTER HIS CRASH, CRUZ. HE'S OUT THERE. AND HE'S BEEN AN ENORMOUS HELP.
EVERYONE CLUSTERED AROUND THE SCREEN. THE ENGINEERS MUTTERED AMONG THEMSELVES.
BUT --
WE COULDA BUILT THAT DINGUS IN THE BASE, WITH ALL OUR EQUIPMENT.
BUT NOT HERE, NOT UNDER THESE CONDITIONS...
SURE WE CAN.
I USED TO JURY-RIG SALVAGED ELECTRONICS IN MY GARAGE, WITH LESS THAN WHAT WE'VE GOT HERE. AND THE ENGINEERS HERE ARE WAY BETTER THAN ME.
MAYBE IT WON'T BE A GOOD JOB. AND MAYBE IT WON'T LAST --

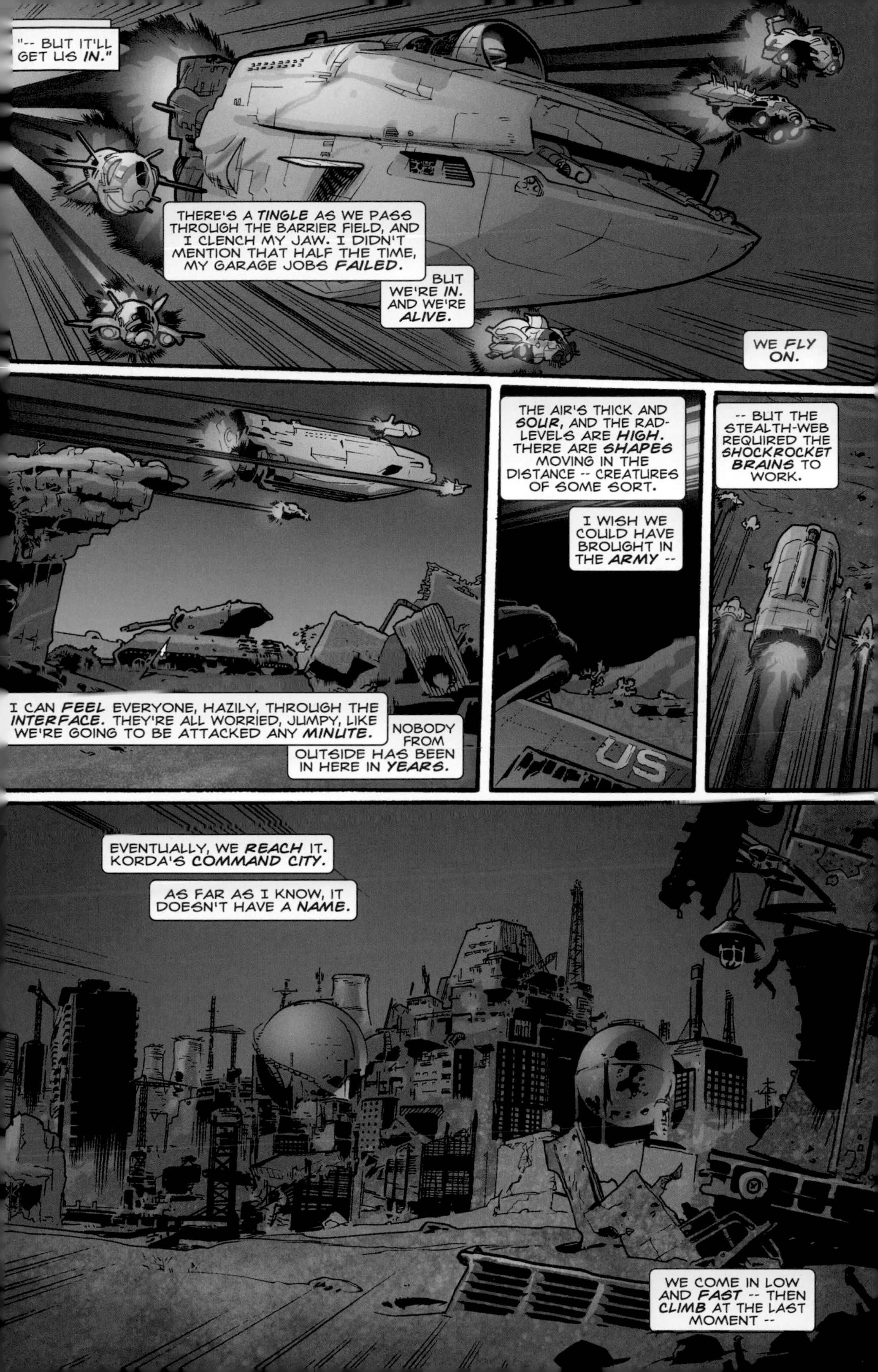
"-- BUT IT'LL GET US IN."
THERE'S A TINGLE AS WE PASS THROUGH THE BARRIER FIELD, AND I CLENCH MY JAW. I DIDN'T MENTION THAT HALF THE TIME, MY GARAGE JOBS FAILED.
BUT WE'RE IN. AND WE'RE ALIVE.
WE FLY ON.
I CAN FEEL EVERYONE, HAZILY, THROUGH THE INTERFACE. THEY'RE ALL WORRIED, JUMPY, LIKE WE'RE GOING TO BE ATTACKED ANY MINUTE.
NOBODY FROM OUTSIDE HAS BEEN IN HERE IN YEARS.
THE AIR'S THICK AND SOUR, AND THE RAD-LEVELS ARE HIGH. THERE ARE SHAPES MOVING IN THE DISTANCE -- CREATURES OF SOME SORT.
I WISH WE COULD HAVE BROUGHT IN THE ARMY --
US
-- BUT THE STEALTH-WEB REQUIRED THE SHOCKROCKET BRAINS TO WORK.
EVENTUALLY, WE REACH IT. KORDA'S COMMAND CITY.
AS FAR AS I KNOW, IT DOESN'T HAVE A NAME.
WE COME IN LOW AND FAST -- THEN CLIMB AT THE LAST MOMENT --

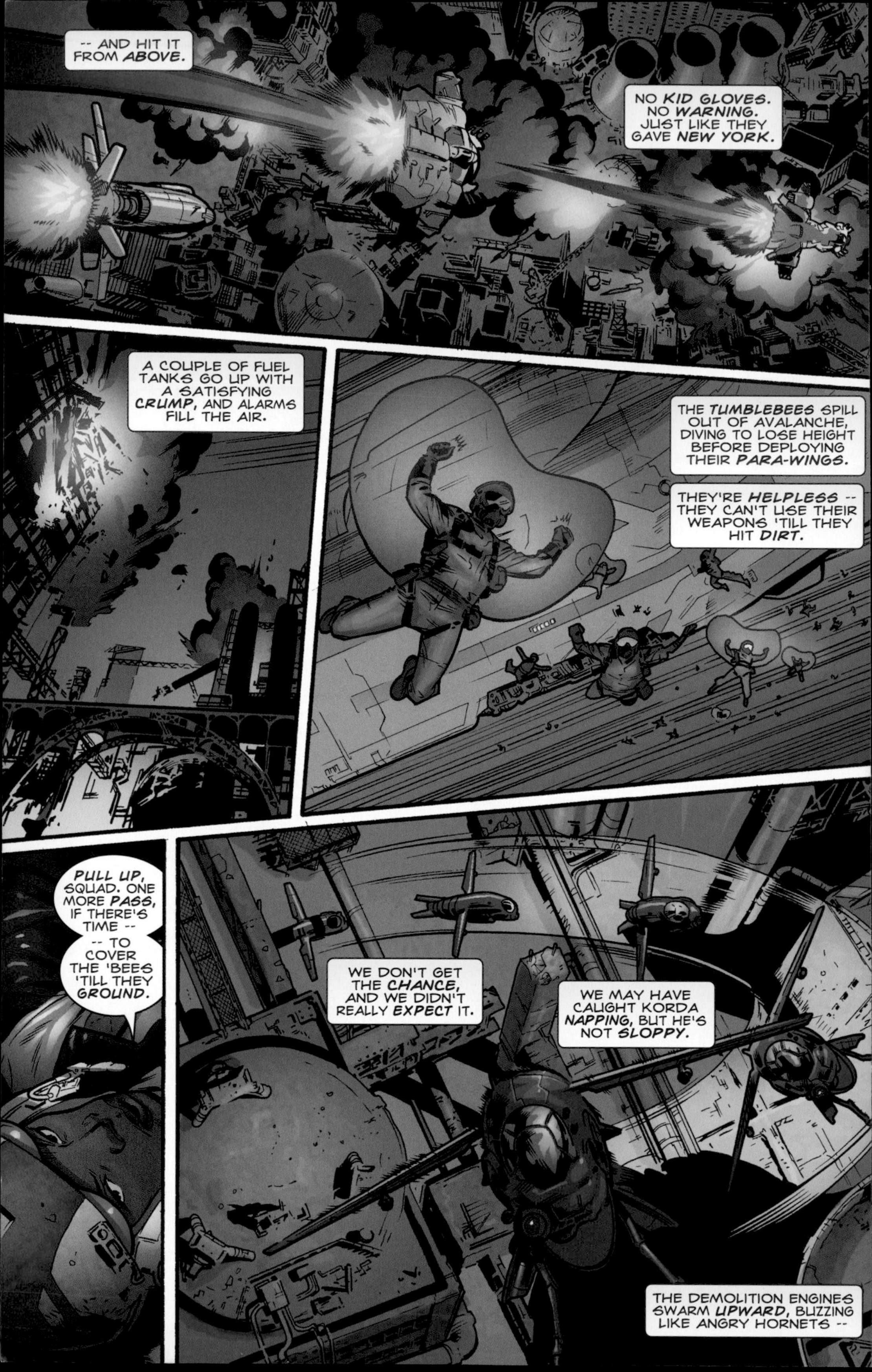

-- AND HIT IT FROM ABOVE.
NO KID GLOVES. NO WARNING. JUST LIKE THEY GAVE NEW YORK.
A COUPLE OF FUEL TANKS GO UP WITH A SATISFYING CRUMP, AND ALARMS FILL THE AIR.
THE TUMBLEBEES SPILL OUT OF AVALANCHE, DIVING TO LOSE HEIGHT BEFORE DEPLOYING THEIR PARA-WINGS.
THEY'RE HELPLESS -- THEY CAN'T USE THEIR WEAPONS 'TILL THEY HIT DIRT.
PULL UP, SQUAD. ONE MORE PASS, IF THERE'S TIME --
-- TO COVER THE 'BEES 'TILL THEY GROUND.
WE DON'T GET THE CHANCE, AND WE DIDN'T REALLY EXPECT IT.
WE MAY HAVE CAUGHT KORDA NAPPING, BUT HE'S NOT SLOPPY.
THE DEMOLITION ENGINES SWARM UPWARD, BUZZING LIKE ANGRY HORNETS --

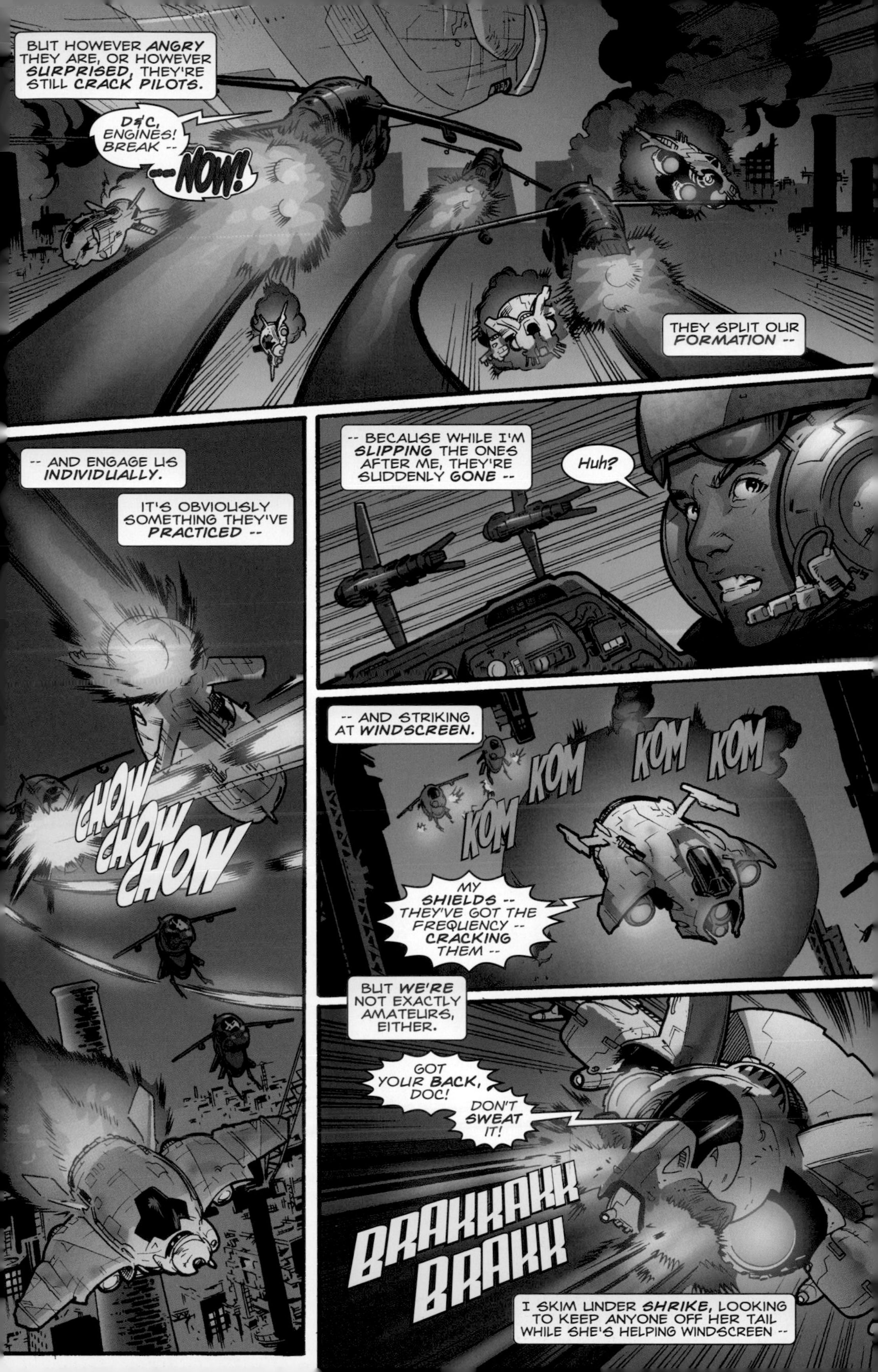
BUT HOWEVER ANGRY THEY ARE, OR HOWEVER SURPRISED, THEY'RE STILL CRACK PILOTS.
D&C, ENGINES! BREAK --
-- NOW!
THEY SPLIT OUR FORMATION --
-- AND ENGAGE US INDIVIDUALLY.
IT'S OBVIOUSLY SOMETHING THEY'VE PRACTICED --
CHOW CHOW CHOW CHOW
-- BECAUSE WHILE I'M SLIPPING THE ONES AFTER ME, THEY'RE SUDDENLY GONE --
Huh?
-- AND STRIKING AT WINDSCREEN.
KOM KOM KOM KOM KOM
MY SHIELDS -- THEY'VE GOT THE FREQUENCY -- CRACKING THEM --
BUT WE'RE NOT EXACTLY AMATEURS, EITHER.
GOT YOUR BACK, DOC!
DON'T SWEAT IT!
BRAKKAKK BRAKK
I SKIM UNDER SHRIKE, LOOKING TO KEEP ANYONE OFF HER TAIL WHILE SHE'S HELPING WINDSCREEN --

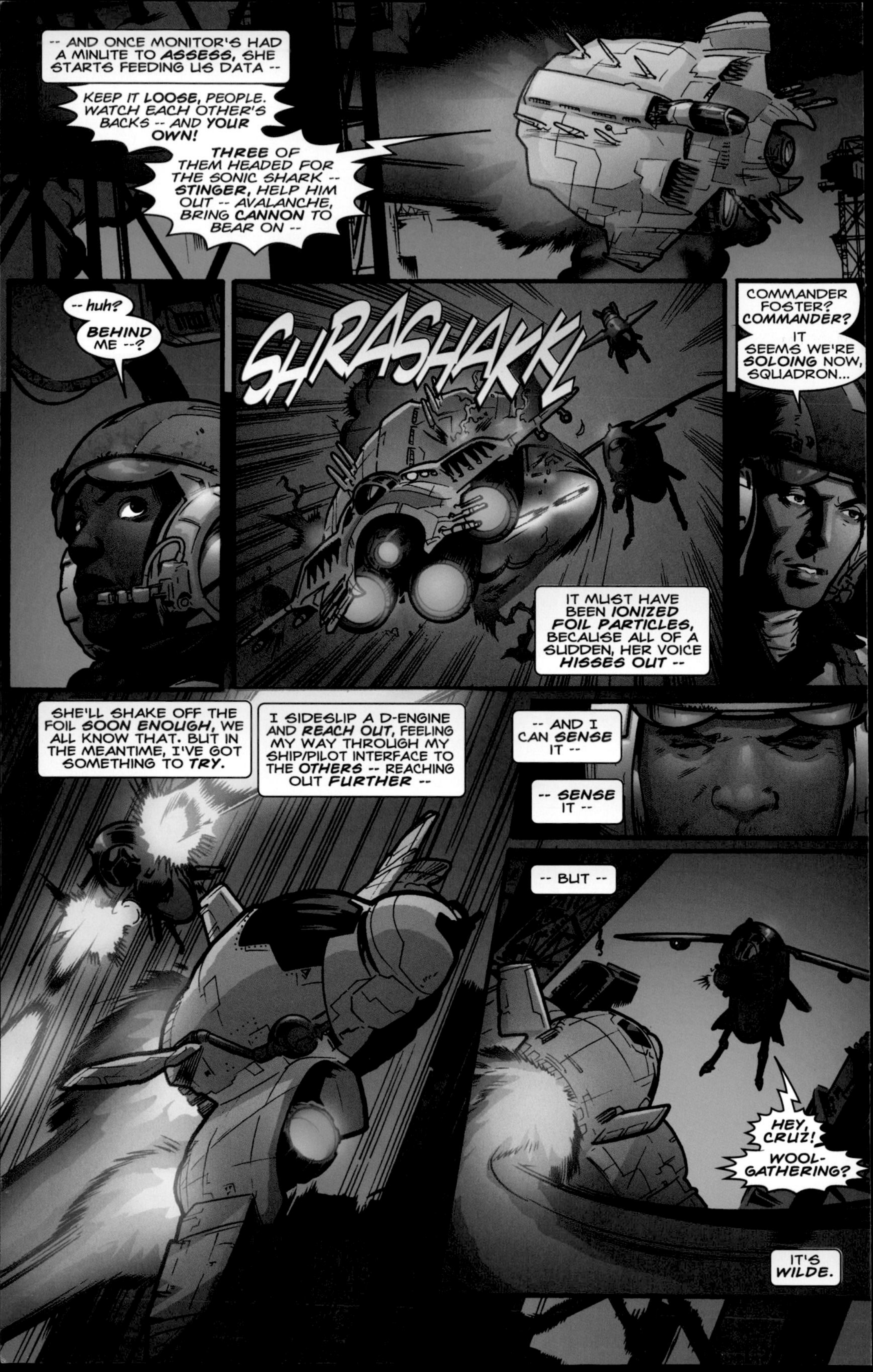
-- AND ONCE MONITOR'S HAD A MINUTE TO ASSESS, SHE STARTS FEEDING US DATA --
KEEP IT LOOSE, PEOPLE. WATCH EACH OTHER'S BACKS -- AND YOUR OWN!
THREE OF THEM HEADED FOR THE SONIC SHARK -- STINGER, HELP HIM OUT -- AVALANCHE, BRING CANNON TO BEAR ON --
-- huh?
BEHIND ME --?
SHRASHAKK!
IT MUST HAVE BEEN IONIZED FOIL PARTICLES, BECAUSE ALL OF A SUDDEN, HER VOICE HISSES OUT --
COMMANDER FOSTER? COMMANDER?
IT SEEMS WE'RE SOLOING NOW, SQUADRON...
SHE'LL SHAKE OFF THE FOIL SOON ENOUGH, WE ALL KNOW THAT. BUT IN THE MEANTIME, I'VE GOT SOMETHING TO TRY.
I SIDESLIP A D-ENGINE AND REACH OUT, FEELING MY WAY THROUGH MY SHIP/PILOT INTERFACE TO THE OTHERS -- REACHING OUT FURTHER --
-- AND I CAN SENSE IT --
-- SENSE IT --
-- BUT --
HEY, CRUZ! WOOL-GATHERING?
IT'S WILDE.

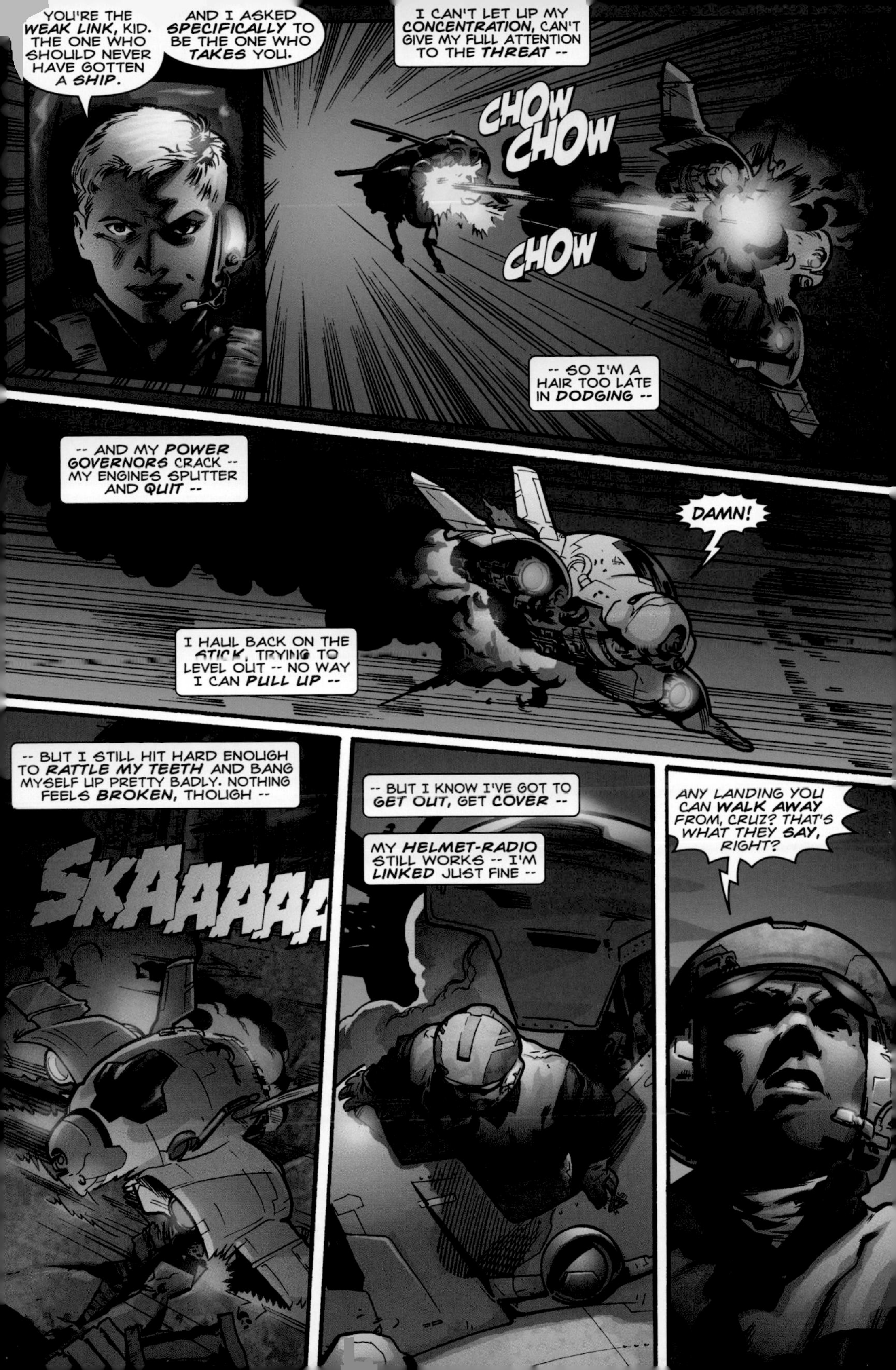
YOU'RE THE WEAK LINK, KID. THE ONE WHO SHOULD NEVER HAVE GOTTEN A SHIP.
AND I ASKED SPECIFICALLY TO BE THE ONE WHO TAKES YOU.
I CAN'T LET UP MY CONCENTRATION, CAN'T GIVE MY FULL ATTENTION TO THE THREAT --
CHOW CHOW
CHOW
-- SO I'M A HAIR TOO LATE IN DODGING --
-- AND MY POWER GOVERNORS CRACK -- MY ENGINES SPUTTER AND QUIT --
DAMN!
I HAUL BACK ON THE STICK, TRYING TO LEVEL OUT -- NO WAY I CAN PULL UP --
-- BUT I STILL HIT HARD ENOUGH TO RATTLE MY TEETH AND BANG MYSELF UP PRETTY BADLY. NOTHING FEELS BROKEN, THOUGH --
SKAAAAAA
-- BUT I KNOW I'VE GOT TO GET OUT, GET COVER --
MY HELMET-RADIO STILL WORKS -- I'M LINKED JUST FINE --
ANY LANDING YOU CAN WALK AWAY FROM, CRUZ? THAT'S WHAT THEY SAY, RIGHT?

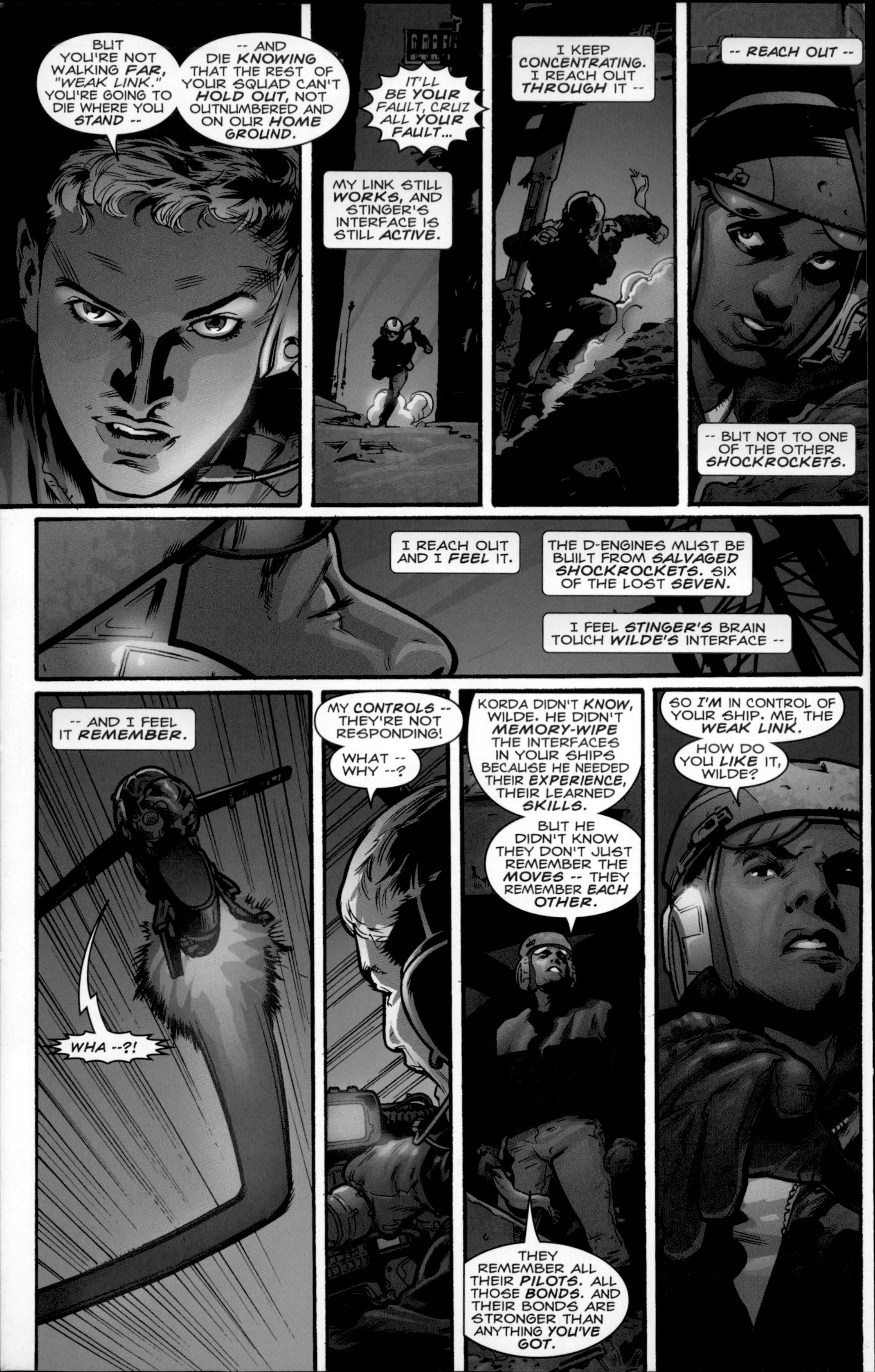
BUT YOU'RE NOT WALKING FAR, "WEAK LINK." YOU'RE GOING TO DIE WHERE YOU STAND --
-- AND DIE KNOWING THAT THE REST OF YOUR SQUAD CAN'T HOLD OUT, NOT OUTNUMBERED AND ON OUR HOME GROUND.
IT'LL BE YOUR FAULT, CRUZ ALL YOUR FAULT...
MY LINK STILL WORKS, AND STINGER'S INTERFACE IS STILL ACTIVE.
I KEEP CONCENTRATING. I REACH OUT THROUGH IT --
-- REACH OUT --
-- BUT NOT TO ONE OF THE OTHER SHOCKROCKETS.
I REACH OUT AND I FEEL IT.
THE D-ENGINES MUST BE BUILT FROM SALVAGED SHOCKROCKETS. SIX OF THE LOST SEVEN.
I FEEL STINGER'S BRAIN TOUCH WILDE'S INTERFACE --
-- AND I FEEL IT REMEMBER.
WHA --?!
MY CONTROLS -- THEY'RE NOT RESPONDING!
WHAT -- WHY --?
KORDA DIDN'T KNOW, WILDE. HE DIDN'T MEMORY-WIPE THE INTERFACES IN YOUR SHIPS BECAUSE HE NEEDED THEIR EXPERIENCE, THEIR LEARNED SKILLS.
BUT HE DIDN'T KNOW THEY DON'T JUST REMEMBER THE MOVES -- THEY REMEMBER EACH OTHER.
THEY REMEMBER ALL THEIR PILOTS. ALL THOSE BONDS. AND THEIR BONDS ARE STRONGER THAN ANYTHING YOU'VE GOT.
SO I'M IN CONTROL OF YOUR SHIP. ME, THE WEAK LINK.
HOW DO YOU LIKE IT, WILDE?

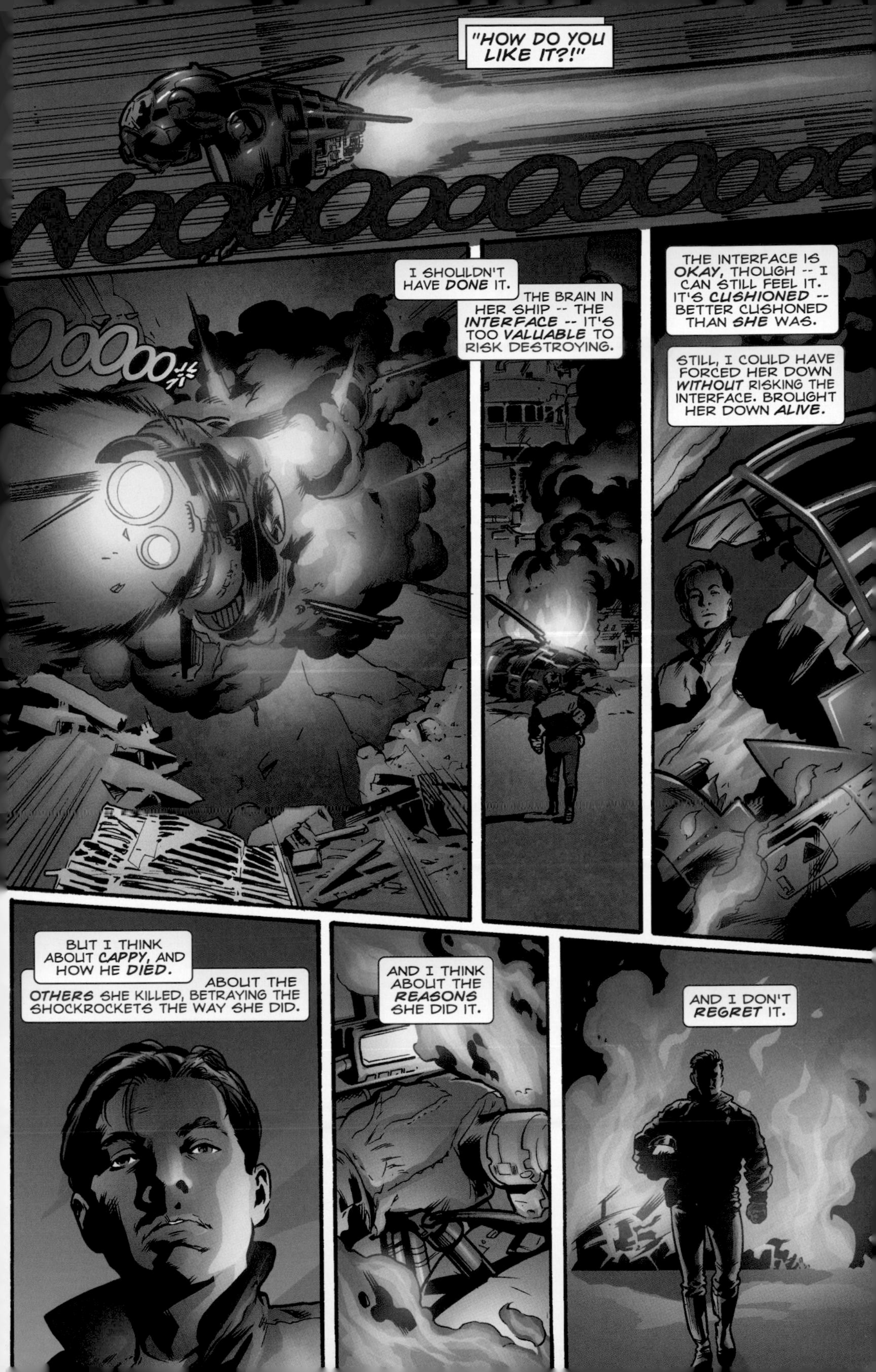
"HOW DO YOU LIKE IT?!"
NOOOOOOOOOOOOOOOOOOOOO
I SHOULDN'T HAVE DONE IT.
THE BRAIN IN HER SHIP -- THE INTERFACE -- IT'S TOO VALUABLE TO RISK DESTROYING.
THE INTERFACE IS OKAY, THOUGH -- I CAN STILL FEEL IT. IT'S CUSHIONED -- BETTER CUSHIONED THAN SHE WAS.
STILL, I COULD HAVE FORCED HER DOWN WITHOUT RISKING THE INTERFACE. BROUGHT HER DOWN ALIVE.
BUT I THINK ABOUT CAPPY, AND HOW HE DIED.
ABOUT THE OTHERS SHE KILLED, BETRAYING THE SHOCKROCKETS THE WAY SHE DID.
AND I THINK ABOUT THE REASONS SHE DID IT.
AND I DON'T REGRET IT.

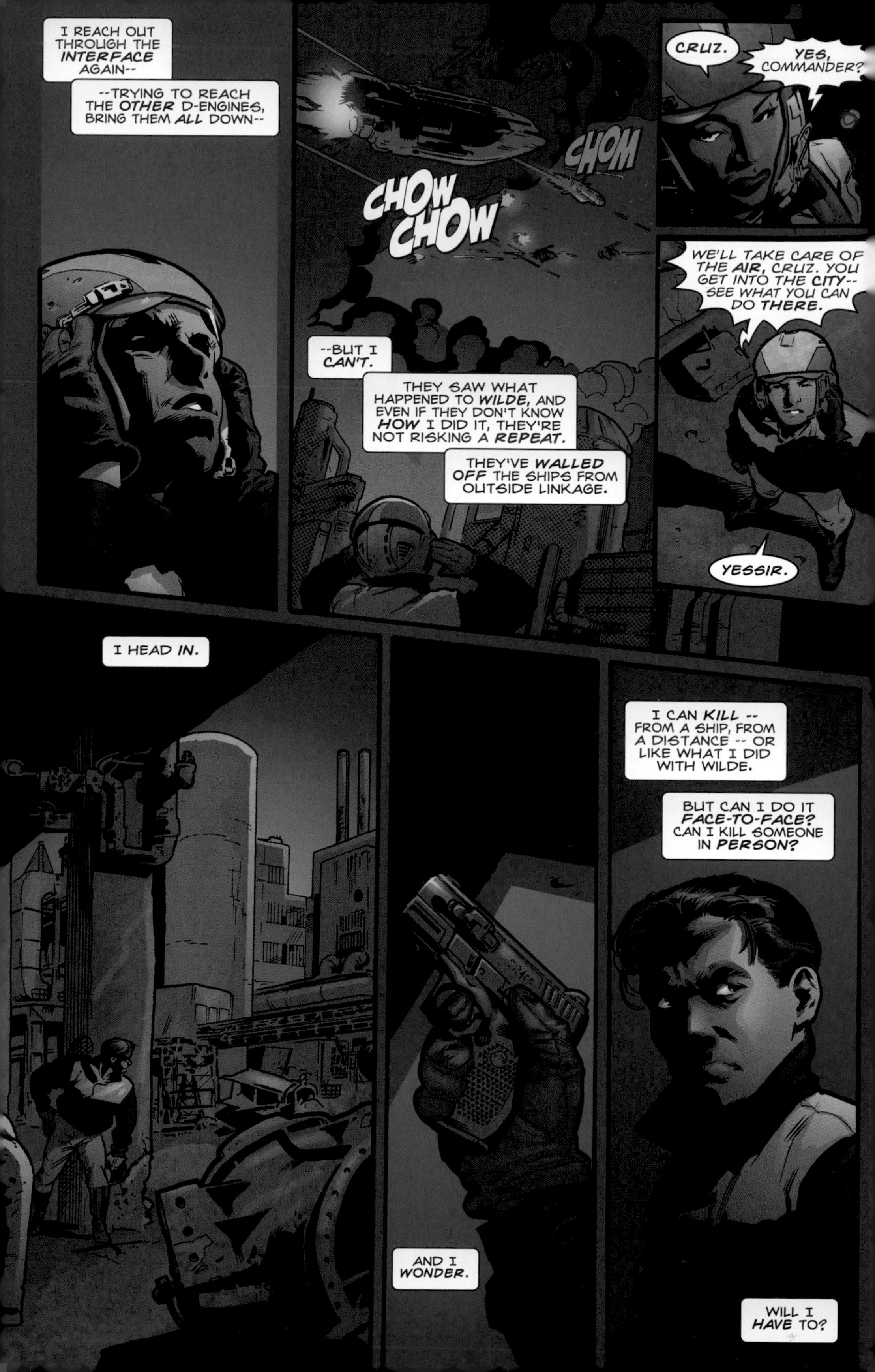

I REACH OUT THROUGH THE INTERFACE AGAIN--
--TRYING TO REACH THE OTHER D-ENGINES, BRING THEM ALL DOWN--
CHOM
CHOW CHOW
--BUT I CAN'T.
THEY SAW WHAT HAPPENED TO WILDE, AND EVEN IF THEY DON'T KNOW HOW I DID IT, THEY'RE NOT RISKING A REPEAT.
THEY'VE WALLED OFF THE SHIPS FROM OUTSIDE LINKAGE.
CRUZ.
YES, COMMANDER?
WE'LL TAKE CARE OF THE AIR, CRUZ. YOU GET INTO THE CITY-- SEE WHAT YOU CAN DO THERE.
YESSIR.
I HEAD IN.
AND I WONDER.
I CAN KILL -- FROM A SHIP, FROM A DISTANCE -- OR LIKE WHAT I DID WITH WILDE.
BUT CAN I DO IT FACE-TO-FACE? CAN I KILL SOMEONE IN PERSON?
WILL I HAVE TO?

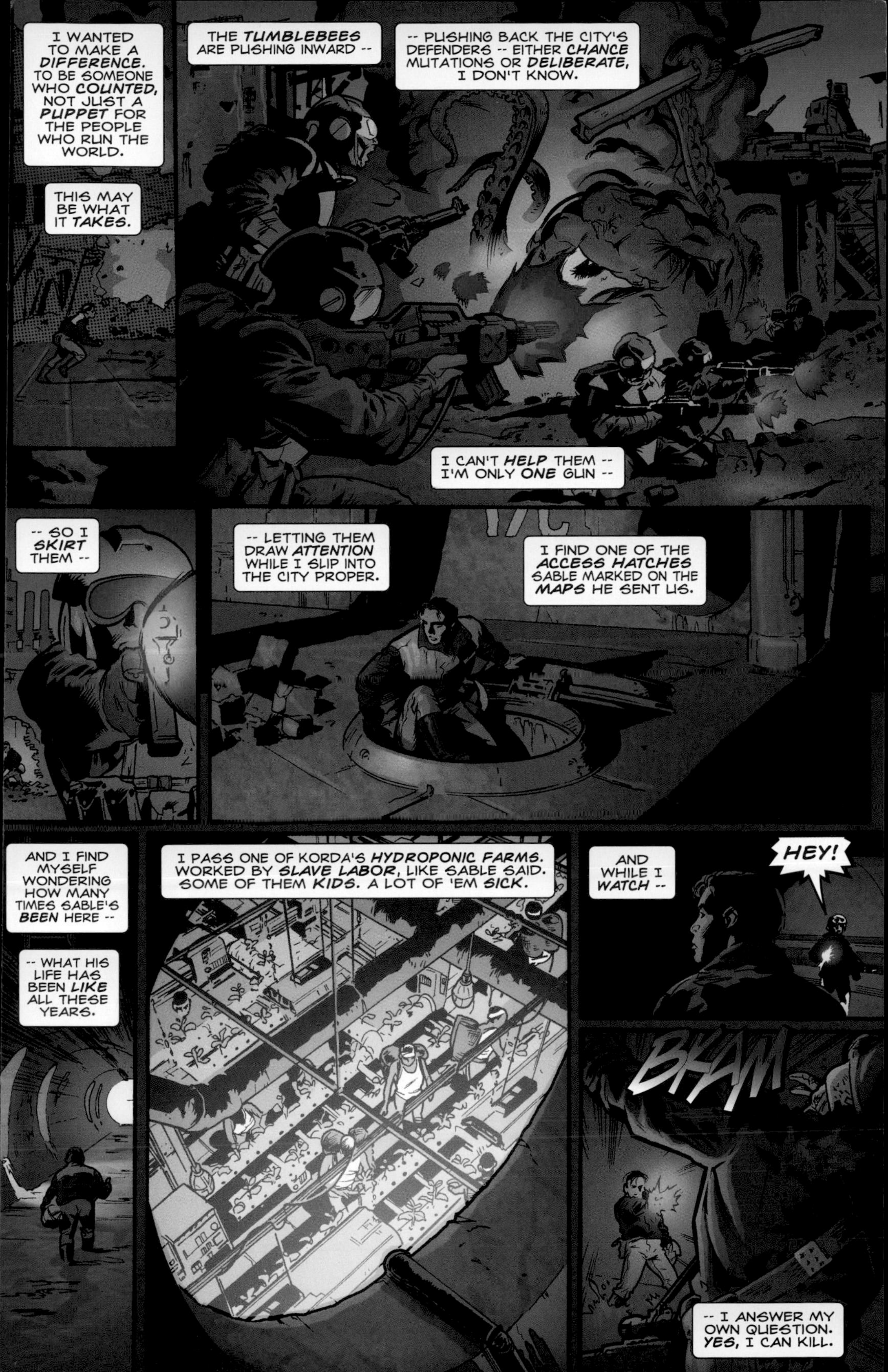

I WANTED TO MAKE A DIFFERENCE. TO BE SOMEONE WHO COUNTED, NOT JUST A PUPPET FOR THE PEOPLE WHO RUN THE WORLD.
THIS MAY BE WHAT IT TAKES.
THE TUMBLEBEES ARE PUSHING INWARD --
-- PUSHING BACK THE CITY'S DEFENDERS -- EITHER CHANCE MUTATIONS OR DELIBERATE, I DON'T KNOW.
I CAN'T HELP THEM -- I'M ONLY ONE GUN --
-- SO I SKIRT THEM --
-- LETTING THEM DRAW ATTENTION WHILE I SLIP INTO THE CITY PROPER.
I FIND ONE OF THE ACCESS HATCHES SABLE MARKED ON THE MAPS HE SENT US.
AND I FIND MYSELF WONDERING HOW MANY TIMES SABLE'S BEEN HERE --
-- WHAT HIS LIFE HAS BEEN LIKE ALL THESE YEARS.
I PASS ONE OF KORDA'S HYDROPONIC FARMS. WORKED BY SLAVE LABOR, LIKE SABLE SAID. SOME OF THEM KIDS. A LOT OF 'EM SICK.
AND WHILE I WATCH --
HEY!
BRAM
-- I ANSWER MY OWN QUESTION. YES, I CAN KILL.

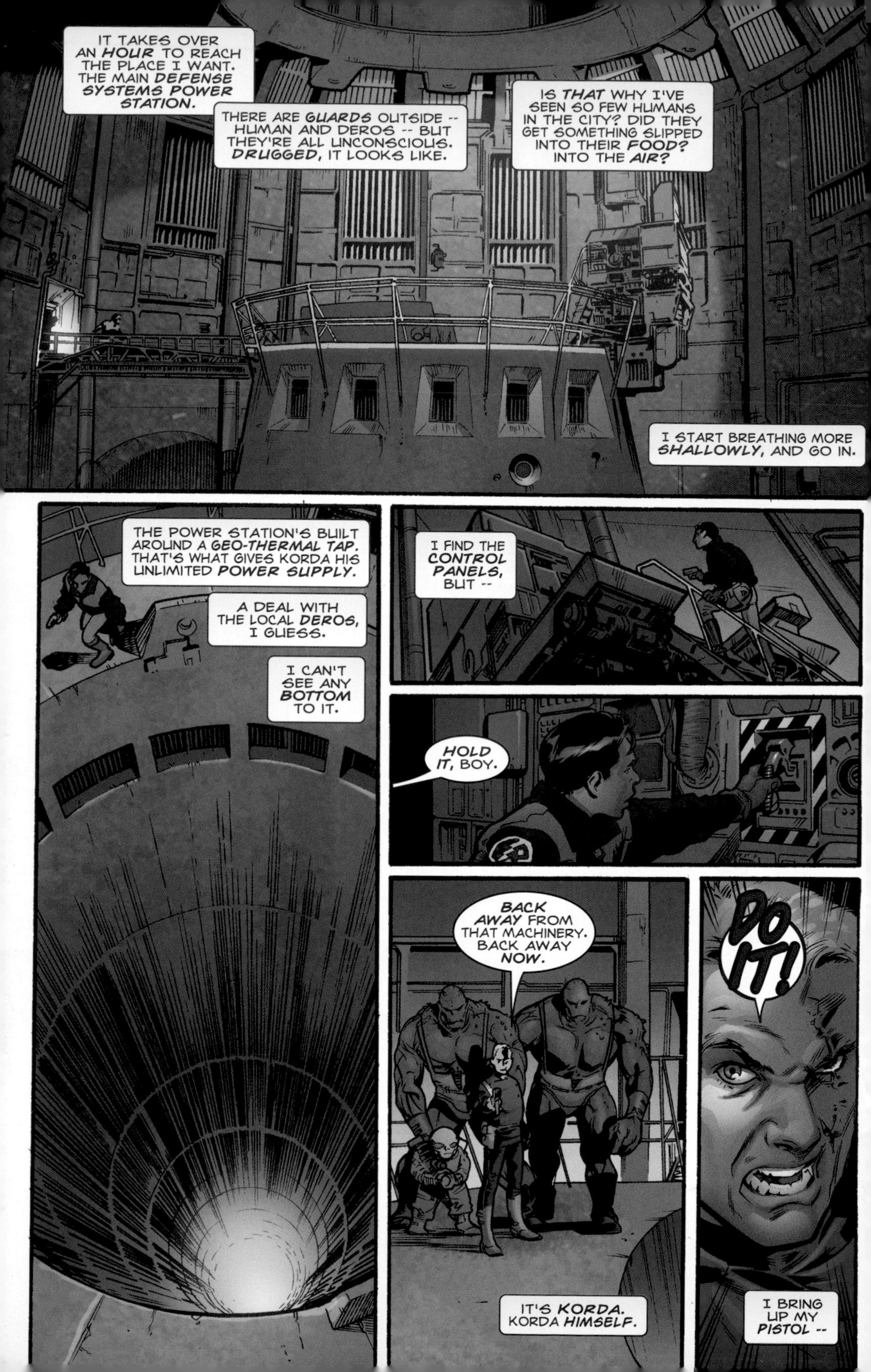
IT TAKES OVER AN HOUR TO REACH THE PLACE I WANT. THE MAIN DEFENSE SYSTEMS POWER STATION.
THERE ARE GUARDS OUTSIDE -- HUMAN AND DEROS -- BUT THEY'RE ALL UNCONSCIOUS. DRUGGED, IT LOOKS LIKE.
IS THAT WHY I'VE SEEN SO FEW HUMANS IN THE CITY? DID THEY GET SOMETHING SLIPPED INTO THEIR FOOD? INTO THE AIR?
I START BREATHING MORE SHALLOWLY, AND GO IN.
THE POWER STATION'S BUILT AROUND A GEO-THERMAL TAP. THAT'S WHAT GIVES KORDA HIS UNLIMITED POWER SUPPLY.
A DEAL WITH THE LOCAL DEROS, I GUESS.
I CAN'T SEE ANY BOTTOM TO IT.
I FIND THE CONTROL PANELS, BUT --
HOLD IT, BOY.
BACK AWAY FROM THAT MACHINERY. BACK AWAY NOW.
IT'S KORDA. KORDA HIMSELF.
DO IT!
I BRING UP MY PISTOL --

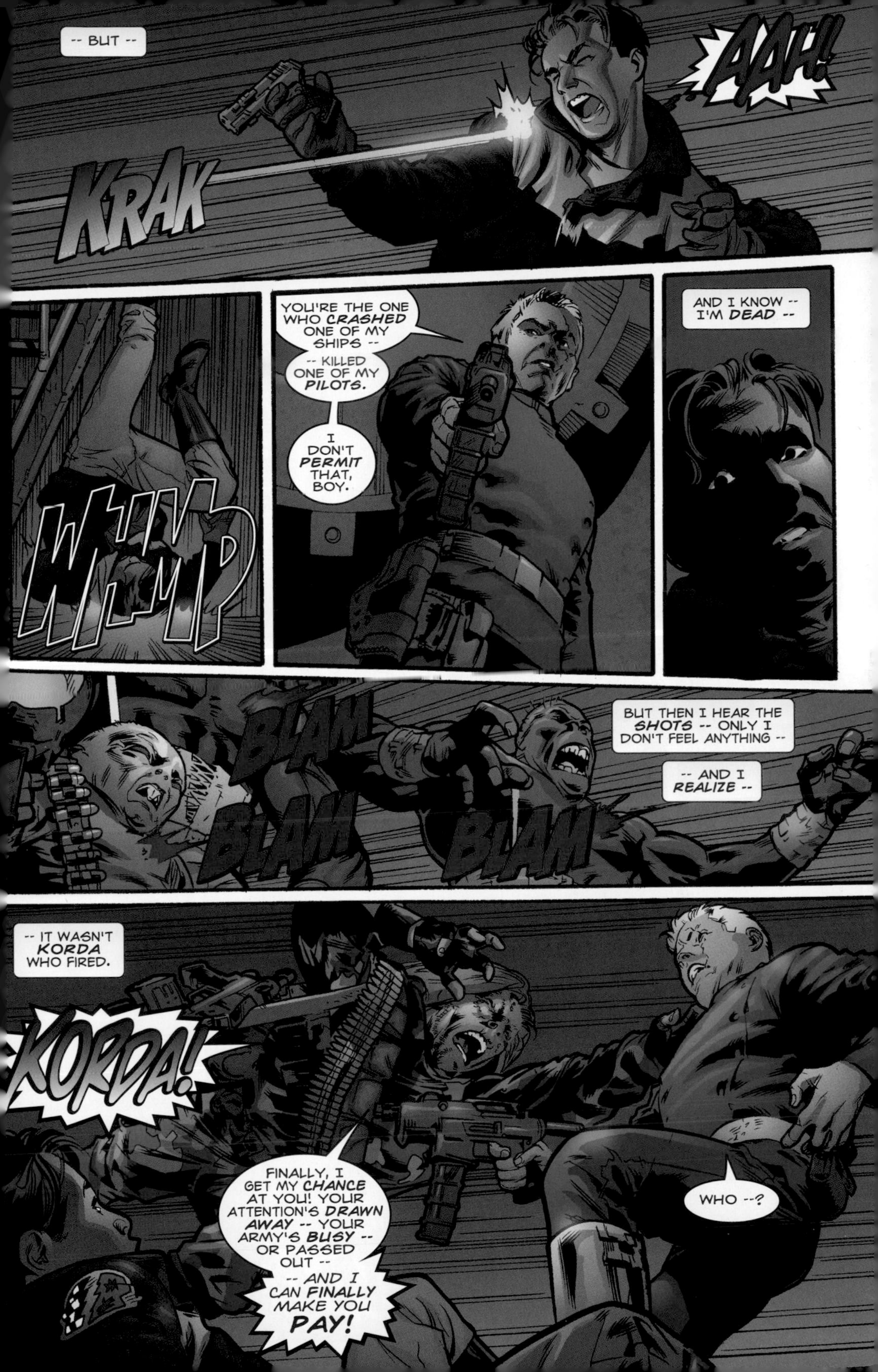
-- BUT --
AAH!
KRAK
WHUMP
YOU'RE THE ONE WHO CRASHED ONE OF MY SHIPS --
-- KILLED ONE OF MY PILOTS.
I DON'T PERMIT THAT, BOY.
AND I KNOW -- I'M DEAD --
BLAM
BLAM
BLAM
BUT THEN I HEAR THE SHOTS -- ONLY I DON'T FEEL ANYTHING --
-- AND I REALIZE --
-- IT WASN'T KORDA WHO FIRED.
KORDA!
FINALLY, I GET MY CHANCE AT YOU! YOUR ATTENTION'S DRAWN AWAY -- YOUR ARMY'S BUSY -- OR PASSED OUT --
-- AND I CAN FINALLY MAKE YOU PAY!
WHO --?

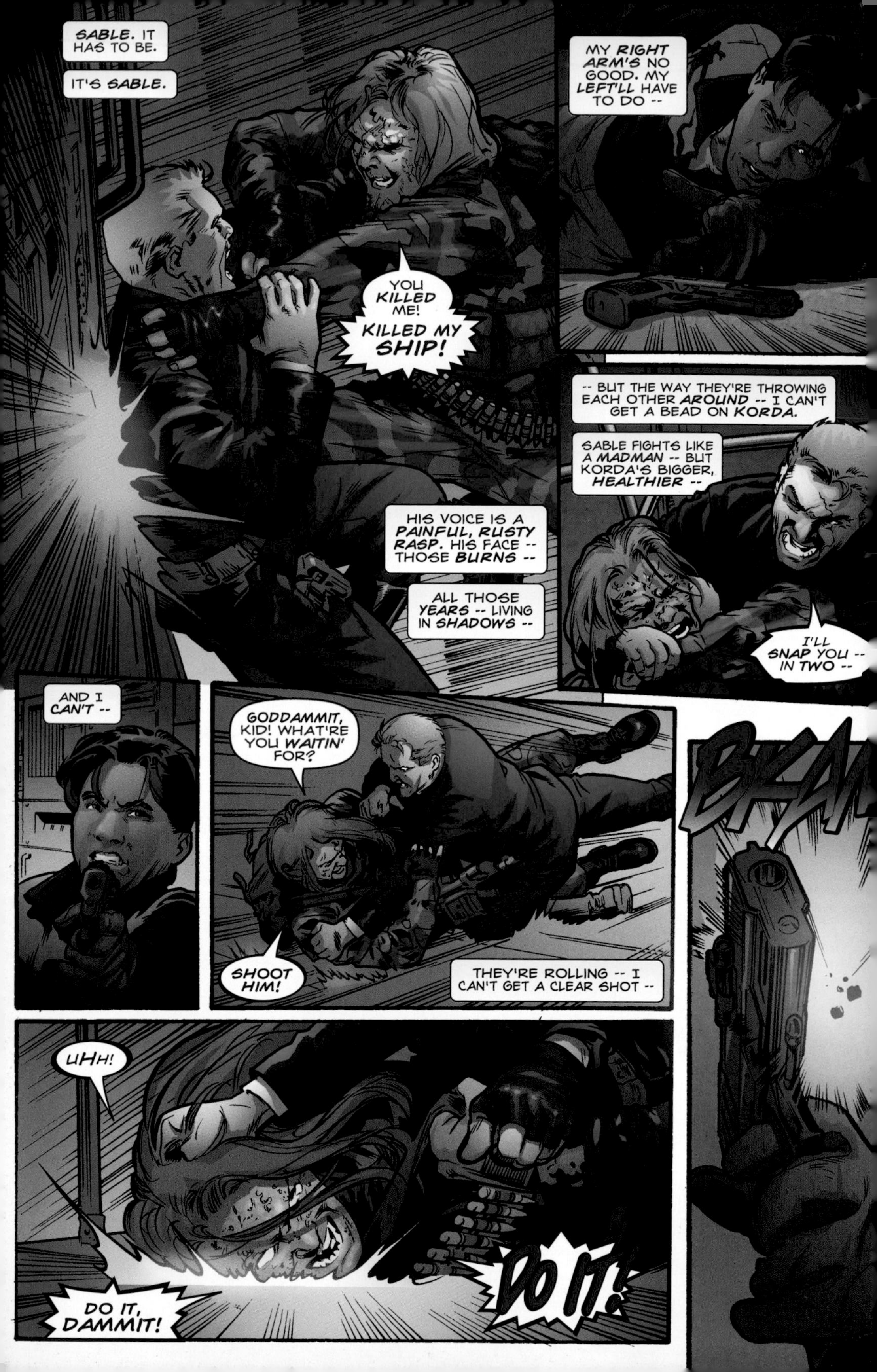
SABLE. IT HAS TO BE.
IT'S SABLE.
YOU KILLED ME!
KILLED MY SHIP!
HIS VOICE IS A PAINFUL, RUSTY RASP. HIS FACE -- THOSE BURNS --
ALL THOSE YEARS -- LIVING IN SHADOWS --
MY RIGHT ARM'S NO GOOD. MY LEFT'LL HAVE TO DO --
-- BUT THE WAY THEY'RE THROWING EACH OTHER AROUND -- I CAN'T GET A BEAD ON KORDA.
SABLE FIGHTS LIKE A MADMAN -- BUT KORDA'S BIGGER, HEALTHIER --
I'LL SNAP YOU -- IN TWO --
AND I CAN'T --
GODDAMMIT, KID! WHAT'RE YOU WAITIN' FOR?
SHOOT HIM!
THEY'RE ROLLING -- I CAN'T GET A CLEAR SHOT --
UHH!
DO IT, DAMMIT!
DO IT!

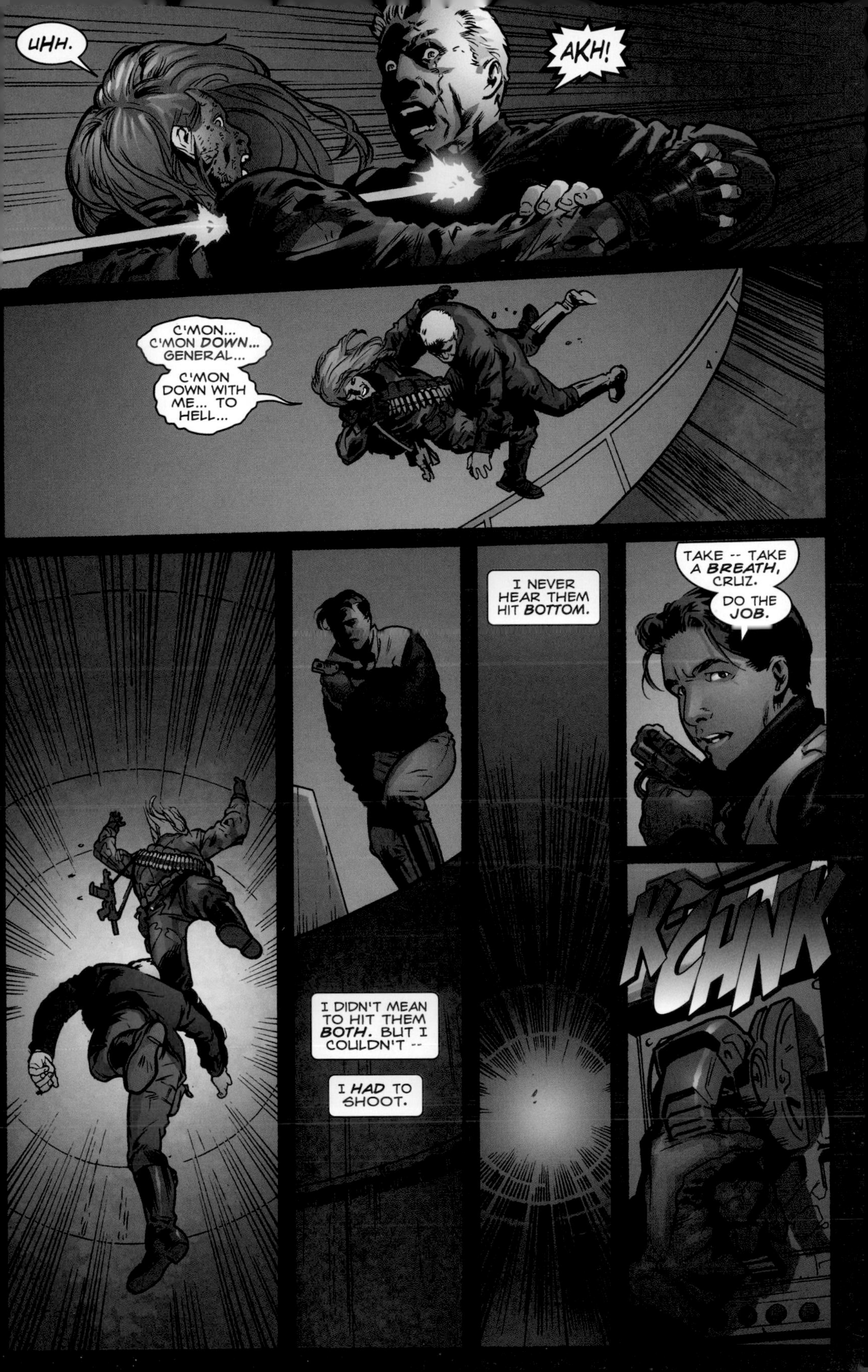
UHH.
AKH!
C'MON... C'MON DOWN... GENERAL...
C'MON DOWN WITH ME... TO HELL...
I NEVER HEAR THEM HIT BOTTOM.
TAKE -- TAKE A BREATH, CRUZ.
DO THE JOB.
I DIDN'T MEAN TO HIT THEM BOTH. BUT I COULDN'T --
I HAD TO SHOOT.
K-CHUNK

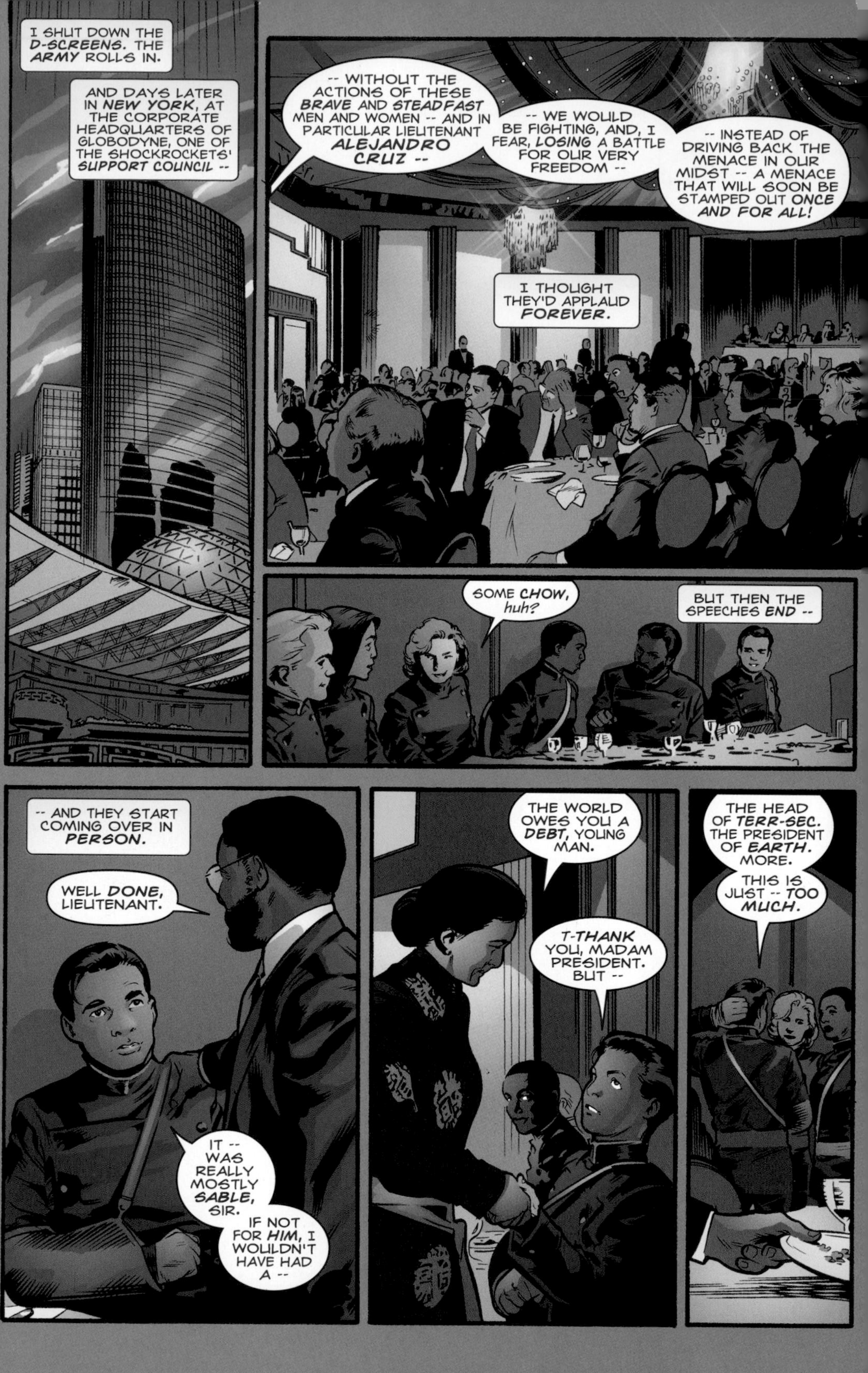
I SHUT DOWN THE D-SCREENS. THE ARMY ROLLS IN.
AND DAYS LATER IN NEW YORK, AT THE CORPORATE HEADQUARTERS OF GLOBODYNE, ONE OF THE SHOCKROCKETS' SUPPORT COUNCIL --
-- WITHOUT THE ACTIONS OF THESE BRAVE AND STEADFAST MEN AND WOMEN -- AND IN PARTICULAR LIEUTENANT ALEJANDRO CRUZ --
-- WE WOULD BE FIGHTING, AND, I FEAR, LOSING A BATTLE FOR OUR VERY FREEDOM --
-- INSTEAD OF DRIVING BACK THE MENACE IN OUR MIDST -- A MENACE THAT WILL SOON BE STAMPED OUT ONCE AND FOR ALL!
I THOUGHT THEY'D APPLAUD FOREVER.
SOME CHOW, huh?
BUT THEN THE SPEECHES END --
-- AND THEY START COMING OVER IN PERSON.
WELL DONE, LIEUTENANT.
IT -- WAS REALLY MOSTLY SABLE, SIR.
IF NOT FOR HIM, I WOULDN'T HAVE HAD A --
THE WORLD OWES YOU A DEBT, YOUNG MAN.
T-THANK YOU, MADAM PRESIDENT. BUT --
THE HEAD OF TERR-SEC. THE PRESIDENT OF EARTH. MORE.
THIS IS JUST -- TOO MUCH.

'JANDRO!

Huh?

CONGRATULATIONS, SON!

WOO-HOO!

VIVA EL PILOTO!

♪♪

THEY FLEW MY *FAMILY* IN.

AND *POPPY* --

BEEN HEARIN' A *LOT* ABOUT WHAT YOU AND THE OTHERS DID, 'JANDRO. HEARIN' YOUR *NAME* A LOT.

SO -- -- GOOD GOING, SON.

YEAH. WAY TO GO, KID.

I GET *AWAY*, AFTER A WHILE -- GET *OUT*, TO THE *UPPER FLOORS*. I NEED SOME *AIR*.

BUT I STILL FEEL *OVERWHELMED*, OVERLOADED --

AND THEN --

-- NOBODY'S AROUND --

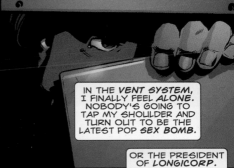

IN THE *VENT SYSTEM*, I FINALLY FEEL *ALONE*. NOBODY'S GOING TO TAP MY SHOULDER AND TURN OUT TO BE THE LATEST POP *SEX BOMB*.

OR THE PRESIDENT OF *LONGICORP*.

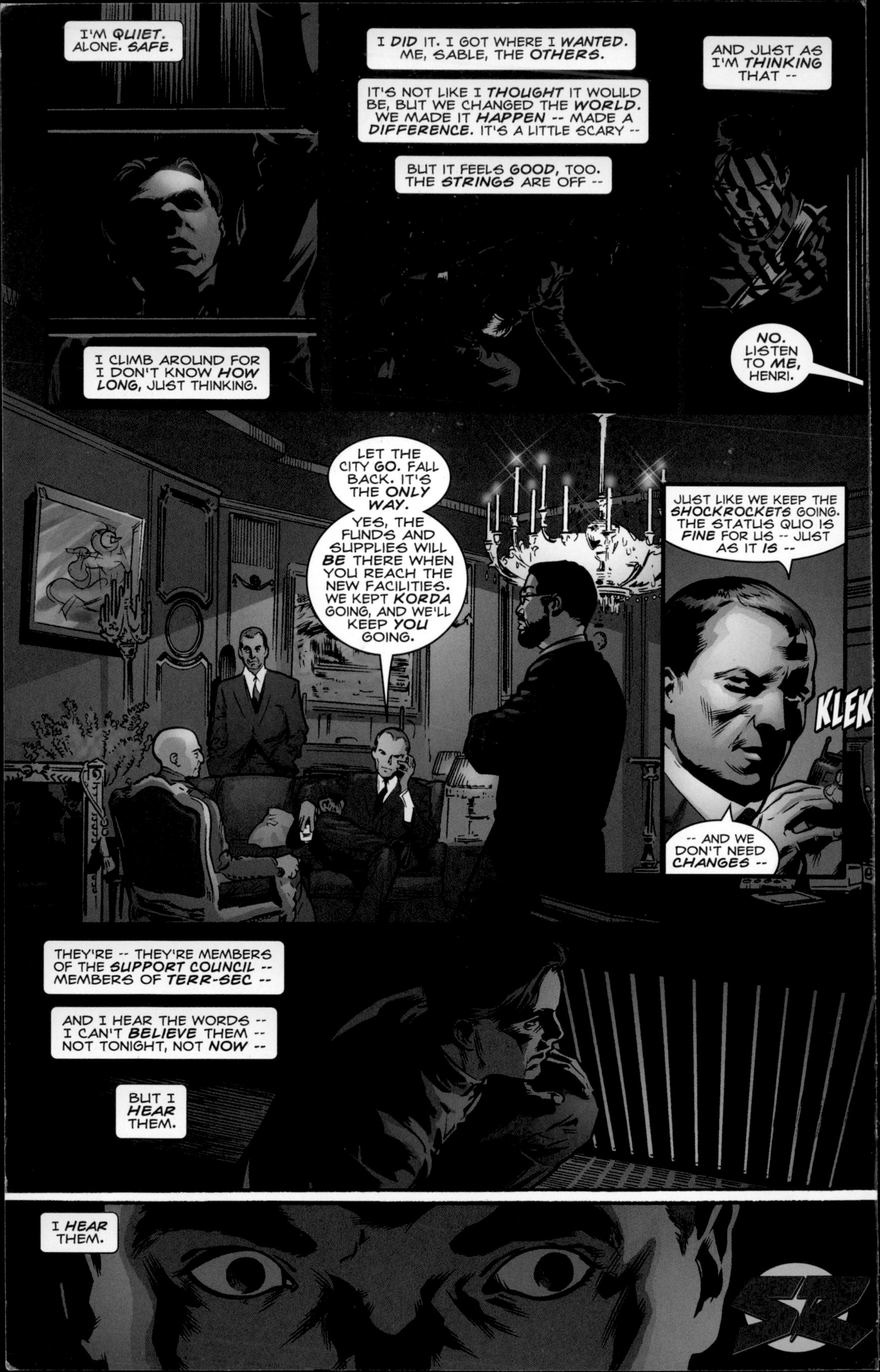
I'M QUIET. ALONE. SAFE.
I CLIMB AROUND FOR I DON'T KNOW HOW LONG, JUST THINKING.
I DID IT. I GOT WHERE I WANTED. ME, SABLE, THE OTHERS.
IT'S NOT LIKE I THOUGHT IT WOULD BE, BUT WE CHANGED THE WORLD. WE MADE IT HAPPEN -- MADE A DIFFERENCE. IT'S A LITTLE SCARY --
BUT IT FEELS GOOD, TOO. THE STRINGS ARE OFF --
AND JUST AS I'M THINKING THAT --
NO. LISTEN TO ME, HENRI.
LET THE CITY GO. FALL BACK. IT'S THE ONLY WAY.
YES, THE FUNDS AND SUPPLIES WILL BE THERE WHEN YOU REACH THE NEW FACILITIES. WE KEPT KORDA GOING, AND WE'LL KEEP YOU GOING.
JUST LIKE WE KEEP THE SHOCKROCKETS GOING. THE STATUS QUO IS FINE FOR US -- JUST AS IT IS --
KLEK
-- AND WE DON'T NEED CHANGES --
THEY'RE -- THEY'RE MEMBERS OF THE SUPPORT COUNCIL -- MEMBERS OF TERR-SEC --
AND I HEAR THE WORDS -- I CAN'T BELIEVE THEM -- NOT TONIGHT, NOT NOW --
BUT I HEAR THEM.
I HEAR THEM.